Our Lives,
Our Fortunes
and Our Sacred Honor

ALSO BY RICHARD R. BEEMAN:

Plain, Honest Men: The Making of the American Constitution

The Penguin Guide to the United States Constitution

The Varieties of Political Experience in Eighteenth-Century America

The Evolution of the Southern Backcountry

Patrick Henry: A Biography

The Old Dominion and the New Nation, 1788–1801

Editor, with Stephen Botein and Edward Carter II:
*Beyond Confederation: The Origins of the
American Constitution and National Identity*

Series Editor, The Penguin Civic Classics:
*The Declaration of Independence and Constitution;
Common Sense; Selected Essays of the Federalist Papers;
Selected Speeches by Abraham Lincoln;
Great American Speeches from the Founding to the Present;*
and *Major Supreme Court Decisions*

OUR LIVES,
OUR FORTUNES
AND OUR SACRED HONOR

THE FORGING *of*
AMERICAN INDEPENDENCE,
1774-1776

RICHARD R. BEEMAN

BASIC BOOKS
A MEMBER OF THE PERSEUS BOOKS GROUP
NEW YORK

Set in 11.5 point Adobe Caslon Pro by the Perseus Books Group

Library of Congress Cataloging-in-Publication Data

Beeman, Richard R.
   Our lives, our fortunes and our sacred honor : the forging of American independence, 1774–1776 / Richard R. Beeman.
      pages   cm
   Includes bibliographical references and index.
   ISBN 978-0-465-02629-6 (hardcover) — ISBN 978-0-465-03782-7 (e-book) 1. United States—History—Revolution, 1775–1783. 2. United States. Continental Congress—History. 3. United States—Politics and government—To 1775. 4. United States—Politics and government—1775–1783. 5. Revolutionaries—United States—Biography. 6. United States—History—Revolution, 1775–1783—Biography. 7. Statesmen—United States—Biography. I. Title.
E210.B43 2013
973.3—dc23   2013001875

10 9 8 7 6 5 4 3 2 1

For Mary

CONTENTS

CAST OF CHARACTERS

The Main Players

John Adams: Fiercely intelligent and fiercely opinionated, he took great pride in his reputation as the "Atlas of Independence." While many of his fellow delegates no doubt admired his commitment to high principle, on many occasions they must have rolled their eyes at his flights into high dudgeon. Adams was an active participant in the Congress from the moment it first convened and stayed around long enough to serve on the drafting committee of the Declaration of Independence. His ideas and emotions were always on display, and, because he was a compulsive correspondent and diarist, he has left us with the most vivid accounts of the events of the forging of American Independence.

Samuel Adams: The Massachusetts Tory Peter Oliver believed that if an artist "wished to draw the Picture of the Devil . . . he would get Sam Adams to sit for him." British officials in the Bay Colony and in London believed that John Adams's older second cousin was capable of turning "the minds of the vulgar . . . into any course that he might chuse." When Sam Adams appeared at the First Continental Congress in September 1774, he surprised the delegates by his somber, logical exegesis on the imperial crisis. The interplay between Sam and John Adams at the Continental Congress had some fascinating twists and turns, with Sam, not John, more often recognizing the importance of gently persuading, rather than badgering, the more reluctant colonies to embrace the decision for independence.

John Dickinson: When he took his seat in the Continental Congress as a delegate from Pennsylvania in October of 1774, Dickinson, along with Boston's Sam Adams, was probably the most well-known defender of American liberty. Dickinson earned that reputation not by his radical activism on the streets of his city, but by the power of his intellect. At the heart of Dickinson's defense was his devout belief in what he called "the principles of the true English constitution." It was that devotion to finding a path toward reconciliation with Great Britain that would set Dickinson and John Adams on opposing courses. When George III failed to change his policies, Dickinson continued to plea for conciliation, delivering a heart-rending speech in the Congress on July 1, 1776, opposing independence. Although he voted against independence and refused to sign the Declaration, he remained a steadfast American patriot, joining the Pennsylvania militia as a brigadier general.

Thomas Jefferson: Next to George Washington, there is no actor in the drama of independence more familiar to Americans. But in September 1774, Thomas Jefferson was still a young, relatively little-known member of the Virginia House of Burgesses. He was not one of the key political powers either in America or even in his home colony of Virginia. He was not elected to serve in the First Continental Congress, and only turned up at the Second Continental Congress in June 1775, elected as an alternate, two months after it had convened. The story of how Jefferson, neither an effective orator nor a political heavyweight in a colony replete with prestigious politicians, became the primary author of the Declaration of Independence, is a fascinating combination of intellectual skill, political maneuvering, and fortunate timing.

King George III: He was not the devil or the tyrant that the American revolutionaries of 1776 made him out to be. Nor was he the incompetent, bumbling, and possibly mentally unstable king portrayed in subsequent histories of the American Revolution. The earnest, modestly intelligent, and somewhat shy and insecure twenty-two-year-old George inherited an enormous responsibility at the death of his grandfather, King George II, in October of 1760. Although George II had often been content to leave matters of imperial policy to his chief ministers in Parliament, his grandson played a more active role in attempting to mediate among the oft-conflicting views of his ministers. By December of 1775, as Americans were becoming more emphatic in denying Parliament's authority over their affairs, the one person whose decisions were capable of producing either reconciliation or revolution was King George III.

Thomas Paine: Born the son of a poor Quaker corset-maker in Thetford, England, he first set foot on American soil on November 30, 1774. (In fact, he may not have actually had his feet on the ground that day, as he was so sickened by the voyage, he had to be carried off his ship and taken to a nearby boardinghouse.) With a modest letter of recommendation from Benjamin Franklin, he soon secured employment as a journeyman writer for *The Pennsylvania Magazine*. On January 10, 1776, with little in his previous writings to suggest the monumental place he would assume in the history of the American Revolution, Thomas Paine published *Common Sense*. Paine's pamphlet would not only accelerate the Americans' movement toward independence, it would also change the course of history.

George Washington: When Colonel Washington arrived in Philadelphia to attend the First Continental Congress, his fellow delegates immediately flocked to take his measure. His military reputation, as well as his imposing physical presence (he was six feet three), were already becoming the stuff of legend. Washington attended both the First and Second Continental Congresses, appearing at the Second, in the immediate aftermath of the battles of Lexington and Concord, in the full dress uniform of a colonel in the Virginia militia. Had anyone else appeared at a civilian gathering in military uniform, those assembled would have regarded the man so attired either as odd or as pathetically ambitious in his quest for high military appointment. But Washington was Washington, and no one looked askance. The decision of the Congress to appoint Washington commander in chief of the still-unformed Continental Army, though opposed by a few from New England, would mark a decisive step on the road to independence.

Important Participants

Samuel Chase: Although the congressional delegation from Maryland wavered on the question of independence up until near the very end, he had been a militant defender of American rights from the moment of his entry into the First Continental Congress in September of 1774. He was a vigorous advocate of a total boycott on all trade with Great Britain, and, in June of 1776, he returned to Maryland and mobilized the people there in a campaign to persuade the members of that colony's convention to authorize their delegates to the Congress to vote in favor of independence. His effort was successful, and on the morning of July 2, after riding 150 miles in two days, he walked into the Congress to announce Maryland's support of the resolution for independence.

James Duane: A highly successful New York lawyer, Duane was a consistent advocate of "moderation" in the conflict with Great Britain. In spite of opposition from many of the more radical patriots in New York, he was elected a delegate to the First Continental Congress. As a member of the committee on rights, he attempted to narrow the Americans' claim to autonomy from all British authority, clashing with the two Adamses and Patrick Henry in the process. Although he was not present in the Congress in July of 1776, he did, reluctantly, endorse the decision for independence.

Lord Dunmore: John Murray, the Fourth Earl of Dunmore, was the royal governor of Virginia from September 1771 until he was forced to flee the colony in January of 1776 by an assault from the Virginia militia. Dunmore was a firm, and highly unpopular, defender of British authority in Virginia and is best known for his notorious proclamation of November 1775 in which he offered freedom to any Virginia slaves who fled their masters to fight on the side of the British.

Benjamin Franklin: When Franklin returned from England in May of 1775 and immediately joined the Pennsylvania delegation to the Second Continental Congress, he was unquestionably the most famous man in America, and also the most famous American in all of Europe. In the Congress he was a strong advocate of inter-colonial union, and he would serve on the committee charged with drafting the Declaration of Independence. Virtually every year of Franklin's life contains something interesting, but the years leading up to independence are particularly extraordinary, for Franklin's natural impulses toward diplomacy and compromise were at war with his growing identity as an "American." Franklin would serve as an important, though not always successful, intermediary between John Adams and John Dickinson.

General Thomas Gage: A British army officer who had fought alongside George Washington during the French and Indian War, Gage served as commander of the British forces in North America. In 1774, in the aftermath of the passage by Parliament of the Coercive Acts, he was appointed military governor of Massachusetts. His attempt to confiscate patriot arms and ammunition in the towns of Lexington and Concord led to the battle that started the Revolutionary War. After failing to convince his superiors in London of the magnitude of the American opposition to British policies, Gage was eventually replaced as military governor and commander of British forces in 1775.

Joseph Galloway: The speaker of the Pennsylvania Assembly when the First Continental Congress convened in September 1774, Galloway was Franklin's closest political ally in Pennsylvania during the period of the early 1760s and early 1770s, but the two men would take very different paths in the two years leading to independence. Unlike Franklin, whose public persona was marked by a plain style and good humor, Galloway's manner—austere, even arrogant—did not win him many friends in the Congress. After the defeat of his proposal for a Plan of Union between the colonies and Great Britain, Galloway became more adamant in opposing any steps that might lead toward independence. When Galloway made the fateful decision to oppose independence and become a Tory, he would provide important, and disastrous, advice to royal officials in London, assuring them that they would be able to recruit a substantial army of American colonists loyal to the Crown in their efforts at putting down the rebellion.

John Hancock: He is, of course, known for his "John Hancock," his outsized signature at the top of the Declaration of Independence. Succeeding Peyton Randolph of Virginia as president of the Continental Congress in May 1775, Hancock was responsible not only for moderating the discussion in the Congress but also for overseeing the ever more complicated actions of the Congress respecting the American military effort. Hancock's relationship with his fellow Massachusetts delegates John and Sam Adams was occasionally a bumpy one, for the two Adamses were not convinced of Hancock's devotion to the cause of independence.

Patrick Henry: The fiery Virginia orator was one of the few members of the First Continental Congress to arrive with independence firmly in mind, declaring, to the alarm of many, that he considered America's connection with Great Britain dissolved and the colonies now living in "a state of nature." When he returned to Virginia after the First Congress had adjourned, he would find that he had a price on his head, with the royal governor, Lord Dunmore, denouncing Henry and his "deluded followers" as traitorous rebels. At the time of the drafting of the Declaration of Independence, Henry was back home preparing to become the first governor of the independent Commonwealth of Virginia. Although absent from the Congress for that climactic event, he played in important role in making it possible.

John Jay: A member of one of the wealthiest and most socially prominent families in New York, Jay, after attending King's College (later Columbia University) and then qualifying for the bar, quickly became a leader both in New York's legal profession and in the city's social scene. Serving in both the First and Second Continental Congresses, he used his high intelligence and political clout to slow the path toward independence. In the spring and early summer of 1776, Jay was back in New York working tirelessly to persuade his colony's political leaders to oppose independence. Like his colleague James Duane, however, Jay would ultimately support independence once the Congress had made its decision and, indeed, would become one of the key negotiators of the treaty of peace with Great Britain at the end of the Revolutionary War.

Richard Henry Lee: Often overshadowed by his more famous Virginia counterparts—Jefferson, Washington and Patrick Henry—in the run-up to independence, Lee was Virginia's most active member of the Continental Congress. John Adams, when he first met Lee in Philadelphia's City Tavern on September 2, 1774, was much impressed, calling the tall, spare Virginian a "Masterly Man." Lee would quickly join forces with the New Englanders to push for bold measures in opposing British oppression and, on June 7, 1776, would propose to the Continental Congress the resolution that, when adopted on July 2, set America on the road to independence.

Lord North: Frederick North, the Second Earl of Guilford, more commonly known as Lord North, was the chief minister of King George III from 1770 to 1782. In that position, he attempted to find a path toward reconciliation between the British and American colonial governments, but since he was never willing to yield on the question of the superior authority of king and Parliament over the colonies, those efforts ultimately led nowhere.

John Rutledge and Edward Rutledge: Both members of South Carolina's wealthy and prestigious Rutledge family had obtained their legal educations at the Inns of Court in London. John Rutledge, the elder of the two brothers, was South Carolina's most influential politician—eventually earning the imposing, but affectionate, sobriquet of "Dictator John." His younger brother Edward was just beginning his political career, but after John returned to South Carolina in November of 1775, it would be Edward who would be an important ally of men like John Dickinson in arguing in the Congress for moderation, hoping that some sort of reconciliation with Great Britain could be achieved. Yet when the moment of decision came, Rutledge stood firmly in the patriot camp. Indeed, as leader of the South Carolina delegation, his support of independence was a crucial element in the decision for independence. But his support came with a catch. When Rutledge and his fellow South Carolinians saw the first draft of Jefferson's Declaration, they quickly spotted the item condemning the slave trade as immoral and contrary to American principles of liberty. That item was, according to Jefferson, "struck out in complaisance" to men like Rutledge, who, far from abolishing the slave trade, wished to expand it.

Roger Sherman: This Connecticut politician was by the testimony of many of his colleagues one of the most physically ungainly specimens ever put on God's earth. According to John Adams, his manner was "the reverse of grace," yet in the same breath Adams declared him to be "one of the soundest and strongest pillars of the Revolution." Jefferson echoed the praise, describing him as "a man who never said a foolish thing in his life." Sherman, one of the few members of the Continental Congress who started his career in poverty— he was the son of a poor shoemaker who died when Sherman was just a young man. His down-to-earth manner and common-sense approach to the imperial crisis earned him a place alongside Jefferson, Franklin, Adams and Robert Livingston on the committee charged with drafting the Declaration of Independence.

THE CONTINENTAL CONGRESS:
A CHRONOLOGY

December 16, 1773—Boston Tea Party.

January 29, 1774—Lord Wedderburn confronts Benjamin Franklin in the "cockpit."

March–May 1774—Parliament passes the Coercive Acts in response to the Boston Tea Party.

May–June 1774—Boston Committee of Correspondence proposes a Solemn League and Covenant boycotting all British goods.
Political Leaders in Pennsylvania and New York call for a meeting of a "general congress" in response to the Coercive Acts.

September 5, 1774—First Continental Congress meets in Carpenters' Hall in Philadelphia.

September 18, 1774—Congress endorses the Suffolk Resolves.

September 27, 1774—Congress agrees to ban imports from Great Britain.

September 28, 1774—Joseph Galloway presents his "Plan of Union."

September 30, 1774—Congress agrees to ban exports to Great Britain, Ireland and the West Indies.

October 14, 1774—Congress adopts a Declaration of Rights and Grievances.

October 20, 1774—Congress approves of the creation of the Association.

October 21, 1774—Congress approves an address to the people of Great Britain.
Congress approves an address to the people of the colonies.

October 26, 1774—Members of Congress sign Address to the King. Congress adjourns, to reconvene on May 10, 1775, if the king and Parliament fail in a "redress of grievances."

January 1775—King George III receives and rejects First Congress's petition.

March 1775—The King's chief minister, Lord North, formulates a "peace plan."

April 19, 1775—Battles of Lexington and Concord.

May 10, 1775—Second Continental Congress convenes in the Assembly Room of the Pennsylvania State House, electing Peyton Randolph president.

May 18, 1775—Congress receives news of the capture of Fort Ticonderoga.

May 24, 1775—Congress elects John Hancock president.

June 9, 1775—Congress authorizes Massachusetts to organize its own government free of royal control.

June 14, 1775—Congress resolves to organize a Continental Army.

June 15, 1775—Congress appoints George Washington commander of the Continental Army.

June 17, 1775—Battle of Bunker Hill.

June 22, 1775—Thomas Jefferson arrives in Philadelphia as a delegate to the Congress.

July 5, 1775—Congress approves an Olive Branch Petition to the king.

July 6, 1775—Congress approves a "Declaration on Taking Arms."

July 31, 1775—Congress responds to Lord North's "peace plan."

August 2, 1775—Congress temporarily adjourns until September 5, 1775.

August 23, 1775—King George III issues his Proclamation for Suppressing Rebellion and Sedition.

September 13, 1775—Congress reconvenes. The colony of Georgia sends a full delegation for the first time, adding the thirteenth member to the "united colonies."

October 13, 1775—Congress authorizes fitting out of armed vessels, marking the beginning of the creation of an American navy.

November 7, 1775—Lord Dunmore, royal governor of Virginia, issues his proclamation promising freedom to slaves willing to fight on the side of the British.

November 9, 1775—Congress receives report of king's rejection of the Olive Branch Petition.

November 1775—In the absence of British authority in those colonies, Congress authorizes New Hampshire and South Carolina to organize their own governments.

December 22, 1775—Parliament and the King approve the Prohibitory Act, effectively declaring war on the American colonies.

January 1776—The Continental Army suffers devastating defeats in Montreal, Canada.

January 10, 1776—Thomas Paine publishes *Common Sense.*

January–May 1776—The individual colonial legislatures discuss, and differ, on the question of independence from Great Britain.

March 4, 1776—General Washington and his troops occupy Dorchester Heights in Boston; British evacuate the city.

March–May 1776—The "phantom" British peace commissioners fail to arrive.

May 15, 1776—The Virginia Convention instructs its delegates to the Continental Congress to place before that body a resolution for independence.

June 7, 1776—Virginia delegate Richard Henry Lee introduces a resolution for independence.

June 11, 1776—Congress appoints a committee to prepare a declaration of independence, with Thomas Jefferson as chair of the committee.

June 28, 1776—Draft of the Declaration of Independence is presented to Congress.

July 1, 1776—Congress begins debate on Lee's resolution for independence.

July 2, 1776—Congress adopts Lee's resolution for independence.

July 2–4, 1776—Congress debates, and edits, the draft of the Declaration of Independence.

July 4, 1776—Congress adopts the Declaration of Independence.

INTRODUCTION

O
N JULY 3, 1776, a tired, but jubilant John Adams sat down at
his desk in Sarah Yard's boarding house on the corner of Second and Market Streets in Philadelphia to write to his beloved wife,
Abigail. He had much to tell. The previous day, the Second Continental Congress had agreed to a resolution affirming that "these
United Colonies are, and of right ought to be, free and independent
states" and renouncing all allegiance to the British crown. Adams re-
joiced in the "Suddenness, as well as Greatness of this Revolution"
and proclaimed, "It is the Will of Heaven, that the two Countries
should be sundered forever." For many months leading up to that
fateful moment, he had worked hard to persuade his fellow delegates
to the Congress—indeed, he had often begged and cajoled them—to
take that fateful step. Now, at last, no doubt with relief as well as jubilation, he was able to send Abigail the news of his success.[1]

Later that day, still in a state of jubilation, John wrote Abigail
again, and envisioned future commemorations of America's decision
for independence. He predicted that "The Second Day of July 1776,
will be the most memorable Epocha, in the History of America. I
am apt to believe that it will be celebrated, by succeeding Generations, as the great anniversary Festival." While his prediction about
the date of the "great anniversary Festival" was off by two days,
Adams was correct in proclaiming that the decisions made during
those days in early July would reverberate through the ages. In the
decades following adoption of the Declaration of Independence, as
Fourth of July celebrations became an important American ritual, it

1

would become commonplace for American politicians and civic leaders to mount the speaker's rostrum to invoke the "will of heaven"—to depict the American Revolution, and the creation of a democratic American nation that came into being in the aftermath of that Revolution, as part of a divine plan, the inevitable result of the efforts of a virtuous citizenry dedicated to freedom.[2]

In retrospect, it may seem that America's decision to declare its independence from Great Britain, whether directed by the will of heaven or through some other more prosaic, but equally inexorable, force, was somehow inevitable. But it seemed anything but inevitable in September of 1774, when the First Continental Congress began the task of forging a united front against British threats to American liberties. It would take twenty-two agonizing months, from the opening session of the Congress on September 5, 1774 until those fateful days in early July of 1776, for the delegates to the Congress to reach the decision for independence. Many of those casting their vote in favor of independence on July 2 did so with a combination of fear, reluctance and even sadness. In their letters to friends and family, most seemed convinced that they had made the right decision, but they also expressed uncertainty about what lay ahead. John Adams himself, in the midst of his rejoicing, acknowledged that it might also be the will of heaven that "America shall suffer Calamities still more wasting and Distresses yet more dreadful." Abraham Clark, one of the delegates from New Jersey, a colony that had only come around at the last minute to support independence, was apprehensive, too. "We are," he wrote, "now embarked on a most Tempestious Sea, Life very uncertain, Seeming Dangers Scattered Thick Around us." And Pennsylvania's Robert Morris, who voted against the resolution for independence on July 2, but then reluctantly signed the Declaration several weeks after it was officially adopted, was overcome with sadness that his colleagues had taken such a drastic step; he continued to believe that "the Interest of Our Country and the Good of Mankind" would have been better served had the Congress gone that extra mile to achieve some sort of reconciliation with their mother country.[3]

To understand the radical nature—indeed, the audacity—of the Americans' decision for independence, we need to put ourselves back into the minds and hearts of those delegates who traveled to Philadelphia for the opening of the First Continental Congress in September of 1774. That Congress was, in the words of John Adams, "a gathering of strangers," a group of men who brought with them widely differing interests and cultural perspectives, and very little sense of themselves as "Americans." Whether through their reading of their local newspapers or of the most recently published and avidly sought-after fashion magazines from London, the residents of Massachusetts, Virginia or South Carolina were much more familiar with the customs, fashions and contemporary happenings in their mother country than they were with events in neighboring colonies. As South Carolinian John Drayton observed, the residents of his colony were "too much prejudiced in favour of British manners, customs and knowledge, to imagine that elsewhere than in England, anything of advantage could be obtained." Why then should the residents of his colony even bother to get to know anything about not only the manners and customs but also the aspirations of the residents of any other American colony?[4]

Perhaps the only thing that bound American colonists together at that moment in 1774 was their common identity as subjects of the British Crown and their loyalty, indeed, their love, of the British monarch. Beginning in the early eighteenth century, it had become standard practice to hang portraits of British monarchs and royal officials in the colonies' legislative chambers and even in their country courts and town halls. As the power, prestige, and territorial expanse of the British empire grew over the course of the eighteenth century, Americans' pride in their empire, and in their king, increased as well. Towns across America began to stage public ceremonies honoring the king's birthday. As entrepreneurial printers began to reproduce large quantities of portraits of King George III, it became commonplace—even fashionable—for Americans of all social classes to display those portraits in their homes. Benjamin Franklin's wife, Deborah, writing to her husband while he was serving as a colonial agent in London, reported with pride that she had decorated the main room of their house in Philadelphia "with brother John's picture and one of the King and Queen."[5]

One of the most dramatic examples of this devotion to the monarch, even as their relationship with the British Parliament began to deteriorate, occurred in October of 1768, when Benjamin Rush, the highly respected Philadelphia physician—and, later, a signer of the Declaration of Independence—visited the grand assembly room of the House of Lords in London. There he found himself gazing at the ornate golden throne of King George III. "I felt," he reported, "as if I walked on sacred ground." He stood, transfixed, overcome with "emotions I cannot describe." In an act of uncommon boldness, Rush asked his guide if he might be permitted to sit upon the throne. The guide initially told him that that was out of the question, but such was the intensity of Rush's appeal, that the guide reluctantly agreed to allow him to. When Rush first sat down on the throne, he was so overwhelmed with feeling, with "such a crowd of ideas" passing through his mind, that he could barely make sense of his experience. But, truly, he recalled, "this is the golden period of the worldly man's wishes. His passions conceive, his hopes aspire, after nothing beyond this Throne."

Rush next went to the chamber of the House of Commons, where he felt nothing but anger. This was the body that had recently enacted the much-detested Stamp Act and Townshend Duties. This was the "place where the infernal scheme for enslaving America was first broached. Here the usurping Commons first endeavored to rob the King of his supremacy over the colonies and to divide it among themselves."[6]

Between 1768 and the early fall of 1774, when the delegates to the First Continental Congress convened in Philadelphia, the conflict escalated still further, but even then, nearly all of the delegates who arrived in Philadelphia to attend that Congress were still holding on to the distinction made by Rush that October in London. However much they may have held the British Parliament in contempt, however overheated their rhetoric about the intent of the Parliament and the king's ministers in Parliament to "enslave them," they, like most of their fellow colonists, found themselves torn by mixed emotions— outrage at British invasions of American liberty and love for their mother country and their king. *Our Lives, Our Fortunes and Our Sacred Honor* begins with a brief account of the escalating conflict between the American colonies and the British imperial government during the years between 1763 and the fateful night of December 16, 1773, when a group of "Mohawk Indians" threw 90,000 pounds of East India Company tea in Boston Harbor. The outraged British reaction to that Tea Party in Boston—embodied in a series of punitive parliamentary laws that came to be known as the "Coercive Acts"—moved the conflict to new heights. But the thirteen American colonies were by no means united on how to combat those new threats to their liberties. Chapter Two describes first the indecision and then the reluctant agreement among the colonies to call a "general congress" to discuss the best means of defending American liberties while at the same time searching for a path toward reconciliation with their "mother country." The next twenty-three chapters tell the story of the deliberations of that Congress during the critically important months between September 5, 1774, and July 4, 1776—during which time America's political leaders worked their way through the often agonizing process that ultimately led to their audacious leap toward independence—shedding both their provincial and their imperial British identities and, in the process, transforming themselves into leaders of an *American* cause.[7]

Many of the principal characters in the drama of the decision for independence are familiar to most Americans. The passionate, mercurial and, in the eyes of many delegates, occasionally obnoxious John Adams seems to have been on center stage at nearly every moment in the drama. John's older cousin Sam, reputed to be a wild-eyed radical, surprised many by the quiet and patient way in which he worked to persuade the more reluctant delegates that independence from England was the correct path. Few of the delegates to the Congress had ever met the reserved but powerfully dignified George Washington. From the moment of his arrival in Philadelphia, however, his very presence inspired respect, even awe. And Thomas Jefferson, a relative newcomer to the proceedings, in spite of his poor oratorical talents, would provide the elegant words that would justify American independence.

There were many other actors in the story who deserve greater attention than they have received. The Congress's secretary, Pennsylvania's Charles Thomson, was an abysmal record keeper, but he was also a powerful advocate for independence in a Pennsylvania delegation that dragged its feet on that question until the very end; he would come to be admired as the "Sam Adams of Philadelphia." Virginia's Richard Henry Lee—the most active and outspoken member of his delegation—introduced the resolution for independence into the Congress and was an indispensable ally to the Adamses in persuading the delegates to sever their ties to Great Britain. Christopher Gadsden, an outlier radical in a South Carolina delegation dominated by wealthy and conservative planters, not only provided important support for the New Englanders in the Congress but also rallied the forces for independence on the streets of Charleston. Edward Rutledge, the leader of the South Carolina delegation and one of John Adams's least favorite people, was an unrestrained Anglophile who enjoyed flaunting his Oxford University education and his subsequent legal training at the Middle Temple in London. He sat on the fence until the day before the July 2 vote, finally adding his support to the cause of independence. While Samuel Chase's fellow Maryland delegates were marking time until receiving word from their legislature on how to vote on the question of independence, the Annapolis lawyer traveled back home and organized a grassroots campaign to pressure the legislature into supporting the resolution for independence. And then there was that recent English immigrant who was not even a member of the Congress, Thomas Paine. Paine's life to that point had consisted of one failure after another. When he left England for America in the fall of 1774, no one could have imagined the impact he would have, both in his newly adopted home and around the world. In January of 1776, just a little over a year after his ship landed at the port of Philadelphia, he published *Common Sense*, a pamphlet that would change the course of history.

Of course there were some actors in this drama, among them many equally sincere and equally honorable, who made different choices. Not enough attention—or respect—has been given to those who dissented from the decision for independence. Joseph Galloway, the most powerful politician in Pennsylvania when the Continental Congress first convened in early September 1774, was not the most charming or most likable man in Philadelphia that summer, but during the first session of the Congress he would introduce what may have been the most promising and creative proposal for ending the constitutional crisis with England—a Plan of Union calling for the creation of a special congress in which both Great Britain and the colonies would be represented. When his proposal was defeated—by some accounts by only a single vote—Galloway would devote all of his energies to thwarting any move toward independence. Once independence was declared, he would try, unsuccessfully, to mobilize the American colonists into a loyalist army committed to putting an end to the American "treason" and then, in 1778, would flee with his daughter to England to try, again unsuccessfully, to lead the American Loyalist movement there.

There is one other character whose central role in this drama has not been given its due; indeed, he has sometimes been vilified as either misguided or simply cowardly. As the First Continental Congress began its deliberations, Pennsylvania's John Dickinson was widely respected as the most astute constitutional theorist in all of America. Admired by nearly all (with the notable exception of his chief adversary, John Adams) for his integrity and devotion to principle, on July 2 Dickinson would speak movingly, and unsuccessfully, in favor of further attempts at reconciliation and *against* independence. He voted against the resolution for independence and refused to sign the Declaration of Independence, but having voted his conscience, he immediately departed the Congress to serve as a major general in the patriot army. Dickinson predicted that his stand against independence would harm his reputation for all of eternity. I hope that this narrative of the journey toward independence will help explain the reasons for Dickinson's actions and in doing so resurrect the good reputation of this highly principled Pennsylvanian.

One of the recurring themes in this account of the decision for independence is the importance of *leadership*. In my previous work, *Plain, Honest Men: The Making of the American Constitution*, I sought to demonstrate the varieties of leadership represented by those men who gathered together in Philadelphia in the summer of 1787: the deep and thoughtful scholarly deliberation of James Madison and James Wilson; Gouverneur Morris's brilliant, but sometimes combative advocacy of a vastly strengthened central government; the Connecticut delegate Roger Sherman's dogged, practical-minded negotiations aimed at resolving the differences between large- and small-state delegates; and George Washington's reserved, but powerful, command over every day of the proceedings during that summer. The outcome—the creation of a "more perfect," if not *entirely* perfect, union—was in large measure the result not only of the individual leadership qualities of the convention delegates, but also of the collective leadership they displayed as they came together in a spirit of collaboration and compromise.

As we will see in the coming pages, the types of leadership on display in the Continental Congress during the months leading to independence were at least as varied as those at the Constitutional Convention of 1787—the fiery oratory of Patrick Henry; the indefatigable behind-the-scenes political maneuvering of John and Sam Adams; and the powerful and elegant literary gifts of Thomas Jefferson. But the challenges facing the revolutionaries of 1776 were not only more formidable, but also less predictable. The thirty-nine "Founding Fathers" who signed the Constitution in September of 1787 had as their starting point the successful outcome of the bold actions of their predecessors in 1776. The fifty-six men who signed the Declaration of Independence, five of whom also later signed the Constitution, had no past precedents, no examples of previous occasions in which Americans from all of the colonies had engaged successfully in a common cause, to guide them. In even contemplating the unprecedented act of a people's revolution against duly constituted authority, they were setting sail on uncharted waters.

The delegates to the Continental Congress faced other leadership challenges as well. At every stage during the twenty-two months of their service, and in spite of the oath of secrecy they had taken requiring that they not reveal the details of their deliberations in the Congress, the delegates knew that they were responsible to the people of America in whose name they were acting. As they first convened, it may well have been the case that many of the delegates represented the leading edge of public opinion. But as the months dragged on, as the people of America mobilized to enforce a boycott of all British trade in America and, beginning in April of 1775, as ordinary Americans put their lives on the line in outright war against a British adversary, many of the delegates discovered that leadership consisted of paying closer attention to those on the front lines of the conflict with

Great Britain. America on the eve of the Revolution was by no means a fully *democratic* society, but the very act of declaring independence in the name of the people would move both leaders and ordinary Americans closer to recognizing the practical implications of their invocation of principles of democracy and popular sovereignty.

The story of American independence is not just about the thoughts and actions of individuals. One of the other important themes of this book is that of the evolution of American institutions and, indeed, American identity. When the Continental Congress first convened, it was an ad hoc extra-legal body with limited power and authority. It was, consonant with the eighteenth-century meaning of the word "congress," a body composed of delegates obliged to follow the instructions given them by their separate and autonomous legislatures. While its delegates might pass resolutions and draft petitions, it did not have the power to *legislate*, much less the power to raise an army or fight a war. But from the fall of 1774 to the summer of 1776 the Continental Congress would begin to lay claim to both legislative and executive powers, and, in the process, would ultimately transform the very meaning of the word "congress." The story of the complete transformation of the "continental" congress into an *American* congress armed with the sovereign power to "establish justice, insure domestic tranquility, provide for the common defence, promote the general Welfare, and secure the Blessings of Liberty" is one that would not begin to achieve full reality until the creation of a new federal government under the United States Constitution. But the beginning of that story—with enormous political and constitutional implications that continue to affect our lives even today—occurred with the convening of the First Continental Congress in September of 1774.

The final paragraph of the Declaration of Independence spoke for the first time of "the united States of America," making the pledge of "our Lives, our Fortunes and our sacred Honor" on behalf of all of the American people. In truth, it was more an expression of hope than a description of reality, but it marked the beginning of the journey toward becoming a truly American nation. President Barack Obama, in his first Independence Day celebratory address from the White House on July 4, 2009, recognized the radical character of that fateful step. He astutely pointed to the "extraordinary audacity it took . . . for a group of patriots to cast off the title of 'subject' for 'citizen,' and to put ideas to paper that were as simple as they were revolutionary: that we are equal; that we are free; that we can pursue our full measure of happiness and make of our lives what we will."

Audacious it was. It was certainly among the most important and far-reaching decisions in the history of the Western world. It marked the first attempt by a colonial people to determine their own political destiny. It was the first revolution based on the principle of popular sovereignty, the notion that since governments are based on the consent of the people, it is also "the Right of the People to alter or abolish" that government if it ceases to serve the purposes for which it was created. More expansively, but also more tentatively, Americans, in their Declaration of Independence, held out the hope of a democratic and egalitarian future. The Americans' success in gaining their independence, achieved only after eight years of exhausting and bloody warfare, would send a message to the rest of the world, changing the course of history in the process. It is a message that still reverberates all over the globe today.

ONE

THE GENESIS OF
REVOLUTION, 1763–1774

The Turning Point

They came, seven thousand strong, from the neighborhoods of Boston and the surrounding countryside. They streamed down the streets of the south side of Boston, heading toward Griffin's Wharf. Few among them, it is likely, on that cold, clear night of December 16, 1773, would ever forget what they were about to see.

Joshua Wyeth, a sixteen-year-old journeyman blacksmith, was one of those who turned the tide of history that night. He and his fellows dressed up as Mohawk warriors to disguise their identity. Within the three fifty-man groups there were a few well-established artisans or middle-class merchants, including the prominent Boston silversmith Paul Revere. But most were young apprentices, journeymen and merchant seamen. They smeared their faces with grease or lamp black, so that, in Joshua Wyeth's words, "our most intimate friends among the spectators had not the least knowledge of us. We sure resembled devils from the bottomless pit rather than men."[1]

At about 6:15 they carefully, quietly boarded three ships—the *Dartmouth*, the *Eleanor* and the *Beaver*. All three had been built in America, primarily for the purpose of whaling, and were owned by Americans. But on that night they were under the command of captains from the British East India Company, and their cargo was *not* whale oil. In the ships' holds were 342 wooden chests, each weighing

400 pounds, containing in all 92,600 pounds of tea from India. In Wyeth's recollection, the men "were merry . . . at the idea of making so large a cup of tea for the fishes," but they also realized that stealth and discipline were essential to the success of their mission. It was serious business, and they spoke "no more words than were absolutely necessary." And it was hard work, chopping the wooden chests open and heaving them overboard. Another of the band, Samuel Nowell, a ship's carpenter, recalled: "I was then young, enterprising, and courageous. And I presume my broad axe was never more dexterously used than while I was staving the Chests and throwing them overboard."[2]

As the crowd on the wharf watched, they could hear the steady chopping of the hatchets, and by nine o'clock that evening, the work was done. To avoid the accusation that they were a disorderly mob run amok, they took special care to prevent any unnecessary breakage and any theft. When a padlock in the captain's cabin of one of the ships was accidentally broken, one of the participants was sent into town to secure a replacement. And when one of the party attempted to make off with some of the loose tea by hiding it in the lining of his coat, his co-conspirators stripped him, covered him in mud, and gave him "a severe bruising in the bargain." Only their desire to avoid any further disturbance kept him from being tarred and feathered.[3]

There was a palpable sense of excitement, of ebullience, in the crowd at the wharf on that moonless night as they strained to see the tea sink into the water. But there was also a sense of restraint. The Massachusetts *Gazette*, reporting on the events of the evening, noted with some amazement that "the town was very quiet during the whole evening and the night following." It seemed that virtually everyone in the town understood that something extraordinary had occurred, that it was a time for solemn contemplation rather than raucous celebration. Few, if any, realized that they had stood witness to the beginning of a revolution.[4]

The Beginnings

A decade earlier it would have been difficult for anyone in America to have predicted, or even imagined, the sense of crisis that existed among Americans during the lead-up and in the aftermath of the

Boston Tea Party. Although individual American colonies and their political leaders had engaged in occasional skirmishes over a variety of economic or government policies during the seventeenth and early eighteenth centuries, on the whole, the weight of "imperial" authority had rested very lightly on American shoulders. Colonial legislatures, and the provincial leaders who served in those legislatures, enjoyed remarkable autonomy; indeed, there was good reason for the members of America's provincial ruling class to feel that they had achieved a status nearly equal to that of their counterparts in the British Parliament. And the unofficial, but nevertheless very real, British policy of "salutary neglect" had allowed for a burgeoning American commercial economy that sometimes operated in technical violation of British navigation laws.[5]

But this would all begin to change in the year 1763. The origins of the Americans' conflict with their mother country lay in those two things that have caused trouble since time immemorial: money and taxes. The British government, in the aftermath of a successful but costly war with France (as well as against some of France's Indian allies in North America), found itself with a vastly expanded empire west of the Appalachian mountains and in Canada. That was the good news. The bad news was that the costs of that war had left the government deeply in debt; given the need to protect their newly won gains, the king and members of Parliament could see the prospect of even deeper debt on the horizon. In their view, the Americans should surely pay their fair share of the costs of the war and its aftermath, for they would ultimately find in those newly acquired lands new sources of opportunity.

Of course, the Americans were not likely to see things that way. They too had made many sacrifices of blood and treasure during the Seven Years' War. And a young colonel from Virginia, George Washington, had earned an international reputation for his bravery as a commander of a Virginia militia regiment during that war. From the Americans' point of view, the conclusion of the Seven Year's War marked a time when they could begin to enjoy the relative peace in a world in which the threat of French intrigue and Indian warfare on their borders was substantially diminished. At precisely the time when royal officials in London were concluding that the Americans should start to pay their fair share of the costs of the empire from which they had enjoyed such great benefit, most Americans, weary of sacrifice and feeling more "independent" of the need for Great Britain's help in protecting their frontier, were hardly in a mood to increase their financial contributions to royal officials back in London.

Beginning in 1764 and 1765, the British Parliament began levying new taxes on the colonies aimed not merely at the regulation of trade but at raising a revenue to pay for the increased costs of managing their expanding empire. In 1764, the king's chancellor of the exchequer George Grenville presented to Parliament a bill that actually lowered the tax on foreign molasses imported into America from six pence per gallon to three pence. Knowing, however, that Americans had been smuggling molasses and therefore paying no duty on the commodity, Grenville also made it clear that, by tightening the enforcement of existing customs regulations, British customs collectors would actually collect the tax and therefore add to the revenue in the British treasury. Parliament quickly passed the so-called Sugar Act, and the reformulation of British tax policy had begun. In 1765, Grenville and the British Parliament moved forward with a more far-reaching piece of legislation, the Stamp Act, which imposed a tax affecting many of the internal operations of the American economy, including taxes on a variety of commercial and legal documents. In fact the amount of the taxes was not so large as to present much of an economic burden to Americans, but both the purpose of the taxes—to raise a revenue for the British treasury—and the means by which the taxes were imposed—enacted by a distant Parliament in which the colonists had no representatives and without their consent—were deeply offensive to Americans. Citing the principles of the unwritten, but deeply revered, "English constitution," Americans protested the taxes on the grounds that they violated the principle of "no taxation without representation."[6]

Protests against parliamentary taxation began in an orderly way—with the political leaders in the colonies' provincial assemblies sending petitions to Parliament asking for the repeal of what they considered to be the unconstitutional and burdensome taxes. Beginning in Boston, ordinary folks in America's cities and towns engaged in other forms of protest. Street marches and demonstrations gradually escalated into full-scale economic boycotts of British goods and, occasionally, the destruction of British property and violence aimed at the British officials charged with enforcing the new imperial policies.

What began as a constitutional debate between English and colonial political leaders was becoming something more volatile—an intensely personal conflict between British officials and ordinary folks on the streets of cities like Boston, New York and Philadelphia. American resistance bred reaction, with the British responding by sending more troops to restore order in their increasingly restive colonies. Parliament was provoked into passing additional legislation—not merely taxes, but other measures, including an order requiring that Americans provide lodging for British troops in their homes—an order that even further inflamed public opinion against the increasing parliamentary "tyranny."

During the period between 1764 and 1773, this escalation of popular resistance, followed by British attempts both to repress the resistance and punish the resisters, was confined principally to American seaport cities and a few colonial capitals of government. And, at least in the eyes of British officials in London, the town of Boston was not only the most obstreperous and violent of those centers of resistance but almost certainly the prime instigator. And again from the British point of view, the blame for Boston's central role in the conflict could be laid at the door of just a few fanatical, self-interested demagogues who had made that town a many-headed "Hydra" of protest.[7]

"Picture of the Devil"

Public enemy number one, to royal officials both in Boston and in London, was a shabbily dressed, but tireless and brilliant political agitator named Samuel Adams. Peter Oliver, who would become one of the most outspoken of Massachusetts' Loyalists, later would say of Adams that if one "wished to draw a picture of the Devil, that he would get Sam Adams to sit for him."

The route that Adams had taken to achieve his fame (or, from the British point of view, infamy) had been circuitous. The son of a moderately prosperous Boston brewmaster and local politician, also named Samuel Adams, the younger Sam Adams's family lineage was distinguished enough that when he entered Harvard in 1736 at the age of fourteen, his class rank, determined not by academic merit but by his family's social status, was number five in a class of twenty-two. At the urging of his father, he studied theology during his undergraduate years, but even then his natural inclination was toward politics. After graduating from Harvard in 1740, he spent a few years halfheartedly attempting to begin a career in business, but then he returned to his alma mater in 1743, where he focused his intellectual efforts on political philosophy, writing his master's thesis on the subject of "Whether it be lawful to resist the Supreme Magistrate, if the Commonwealth cannot be otherwise preserved."[8]

Although Adams remained a devout Puritan all of his life, he was not drawn either to the clergy or, indeed, to any other occupation likely to earn him a living. For many years after his graduation from Harvard he seemed a young man adrift. Upon his father's death in 1748, Sam inherited a modest fortune. He took over the management of his father's brewery, but it was clear to all around him that he had neither the talent nor the inclination to keep the business thriving. The brewery went quickly downhill and, with it, the inheritance from his father. In 1758, virtually all of the Adams estate—the brewery, his house and a variety of other modest landholdings—were put up for auction by the town sheriff. Showing a flash of the skills that he would use so effectively during the revolutionary crisis, Adams swung into action, appearing in person at the auction, scaring off potential bidders on the property by threatening to sue anyone who set foot on his property. He averted foreclosure, but holding onto the property did little to improve his precarious financial position; the brewery would soon fail altogether, and his house fall into disrepair. Adams's personal life during those years provided equal cause for despair. In 1749, at the age of twenty-seven, he married the twenty-four-year-old Elizabeth Checkley, and they immediately set out to create a large family. Over the course of the next six years Elizabeth would give birth to five children. This was an age, however, when infant mortality was extremely high, and only two of Elizabeth's children survived beyond the age of three months. And, when Elizabeth gave birth to a stillborn son in July of 1757, she was so weakened by the delivery that she died a few weeks later, at the age of thirty-two, leaving Adams a widower, a single parent of two children and the proprietor of a declining brewery business.[9]

In the midst of his financial and personal travail, Adams was beginning to involve himself in the civic affairs of his hometown of Boston, earning a reputation as an intelligent and reliable public servant. He volunteered to serve on a variety of committees, one overseeing the operation of a local school and another charged with the task of inspecting the town's chimneys. He was also developing a following as an eloquent and persuasive journalist, writing on a variety of civic and political issues. As early as 1756 he began to write newspaper essays questioning the excessive concentration of power in the hands of Massachusetts' royal governor, William Shirley. Adams had also become a member of several of Boston's political clubs, including the influential Boston Caucus, a group of Boston residents who regularly supported the prerogatives of provincial political leaders against those of royal government officials. In 1760, he had become sufficiently prominent in local politics that the Boston town meeting asked him to help in the drafting of instructions for the town's four members of the Massachusetts House of Representatives.

Adams was rewarded for his local political activism in 1756 by being elected one of the town's four tax collectors, a potential, though somewhat risky, path toward a more influential career as a public servant. Whether through inattention to duty or, perhaps, excessive charity, he proved an abysmally poor collector of the town's tax revenues. A report issued by the town in March of 1763 indicated that of the £4,000 in taxes that remained uncollected during the previous year, Adams was responsible for £2,200 in those tax arrears. As much as his casual approach to tax collection may have appealed to some of his fellow residents, the Boston officials responsible for balancing the town's budget were not pleased, and Adams was soon thereafter relieved of his responsibilities.[10]

At that moment, at the dawn of America's impending conflict with Great Britain, Sam Adams, though undeniably smart, articulate, well-educated and reasonably well-connected, had not yet found his calling. Idling his time away in Boston's taverns and coffeehouses talking politics and writing occasional newspaper pieces, Adams did not seem destined for fame. He and his second wife, Elizabeth Wells, the twenty-four-year-old daughter of a family friend, lived in the run-down house left him by his father. Anyone who encountered Adams on the street at that time would have found him wearing tattered, ill-fitting cast-off clothes collected either by his frugal new wife or donated by neighbors.

The Imperial Crisis and Sam Adams's Rise to Fame

Sam Adams's life would began to change dramatically when news of Great Britain's first serious steps to tighten up on the financial administration of its empire—the enactment by Parliament of first the Sugar Act, and later the Stamp Act—reached Boston. The Stamp Act would prove particularly vulnerable to political attack, because its imposition of taxes on virtually all legal, commercial and public documents would have their greatest impact on such highly vocal occupational groups as lawyers, merchants and newspaper printers. Adams, whose writings about local politics had already gained him a modest following, was ready to seize the opportunity to enhance his reputation as a defender of American liberty. At the request of the Boston town meeting, he helped to draft the town's first response to Parliament's newly announced intention of levying new taxes on the colonies. And he began to shift his formidable writing skills into high gear, authoring an ever increasing number of pamphlets denouncing royal encroachments on American liberties. Lieutenant Governor Thomas Hutchinson, who would soon become one of Adams's principal targets, grudgingly acknowledged Adams's increasing literary skills during this period, noting, however, that much of the improvement consisted of the "talent of artfully and fallaciously insinuating into the minds of his readers a prejudice against the characters . . . he attacked."[11]

Already a member of politically active organizations such as the Boston Caucus, Adams became closely associated with (though never a formal member of) a group of politically radical shopkeepers and artisans known as the Loyal Nine, formed in response to the passage of the Stamp Act. As the leader of that group's successor organization, the Sons of Liberty, Adams mobilized not only working and middle-class Bostonians but also the city's growing population of unemployed and underemployed sailors, semiskilled and unskilled workers in a protest movement the likes of which America had never seen.

The new protest movement erupted with ferocity in August of 1765. That month, a humble shoemaker named Ebenezer McIntosh led his 2,000-man gang, the South End Mob, in the coerced resignation of the man assigned the job of collecting the Stamp Tax, Andrew Oliver. Oliver's resignation, which was quickly followed by the mob's demolition of the new customs house and then, a few days later, the destruction of the home of Lieutenant Governor Hutchinson, made it abundantly clear to British officials just how powerless they were in the face of an enraged citizenry. When the royal governor, Francis Bernard, ordered the arrest of McIntosh, Boston's sheriff, Stephen Greenleaf, ruefully noted that if he were to arrest McIntosh, royal officials would soon discover that there were not any government buildings left standing in the town. An embarrassed Bernard, defending his inaction to his superiors back in London, admitted that "the mob was so general and so supported that all civil power ceased in an Instant, and I had not the least authority to oppose or quiet the Mob." With Bernard's admission of defeat, British attempts to enforce the Stamp Act in Boston effectively came to an end.[12]

Boston's example would not be lost on Great Britain's other colonies in America. Although resistance to the Stamp Act outside of Boston may not have been as violent or as dramatic, it was in the end equally effective. The British Parliament, with many of its members gritting their teeth and vowing to continue their attempt to tax the colonies, repealed the Stamp Act in February of 1766.

American opposition to the Stamp Act in Boston and elsewhere set a pattern that would be repeated during the years from 1766 to 1773. The British Parliament, at the urging of the King's Ministry, a group of the king's chief advisers who acted as his chief operatives in Parliament, would attempt to assert its authority over the colonies, and the colonies would successfully resist. The British would make a tactical retreat but would continue to assert their theoretical right, as they did in the Declaratory Act in 1766, to "legislate for the American colonies in all cases whatsoever." This pattern of royal assertion, colonial resistance and royal retreat had other consequences. As Americans of all social classes continued to clash with British royal officials and British soldiers, the conflict escalated from a clash of constitutional principles and economic interests to one with an *intensely personal* dimension. Royal officials like Thomas Hutchinson came to despise men like Sam Adams, who seemed to spend every waking moment making their lives miserable. British soldiers, charged with keeping order and greatly outnumbered by unruly members of tireless mobs, felt increasingly angry and beleaguered. And those feelings were reciprocated by their American antagonists.

The most concerted and well-organized forms of American opposition during the years 1766–1773 occurred in America's seaport cities, where the colonists' economic interests were most directly threatened by the British policies of taxation and commercial regulation and where there were larger concentrations of middle- and lower-class residents capable of exerting a show of force in resisting British policies. Although American resistance occurred in fits and starts, declining and then re-emerging with the appearance of new British provocations, the overall *tone* of that resistance began to change. American grievances against British policies were founded both in economic interest and in constitutional principle. Economic interest was based in the natural desire to avoid any taxes or any form of regulation that might affect Americans' pocketbooks. Constitutional principle was expressed in resolutions and petitions drafted in virtually every American colonial legislature that Parliament did not have the authority to tax the colonies without their consent. Some of the mounting antagonism between the British and the colonists was no doubt a natural consequence of the escalation of the constitutional and economic conflict that divided the two sides. But it was given an added boost by the conscious attempts of men like Sam Adams to organize and energize the opposition. Organizations like Boston's Sons of Liberty would spread to other colonies, serving as a critical mediating force between the sorts of upper-class colonists who served in the provincial legislatures and ordinary townspeople who would make up the rank and file of the resistance movement. Sam Adams proved particularly effective at using a longstanding institution of civic governance, the Boston Town Meeting, as a means of implementing the agenda of the Sons of Liberty. Normally a town meeting would only be called at regularly scheduled times in order to discuss and act on the regular business of the town, which included things like the granting of licenses for taverns and coffeehouses or the enforcement of regulations preventing wild pigs from running through the streets. But in this new, politically volatile environment, Adams's verbal and organizational skills enabled him to arrange for extraordinary sessions of the town meeting in which he and like-minded Boston radicals would rouse the populace to oppose some new British provocation.[13]

However well-organized the opposition in Boston may have been, Sam Adams was acutely aware that the American resistance to British policy needed to be orchestrated and coordinated on an intercolonial basis to be truly effective. As early as 1771 he wrote to Arthur Lee, a Virginian who had published an influential set of essays denouncing the recent British policies, suggesting that "in every colony societies should be formed out of the most respectable inhabitants"; those societies, he believed, could join forces and cause the "enemies of our common liberty . . . to tremble." It would be another year before he would effectuate his plan, but in the fall of 1772, he made his move. At a Boston Town Meeting on November 2, he proposed that "a committee of correspondence be appointed . . . to state the rights of the colonists and of this Province in particular, as men and Christians, and as subjects; and to communicate and publish the same to the several towns and to the world." After several hours of debate, the Bostonians endorsed Adams's proposal. Adams wasted no time. The Boston Committee of Correspondence held its first meeting the next day, and from that meeting would emerge plans to organize similar committees in towns all across Massachusetts, and then to widen the network to other colonies. It was the beginning—the bare beginning—of a coordinated, *American* resistance movement.[14]

Not everyone in the colony was pleased. Daniel Leonard, a Massachusetts lawyer who would eventually cast his lot with the Tories, described Adams's actions as the "foulest, subtlest, and most venomous serpent ever issued from the egg of sedition." Thomas Hutchinson, promoted to the position of royal governor of Massachusetts in 1771, was equally unhappy, but in a letter to Lord Dartmouth, one of King George's chief advisers, he grudgingly acknowledged the popularity of

Adams's proposals, advising the king to ban any further town meetings in Boston, which he believed to be the source of all of the spirit of rebellion that Adams was fomenting.[15]

But spread it did. Not only did other Massachusetts towns form similar committees, but, one by one, nearly all of the colonies followed suit—Virginia, in March of 1773, followed by Rhode Island, Connecticut, New Hampshire and South Carolina a few months later. By the time the Massachusetts "Mohawk Indians" had their tea party on December 16, 1773, New York and Pennsylvania, the perennial laggards in the resistance to British policy, were beginning to organize committees of their own.[16]

The Tea Act and Its Consequences

It was in this context of growing political activism in Boston and a heightened alertness on the part of other colonies that rumors began swirling in America in the spring of 1773. The British, it was said, intended to give a monopoly on the trade in tea to its principal, but financially troubled, commercial enterprise in South Asia, the East India Company. In the past the company had been required to send its ships through English ports before traveling to America, but by the terms of the Tea Act, which went into effect in 1773, it was allowed to transport the tea it obtained in the India trade directly to the American colonies, thus lowering its costs. By early October Americans learned that the British Parliament had not only awarded a monopoly to the company, but also that the royal government intended to levy taxes on the tea, to be collected in America from Americans, once the East India Company had landed the tea on American shores. The members of Parliament who voted in favor of the act thought it would be a win-win situation, for not only would it help the East India Company to carry out its trade more efficiently, but it might also actually serve to lower the price of tea in America, since the company would no longer have to pay taxes levied on its trade in England. But there were two problems with this reasoning. First, most Americans were accustomed to buying tea smuggled in from Holland—tea on which they paid *no taxes*. And perhaps of greater importance, many Americans, and, in particular, nearly all

American merchants, recognized that not only would the granting of a monopoly to the East India Company shut them out of the tea trade altogether, but it could also, in the long run, leave the Company free to charge whatever price they wished for their imported tea.

As soon as he heard news of the passage of the Tea Act, Sam Adams began to organize the opposition to its implementation. On Friday, November 5, he and other Boston radicals organized a town meeting in Faneuil Hall, Boston's principal marketplace and meeting hall. The wealthy and prominent Boston merchant John Hancock moderated the meeting, though given Hancock's previous history of confrontational opposition to British customs policies, few could doubt that the outcome of the meeting would be anything but moderate. The citizens vowed "a virtuous and steady opposition to this ministerial plan of governing America" and made clear their opposition to any attempt either to unload or sell the tea in Boston.[17]

On Sunday, November 28, the first of the three East India Company ships, the *Dartmouth*, sailed into Boston Harbor. News of its arrival spread quickly, prompting both the Boston town meeting and the Boston Committee of Correspondence to take the unusual step of meeting on the Sabbath. By the next morning, Sam Adams and the collection of merchants, artisans and shopkeepers comprising the Sons of Liberty had plastered the town with posters warning their fellow citizens that "The Hour of Destruction or of Manly Opposition to the Machinations of Tyranny Stares you in the Face!" On that same day, Boston's citizens gathered once again. They initially met at Faneuil Hall, but when the crowd of more than 2,500 overwhelmed the space available, they moved the meeting to the Old South Meeting House, where more than 5,000 of Boston's approximately 18,000 residents—nearly every adult male in the city—gathered to do everything possible to see to it that the tea be sent back to England and that the taxes on the tea remain unpaid.[18]

With the arrival of two additional East India Company ships, the *Beaver* and the *Eleanor*, during the next two weeks, the stakes were raised higher. Governor Hutchinson, who had become the most detested symbol of British authority in Boston, was determined to prevent Sam Adams and the Sons of Liberty from defying British authority yet again. Intent on forcing the colony into complying with the Tea Act, he arranged to have the East India Company tea consigned to and then sold by the only residents of Boston willing to do so—members of his own family. But he had not yet figured out a way to get the tea unloaded from the East India Company ships, for the Boston patriots put out the word that anyone cooperating with the East India Company in unloading their cargo would suffer the fate of "wretches unworthy to live and will be made the first victims of our just Resentment."[19] Everyone knew that the critical moment would fall sometime before midnight on December 16, for that would be the last day that the ships could lie in the harbor without paying the customs duty. At that point, Hutchinson faced the choice either of making some sort of move to unload the tea or of having the East India ships return to England with their full cargo still on board. And so it was that the three small groups of "Mohawk Indians" gathered on Griffin's Wharf that fateful night.

Sam Adams's younger cousin John was merely one of the witnesses and not a participant, but he was powerfully impressed by what he saw. Writing in his diary immediately after the event, John commented, approvingly, that "This destruction of the tea is an event so bold, so daring, so firm, intrepid & inflexible, and it must have so important Consequences, and so lasting, that I cannot but consider it an Epocha in History." And though he had on previous occasions made known his disapproval of mob violence, he declared that those involved in the Boston Tea Party had demonstrated "a Dignity, a Majesty, a Sublimity . . . that I greatly admire."[20]

The other American port cities that were potential recipients of the East India Company tea—New York, Philadelphia and Charleston, South Carolina—soon joined their Boston brethren in refusing to accept the company's shipments. Although their resistance was not accompanied by either the drama or the systematic destruction of the tea that occurred in Boston, in each of those cities a determined citizenry prevented the East India Company ships from unloading their tea, forcing them to turn around and head back to England with their undelivered cargo.[21]

The financial loss suffered by the East India Company by the destruction of the tea in Boston was not insignificant—the East India Company estimated the loss at £9,659, which would be the equivalent of more than £1,000,000 today. But more important than the financial loss was the open defiance shown by the Bostonians. The Boston Tea Party would prove to be the final straw for royal officials both in America and London. Governor Hutchinson, who had suffered a steady stream of indignities at the hands of Boston radicals from the time of the demolition of his home in the summer of 1765 onward, was determined to punish the culprits. To fail to do so, he reasoned, would be to allow all property rights to be trampled by "a lawless and highly criminal assembly."[22]

News of the events in Boston did not reach London until late January, and, not surprisingly, the king, his ministers and the members of Parliament were not pleased. As one member of Parliament declared: "The town of Boston ought to be knocked about the ears and destroyed." Perhaps not everyone wished to go that far, but there was solid consensus in Parliament and among the king's ministers that some sort of dramatic action against Boston's "criminal fanatics" was necessary if England was going to be able to maintain even a semblance of authority over her colonies.[23]

The British Respond, and
Benjamin Franklin Pays the Price

The most immediate victim of the British ministry's outrage over the Boston Tea Party was a man who, in his capacity as colonial agent to Parliament for the colonies of Pennsylvania and Massachusetts, had attempted to walk a fine line between defense of colonial rights and amicable relations with key British officials. On January 29, two days after official word of the Tea Party had reached England, Benjamin Franklin was summoned into an anteroom in the Privy Council chamber, nicknamed the "cockpit," the place for cockfighting. As Franklin entered he saw it was packed with nearly every important member of British officialdom—Lord Dartmouth and Lord Hillsborough, who had already formed a bitter animus toward the much-heralded American scientist and diplomat; Lord North, the chief architect of an increasingly punitive policy toward the Americans; and even the Archbishop of Canterbury. There were a few friendly faces—the Irish politician and philosopher Edmund

Burke and Franklin's longtime friend and fellow scientist Joseph Priestley—but looking at the cast of assembled characters, Franklin could have had no doubt that he had not been summoned for polite conversation.

Franklin was led to a long table at the center of the room, where he faced the members of the Privy Council. Ostensibly there to hear a petition from Massachusetts residents asking for the removal of Governor Hutchinson from office, the Privy Councilors had in fact gathered to indict Franklin for having illegally received, transmitted and connived in the publication of letters from Governor Hutchinson and other royal officials in Massachusetts. Lord Alexander Wedderburn, the solicitor general, took the role of Franklin's designated inquisitor. In a controlled tirade that lasted for well over an hour and that Franklin later likened to "bull-baiting," Wedderburn delivered to the esteemed doctor a public and humiliating dressing-down. He accused Franklin of being the "mover and prime conductor" of a conspiracy against the royal government in Massachusetts; he labeled the American a common thief, who had "forfeited all the respect of societies and of men." Pounding on the table, Wedderburn claimed that Franklin, far from being a servant of the colonial governments of Pennsylvania and Massachusetts, was instead behaving like "the minister of a foreign independent state," all with the intent of moving forward "the idea of a Great American Republic." As Wedderburn continued his verbal assault, the crowd of British courtiers packed into the cockpit cheered the solicitor general and mocked Franklin. The American, dressed in a simple velvet suit, kept his emotions firmly under control. As one of those present observed, "the Doctor . . . stood conspicuously erect, without the smallest movement of any part of his body. The muscles of his face had been previously composed as to afford a placid tranquil expression of countenance, and he did not suffer the slightest alteration of it to appear."[24]

Although Franklin had probably crossed an ethical line in disseminating some of Governor Hutchinson's private letters, Wedderburn was wholly off the mark in accusing him of fomenting rebellion against the king. Franklin, at least at that moment, was emphatically *not* an advocate of American independence. Indeed, when he learned of the Boston Tea Party, he deplored the "violent injustice" of the event, arguing that the Bostonians should make voluntary restitution for the value of the tea. But Wedderburn's attack, carried out in full view of the highest officials in England, would mark the beginning of Franklin's transformation from conciliator to revolutionary.

After Wedderburn had finished his tirade, he called on Franklin to testify, but, according to the official record of the hearing, "Dr. Franklin being present remained silent, but declared by his counsel that he did not choose to be examined." In what was a foregone conclusion, the Privy Council rejected the Massachusetts petition for the removal of Governor Hutchinson, but Wedderburn and his fellow Privy Councilors had won a pyrrhic victory. However much they may have enjoyed Franklin's public humiliation, their behavior would strain the affections of the one man in America capable of bringing about a reconciliation between Great Britain and her colonies. Franklin was a man of carefully cultivated self-control and humility, but he was also a man of intense pride. He would never forget or forgive those British officials who had watched his public humiliation so smugly. From that moment forward, Benjamin Franklin would become an ardent defender of American, not British imperial, interests.[25]

The Coercive Acts

On the same day that Lord Wedderburn publicly humiliated Dr. Franklin, the king's chief ministers, led by Lord Frederick North, chancellor of the exchequer and first lord of the treasury, began discussions on how to respond to the Boston Tea Party. All of the members of the ministry were convinced that they must respond decisively if the British government was going to "secure the Dependance of the Colonies on the Mother Country." North realized that the dispute was no longer one over taxes but over "whether we have, or have not any authority in that country." But the British imperial bureaucracy was a slow-moving beast, and it was more than a month before the ministry decided on a course of action. Although by that time the British had learned of resistance to the East India Company in other American port towns, they remained fixated on the "New England fanatics" in Boston. Consequently, on March 14 North recommended to Parliament the enactment of the first of a series of bills aimed at reducing the Bostonians to a state of submission. The Boston Port Bill proposed that no ships engaged in either foreign or coastal trade be allowed to enter the port—an order to remain in effect until the Bostonians made full restitution to the East India Company for the value of the tea they had destroyed. Lord North was convinced that if he could bring Boston to heel, others inclined to follow that town's example would soon fall into line; in defending the Boston Port Bill, he emphasized that the measure was in fact a moderate one, for it penalized Boston and Boston alone. Moreover, he reasoned, other colonies might well be tempted to take advantage of the Boston port closure in order to increase the volume of trade in their own ports, thus further marginalizing the Boston resistance. The bill moved swiftly through Parliament, and by the end of March the king had endorsed it as well.

Between the end of March and the end of June Parliament passed other acts aimed at punishing not only Boston, but the entire colony of Massachusetts. That legislation came to be known derisively in America as the Coercive Acts. It included a bill, the Massachusetts Government Act, which vastly strengthened the power of the Massachusetts royal governor to appoint and remove most civil officials, prohibited the calling of town meetings without permission from the Crown and significantly reduced popular influence over the selection of juries. Another act, the Impartial Administration of Justice Act, stipulated that any royal official accused of a crime in Massachusetts might demand to be tried in England rather than before hostile juries in Massachusetts. In a further move signaling just how intent the king and Parliament were to enforce their version of the rule of law in Massachusetts, the king replaced the beleaguered outgoing governor, Thomas Hutchinson, who had made it clear that he was ready not only to give up the governorship but also to leave North America altogether. The decision to replace Hutchinson with General Thomas Gage, the commander of the British army in North America, seemed to mean to many in the colony that the king was intent on converting their government into a military dictatorship.

The British Parliament also passed a bill that required Massachusetts residents to provide housing and provisions for British troops in their own homes. Considering the fact that many of the same men behind the Boston Tea Party had been conducting informal guerrilla warfare against British soldiers for the past several years, taunting and threatening them, pelting them with rocks and snowballs, the Quartering Act was not merely provocative but also perfectly calculated to stir up a powerful reaction on the streets of Boston.[26]

Action and reaction: That had been the dynamic of events shaping relations between royal officials in London and the American colonists since Parliament passed the Sugar Act in 1764. But the Coercive Acts, enacted in reaction to the bold actions of Sam Adams and his radical followers in Boston that night of December 16, raised the conflict to an entirely new level. Anyone with eyes to see could have predicted that the Americans would not meekly acquiesce to the Coercive Acts. It remained to be seen what form the American response would take.

TWO

THE QUEST FOR A UNIFIED
AMERICAN RESISTANCE

FROM 1764 TO early 1774, as the British tightened the reins of imperial rule, the political leaders of the American colonies were for the most part determined to resist. They also agreed that the Tea Act, giving the English East India Company a monopoly on all tea sold in the colonies, was yet another dangerous step in the destruction of America's liberties. Indeed, the success of Boston's radicals in thwarting implementation of the Tea Act had emboldened citizens in New York, Philadelphia and Charleston to band together to turn back the East India Company ships in their towns. But in those cities, successful resistance to the Tea Act had occurred without resort to the destruction of property. Why, many asked, had it been necessary for the Bostonians to go to such extraordinary lengths?

Indeed, in nearly all of the earlier acts of resistance in America, most colonies managed to successfully obstruct British policy without the drama and disorder occurring in Boston. In the resistance to the Stamp Act in Boston, the mob had sometimes seemed to have taken over control of the town. In Virginia, opponents of the Stamp Act followed a very different path. Soon after Virginia's provincial assembly, the House of Burgesses, passed resolutions declaring the Stamp Act unconstitutional, political leaders in that colony gathered to confront the British officials charged with enforcing the act with a determined, but also genteel, demeanor. As a frustrated royal Governor

Francis Faquier described the encounter, a "mob" approached Hugh Mercer, the man selected by British royal officials to implement the Stamp Tax in the colony, on the town green in Williamsburg and advised him of the error of his ways. But the mob, Faquier marveled, was unlike any he had ever seen, for "it was chiefly if not altogether Composed of Gentlemen of Property in the Colony, some of them at the head of their respective Counties, and the Merchants of the Country." Mercer, when confronted by individuals whom he considered his peers, indeed, his friends, promptly resigned his commission, whereupon the members of the "mob" gave him a round of huzzahs and repaired to the nearest tavern to drink toasts to his good health and to American liberty.[1] Genteel Virginians and fanatical Bostonians! Whatever outrage the colonists may have felt about Parliament's passage of the Coercive Acts, many Americans nevertheless could not hide their resentment that it was the radical behavior of the Bostonians that had put all of the colonies in the position in which they now found themselves. Pennsylvania's Joseph Galloway, for example, pointed to the "riotous conduct of the New Englanders" as the cause of Parliament's punitive actions; if the "republican mobs" and "lawless Presbyterians" of Boston had not run amok, the American colonies, Galloway lamented, might not have found themselves in their present predicament.[2]

It is hardly surprising therefore that in the late spring of 1774, Sam Adams and the Boston Committee of Correspondence called for all of the colonies to embrace a "Solemn League and Covenant." That very phrase reflected the Puritan values that lay at the foundation of the initiative, but, in practical terms, it amounted to a proposal for a total boycott of British trade, closing American ports to all English ships and refusing to purchase any English goods. The proposal met with a cool reception in some quarters. Although many colonists were prepared to unite in expressions of sympathy for Boston, whose port was now blockaded by a fleet of ships from the British Royal Navy and five regiments from the British Royal Army, they were not so eager to jeopardize their own economic well-being by closing their ports to the ships of their principal trading partner.[3]

New York Responds

Boston needed New York and Philadelphia. If any attempt at a thoroughgoing boycott of British goods was to be successful, those seaport towns, which lagged behind Boston in their commitment to common action in resisting British policies, would have to sign on. If they did not, not only would the overall effect of the boycott be drastically diminished, but it would also be possible for British goods entering those ports to be shipped overland to other colonies, effectively negating any effect of a boycott. And so, even before he had officially proposed his Solemn League and Covenant in Boston, Adams wrote to two of the most militant members of the New York Committee of Correspondence, Isaac Sears and Alexander McDougall, asking if they could help mobilize the merchants of their town to go along with his plan for a colony-wide boycott of British goods. At that time, the New York committee consisted of a mixture of radicals like Sears and McDougall and some of the more conservative merchants who had resisted past attempts at imposing a boycott on British trade. When the New York Committee of Correspondence met on May 16, 1774, to craft a response to the Coercive Acts, many of the most prominent merchants still wanted to moderate the confrontation with Great Britain. Fearing that the New York committee was too much under the sway of radicals like Sears and McDougall, the more conservative New Yorkers arranged for the fifteen-person committee of radicals to be expanded into a Committee of Fifty-one. Although Sears and McDougall were included on this new, enlarged committee, most of its members were inclined toward moderation, not confrontation.[4]

When the Committee of Fifty-One had its first meeting on May 23, Sears and McDougall asked it to consider endorsing a complete boycott of all British trade. Gouverneur Morris, a twenty-two-year-old graduate of New York's King's College (later Columbia University) and thirteen years later to become one of the most influential members of the Constitutional Convention of 1787, was in the gallery observing the jockeying for position between radicals and conservatives that evening. Morris himself was a scion of one the wealthiest and most privileged families of New York's Hudson Valley, but, as he witnessed the clash of ideas and interests between the wealthiest and the ordinary citizens of the city, his sympathy appeared to be with the latter. "I stood in the balcony," he wrote, "and on my right hand were ranged all the people of property and on the other, all the tradesmen &c. who thought it worth their while to leave their labour for the good of the Country." As Morris observed, "The mob [began to] think and reason" and the "gentry began to fear this." But, Morris noted, the "gentry" held most of the cards. In the discussion and decision that followed, the New York committee, now led by more traditionally minded politicians such as John Jay, James Duane and James DeLancey, agreed that their colony should come to Boston's aid. But rather than explicitly endorsing the call for an inter-colonial boycott of all British trade, they instead proposed the convening of an inter-colonial congress to *discuss* the best course of action. Such a congress, likely to be composed of the most distinguished political leaders of each of the colonies, would, many among the Committee of Fifty-One reasoned, be more deliberative and less prone to be swayed by the immediate passions of the moment.[5]

For astute observers like Gouverneur Morris, both the character of the debate and the decisions of the Committee of Fifty-One on that day suggested that New York's resistance to the recent British threats was anything but unified; the varied reactions of New York's citizens to those threats revealed a colony divided by interests, ideology and social class. If the dynamic of events in New York were any indication, the challenges facing any effort to bring Americans together in common cause in defense of their liberties would be formidable indeed.

Drama in Philadelphia

Like many of New York's leading merchants and politicians, the political leaders of Philadelphia were widely suspected of having dragged their heels in earlier protests against the Stamp Act and, later, the Townshend Duties, a new set of taxes imposed by Parliament in 1767 on a long list of goods imported into America. Now, once again they were leaning toward caution in the aftermath of the Coercive Acts. On May 19, 1774, the Massachusetts silversmith and Tea Party participant

Paul Revere completed the first of his famous rides. The Boston Committee of Correspondence sent him to Philadelphia to deliver a plea, most likely drafted by Sam Adams, for that city's Committee of Correspondence to support Boston's cause. "The single question," Adams wrote "is whether YOU consider Boston as now suffering in the common cause." If that was the case, he argued, then "suspending your trade with Great Britain . . . will be a great, but necessary sacrifice to the cause of liberty." A few of the radicals on Philadelphia's Committee, among them Charles Thomson, Thomas Mifflin and Joseph Reed, may have been prepared to throw their support behind the proposal for a boycott, but they were well aware that many of the most powerful political groups in the city were suspicious of the Bostonians. Among those were the leaders of the Pennsylvania Assembly, including the Speaker, Joseph Galloway, a sizable number of the city's merchants, who had long been uneasy about any measure that might disrupt their trade, and members of the Society of Friends, who, according to Charles Thomson, were "principled against war, saw the storm gathering, and therefore wished to keep aloof from danger."[6]

With those fears in mind, Thomson, Mifflin and Reed turned to the one man in the colony whose reputation as a principled, but moderate, opponent of recent British policies exceeded that of any other, not only in Pennsylvania, but perhaps in all of America. Whereas Sam Adams had gained a reputation as the boldest and most visible political activist in America, John Dickinson was widely recognized as the most intellectually astute and carefully modulated defender of America's constitutional liberties. In 1767–1768, in response to Parliament's enactment of the Townshend Duties, Dickinson had written a series of essays, *Letters from a Farmer in Pennsylvania,* which had, at least from the American point of view, utterly demolished the validity of the Parliament's claim to have a constitutional right to tax the colonies. While Dickinson would come to play a vitally important, if controversial, role in the movement for independence, at that particular moment, in the late spring of 1774, the wealthy, genteel and well-educated lawyer had kept his own views about America's growing crisis with England to himself.[7]

On May 18 Thomson paid a visit to Dickinson to try to persuade him that "now was the time to step forward." The following day, May

19, Paul Revere arrived in Philadelphia with the resolutions from the Boston Committee of Correspondence asking for support of the boycott on British trade. Prompted by the news from Boston, Thomson, Reed and Mifflin arranged for a public meeting to be held the following evening at City Tavern, the city's largest and most popular hostelry, to discuss Boston's plight and the best way to respond to it. On the morning of May 20, the three men paid another call on Dickinson at his stately home, Fair Hill, two miles outside of Philadelphia, to enlist his aid in a plan "to sound the sentiments of the people, but not to cause divisions or create parties."[8]

The plan, as they outlined it to Dickinson, was for Reed, a lawyer trained in England who had recently set up practice in Philadelphia, and Mifflin, a young merchant from one of Philadelphia's wealthiest Quaker families, to take the lead at that evening's public meeting. Each would make speeches expressing sympathy for Boston, and then Thomson, who was widely known as being a "rash man," would make a fiery speech pleading for unequivocal support of the resolutions from the Boston Committee of Correspondence. The three men knew that Thomson's plea was likely to be rejected by most of the men present at that meeting, and therefore the key element in their plan was to persuade Dickinson to speak immediately after Thomson, opposing Thomson's radical plan and instead press "for moderate measures, and thus, by an apparent dispute, prevent a further opposition, and carry the point agreed upon." Dickinson was uneasy about the plan, and according to Reed, it was only after "a generous circulation" of glasses of wine from Dickinson's own cellar, and further pleading by the three visitors, that he agreed to participate.[9]

On the evening of May 20, between two and three hundred men "of all ranks and interests" jammed into the Long Room of City Tavern to decide on a response to the Boston resolutions. The Long Room was by far the largest space in the tavern, taking up nearly the whole of the second floor, but it was still a very close and uncomfortable space given the size of the crowd and the unusual warmth of that May evening. The proceedings initially unfolded as scripted, with Reed first speaking in support of Boston "with temper, moderation, but in pathetic terms," and then Mifflin echoing Reed's sentiments but "with more warmth and fire." At that point the carefully orchestrated drama unraveled a bit. Thomson began an impassioned plea for full support of Boston, but in the middle of his speech, overcome by the intense heat in the overcrowded room and lack of sleep during the previous two nights, he fainted dead away. His speech nevertheless had its effect. According to his recollection, after he was revived, the crowd in the room had been thrown into a state of "tumult and disorder past description," with the more conservative merchants and Quakers railing against "the violence of the measures proposed." At that point Dickinson stepped up to the head table and the front of the room and, speaking with what one of the attendees described as "great coolness, calmness, moderation, and good sense," proposed both that a petition be sent to Deputy Governor John Penn asking for an immediate summoning of the Pennsylvania Assembly into session and that a Committee of Correspondence be appointed in order to send a letter of support to Boston. Both of these proposals seemed to satisfy most of the people in the room, but at that moment Dickinson apparently left the meeting, leaving those crowded into the room to argue about the composition of the committee. At that point, the two opposing sides each nominated their own slates of committee members—one composed of those inclined toward supporting Boston's call for the boycott of British goods and the other made up of those favoring more tepid language offering Boston moral support but little else. In the end, those gathered in the room decided simply to combine the two slates, resulting in a reconstituted, nineteen-member Committee of Correspondence, relatively evenly divided between radicals and conservatives, with radicals like Thomson, Mifflin and Reed, moderates like John Dickinson and conservative merchants such as Thomas Wharton and Henry Drinker.[10]

When the committee met the following day, the letter of support for Boston they drafted reflected the divisions that had surfaced but then had been temporarily submerged by Dickinson's attempts at moderation the night before. Although we have no record of what transpired in that secret meeting, Dickinson himself almost certainly carried the burden of trying to broker some sort of compromise position between the radical and conservative Philadelphians. The letter, most likely written by Dickinson, expressed the Philadelphians' sympathy with Boston's plight and spoke of all of the colonies being united "in common cause" with the suffering Bostonians. But at the same time, its tone was restrained, even condescending. It urged the Bostonians to exercise "prudence and moderation" and noted that the very seriousness of the crisis required not immediate action but "more mature deliberation." That mature deliberation could be best accomplished, the Philadelphia Committee of Correspondence wrote, by the calling of "a general Congress of Deputies from the different Colonies, clearly to state what we conceive our rights and to make claim or petition of them to his Majesty, in firm, but decent and dutiful terms." Although the Philadelphia response did not reject outright a boycott of trade with Great Britain, it made clear that such a boycott should be a "last resource" if the petition to the king failed to produce a favorable result. The Philadelphia response, which clearly fell short of what radicals like Thomson, Reed and Mifflin desired and went further than many of Philadelphia's mercantile and political leaders would have preferred, was in some senses precisely the sort of "decent and respectful" communication that moderates such as John Dickinson thought most appropriate at the time.[11]

Coalescence

Upon reading a report from Charles Thomson, Sam Adams felt disappointment with the moderate response from the Philadelphia meeting. Thomson and Thomas Mifflin tried to console him by emphasizing the positive effects that the calling of a congress might have, but he was not persuaded. He agreed that the calling of a congress was an "absolute necessity" but lamented that it was nevertheless insufficient. "From the length of time it will take to bring it to pass," Adams conjectured, "I fear it cannot answer for the present Emergency." Only a thoroughgoing boycott of trade with Britain, implemented immediately, could prevent the British from starving Boston into submission.[12]

The Bostonians would receive more encouraging news further south. At a meeting in Annapolis, Maryland, about events in Philadelphia, a group of citizens, including some of the colony's most powerful political leaders, pledged their support for a thoroughgoing boycott of British goods in support of Boston. And, crucially, the political leaders of Virginia, unlike their counterparts in New York and Pennsylvania, were united in their determination to support Boston's cause. In mid-May of 1774 Virginians learned of the passage of the Boston Port Bill. Some younger burgesses, including Patrick Henry, Richard Henry Lee, George Mason and a relative newcomer to the political scene, Thomas Jefferson, "cooked up a resolution" to designate June 1, when the act was to take effect, as a day of "fasting, humiliation, and prayer." On May 26, Virginia's royal governor, John Murray, Earl of Dunmore, ordered the House of Burgesses dissolved for what he considered to be an act of disrespect to "his Majesty and the Parliament of Great Britain," but that did not prevent the burgesses from meeting in an extra-legal session in Williamsburg's Raleigh Tavern the following day, at which time they passed resolutions denouncing the governor for his actions and agreeing to a partial boycott of British imports from the East India Company. On May 30, after Speaker of the House Peyton Randolph received a formal request from Sam Adams and the Boston Committee of Correspondence asking Virginia to join Boston in a total boycott of British Goods, the House of Burgesses, again meeting in a rump session, agreed to convene a special convention on August 1 to appoint delegates to the "general Congress" recently proposed by New York and Pennsylvania and, equally important, to consider whether to support the plan for a general boycott.[13]

Virginia's commitment to support a "general Congress" may have been decisive in persuading other southern colonies to send delegates as well, thus assuring that a truly "Continental" Congress would become a reality. And, when the Virginia Convention met in early August and threw its support behind a total boycott of all English goods, Sam Adams and his fellow Bostonians could be sure that when that Congress convened, they would have a powerful ally at their side.[14]

By mid-June of 1774 it was clear that the next step in addressing the threats posed by the Coercive Acts was an inter-colonial congress. It was also clear by that time that all the colonies, except for Georgia, which had been less involved in previous protests against British policies and was also at that time preoccupied by warfare with Indians on its western frontier, would be sending delegates to that Congress. And there seemed to be uniform consent that the Congress would be held in Philadelphia—a logical choice in the sense that Philadelphia, with a population of approximately 28,000 in 1774, was the largest city in America and, if not in the geographic center of the colonies, was more conveniently located than any other important American city. On the other hand, the location may not have pleased Sam Adams and the Bostonians, for they knew all too well Philadelphia's reputation as the most conservative city in America—with a large concentration of merchants and Quakers who seemed prepared to protect either their pocketbooks or their pacifistic principles at the price of American liberty.[15]

Many in New York and Philadelphia clearly intended the Congress as a means of dampening the militant, even revolutionary, ardor of the Bostonians. But as the implications of the Coercive Acts began to sink in, many colonists throughout America were beginning to understand that Boston's plight really could become theirs. And Virginia's strong support of Boston's more aggressive plan of resistance would carry a great deal of weight once the Congress convened. Although it would take almost two years for the fact to reveal itself, the "general Congress," initially conceived by many of its proponents in Philadelphia and New York as a temporizing measure, would ultimately become the principal institutional agency of the world's first popular revolution.

THREE

THE DELEGATES GATHER
IN PHILADELPHIA

MOST OF THEM had never met, never even heard of one another. But during the month of August 1774, many of America's most powerful men were making preparations to embark on an unprecedented journey to an unprecedented gathering. From the forests and mountains of New Hampshire to the rice fields of South Carolina, the political leaders of Great Britain's colonies in North America prepared to head to Philadelphia to attend the "general Congress" charged with the task of responding to the newest, and by far the most serious, British threats to American liberty. They were all aware of the gravity of the business in which they were to engage, but few could have imagined that they would set in motion a series of events that would lead to the first popular revolution in the history of the world.

The Massachusetts, South Carolina and Virginia Delegates Depart

It is perhaps not surprising that the first colonial delegation to leave for Philadelphia to attend the general Congress was from Massachusetts. Ten years earlier it had been that colony's vigorous, and sometimes violent, response to Great Britain's attempts to tax the American colonies that had set in motion the events that had led to the crisis the colonies now faced.

The four delegates from Massachusetts—Sam Adams, John Adams, Robert Treat Paine and Thomas Cushing, all Bostonians—began their 300-mile trip to Philadelphia on August 10. Paine, as a youthful, aspiring merchant, had traveled both to the Carolinas and to Spain and the Azores, and Sam Adams had made a brief trip to New York to attend the Stamp Act Congress nine years earlier, but neither John Adams nor Thomas Cushing had ever traveled outside of their own colony. And with the exception of Cushing, the Massachusetts delegates were, at best, men of modest means. It would have been easier and faster to make the trip to Philadelphia by sea, but the port of Boston had recently been ordered closed by the British government, so that was out of the question. And so, on the day of their departure they crowded into the coach provided by Thomas Cushing and began their journey.[1]

The Massachusetts delegates knew they were heading toward a gathering of some of the wealthiest and most sophisticated men in America, so it's likely that all of them took special care in packing their finest clothing for the trip. But in Sam Adams's case, the selection of apparel had a special significance. In spite of his increasing prominence as one of the leaders of the opposition to British policies in Boston, Adams had always been notoriously unconcerned with his personal appearance. Indeed, he was widely viewed as among the most slovenly dressed residents of Boston. Apparently the Boston Sons of Liberty decided they had to do something about this before they sent their spiritual and political leader off to plead their case. A few weeks before he was due to leave for Philadelphia, Adams was interrupted during his dinner by a "well-known tailor," who asked him if he might take his measurements. Although the tailor "firmly refused" to explain why, Adams agreed. After the measurements were made and Adams and his family sat down again to their dinner, they were interrupted yet again by a knock on the door from the "most approved hatter in Boston," who made a similar request. And then, in succession, there appeared a shoemaker and a wigmaker, each taking the appropriate measurements and each refusing to tell Adams who had sent them. Before Adams departed for Philadelphia, he received a "large trunk" containing a full suit of clothes, two pairs of shoes "of the best style," a set of silver shoe-buckles, six pairs of "the best silk hose," a set of gold knee buckles, a set of gold sleeve-buttons, a gold-headed cane, a red cloak, a new wig and an "elegant cocked hat." The only hint that Adams had of the identity of his benefactors was contained in the embossing upon the buttons of his new suit of clothes, for each of the buttons contained a Liberty Cap, the emblem of the Sons of Liberty. (The Sons of Liberty also arranged to make repairs to his house and to build him a new barn.)[2]

In spite of having to make their trip overland, the Massachusetts delegates began their journey far earlier than was necessary for an on-time arrival at a congress that wasn't due to begin its business until September 5. But the four men did not intend their trip through Massachusetts, Connecticut, New York, New Jersey and Pennsylvania to be a tourist junket. Over the course of the past decade political leaders and street protesters alike in their colony had behaved in ways that seemed calculated to provoke a hostile British response, and the Massachusetts delegates were acutely aware that many in America felt a mixture of sympathy for and annoyance at their colony—sympathy because Massachusetts had been the particular target of Parliament's attempt to punish the rebelliousness through the recent passage of the Coercive Acts and annoyance because many of the colonists still believed that if the extremists of Massachusetts, and Boston in particular, had been more restrained in their actions, the current crisis in Anglo-American relations might have been averted. Their extended trip through New England and the mid-Atlantic would allow them to introduce themselves to many of the leaders of those colonies to begin to make their case and, perhaps, also to get some advance indicators of the support their colony was likely to receive in the Philadelphia congress.

A thousand miles to the south, in Charleston, South Carolina, three extraordinarily rich, powerful and self-confident men prepared for their departure to Philadelphia. John Rutledge combined his skills as a London-trained lawyer and owner of more than 300 slaves working on his five rice plantations to become his colony's most powerful politician. His younger brother Edward, Oxford-educated and similarly trained as a lawyer in London's Middle Temple, had not yet acquired such massive wealth, but with an older brother like John, he was hardly lacking in either influence or prestige. Edward's father-in-law, Henry

Middleton, was another fabulously wealthy low-country planter, owner of some 50,000 acres of land and nearly 800 slaves. Edward Rutledge and Henry Middleton boarded their ship and set sail for Philadelphia on July 30, arriving on August 10. John Rutledge left ten days later on the brigantine *Besey*, headed first for New York, then overland to Philadelphia. If the Massachusetts delegates brought with them their best, but still somewhat dowdy, locally tailored woolen suits and waistcoats, we can be sure that the South Carolinians were well-prepared to show off their superior sense of style with the most up-to-date fashions—probably crafted from silk and linen—from London. And though the New Englanders traveled alone, the two Rutledges and Henry Middleton brought their wives and a full complement of slaves who would serve as their maids and manservants.[3]

The other two South Carolina delegates to the general Congress—Christopher Gadsden and Thomas Lynch—departed on August 15, sailing on the brigantine *Sea Nymph*. Whereas the Rutledges and Henry Middleton had set sail with little fanfare, Gadsden and Lynch were escorted to their ship by hundreds of Charleston's residents. According to the *South Carolina Gazette*, they received "prayers and every mark of respect" as they walked out on Market Wharf in Charleston, and as they boarded their ship, the local militia honored them with a salute of cannon fire. It is not clear how much experience the militia had in staging such a ceremony, and, tragically, some of the powder for the cannon was accidentally ignited, badly burning three men, one of them fatally.

Gadsden, age fifty, a Charleston merchant of only modest means, was viewed by the Rutledge clan as untrustworthy. They thought him too much inclined to demagoguery as he went about rousing opposition to British policies among the "lower sort" of Charleston. Of all of South Carolina's political leaders, he had been the most fervent opponent of Great Britain's attempt to tax the colonies ever since Parliament's passage of the Stamp Act back in 1765. His shipmate, the forty-four-year-old Thomas Lynch, seemed at first glance to have been a more appropriate traveling companion of the Rutledges, for he was one of South Carolina's wealthiest rice planters. But Lynch, like Gadsden, considered himself a representative of the common people. According to Connecticut congressional delegate Silas Deane,

Lynch was "plain and sensible" in his appearance, preferring to wear clothing that was "the manufacture of this country"; and, unlike many of his "powdered" South Carolina counterparts, he wore his hair "straight." Most important, he had consistently advocated taking bold steps to protest the recent actions of the British Parliament. He felt much more comfortable traveling with Gadsden than with the Rutledges and Henry Middleton.[4]

On August 30, the Virginia radical Patrick Henry arrived at Mount Vernon, the stately plantation of Colonel George Washington. He was joined that day by two of the most respected figures in the Virginia House of Burgesses, George Mason, Washington's good friend and neighbor, and Edmund Pendleton, a Virginia lawyer of a more conservative bent. Henry, born, raised and propelled to political power by his quick wit and silver tongue in the Virginia Piedmont, had never before experienced life at a plantation as luxurious, expansive and bustling with activity—almost like a small village. And Washington no doubt gave his guest a full tour, riding amidst fields devoted to the cultivation not only of tobacco, but also of flax and wheat, and the grazing of cattle and sheep, touring the Colonel's gristmill and distillery and, most impressive of all, viewing the vast expanse of the Potomac River from the veranda of the gracious main house.[5]

It is hard to imagine two men more different in social background, personal temperament and public personae than Patrick Henry and George Washington. From the moment that news of the passage of the Stamp Act by the British Parliament in 1765 reached America, Henry had stirred up a ruckus in the Virginia House of Burgesses, delivering fiery speeches denouncing British attempts to rob Americans of their liberties. Although by 1774 Henry had already served as a burgess for nine years, many of his more conservative Virginia colleagues still regarded him as both a newcomer and a rabble-rouser. Everyone who ever encountered Washington was struck by his physical presence—not merely his six-foot-three-inch height, but by his relaxed, but reserved and self-confident demeanor. Washington not only had served in the House of Burgesses for a longer period of time than Henry—sixteen years—but he had also earned the universal respect of his colleagues as a man of uncommon self-restraint, thoughtfulness and judgment. Yet on virtually every issue from 1765 to 1774, Washington had supported Henry's radical positions—allowing his more volatile Virginia colleague to make the impassioned speeches while he remained silent—but ultimately, both inside the House of Burgesses and out of doors, making it clear that he was on Henry's side.

Henry and Washington, joined by Mason and Pendleton, ate, drank and talked well into the night and then, after a good night's sleep and further conversation the next morning and afternoon, they mounted their horses at around three in the afternoon, with the three congressional delegates preparing to head to Philadelphia and Mason to return to his nearby plantation a few miles away. As they were about to set off, Martha Washington, knowing that her husband and Henry were of the same mind, offered the more conservative Edmund Pendleton a bit of advice: "I hope you will stand firm. I know George will."

There were others in the riding party as well. Henry, Washington and Pendleton were accompanied by three slaves who would serve as manservants to them during their time in Philadelphia.[6]

The Delegates Arrive in Philadelphia

Edward Rutledge and Henry Middleton would be the first delegates from outside of Pennsylvania to arrive in Philadelphia. Sometime during the day on August 10 they sailed up the Delaware River into the port of Philadelphia. All of Pennsylvania's delegates lived in Philadelphia, so they had no journey at all to make. Most of Philadelphia's 28,000 residents—the largest population of any city in America— lived within a few blocks of the riverfront, and, as a consequence, the city's prospect from aboard ship was far more impressive than any view of it by land.

As they pulled into port, Edward Rutledge and Henry Middleton could see the rooftops of the city's principal buildings: the Pennsylvania State House, the Academy of Philadelphia (later to become the University of Pennsylvania), the American Philosophical Society, the Court House, the Pennsylvania Hospital and the new city jail, as well as the steeples of the city's numerous churches. Both men had spent some of their youth and early adulthood in London, so perhaps they were less than overwhelmed by the architecture and scale of what was, by English standards, really only a medium-sized town. But by the provincial standards of rural America, and compared to Charleston, with a population of 11,000, more than half of whom were slaves, it was an impressive sight nonetheless. Since the Rutledge and Middleton entourage arrived in Philadelphia ahead of all of the other out-of-town delegates, they immediately took up lodging at Frye's Tavern, considered the city's finest, if not the largest, of Philadelphia's hostelries. They also reserved some rooms for the later-arriving John Rutledge. The retinue of those three South Carolina delegates was so large that they took up most of the space in the tavern, much to the chagrin of delegates from other colonies who had been hoping to lodge there as well.[7]

Gadsden and Lynch arrived in Philadelphia on August 22. They found lodging in the home of Mrs. Mary House, a "genteel and sensible" recently widowed forty-year-old, who, with the death of her husband and the impending marriage of her daughter Eliza, had decided to take in boarders. Mrs. House's boardinghouse would become the home away from home for a variety of members of the Continental Congress, including Silas Deane and Eliphalet Dyer, both of Connecticut.

The Massachusetts Delegates Arrive in Philadelphia

On August 29, at dusk, the four Massachusetts delegates reached the small Pennsylvania town of Frankford, five miles outside of Philadelphia. Their nineteen-day "listening tour" of the Northeast had been on the whole gratifying. According to John Adams, the Massachusetts delegates were greeted with enthusiasm in virtually all of their various stopping places along the way. He made particular note of the reception his party received in New Haven, where, he exulted, "as we came into the Town all the Bells in Town were sett to ringing, and the People—Men, Women and Children—were crowding at the Doors and Windows as if it was to see a Coronation!" Perhaps the only downbeat note in his report of his travels was his reaction to the manners and mood of the people of New York City. Adams was well aware that New York, along with Philadelphia, had often expressed disapproval of the "radical fanatics" of Boston, and as Adams surveyed the scene in that city, he could not resist observing that "with all the Opulence and Splendor of this City, there is very little good Breeding to be found. We have been treated with an assiduous Respect. But I have not seen one real Gentleman, one well bred Man, since I came to Town."[8]

And so that evening of August 29, as the party of Bostonians reached the outskirts of Philadelphia, they were greeted warmly by "a Number of . . . Gentleman came out of Phyladelphia to meet us." Included in the welcoming party was Thomas Mifflin, one of the Pennsylvania delegates certain to join in common cause with the Bostonians; Thomas McKean, a delegate from Delaware; Nathaniel Folsom and John Sullivan, the delegates from New Hampshire; and John Rutledge. The Bostonians had had a long ride beginning in Trenton, New Jersey, and it had been a hot, sultry day. As they were escorted into town by their welcoming party, they felt "dirty, dusty, and fatigued." The prospect of the city as they arrived overland, from the north, was far less impressive than that of an approach by water. Philadelphia may have been America's largest city, but the Bostonians, as their coach bumped along the dusty road through fields of wheat and corn, were unaware that they were even approaching a town of any size until they were right on top of it.[9]

When their carriage finally dropped them off at the City Tavern, on Second Street, just above Walnut, they received a hearty, raucous welcome from a large contingent of delegates from many of the other colonies who had gathered there. City Tavern, referred to variously as the New Tavern or Smith's after its proprietor, Daniel Smith, had quickly become the unofficial gathering place for delegates as they arrived in town. Even though no one there had ever actually met them, the Massachusetts delegates were considered something like celebrities, coming as they did from Boston, that "hotbed of sedition." Virtually all of the delegates to the Congress were eager to take the measure of the "New England fanatics." At least one of those delegates, the ultraconservative Joseph Galloway of Pennsylvania, was polite, but cautious in his assessment of them. He noted that, upon first impression, they were "in their Behaviour and Conversation very modest," but he also noticed that they had already begun "to throw out Hints, which, like Straws and Feathers, tell us from which Point of the Compass the Wind comes." Galloway, who had already been outspoken in his dismay at the upheaval caused by the radical actions of the New Englanders, plainly did not wish to have the upcoming Congress controlled by the "wind" from Massachusetts.[10]

After a long evening of drinking and dining—"a Supper . . . as elegant as ever was laid upon a Table," John Adams enthused—the Massachusetts delegates departed from City Tavern just before midnight. They crossed the street and checked into the much more modest lodgings of Sarah Yard's Boarding House on the corner of Second and Market Streets. The Bostonians, like most of their fellow delegates, would have to become accustomed to accommodations in tiny rooms like those in Mrs. Yard's boardinghouse for the remainder of their stay in Philadelphia. John Adams would live in that cramped room at the boardinghouse for most of the next four years.[11]

George Washington, Patrick Henry and Edmund Pendleton rode into Philadelphia in the late afternoon of September 4, a cool, cloudy Sunday. On previous occasions, Washington had traveled to both Boston and Philadelphia, but it was Henry's and Pendleton's first time outside of Virginia. The three Virginians would be the last delegates to arrive before the Congress began the following morning. The other Virginia delegates—Richard Bland, Benjamin Harrison, Richard Henry Lee and Peyton Randolph—had arrived a few days earlier. (The North Carolina delegates did not leave their colony until after the proceedings had begun and did not show up at the Congress until September 14.) As they approached Philadelphia, Washington, Henry and Pendleton crossed the Schuylkill on a flatbed ferry, which with its ropes and pulleys hauled them and their horses across. They were met by cheering crowds organized by the city's Sons of Liberty, and then made their way to City Tavern. Richard Henry Lee, the Virginian who would eventually introduce a resolution for independence into what by then was being called the Continental Congress, greeted the three men enthusiastically and proceeded to introduce them to the delegates from other colonies.[12]

Patrick Henry, author of the "Virginia Resolves" protesting the Stamp Act, had already earned a reputation as an orator of unusual style and ability, and within a week of his arrival, he was being referred to by some delegates as "the Demosthenes of America." But those gathered at the City Tavern that evening were certainly most interested in taking the measure of the forty-two-year-old Colonel Washington. Several delegates, writing back home to family and friends following that evening, went on at length not only about his commanding stature, but also his personal manner. Like virtually everyone who encountered him, the delegates were impressed, even awestruck, by his physical appearance—not only his height, but also his countenance—serious, yet youthful, firm, yet friendly. Writing home to his wife, Connecticut's Silas Deane described Washington as "modest," "cool in countenance," impressively "soldierlike" and then went on to repeat a story—most likely apocryphal, that such was Washington's devotion to the patriot cause that on hearing of the passage of the Coercive Acts he had offered to raise an army of a thousand men at his own expense for the defense of his country. Although unlike Henry or Richard Henry Lee, Washington did far more listening than talking, and though Washington had never aspired to a position of political leadership within his own Virginia House of Burgesses, there could be no doubt in anyone's mind that Washington appeared the ideal paragon of a true leader.[13]

After leaving the tavern, Washington would spend his first night in Philadelphia at the home of Doctor William Shippen and thereafter would board, along with his slave Billy Lee, at the Harp and Crown, a tavern located on Third Street, just below Arch Street, a few blocks from Carpenters' Hall. Patrick Henry followed his fellow Virginia delegate and political ally Richard Henry Lee to the handsome townhouse of Lee's brother-in-law, where both delegates would make their lodgings during their time in Philadelphia.[14]

The men who traveled from Massachusetts, South Carolina and Virginia to Philadelphia represented only three of the thirteen delegations that would eventually gather to deliberate on the next steps to be taken in what was becoming a rapidly escalating conflict with England. Like their counterparts from the other ten colonies, they came to Philadelphia with the fear that their colony's relationship with their mother country had reached a state of genuine crisis. But in spite of their anger at the recent actions of the British Parliament—in particular, the parliament's passage of the Coercive Acts—they also carried with them a sense of hope—hope that their longstanding and generally affectionate relationship with Great Britain could be restored. With the exception of perhaps a few of those "fanatical New Englanders," they did consider themselves to be loyal—even loving—subjects of the King of England.[15]

They had not come to Philadelphia to wage a revolution. Their first, indeed their only, task was to find a path toward reconciliation. As they arrived in Philadelphia in late August and early September of 1774, many of them must have wondered how things had reached such a state of crisis. How had a relationship that had been so harmonious, so mutually beneficial to both Crown and colonies, deteriorated so badly, and so quickly?

The Delegates Explore Philadelphia

Like anyone arriving in a great city for the first time, the delegates set out to explore Philadelphia. The founder of Pennsylvania, William Penn, had laid out a plan for Philadelphia that had the city's streets arranged in a perfect grid, stretching from the Delaware to the Schuylkill rivers. In fact though, in 1774, nearly a century after its founding, Philadelphia's population was crammed into a space occupying only about a quarter of that area. The main part of the city was roughly the size of a small New England town but with ten times the population, and so perhaps the first thing that caught their attention was the sheer concentration of humanity within that relatively small space. The city occupied the area from Front Street bordering the Delaware River in the east, westward to Sixth Street in the West, and running north and south from Arch Street to South Street, and within those confines lived most of the city's residents.

Because Philadelphia's population was growing more rapidly than any town in America at that point, more and more of the city's residents crammed themselves into small houses and shacks in makeshift alleys that ran between the more carefully laid-out main streets. In that sense Philadelphia provided the visiting delegates with a glimpse of America's future—a city in which the contrasts between prosperity and poverty were impossible to ignore.[16]

Arriving delegates must also have been struck by Philadelphia's ethnic and religious diversity. Boston was overwhelmingly English in its makeup. New York was growing more diverse, with its mixture of English, Dutch, increasing numbers of other European immigrants and a growing African slave population. But Philadelphia, within its roughly forty blocks, had brought together rich and poor, slave and free, English, Irish, German and African, Quaker, Anglican, Presbyterian, Lutheran, Catholic and Jew. The city's richest and most powerful residents lived in imposing townhouses on the main streets, but they could easily see and hear the dynamic commotion of the great mass of Philadelphia's other inhabitants, of all religions and ethnicities, clustered tightly in makeshift shacks located in the alleys immediately behind those houses. And, modern-day plumbing being something that lay in the distant future, the smell emanating from the improvised outhouses, not to mention from the open sewer on Dock Street running through the heart of the town, was not something anyone used to living in the expansive environment of the countryside would be likely to miss.

Philadelphia in 1774 was not only a city whose population was expanding more rapidly than that of any other in America, but also which was enjoying a prosperity greater than any other city. In 1774 Philadelphia's residents, about a thousand of whom were African slaves and another thousand free blacks, lived in some 6,000 houses, with more than 500 new houses added each year. In 1774 alone, Philadelphians built more houses than Bostonians were able to construct in an entire decade. A few of those houses were genuinely impressive structures. Located on the south side of Market Street between 5th and 6th Streets, the mansion owned by Richard Penn, grandson of the colony's founder, William Penn, was as lavish as any home in any city in America.[17]

In the days immediately following his arrival, John Adams would frequently evince his awe at the city's opulence and sophistication. He was particularly impressed by the Pennsylvania Hospital, located at Eighth and Pine Streets. Medical practice anywhere in America was in a pretty primitive state, with most ordinary illnesses being treated either by purgatives, sweating or bleeding, and typical surgical procedures occurring with little or no anesthesia, and amputation being the norm rather than the exception. But primitive as it may have seemed to a twenty-first century patient, it was improving. And Pennsylvania Hospital, co-founded by Benjamin Franklin and Dr. Thomas Bond, was leading the way. It was probably America's first teaching hospital, in which doctors received carefully planned clinical training rather than serving a haphazard apprenticeship. And it pioneered in treating the mentally, as well as the physically, ill. Recording his impressions in his diary after a tour of the hospital, John Adams went on and on about the range of activities occurring within the hospital, showing a particular fascination for the "lower Rooms under Ground," in which "the Cells of the Lunaticks, a Number of them, some furious, some merry, some Melancholly" were to be found. Although Adams's description may sound Dickensian to a twenty-first century reader, the very fact that the mentally ill were being treated in a hospital rather than simply being confined to the basements of their homes was a step forward in American medical practice. Apart from the hospital, Philadelphia may have had more trained doctors than any city in America, and many of the delegates to the Congress, mindful of periodic outbreaks of smallpox in the city and having access for the first time to doctors capable of treating them, ventured to try the still-untested method of inoculation while they were in the city.[18]

By far the most imposing building in the city was the State House. Designed by Andrew Hamilton and Edmund Woolley in 1732, it had taken more than two decades to complete. With its imposing bell tower and the bucolic park and gardens surrounding it, it may have been the most impressive public building in all of America. Some of that beauty and dignity was undermined a bit by the immense building standing directly in front of the State House. The Walnut Street Jail, still under construction in 1774, was a massive three-story structure that loomed over the State House, and the residents of the jail, taken to hanging out the windows and raining insults on passersby, made the overall scene in that neighborhood a bit less inviting.[19]

The delegates may have been most impressed by the number of cultural and intellectual institutions in the city. Three of the most prominent of those had all been created by the city's leading citizen,

Benjamin Franklin. The Library Company of Philadelphia, America's first public library, had its headquarters on the second floor of Carpenters' Hall, the building in which the delegates would meet during the next three months. The College of Philadelphia, later to be known as the University of Pennsylvania, was founded by Franklin as his city's answer to Harvard, Yale and Princeton. Unlike its counterparts to the north, and consistent with Franklin's own intellectual and philosophical beliefs, the college was intended to be America's first secular institution of higher learning, with a curriculum aimed at combining a knowledge of ancient languages and ancient history with the "useful knowledge" to be gained by the study of subjects such as mathematics, natural science and the history of commerce and manufacturing. And, standing right next to the State House, was the American Philosophical Society, intended by its founder to be the American equivalent of the Royal Society of London, of which he was a proud member. The cultural and intellectual institutions of Philadelphia could hardly compete in scale or prestige with those of London, but they were nevertheless indicative of a combination of economic vitality and cosmopolitan, cultural ambition unmatched in any other city in America.[20]

On a far different level, most of the delegates, with the possible exceptions of a few of the New Englanders, must also have been pleased to see that there was no shortage of places in which they could find opportunities for the convivial consumption of alcohol. Philadelphians, like most Americans, had a marked fondness for drink. Starting their day with a glass of beer and continuing on through the afternoon and evening with cider, wine, port and rum, Philadelphians consumed an amount of alcohol that is simply astonishing by today's standards. Consequently, the one, truly ubiquitous commercial institution in the city was the tavern, of which there were no fewer than 110 in 1774. Taverns were spread throughout the city—indeed, it would have been impossible to walk even a block without encountering one—but they were particularly concentrated around the public market, for that was the area in which an enterprising tavern keeper was most likely to attract a clientele. In general, taverns were of three types. The largest and most genteel—taverns like Smith's City Tavern, the Indian King, the Indian Queen and the London Coffee House—served as dining places and watering holes for the city's elite, as well as providing lodging for travelers who expected a bit more than a bare room and bed. Overwhelmingly, the delegates to the Congress lodged during their time in Philadelphia either in these genteel taverns or in some of the city's more respectable boarding-houses. The boardinghouses may have served breakfast but in general did not serve dinner, so most of the delegates either took their main meals in the city's finest taverns or, as was often the case, by invitation in the homes of some of the city's most prominent citizens. A level below the genteel taverns were those like the Black Horse or the Anvil and Double Cross Keys, which also provided food, drink and lodging, but were not as finely furnished. We know that many of the delegates from the South brought one or more slaves with them, and though we have little record of where those slaves were lodged, it is likely that they either stayed in this second level of tavern or in some of the smaller, less commodious boardinghouses that dotted the city's streets and alleys.[21]

Like every city and town of any size in America, Philadelphia boasted a public market, but it was surely the largest, and perhaps the most boisterous, in all of America. It was a covered market, with walls and roofs, and stretched along Market Street (or High Street as it was sometimes called) all the way from Second Street to Fifth Street. The stalls from Second through Fourth Streets were devoted mainly to the selling of meat and fish. The butchers often slaugh-tered their animals on the spot, and the patrons were frequently forced to stand in the pools of blood while they made their pur-chases. On a hot day—and it was very hot during those early days in September—it was not unusual to see animals' carcasses completely covered with flies. When the butchers wanted to get rid of the car-casses, they would throw them in the creek (we would call it an open sewer) at nearby Dock Street. Dock Street Creek was a notoriously filthy, smelly, unhealthy part of the city, the recipient not only of ani-mal carcasses, but also the waste products of neighborhood brewing establishments and soap boilers, not to mention the constant flow of excrement that made its way into the creek from the neighboring privies scattered all over the city.[22]

Silas Deane, a delegate who hailed from the small town of Wethersfield, Connecticut, south of Hartford, was no doubt one of those unaccustomed to such sights and smells, and, clearly, he didn't like them. He displayed some of the provincial pride common among the New Englanders, and his first impressions of Philadelphia were unrelentingly negative. He complained about the quality of the roads leading into it and the unimpressive vista as he was approaching the city. Writing to his wife, he complained that there was more "grass and verdant Meadows" in the immediate vicinity of Hartford, Connecticut, than there was on the sixty miles of road leading into Philadelphia. Nor did Deane think much of the High Street Market. He visited it on September 2, a particularly warm day, and the New Englander complained bitterly about not only the heat, but about the quality of the fruit, vegetables, fish, fowl and beef to be purchased there. Apparently Deane was not reticent about sharing with the city's residents his low opinion about virtually everything he saw in Philadelphia, an impulse that hardly won him any friends among those attending the market that day. Deane's opinion of the city would improve over time, but his initial comments were symptomatic of an obstacle the delegates to the Congress would have to overcome: a reflexive provincialism that militated against efforts to work together to find a common solution to the imperial crisis which they were confronting.[23]

Forty-five of the fifty-six delegates to the First Continental Congress had arrived in Philadelphia by September 5, the day it commenced. It was a remarkable feat since many colonies had not even elected their delegates until late July or early August—a relatively short time between the decision to hold a general congress in the first place and the distances that many had to travel to attend it.

In addition to the delegates from Massachusetts, Virginia and South Carolina, whose travels and initial impressions of the city we have already observed, the other delegates present that opening day were John Sullivan and Nathaniel Folsom from New Hampshire; Stephen Hopkins and Samuel Ward from Rhode Island; Eliphalet Dyer, Silas Deane and Roger Sherman from Connecticut; James Duane, John Jay, Philip Livingston, Isaac Low and William Floyd of New York; James Kinsey, William Livingston, John Dehart, Stephen Crane and Richard Smith of New Jersey; Caesar Rodney, Thomas

McKean and George Read from Delaware; and, the Congress's hosts, the delegates from Pennsylvania—Joseph Galloway, Samuel Rhoads, Thomas Mifflin, Charles Humphreys, John Morton and Edward Biddle.[24]

The Delegates to the First Congress: A Collective Profile

Although most of the delegates to the Congress had entered into the city as strangers, nevertheless, as a group they had much in common. Pennsylvania's deputy governor, John Penn, described them as "the ablest & wealthiest men in America" and believed they would express the views "not . . . of a Mob but of the first & best people in all the Colonies." Penn was right. Nearly all of the delegates were wealthy, and nearly every delegation could count among its members an individual—Thomas Cushing of Massachusetts, Samuel Ward of Rhode Island, John Jay and Philip Livingston of New York, Governor William Livingston of New Jersey, John Dickinson of Pennsylvania, Peyton Randolph, Richard Henry Lee, Richard Bland and Benjamin Harrison of Virginia, the Rutledges and Henry Middleton of South Carolina—who were among the wealthiest residents in his colony.

Reflecting an occupational bias that would persist in American politics up to the present day, thirty-two of the fifty-six delegates who would eventually take part in the sessions of the First Continental Congress were lawyers. That number is somewhat misleading, for only about half of them earned their living by practicing law; the rest were planters or merchants or simply subsisted on inherited wealth as "gentlemen." Then, as now, ambitious men pursued legal training not only as a vocation but as a useful path toward financial and political success. Not surprisingly, the majority of the delegates from the South were planters, although, again, among that group of twenty-three, at least ten could claim training in the law.[25]

The one delegate whose occupation is most difficult to describe was also the one with most modest economic attainment—Sam Adams. Although he had from time to time made a meager living as a highly unsuccessful tax collector, perhaps the best occupational label for Boston's most visible resident was "professional politician," or, in the eyes of the British, "professional agitator."

At a time when a college education was a rarity, even among the wealthy, fifteen of the delegates had attended college and five had studied law at the Inns of Court in London. Among the New Englanders, all four of the Massachusetts delegates had attended Harvard, and two of the three Connecticut delegates—Eliphalet Dyer and Silas Deane—had attended Yale; the third Connecticut delegate, Roger Sherman, who began his career as a shoemaker, had no formal education beyond a few years in grammar school. Among the New York delegates, John Jay attended King's College (soon to become Columbia), and Philip Livingston attended Yale. New Jersey's William Livingston, the son of Philip Livingston, followed in his father's footsteps and also attended Yale. Among the Pennsylvania delegates, only Thomas Mifflin could boast of a college degree, having attended the College of Philadelphia. When John Dickinson joined the Pennsylvania delegation in mid-October, he would bring to six the total number of congressional delegates with legal training at the Inns of Court. Among the Marylanders, Robert Goldsborough attended the College of Philadelphia and then went to England where he acquired his legal training at the Inns of Court; his fellow Maryland delegate William Paca received bachelor's and master's degrees from the College of Philadelphia. Three of the Virginians—Richard Bland, Benjamin Harrison and Peyton Randolph—attended the College of William and Mary (although Harrison never received his degree) and Peyton Randolph went on to study law at the Inns of Court. Although Richard Henry Lee did not have a college degree, beginning at the age of sixteen he spent two years at the Queen Elizabeth Grammar School in Wakefield, England, probably the equivalent of an education at any of America's colleges at the time. William Hooper, one of the delegates from North Carolina who would join the Congress in the coming week, had grown up in Boston and was the lone delegate outside of Massachusetts to boast a Harvard degree. Finally, three of the South Carolinians, as we have seen, pursued their legal training at the Middle Temple in the Inns of Court in London, and two of them, Edward Rutledge and Thomas Lynch, could lay claim to being the only members of the Congress to have spent some of their undergraduate years studying at Oxford and Cambridge respectively.[26]

There were a few whose principal means of education came in the "school of life." Patrick Henry's formal education stopped when he was ten. New Hampshire's John Sullivan was the son of a poor Irish immigrant, but by the time he traveled to Philadelphia he had built a substantial fortune from a successful legal practice. Roger Sherman of Connecticut, though he had by 1774 become a surveyor and public officeholder of moderate means, had started his life in relative poverty and probably attended only a few years of common school, and John Morton was a self-educated, middle-class farmer living just outside of Philadelphia.

For the most part, the delegates shared a common cultural and religious experience. Every one of the fifty-six delegates who would eventually attend at least some of the sessions of the First Continental Congress had been born within the thirteen North American colonies. Among the fifty-six congressional delegates, thirty-eight could trace their primary ethnic heritage to England, seven to Ireland, three to Scotland, with the remainder having family connections in Holland, Sweden and Switzerland.[27]

The delegates' religious affiliations largely reflected the religious composition of the colonies they were representing. The thirty-one Anglicans came largely from the middle and southern colonies, the eight Congregationalists from New Hampshire, Massachusetts and Connecticut, the five Presbyterians from the middle colonies, four of the five Quakers came, predictably, from Pennsylvania, the lone Baptist came from Rhode Island and two of the nine New York delegates—Simon Boerum and John Haring—were members of the Dutch Reformed Church. Five of the delegates did not leave a record of any religious preference.[28]

The average age of the delegates was a little over forty-five, pretty close to the average age of the adult population of America as a whole at that time. But averages do not tell the whole story—the age range among the delegates was considerable—from twenty-four (Edward Rutledge of South Carolina) to sixty-seven (Stephen Hopkins of Rhode Island). There were relatively few delegates at the older end of the age spectrum—Stephen Hopkins and William Livingston at age sixty-three were the only delegates over sixty. The very young delegates—Rutledge at twenty-four, John Jay at twenty-eight—probably owed their selection more to impressive family connections than to distinguished records of achievement or of public service. In that regard, there was a slight concentration of younger delegates from the southern colonies, where a family's social and economic standing often guaranteed service in high political office.

The most notable characteristic shared by nearly all the delegates was a record of past service in the politics of their home colonies. Indeed, the distinction of those records no doubt caused them to be selected to serve in the Congress in the first place. Forty-nine of the fifty-six delegates had served in the provincial assemblies of their colonies, and thirteen had served as Speaker of their assemblies, a position generally considered to be the highest elective office in their provinces. Most Americans thought of their elected assemblies as the provincial equivalents of the British Parliament and that members of those assemblies possessed the rights and prerogatives of members of Parliament. The men who had served in the provincial assemblies during the period from 1765 to 1774 had not only confronted the constitutional challenges to the interests and liberties of their constituents posed by British policies but also come to view parliamentary encroachments on their legislative prerogatives as both a violation of their constitutional rights and a personal affront to their dignity and prestige.[29]

In addition to service within their own colonies, ten of the delegates to the First Continental Congress—Sam Adams, John Dickinson, Eliphalet Dyer, Christopher Gadsden, Philip Livingston, Thomas Lynch, Thomas McKean, John Morton, Caesar Rodney and John Rutledge—were among the twenty-eight delegates from nine colonies who had attended the Stamp Act Congress in New York City in October of 1765. Those ten delegates had acquired at least some superficial familiarity with one another during the two weeks the Stamp Act Congress was in session. In a sense, the "general Congress" in Philadelphia that was to begin on September 5, 1774, was similar to the Stamp Act Congress. Both had been called in response to specific pieces of parliamentary legislation—the Stamp Act and the Coercive Acts. But surely most of the delegates gathered in Philadelphia realized just how much higher the stakes were now. While some may have held out a hope that their meeting might not last much longer than the two weeks of the Stamp Act Congress, most probably understood that the extent and the complexity of issues that they were likely to face would go far beyond the limited set of resolutions that came out of the Stamp Act Congress.

However inapt the comparison between the Stamp Act Congress and the upcoming Continental Congress may be, the men who were about to gather together in Philadelphia in September of 1774—both those who had attended the Stamp Act Congress and those who had not—shared an important common ground. Perhaps more than any group of men in America, they shared a common sense not only of the constitutional issues at stake in the conflict with England, but also an intensely personal interest in defending their legislative prerogatives. The men about to gather together in Philadelphia were mostly, though not exclusively, strangers to one another, but their common experience as legislators, more than matters of age, education, wealth, ethnicity or religion, would provide them with a solid foundation on which to build, in the first instance, a new legislative body—an American "Congress"—and, eventually, a new nation.

FOUR

TWO DIFFERENT
PATHS TO LIBERTY

John Adams and John Dickinson

JOHN ADAMS'S AFTER-the-fact assessment of the composition of the First Continental Congress—that it consisted of "a third tories, another third whigs, and the rest mongrels"—was both glib and technically inaccurate. But like much of his hyperbole, it contained an element of truth. As we have seen, the delegates traveling to Philadelphia from across the vast American landscape arrived with a variety of objectives. Many, but not all of those from New England and Virginia hoped that the Congress would unite their neighboring colonies around a plan for bold resistance to the Coercive Acts; the delegates from New York and Pennsylvania hoped it would lead to a principled but moderate reconciliation with their mother country. Many of the representatives from other colonies—particularly from those colonies that did not have major seaports and were less affected by Great Britain's new taxation policies—had been less engaged in the conflict of the previous decade and therefore came to Philadelphia less certain about the direction in which the Congress should move. They may have been most interested in observing the supposedly "radical" New Englanders first hand as a way of taking their measure about what the next steps should be. Although a few—Sam Adams and perhaps John Adams and Patrick Henry—may have entertained the thought that nothing short of independence could lead to a successful resolution of the

Anglo-American conflict, no one attending the First Continental Congress came to Philadelphia with the goal of independence.

The escalating conflict between Great Britain and the colonies over the course of the months between September 5, 1774, and July 4, 1776, would move nearly all of the delegates to the Congress toward a more militant position. But over those months, there were two individuals whose differing opinions about how to respond to the growing crisis would be particularly important in framing the debate within the Congress.

John Adams, who had a long history of combat with royal officials within the politics of Massachusetts Bay, would consistently advocate responses that were destined to put Americans in an ever-more combative posture vis-à-vis the mother country. John Dickinson, who stood at the pinnacle of a Pennsylvania society that had enjoyed generally cordial relations with the Crown, was no less committed to defending American liberties from encroachments at the hands of a corrupt Parliament and British Ministry. But more moderate in temperament and more deeply respectful of what he saw as the "true principles" of the beloved, but unwritten, English constitution, Dickinson devoted his considerable intelligence and powers of logic to finding a path toward reconciliation.

As the events of the next twenty-two months unfolded, Americans would choose Adams's path, not Dickinson's. It would be Adams who would be able to boast of being the "Atlas of Independence," leaving Dickinson to defend himself against charges of pusillanimity, and even cowardice. In hindsight, it's tempting to cast aside as unrealistic the attempts of men like Dickinson to find a path toward reconciliation that involved neither independence nor submission. But to do so is to ignore the contingent nature of America's revolution against British rule. In order to reach a fair assessment of those men most immediately involved in the decision for independence, we need to make the effort to cast ourselves back nearly 250 years in time and to attempt to inhabit the minds and hearts of the men entrusted with making that decision. One useful way to begin that effort is to acquaint ourselves with the careers and personalities of two of the principal American combatants.[1]

The Irascible John Adams

John Adams, unlike his older cousin Sam, was just beginning to establish his reputation, and his journey to Philadelphia would dramatically change his life. The younger Adams seemed the polar opposite of his cousin. Whereas Sam Adams had drifted aimlessly after graduating from Harvard, John—thirteen years younger and, like Sam, a Harvard graduate—had immediately shown the self-conscious ambition and purposefulness that would characterize his adult life. Although by his own characterization he was a lackadaisical and easily distractible student before entering college, he soon thereafter developed a deep love of learning and an impressive intellectual self-discipline that would stay with him until the day he died. After graduating from Harvard in 1755 he spent a year teaching school in Worcester, Massachusetts, a decision that may have been the only false turn that he made in his career. He hated teaching the "little runtlings" of Worcester, and, no doubt, his pupils reciprocated the feeling. At the end of that year he embarked on the study of law, not so much because of an instinctive love of the law, but because that profession would assure him a steady income and a respectable social position.[2]

While at Harvard, Adams had chafed at the fact that his social standing—he was ranked only sixteen in his class of twenty-five—prevented him from getting the recognition he felt he deserved. He railed against the artificial social distinctions that had enabled the egocentric John Hancock, who had entered Harvard a year ahead of him and was ranked fifth in his class, to enjoy a far more active social life. And his obsessive hatred of Massachusetts's Royal Governor Thomas Hutchinson owed at least as much to Hutchinson's obvious favoritism for people of "high family" in his social and political patronage than it did to his constitutional differences with the governor. Fueled by those resentments, Adams yearned to rise above "the common Herd of Mankind." Beginning right after his graduation from Harvard, Adams began to keep a diary into which he poured his soul, asking himself what it would take to become a "great Man," one who might achieve "immortality in the Memories of all the Worthy." His diary entries reflect not only his considerable aspirations and ambitions but also vanity and insecurity. He was simultaneously plagued by self-doubts about whether his talents were equal to his ambitions and by a self-loathing in which he chastised himself for even aspiring to such lofty goals. His struggle to overcome what he called "my natural Pride and Self Conceit" would be never-ending, and, on the whole, unsuccessful, but those same personality traits would drive him to work tirelessly to meet those goals he set for himself.[3]

In those days, legal training involved an apprenticeship—nearly a form of indentured servitude—to a lawyer in one's region. If Adams had been more well-connected, he might have spent his legal apprenticeship with a prominent Boston lawyer, but, much to his chagrin, he had to settle for what would be two lonely years studying under James Putnam, a Worcester lawyer only a few years older than Adams himself. Putnam devoted so little time to his charge that when Adams completed his studies in 1758, Putnam, perhaps through negligence rather than animus, failed to write a letter of recommendation for him. But Adams nevertheless pursued his studies with diligence, if not passion, and, upon completing his training he set about the task of starting his legal career in his hometown of Braintree, just outside of Boston, but within its judicial district. In spite of the lack of a letter from his mentor, he knocked on the doors of the offices of Boston's leading lawyers, managing to get a hearing from three of the city's most successful attorneys—Jeremy Gridley, Oxenbridge Thatcher and, momentously as things would turn out, James Otis, Jr. With their support, Adams was admitted to the bar and certified as eligible to serve within Boston's judicial district.[4]

Adams's diary entries from this period reveal a young lawyer struggling to cope with the curse of ambition combined with self-doubt. It didn't help when he lost his first case because he had improperly prepared the writ that he presented to the court. Adams, who went through life feeling that the whole world constantly had its eyes on him, felt totally humiliated, believing that the entire Boston legal profession was laughing at his ineptitude. Immediately following this legal setback, he berated himself in his diary, moaning: "I have insensibly fallen into Habits of affecting Wit and Humour, of Shrugging my Shoulders, and moving and distorting the Muscles of my face. My motions are stiff and uneasy, ungraceful, and my attention is unsteady and irregular. These are Reflections on myself that I make. They are faults. Defects, Fopperies, and follies, and Disadvantages." But equally clear was a will to overcome his personal defects, and the very next week he predicted: "I will attempt some uncommon, unexpected Enterprize in the Law. Let me lay the Plan and arouse Spirit enough to push boldly. I swear I will push myself into Business. I will watch my Opportunity, to speak in Court, and will strike with surprise—surprize Bench, Bar, Jury, Auditors, and all. Activity, Boldness, forwardness, will draw attention." But John would struggle to get his legal career launched, so much so that when he found himself falling in love with Hannah Quincy, the daughter of Colonel Josiah Quincy, the wealthiest and most prominent man in Braintree, he put off all talk of marriage on the grounds that he needed to devote his full attention to his legal practice. The consequence of this single-mindedness was that young Hannah found another man to whom to devote her affections, a development that threw Adams into despair and provided him with yet another proof of his own inadequacies.[5]

But gradually his law practice began to take off. He won his first case in front of a jury in the fall of 1760. From that time forward, as his confidence in his abilities as a litigator grew, he spared no effort in seeking to cultivate Boston's most influential lawyers. Those efforts would not only prove helpful to his rise within his profession but, perhaps even more significantly, would lead him into the world of politics. He particularly cultivated James Otis, Jr., one of the most successful lawyers in the Boston judicial district and perhaps the most influential politician serving in the Massachusetts General Court, the colony's provincial legislature. Having been spurned by James Putnam, Adams made a conscious attempt to win Otis's respect. He was particularly admiring of Otis's oratorical skills, which though deeply grounded in careful research and enriched by learned citations to classical literature were, he later recalled, displayed in "a torrent of impetuous eloquence." Although Adams may not have possessed the instinctive charisma that Otis displayed both in the courtroom and on the floor of the legislature, he was so inspired by his senior colleague's prodigious oratorical skills that he worked self-consciously, and successfully, to improve his own abilities as a performer on the public stage. Those efforts enabled Adams to take another step forward in

November of 1761, when his success in the courtrooms of the Boston judicial district earned him a qualification to practice before the Massachusetts Superior Court, giving him access to a new range of cases.[6]

As prospects in Adams's professional life began to brighten, so too, after some five years of neglect, did the outlook on his personal life. John Adams fell in love. Abigail Smith, the daughter of the Congregational minister Reverend William Smith from the neighboring town of Weymouth, Massachusetts, was not only a woman of high intelligence but also, considering the generally dismal opportunities that women of that age had to obtain an education, unusually well-educated. Beginning at the age of eleven, she was tutored by Richard Cranch, a friend of Reverend Smith, receiving an impressive grounding in classical as well as contemporary literature.

It was not love at first sight. Adams had first met Abigail in 1759, when she was only fifteen. He was still in the depths of depression over his unsuccessful wooing of Hannah Quincy, and it was not until the spring of 1763 that the two began their courtship. As was the case with Hannah, Adams took his time, but the two were finally married on October 24, 1764, a partnership that would endure until Abigail's death in 1818 and that would enrich John Adams's life through every trial and tribulation he encountered. Nor is John Adams the sole person who should be thankful for his longtime relationship with his wife Abigail. Historians writing about this period of American history also owe her a huge debt of gratitude, for with her literary skills and her wit, she encouraged a correspondence with her husband John that has produced a rich record both of their personal life and of their reactions to nearly all of the public events of the era in which they lived.[7]

After he graduated from Harvard, John Adams spent an unusual amount of time putting pen to paper—not only preparing legal briefs but recording nearly every one of his thoughts and actions in his diary. In the spring and summer of 1763, he began to put his penchant for writing to a different use, drawing on his knowledge of law and his growing interest in politics (it was nearly impossible for a lawyer practicing in the Boston area *not* to be interested in the politics of that city at that time) to put some of his ideas into print. He began in a light-hearted way: under the pseudonym of "Humphrey Ploughjogger," he wrote a set of satirical essays in which he ridiculed the "grate men" in the colony who "dus nothing but quaril with anuther." He followed these essays with more serious ones speculating on government and human nature. Beginning in August of 1765, he began publishing, in four installments, his "Dissertation on the Canon and Feudal Law." Although he would later claim that the essays played an important role in igniting opposition to the Stamp Act, whose details were just beginning to be known at that time, in fact, they were aimed at more general topics relating to human nature, religion and government—in particular on the dangers of the arbitrary power exercised by religion and government. Even though he did not even mention the Stamp Act until the fourth installment of the essays, published in the *Boston Gazette* on October 21, 1765, he did emphasize that "British liberties are not the grants of princes or parliaments" but rather "inherent and essential, agreed upon as maxims and established as preliminaries, even before Parliament existed." This emphasis on fundamental liberties, while not invoking the English philosopher John Locke's notion of "natural rights," would surface again and again in Adams's writing and would, eventually, provide at least part of the basis for America's justification of independence from Great Britain.[8]

Although most of Adams's early political writings, unlike those of his cousin Sam, were largely theoretical, they did start to change as the full impact of the passage of the Stamp Act began to be felt. His instinctive reaction to the British provocation was pure John Adams, which is to say that it was concerned much less with long-range constitutional implications and much more with possible effects on the still-nascent law practice of John Adams. Boston's resistance to the Stamp Act required not only street protests and boycotts but also the willingness of lawyers to refuse to comply with the act's provisions requiring the use of stamps on all legal documents. Adams took this personally, for the cost of those stamps hit him directly in his own pocketbook. At a time when many of Boston's political leaders were using high-minded rhetoric to encourage their fellow residents to stand up in virtuous opposition to British tyranny, Adams wallowed in self-pity, noting in his diary melodramatically that "I have groped in dark Obscurity till of late, and had but just become known, and gained a small degree of Reputation, when this execrable project was set on foot for my Ruin as well as that of America in general." The detestable Stamp Act seemed aimed directly at the well-being of Mr. John Adams.[9]

But however much Adams may have initially been preoccupied with the effects of the Stamp Act on his own livelihood, he soon found that it offered him a different route to the fame and respect to which he aspired. By the fall of 1765 his reputation as a skillful writer was sufficiently well known that he was asked to draft the town of Braintree's instructions to its delegates to the Massachusetts General Court, commanding them to oppose the act on the grounds that it was unconstitutional and that it would produce "convulsive Change" in their colony's relationship with the mother country. And in January of 1766, Adams published three essays in the *Boston Gazette* elaborating on his opposition to the Stamp Act. Although Adams clearly believed that the act was unconstitutional, his essays opposing it were relatively restrained, for he was inclined to believe it was the result of blundering British ministers and an ill-informed Parliament; surely, reasonable petitions and remonstrances would cause the British government to see the error of its ways. Although Adams's political writings and rhetoric would gradually grow more passionate over time, at this early stage of his entry into the world of politics, his natural instincts were, unlike those of his cousin, cautious and restrained.[10]

John Adams steadfastly supported peaceful, purposeful resistance to the Stamp Act during the spring and early summer of 1765, but when riots erupted on the streets of Boston, he was deeply disturbed. When the Boston mob ransacked the house of Lieutenant Governor Thomas Hutchinson in August of 1765 (an action that may have been actively encouraged by his cousin Sam), Adams recorded in his diary his concern about the "dangerous Tendency and Consequence" of such an "atrocious Violation of the peace." Throughout the years leading up to independence, Adams would wrestle with this tension between his determination to defend America's constitutional rights against British encroachment and his deep distaste for violence and disorder.[11]

In the aftermath of the repeal of the Stamp Act in February of 1766, Adams threw himself into the task of building up a law practice that had been temporarily derailed by the closing of the courts. But as hostilities between the residents of Boston and British royal officials and soldiers escalated after the passage of the Townshend Acts in 1767, Adams was once again drawn into the fray. In 1768 he served as chief defense counsel for John Hancock, the Boston merchant who had been most flagrant in his defiance of the new British acts of trade. Hancock was rewarded for his efforts by having one of his ships, the *Liberty*, seized and by being ordered to pay a £9,000 fine—a huge amount in those days—for having engaged in smuggling. Adams did not entirely approve of Hancock's flaunting of British law and admitted to feeling some disgust at having to take the case, but, enticed by a substantial fee and by the attention the case would no doubt bring to his practice, he agreed to take it on. The case dragged on for several months, but in the end Adams persuaded the British that they lacked the evidence to secure a conviction, and they dropped the charges.[12]

Adams's commitment to the rule of law and peaceful resistance to British policies was put to a further test in the wake of the March 5, 1770, event that came to be known, at least in the minds of American propagandists, as the Boston Massacre. The events of that cold winter night were in some senses little different from many previous instances in which unruly Bostonians gathered to taunt the British soldiers who had been sent to the city to enforce the British version of law and order. They'd been doing it regularly since the passage of the Townshend Duties in 1767. In this case, however, someone in the crowd of 400 protesters threw a club that struck a British soldier, after which, in spite of orders to the contrary by their commanding officer, Captain Thomas Preston, the British soldiers opened fire, killing five Bostonians. The residents of Boston demanded retribution, and by the end of that month Preston and several other soldiers had been indicted by a Boston grand jury on the charge of what today would be called manslaughter. There was no shortage of Boston lawyers ready and willing to serve as prosecutors, but securing a lawyer to defend the hated British soldiers was another matter altogether.

Historians have long speculated about the reasons behind Adams's decision to defend the British soldiers and the consequences of his having done so. Many of the explanations have turned on the behind-the-scenes maneuverings of John's cousin Sam, who was on the one hand determined to prove that even British soldiers could get a fair trial in Boston and, on the other, sufficiently confident of the mood of a Boston jury that even with the excellent counsel provided by his cousin and Josiah Quincy, one of the leading lawyers in Boston and the brother of the prosecuting attorney in the case, Samuel Quincy, the soldiers would in the end be convicted. This may be a sufficient explanation for Sam Adams's role in the affair, but it does not explain why his younger cousin was persuaded to accept the assignment. Some have argued that John Adams's election to a vacant seat in the Massachusetts provincial assembly just three months after the trial—an election in which Sam Adams vigorously supported him—is sufficient explanation of the younger Adams's behavior. Although there may indeed have been some sort of "understanding" between the two Adamses, the fact of the matter is that not only did John agree to take the lead in defending the soldiers, but when the trials finally unfolded, his performance as a defense attorney was much more than perfunctory. Indeed, it was masterful. He insisted that Preston be tried separately from the soldiers accused of actually firing on the rioters. His vigorous cross-examination of the witnesses for the prosecution in Preston's case revealed the full extent of the confusing chaos surrounding the tragedy, casting doubt on whether Preston had ever given the command to fire. And once Preston was acquitted, he secured the acquittal of six of the eight soldiers, who, he argued, were innocent victims of the riotous atmosphere and were only doing what they thought was their duty when they heard the command of "fire" from an unknown source. The other two soldiers were convicted of manslaughter, but then allowed to plead "benefit of clergy," which enabled them to escape all punishment except for the branding of a thumb.[13]

Adams's own explanation for agreeing to serve as defense attorney emphasized his commitment to the right to competent legal counsel, which, he insisted, was an indispensable element of "a free country." If no other Boston attorney would step forward, and if Captain Preston believed that he could not receive a fair trial in Boston, then it was, Adams argued, his moral and professional duty to prove otherwise. Moreover, Adams, no doubt aware that some might accuse him of defending the hated British soldiery simply out of a desire for material gain, insisted that he would take the case only for a token fee of one guinea. In his recounting of the event later in life, Adams would add a few embellishments, emphasizing the risks to his reputation given the intense popular hatred of the British soldiers. In fact, when news of the repeal of the Townshend Duties reached Boston shortly after the events of the Boston Massacre and popular passions had subsided, Adams was able not only to take credit for stepping in to defend the principle of the rule of law but also to enhance his reputation as a highly effective lawyer in the bargain.[14]

The trial of Captain Preston and the British soldiers provided further confirmation that however self-centered Adams was, he was also truly committed to the rule of law. Looking back on the tumult of the years immediately preceding independence, Adams recalled being approached on the streets of Boston by "a common Horse Jockey" who had "sometimes been my Client." The man was, Adams noted, no stranger to the courtroom; he had been brought to trial on numerous occasions for a variety of petty civil and criminal offenses. As he came up to Adams, he greeted him with the exclamation: "Oh! Mr. Adams what great Things have you and your Colleagues done for Us! We can never be gratefull enough to you. There are no Courts of justice now in this Province, and I hope there never will be another!" Adams was appalled. "Are these the Sentiments of such People? And how many of them are there in the Country? Truly, we must guard against this Sprit and these Principles or We shall repent of all of our Conduct."[15]

In spite of these concerns, as Adams made his preparations for his journey to Philadelphia that August, his mood was ebullient. There would be no "common Horse Jockeys" at the Continental Congress, and he must have relished the opportunity to appear on a continental, rather than a merely provincial, stage. As his journey to Philadelphia proceeded, his diary entries, few and far between in previous months, increased and were notable for their detailed and enthusiastic recording of the people, places and landscapes that he saw along the way. He and his fellow delegates were particularly pleased by the favorable reception they received from important local political leaders in the towns along their route. Arriving in New Haven on August 16, he observed: "As we came into the Town all the Bells in Town were sett to ringing, and the People—Men, Women and Children—were crouding at the Doors and Windows as if it was to see a Coronation!"[16]

By the time he arrived in Philadelphia, Adams must have felt great pride that he had ascended to such a high level of prominence and public trust within his home colony. Over the past decade he'd gone from an unknown lawyer scraping to making a living to one of the best-known and most respected lawyers and political activists in a colony filled with such men. Indeed, within the colony of Massachusetts, only his cousin Sam and perhaps John Hancock, could claim reputations superior to his. John Adams, being John Adams, however, must have also been well aware that his reputation at that moment was a purely provincial one, that he was little known outside of his home colony. Although he may have been a man on the way up, he knew that he had much to prove in this new, continental venue.

The Maddeningly Moderate John Dickinson

When the Congress opened for business on September 5, John Dickinson had not even been elected to serve as one of Pennsylvania's delegates. Though he was by then one of the colonies' best-known defenders of their constitutional liberties, he had been essentially blackballed by fellow Pennsylvanian Joseph Galloway. Dickinson had chosen not to serve in the Pennsylvania Assembly during the session when the congressional delegates were selected, and Dickinson's longtime rival in Pennsylvania politics, Galloway, as Speaker of the Assembly, had ruled that only members of that body were eligible for selection. Dickinson had made his name with the publication of *Letters from a Farmer in Pennsylvania*, a series of twelve essays written in 1767–1768 in response to the Townshend Duties. Dickinson acknowledged Parliament's right, dating back to the navigation acts of the mid-seventeenth century, to impose taxes on the colonies for the purposes of regulating within the British Empire, but, relying on his extensive training in international law, he had made a strong case that the acts imposed by Parliament beginning in 1764—the Sugar Act, the Stamp Act and the Townshend Duties—were of an entirely different, and unprecedented character. Their purpose, he correctly pointed out, was to raise a revenue intended to go into British, not American, coffers. Dickinson argued that any tax for the purposes of raising a revenue was, in effect, a gift of the people to their government. And such gifts from the people could only be given with their explicit consent. The new British taxes on the colonies, passed without the consent of the American people, were, Dickinson insisted, contrary to the fundamental principles of the English constitution.[17]

Dickinson's family roots in America went back to the mid-seventeenth century, when his great-grandfather Walter Dickinson, along with several other members of the Society of Friends, immigrated to Virginia from England. From that time forward, the Dickinson family would steadily accumulate lands in Virginia, Maryland and Delaware and generate substantial wealth, principally from the cultivation of tobacco. Through the combination of their wealth and social connections, the Dickinsons would become known throughout the Chesapeake region as pillars of the Quaker religious community. Though many of John Dickinson's contemporaries believed him to be a Quaker, and in spite of his long family association with Quakerism and his marriage to Polly Norris, the daughter of Isaac Norris, one of the most influential Quaker merchants and politicians in Philadelphia, Dickinson formally rejected any formal association with the Quaker meeting, or, indeed, any religious organization.

Dickinson's education both at home and abroad was as distinguished as that of any man in America. Schooled at his family's home in Delaware by an assortment of tutors, he developed at an early age a deep interest in Latin and history. In 1750, when he was eighteen, Dickinson moved to Philadelphia to begin studying law under John Moland, arguably the most eminent lawyer in the city. Dickinson's two years of study and apprenticeship with Moland deepened his interest in the connections between law and history, and it was a combination of intellectual and professional ambition that took him across the Atlantic to embark on three more years of legal study at the profession's most prestigious institution, the Middle Temple in London. When Dickinson returned to Philadelphia in 1757 to begin practicing law, he may well have been the best-trained lawyer in America. At the time the delegates to the First Continental Congress were gathering, Dickinson was dividing his time among three separate residences; he was living at Fair Hill, the family estate of his wife on the outskirts of Philadelphia, he was building a handsome townhouse on Chestnut Street between Sixth and Seventh Streets and he remained the heir to his family's magnificent estate, Poplar Hall, in Kent County, Delaware.[18]

Dickinson's first elected political position was as a member of Delaware's General Assembly in 1759. In those days, the colony of Delaware was often referred to as the "three lower counties of Pennsylvania," and the prominence of Dickinson's family in that region made his election virtually automatic. As his social, professional and political world came increasingly to be centered in Philadelphia, however, he began to focus his attention more acutely on that city. The Dickinson family's social and political clout was not as overwhelming in Philadelphia as it was in Delaware, however, and when John ran for a seat in the Pennsylvania Assembly in 1761, he was defeated. But it would not take long for him to build his reputation on his own merits, and the following year, he won election as a representative from Philadelphia County. During his years of service in the Pennsylvania Assembly he was generally identified with the so-called Quaker Party, the group of legislators who, though dominated by Quakers, also included men like Benjamin Franklin, Dickinson and even his arch-rival, Joseph Galloway.

The one thing that all of the Quaker Party members had in common was a determination to limit the prerogatives of the "proprietor." While most American colonies were "royal" colonies, whose governors were appointed directly by the king, Pennsylvania was a "proprietary" colony. Its governor was always a direct descendant of William Penn, the English Quaker who had been given the original grant of control over all of the lands that would come to be known as Pennsylvania. William Penn's descendants chose not to embrace their ancestor's Quaker religion, becoming Anglicans instead, thus setting up a conflict between many of the Quaker politicians who had come to dominate the colony's provincial assembly and the Anglican members of the Penn family who served as the colony's governors. Dickinson, ever independent, had no fear of breaking with party orthodoxy, and when, in 1764 Franklin and Galloway proposed to eliminate the power of the proprietor by converting Pennsylvania into a royal colony, Dickinson wrote and spoke eloquently against the scheme, observing, presciently as things turned out, that the injustices that might result from royal rule might be worse than those suffered under the proprietor.

The rift between Dickinson and Galloway on that issue became so severe that the two actually came to blows, with Galloway grabbing hold of Dickinson's notably prominent proboscis and striking him with his cane. Dickinson, mild-mannered and so slight of build that he would have been unlikely to emerge victorious in any contest of fisticuffs, managed to deflect the blow from the cane and to deliver a "fair knock on the head" to Galloway with a stick. They were eventually separated by others, but at that moment the political rivalry between the two escalated to an enmity that would last throughout the remainder of their political careers.[19]

As we have seen, in the aftermath of the passage of the Coercive Acts, Dickinson occupied a middle ground between radicals like Charles Thomson, Thomas Mifflin, Joseph Reed and many of the artisans and mechanics of Philadelphia, on the one hand, and the group of conservative Philadelphia merchants and Quakers who continued to dominate the politics of the Assembly, on the other. He became chair of the Philadelphia Committee of Correspondence, drawing up three sets of resolutions laying out the grounds for America's resistance to British policy and issuing a set of instructions to the soon-to-be elected members of Pennsylvania's delegation to the Continental Congress. The instructions were classic Dickinson, urging the delegates on the one hand to be steadfast in providing relief for "our suffering Brethren [in Boston and] obtaining redress of grievances" while, on the other, insisting that a primary purpose of the gathering was to "restore harmony between Great Britain and her colonies on a constitutional foundation."[20]

When it came time for the Pennsylvania Assembly to choose delegates to the Continental Congress, Galloway, as Speaker of the Assembly, pushed through a resolution restricting the delegation to members of the Assembly. Although he would easily have been elected, Dickinson had chosen not to serve in the Assembly that year, so he along with Charles Thomson, the other Philadelphia politician whom Galloway disliked and feared, were deemed ineligible to serve. But even though he was not formally a member of the Congress, Dickinson was, with the sole exception of Benjamin Franklin, who was still in England, the most prestigious politician in Philadelphia, and his conspicuous presence in the city's fashionable homes and taverns during the opening weeks of the Congress's deliberations was noted by everyone.[21]

No one was more cognizant of Dickinson's prestige, reputation and presence than John Adams. The two men could hardly have been more different. Adams—short, pudgy and pugnacious—nearly always wore his emotions on his sleeve. Dickinson, as described by Adams, was "tall, but slender as a Reed." But more important were the emotional differences between the two men. Though both had powerful, incisive intellects, Dickinson's was more controlled; whether in his oratory or his writing, Dickinson strove for both a political and emotional moderation of which Adams was, quite simply, psychologically incapable. But, at that first meeting at least, Adams was nonetheless impressed not only with Dickinson's reputation—he was, after all, the "Farmer in Pennsylvania"—but also by the "Springs of life" within Dickinson that, Adams opined, belied his apparent frailty. Those "Springs of life"—a strong sense of intellectual and moral rectitude that would cause Dickinson to defend with persistence and a carefully modulated passion his own political beliefs no matter how much others might disagree with him—would over the course of the next twenty-two months cause Adams more anguish and frustration than the traits of anyone else in the Congress. During those months, John Adams would discover that one of his most formidable adversaries was not George III or any of the king's ministers, but the mild-mannered "Farmer in Pennsylvania."[22]

FIVE

THE CONGRESS ORGANIZES

P HILADELPHIANS AWOKE on the morning of September 5, 1774, to find the city enveloped in a mist. Light rain would fall most of the day. Those delegates who had wisely decided to stay at the City Tavern were no doubt especially pleased that they had only to walk up to the second floor where they were to meet in the tavern's Long Room, the temporary meeting place of the First Continental Congress until the delegates could agree on a permanent location. Some forty-three of the Congress's fifty-six delegates were in attendance that day (only North Carolina and Georgia went unrepresented), and the room, which had been jammed by over 200 Philadelphians on the day on which the Philadelphia Committee of Correspondence agreed to call for a Continental Congress, easily accommodated the group.[1]

Their first order of business that day would be to choose a permanent meeting place for the new congress, but that item also produced the first bit of tension. The Speaker of the Pennsylvania Assembly, Joseph Galloway, had made clear he wanted the Congress to meet in the Assembly Room of the Pennsylvania State House, the building on Chestnut Street between Fifth and Sixth Streets that would, several decades after Americans had declared their independence, come to be known as Independence Hall. On the surface, his offer of that commodious public space to the new Congress seemed generous. Completed in 1753, it was, after all, Philadelphia's most important public space, the longtime meeting place of the Pennsylvania Assembly. But to the more radical delegates, in particular most of the

New Englanders and a few of the South Carolinians and Virginians, the State House was too closely associated with the Pennsylvania Assembly's more conservative political leaders, who had dragged their feet on questions relating to a united opposition to British policies. And it didn't help that the proposal came from Galloway, who was seen as the leader of Pennsylvania's most reluctant patriots.

Indeed, within a day of his arrival in Philadelphia, on August 30, John Adams had already begun to scout out alternative meeting places, including the newly completed guild hall for the Carpenters' Company of the City, a group of Philadelphia's master builders, located near Fourth and Chestnut Streets. After conversations with South Carolina's Thomas Lynch and Christopher Gadsden and two of the more radical Pennsylvanians—Thomas Mifflin and Thomas McKean—Adams was likely instrumental in forming a coalition of southerners and New Englanders determined to hold the meetings in Carpenters' Hall.[2]

The delegates agreed to go on a brief inspection tour of both Carpenters' Hall and the Assembly Room of the State House. They walked the two and a half blocks from the City Tavern to Carpenters' Hall. A lovely, two-story brick building in the Georgian style recently constructed by Philadelphia's carpenters as a showpiece of their craftsmanship, the hall would have struck all of them as both comfortable and spacious. Thomas Lynch, pushing the radicals' agenda, proposed that the delegates agree then and there, "without further Enquiry" that the guild hall would provide an ideal venue for their meetings. James Duane—one of the conservative delegates from New York who had no doubt already bonded with Galloway—objected, arguing that the Assembly Room of the State House was equally convenient and commodious, and as a public rather than a private hall, it was more appropriate to a meeting of the sort on which they were embarking. He pointedly observed that Galloway, as Speaker of the Pennsylvania Assembly, had been gracious enough to offer the State House for the delegates' use; the very least they could do, he argued, was to inspect the site, as a "piece of respect" due the distinguished speaker. But for the first, and not the last, time, the delegates chose not to pay that respect to Mr. Galloway. By a "great Majority," they decided they would conduct their business in Carpenters' Hall for the remainder of their time in Philadelphia. In fact, from a practical standpoint, it would have made little difference whether the delegates met in Carpenters' Hall or the State House, and the decision not even to walk the two blocks from Carpenters' Hall to the State House must have seemed a great affront to Galloway and his supporters. The decision may have had some symbolic importance to the more radical delegates, but it did little to promote the eventual consensus on other matters that would prove so important to the Congress's success.[3]

The delegates would meet daily, except on Sundays, in the East Room of Carpenters' Hall during the fifty-one days in which the Congress was in session. Meeting on the first floor of the building, they would share the space with one of Benjamin Franklin's many contributions to his adopted city, the new Library Company, America's first lending library, which occupied the second floor of the building.

Once settled in the East Room, the delegates moved immediately, and unanimously, to elect as president of their Congress Peyton Randolph, Speaker of Virginia's House of Burgesses. Randolph, a tall, well-fed Virginian, spent most of his time living in his handsome townhouse in Virginia's colonial capital of Williamsburg. His wardrobe consisted of the latest in English fashions, and he could have been easily mistaken for an English aristocrat rather than a provincial politician. Like the decision on where to meet, the decision to select Randolph seems to have been informally agreed to by a majority of the delegates before they had formally convened, but unlike the decision on where to meet, this one appears to have been arrived at amicably. Randolph's reputation as a man of uncommon distinction and political acumen was already well-known outside of his home colony. His ancestors had begun to set down their roots in Virginia in the mid-seventeenth century, and from that time forward they had been involved in nearly every aspect of the economic, social and political life of the colony. In 1745 Peyton had consolidated the Randolph family's power and authority in the colony by marrying Elizabeth Harrison, herself the eldest child of a union with two powerful Virginia dynasties, the Harrisons and Carters. And in 1748, at the age of twenty-six, he added two important public offices to his portfolio—he was elected a delegate to the House of Burgesses by the voters of Williamsburg and, simultaneously, was appointed by Lieutenant

Governor William Gooch as attorney general of the colony. The practice of holding legislative office in the provincial government while at the same time serving in an appointive office in the royal government was one that typified the generally affable—one might even say cozy—relationship between the royal and provincial leadership classes of Virginia, and Randolph would continue to move easily between those two worlds almost until the moment that independence was declared.[4]

The amiable relationship between royal and provincial political leaders in Virginia began to fray in 1765, when John Robinson, then Speaker of the House but also serving at royal pleasure as the colony's treasurer, was involved in a scandal concerning the lending of government money to some of his closest associates. In 1766, after Robinson's unexpected death, Randolph became Speaker and immediately put an end to the practice of serving in the legislature while at the same time holding high office in the royal government.[5]

As events unfolded, it became clear that Randolph had assumed his colony's most powerful office at precisely the moment when Virginia's cordial relationship with royal officials in London was beginning to deteriorate. During the years between 1766 and 1774, his ability to broker compromises between firebrands like Patrick Henry and Richard Henry Lee and conservative men like Edmund Pendleton and Benjamin Harrison earned him the respect of all. As the leader of the provincial legislature whose petitions and resolutions to Parliament often served as a model for other colonies to follow, Randolph was no doubt seen by many outside of his colony as ideally qualified to be a broker of compromise and consensus in the First Continental Congress. That body would be confronted not only with different attitudes toward the proper means of resisting British policies but also with vast social, economic and cultural differences among delegates from twelve colonies (North Carolina's delegates arrived on September 14, but Georgia's remained absent) spread out over nearly 330,000 square miles of territory.

But it was not Randolph's distinguished lineage and talent for compromise alone that produced his unanimous election as the Congress's president. The New Englanders—particularly John and Sam Adams—were all too aware of their reputations as wild-eyed radicals

who had helped precipitate the present crisis, and they knew that selecting a Virginian—particularly one with the aristocratic bearing
and dignified demeanor of Peyton Randolph—to preside over the
Congress, would serve to set at least some delegates' minds at ease.

Toward a New Conception of a Congress

The delegates' decisions, made with apparent casualness, to call their
gathering a Congress and the moderator of their proceedings a President were freighted with meaning. In Britain, the supreme legislative
body was of course the Parliament; in America, most of the provincial
legislative bodies were called assemblies. The eighteenth-century
meaning of a "congress" signified a meeting of representatives from
separate, autonomous political entities, gathered together for a limited
purpose of formulating a common position on specific issues. As such,
each of the delegations to the Congress felt bound to represent a specific entity—in this case each of the American colonies and, in particular, the provincial assemblies that served as the legislative bodies for
those colonies. An "assembly" or "legislature," by contrast, had more
far-reaching authority to legislate on a wide—indeed, open-ended—
range of issues in the name of the people. Strictly speaking, the First
Continental Congress possessed no formal authority to make any decision binding on the legislatures of the individual colonies. Any legitimacy that the Congress might have would be entirely dependent on
public opinion, as expressed in the provincial assemblies and, increasingly, in the rapidly expanding and more popularly based Committees
of Correspondence. One of the truly significant developments of the
period between 1774 and 1776, and, even more important, of the period from 1776 until the Continental Congress was succeeded by the
First Federal Congress in 1789, was the Congress's gradual acquisition
of legitimacy and, as a consequence of that increased legitimacy, its
gradual extension of authority to include a wide variety of legislative
and administrative functions.[6]

The delegates' sense of their mission and the legitimacy of their
increasing exercise of political power would evolve over both sessions.
This evolution is reflected in the changing way they referred to their
own body. As the delegates gathered on that first day, they called it

either the "general congress," or, more formally, the "Congress." The fact that people often thought of it as a "general congress" even before it began its business suggests that at least some conceived of its mission as extending beyond a single issue. Over time, many delegates would come to refer to it as a "continental congress," using the phrase in a purely descriptive sense to mean the vast geographical area it represented. But by the summer of 1775, when the second session of the Congress was under way, many Americans both within and outside the Congress had begun to refer to it as the "Continental Congress," in capital letters. Although that phrase was never adopted as the official name of the body—it always remained, officially, "The Congress"—the increasing frequency with which it was called the Continental Congress suggests that it was in the process of becoming an institution whose scope of responsibilities and authority was steadily increasing.

The delegates' decision to assign the label of President to Peyton Randolph was consistent with their belief in the limited nature of the authority of both the Congress and its presiding officer. In 1774, the term "president" was understood to signify an individual who presided over the proceedings of either "a temporary or permanent body of persons"—in effect, a chairman or moderator lacking any of the executive authority that we associate with modern-day presidents and prime ministers. The powers of an American "president" would, of course, change dramatically with the ratification of the United States Constitution of 1788, and the nature of the relationship between the American president and Congress would change as well.[7]

The Inconstant Record Keeper

If Randolph's election as president of the Congress proceeded without contention, the next item of business on that first day—choosing a secretary responsible for recording the minutes of the meeting—was another matter. And once again, Joseph Galloway would find himself on the losing side. Galloway had used his influence in the Assembly to prevent his fellow assemblyman, Charles Thomson, whom he considered an incendiary radical, from being elected a delegate to the Congress. But many other delegates, who admired Thomson as one of the leaders of the radical wing of Philadelphia's resistance movement, decided that they would include him in the proceedings by nominating him as the Congress's non-voting secretary. Thinking that he might be able to thwart Thomson's election by putting forward the name of a relatively moderate New Englander, Silas Deane of Connecticut, Galloway sounded out other delegates about that alternative. But he didn't like what he heard; it was pretty clear that most of the delegates preferred the appointment of Thomson. And so, after informal conversations among the delegates in the taverns and boarding-houses of Philadelphia, the venues where much of the business of the Congress would be conducted from that time forward, Thomson was unanimously elected secretary. Deane, who did not seem troubled by being passed over, wrote to his wife that Thomson's election was "highly agreeable to the mechanics and citizens in general," even if it was "mortifying to the last degree to Mr. Galloway."[8]

Charles Thomson had overcome a daunting history of hardship in order to reach the position of secretary of the Continental Congress. He had arrived in America from Ulster, Ireland, in 1739, in a desperate state. His father, John, mourning the recent death of his wife during childbirth and beset by financial problems, set sail for America with his sons, including the nine-year-old Charles, in search of a better life. Just before the ship carrying them to New Castle, Delaware, landed, however, John Thomson died from a shipboard fever. The ship's captain, not wishing to deal with the bother of burying his passenger once they arrived, cast his body into the sea, making sure beforehand to take all of John's money and his few possessions. When they arrived in Newcastle, Charles was separated from his brothers and sent to live with a local blacksmith, who immediately laid plans to make Charles his indentured servant. The boy got wind of the plans and escaped, heading up the post road toward Philadelphia. At that point, something good finally happened to Charles Thomson. Along the way to Philadelphia, he was befriended by a woman who took him under her care and arranged for him to attend a private academy run by Francis Alison, a Presbyterian minister in New London, Pennsylvania, twenty-five miles south of Philadelphia. Thomson would spend the next seven years living and studying with Alison, a man whom Benjamin Franklin praised as possessing "great ingenuity and learning." By 1750, Thomson had been appointed a tutor in classical languages by Franklin, to whom Alison had introduced him, at the Academy in Philadelphia, later called the College of Philadelphia, and still later the University of Pennsylvania. At this point in his life, Thomson could feel grateful that he had escaped from a life as an impoverished orphan and, indeed, had acquired a classical education that might provide him with a foundation for a climb to success. He was clearly a young man with ambition, but he almost certainly did not know what path he might take in order to find the ladder that would enable him to make that climb.[9]

Thomson would continue teaching for the next decade, while at the same time dabbling in local politics. He became particularly interested in what he considered to be the Pennsylvania proprietary government's inhumane policy toward the colony's Indians and in 1759 wrote a lengthy, anonymous pamphlet, *An Enquiry into the Causes of the Alienation of the Delaware and Shawnee Indians from the British Interest.* Although the pamphlet did not endear him to Pennsylvania's proprietary officials, it did win him praise among many of the Quakers in the Pennsylvania Assembly. By 1760, recognizing that a career as a teacher was unlikely to lead him to either wealth or fame, he left his teaching post and began a career as a merchant and, a bit later, as a distiller of rum. Combining an interest in the pursuit of profit with an active engagement in politics, Thomson joined those in Philadelphia who urged firm resistance to British policies every step of the way between the enactment of the Stamp Act in 1765 and the passage of the Coercive Acts in 1774. Working behind the scenes, he had been one of the most active organizers of resistance to the Stamp Act in Philadelphia, and allying himself with John Dickinson, he had been a key organizer of the non-importation agreement in Philadelphia in response to the Townshend Duties.

By 1774, on the eve of Thomson's election as secretary to the Continental Congress, his climb to political prominence had reached a height sufficient to prompt John Adams to label him "the Sam Adams of Philadelphia—the Life of the Cause of Liberty." Some of his more conservative enemies in Pennsylvania described him in less flattering terms as "one of the most violent of the Sons of Liberty (so-called) in America," but as men like Joseph Galloway were beginning to realize, many of the members of the Continental Congress, a body that they had hoped would put the brakes on the radical resistance movement in America, were far more sympathetic to the likes of the Adamses and Charles Thomson than they had anticipated.[10]

Thomson would serve as secretary of the Congress from its opening day on September 5, 1774, until its expiration and supplanting by the First Federal Congress in 1789. Because of the longevity of his service recording, or at least being responsible for recording, all of the business of the Congress, he was in a unique position to observe every important event that occurred in America's first continental legislative body. Alas, he proved to be a less-than-conscientious record keeper, and historians are still puzzling over the precise order of some of the business conducted in the Congress. Even worse, at least from the standpoint of the twenty-first-century historian eager to learn more about the inner workings of the Congress, late in his life Thomson took an even more willful step. He had apparently amassed a large collection of "secret historical memoirs" relating to the Revolution, but when asked if he would write a history of the Revolution, he emphatically declined, claiming that his history would "contradict all the histories of the great events of the Revolution," thereby casting doubt on the virtue and wisdom of those involved in the struggle. It would be better, he asserted, to allow subsequent generations of Americans to live with their myths: "Let the world admire the supposed wisdom and valor of our great men. Perhaps they may adopt the qualities that have been ascribed to them, and thus good may be done." He would prefer, he said, to let America's revolutionary heroes "go down with éclat to Posterity, whose Laurels would be tarnished if I were to write." Nor did he merely refrain from writing that history; he made sure that others would not use his papers to do the same. Beginning in 1815, he proceeded to burn every scrap of information that he had respecting the course of events of the American Revolution! A coup for mythmaking, but a disaster for history.[11]

Instructing the Delegates

After approving Thomson's appointment as secretary, there were certainly many in the New York and Pennsylvania delegations who must have felt some uneasiness about the direction in which the Congress was moving. They may have felt some relief when the Congress turned to more routine business—that of the reading of the credentials and instructions from each of the colonial legislatures to their delegates. However routine that procedural business may have been, the instructions from the colonial legislatures provide us with a striking reminder that the First Continental Congress, far from being conceived by the colonial legislatures as a revolutionary body, was instead one called not just to protest the policies of the British Parliament but also to seek reconciliation with their mother country. The instructions from the colonial legislatures, even in the more radical Virginia and Massachusetts, were strikingly similar. While all of them referred to the need for a redress of American grievances, they also were in accord in desiring the restoration of "that peace, harmony, & mutual confidence which once happily subsisted between the parent country and her Colonies." When we look back on the steady deterioration in the relationship between the Congress and royal officials in London during the twenty-two months that would follow, we might find it tempting to regard these expressions of affection and felicity as insincere boilerplate, but in fact, the overwhelming number of delegates to the Congress did come to Philadelphia with a deep affection for their mother country and were genuinely desirous of finding a path toward reconciliation.[12]

The instructions to the delegation from the Massachusetts General Court, adopted on June 17 and most likely drafted by Sam Adams, were surprisingly mild, joining in the common refrain, expressing the General Court's hope for a "restoration of union & harmony between Great Britain and the Colonies, most ardently desired by all good men." Sam Adams may have had far more ambivalence about the desirability of a "restoration of union & harmony" than most of his fellow delegates, but, ever the shrewd tactician, he realized that moderation, not militance, would likely win Boston and Massachusetts more friends among the delegates attending the Congress.[13]

A few legislatures were more pointed in their criticisms of British policies. The Delaware legislature offered a catalogue of specific British actions that had precipitated the crisis. Its instructions condemned the acts of Parliament that had closed the ports of Boston and essentially imposed a military government on the residents of Massachusetts Bay. In addition, they called particular attention to

British trade policies designed to restrain American manufacturing by making the colonies a captive market for goods made in England. Such policies, the Delaware legislators believed, were meant to take away "the property of the Colonists without their participation or consent."[14]

The Virginia Convention, which had begun to meet in defiance of the order of the Royal Governor, Lord Dunmore, after he had dissolved the colony's legitimate legislature, the House of Burgesses, was the least restrained in its rhetoric. Some of the impassioned language of its instructions was no doubt crafted by men like Richard Henry Lee and Patrick Henry, who were eager to support Boston at all costs. But we must now mention a young and still relatively obscure member of the Convention from Albemarle County. Thomas Jefferson, thirty-one in 1774, had been elected to his first term in the House of Burgesses five years before. By the time the Virginia Convention opened its proceedings in July of 1774, Jefferson had gained considerable respect among his fellow delegates for his intellect and literary skills, but was not yet considered one of the most prominent leaders of that body. Nevertheless, he took it upon himself to draft a set of resolutions defending American rights and defining the limits of Parliament's power over the colonies, a draft he hoped would be endorsed by the Virginia Convention and would then serve as the colony's official position in the upcoming general Congress. Much to his disappointment, on July 11, he was stricken by dysentery on his way to the Convention and had to turn back home to recover. Jefferson's friend and fellow Albemarle County representative John Walker carried a copy of his resolutions to Williamsburg for him, presenting them to Speaker Peyton Randolph, but Jefferson was no doubt frustrated that he did not have a chance to be present to speak on behalf of his literary production.

Jefferson's resolutions are particularly notable in light of the famous document that he would present to the Continental Congress in July of 1776. They condemned the "many unwarrantable encroachments and usurpation, attempted to be made by the legislature of one part of the empire, upon those rights which God and the laws have given equally and independently to all." The young Albemarle County lawyer had no use for humble expressions of affection and devotion to King George III, instead asserting that "his majesty will think we have reason to expect when he reflects that he is no more than the chief officer of the people, appointed by the laws, and circumscribed with definite powers, to assist in working the great machine of government erected for their use, and consequently subject to their superintendance." In a lengthy exegesis—too lengthy given the traditional form of such instructions—in support of his challenge to the king's authority, Jefferson embarked on a careful historical analysis of the "origin and first settlement of these countries," concluding that a long "chain of parliamentary usurpation" was responsible for the mistaken notion that Parliament had any authority at all over the American colonies. He then proceeded, in a manner again similar to his construction of the Declaration of Independence, to provide a catalogue of grievances against the king, whom Jefferson blamed for disallowing "wholesome" laws, dissolving provincial legislatures, the presence of a standing army on American soil and the replacement of civil with military government in Massachusetts. Jefferson's draft concluded with an expression of hope that "fraternal love and harmony" would be restored between Great Britain and its colonies, but it made it clear that that outcome depended on a redress of the colonists' grievances and a recognition that "kings are the servants, not the proprietors of the people." Jefferson's reputation as a defender of American liberties was nowhere near as prominent as that of Patrick Henry or Richard Henry Lee, who had been elected to the Continental Congress at least in part because of their fiery speech-making. But Jefferson's literary efforts, still in their infancy, would ultimately prove more important and earn for him a prominence far greater than anything that his more oratorically skilled colleagues would ever achieve.[15]

The members of the Virginia Convention, when they considered Jefferson's proposed resolutions, were not prepared for such a bold assertion of American rights, nor for such a bold denial of the rights of the king and Parliament. In Jefferson's recollection, the leap was "too long, as yet, for the mass of our citizens." But Jefferson's literary efforts were not in vain. Just a week later some of his friends arranged to publish his ideas in pamphlet form under the title of *A Summary View of the Rights of British America*. The pamphlet would circulate widely throughout the colonies and help to establish Jefferson's reputation as an unusually careful and eloquent defender of America's constitutional liberties. Indeed, Jefferson's *Summary View* would play an important role in his ultimate selection by the Congress as the principal draftsman of the Declaration of Independence.[16]

The final version of Virginia's instructions, adopted on August 1, 1774, was much more concise than Jefferson's lengthy treatise, consisting of just one paragraph. It was slightly more belligerent than the instructions from some of the other colonies, referring to the "rage and ruin of arbitrary taxes," but it too concluded by expressing a desire to move as "speedily as possible to procure the return of that harmony and Union, so beneficial to the whole Empire, and so ardently desired by all British America."[17]

The Son of Thunder

By September 6, the mist and rain of the previous day had given way to warm sunshine as the delegates turned to their first important piece of procedural business—the establishment of rules for voting within the Congress. That discussion would produce the first overt signs of discord among the colonies. The cause of the discord, however, had little to do with the delegates' attitudes toward their attachment to the mother country and everything to do with their calculation of the self-interests of the colonies they were representing.

The man who provoked that discord had become a force to contend with in his home colony of Virginia, and over the course of his career would become legendary as the "son of thunder" because of the extraordinary power of his oratory. But in 1774 he was still relatively little known in other parts of America. Although later in his career he would dress more elegantly, favoring a dramatic, scarlet cloak, Patrick Henry appeared before the Congress wearing a plain, unpowdered wig and dressed in a simple gray suit of country clothing, more nearly resembling—in the recollection of Charles Thomson—a Presbyterian minister "used to haranguing the people." And harangue he did. Though Henry would take his place in history as a passionate defender of the provincial interests of his home state of Virginia and a vocal opponent of any interference from outside authority—whether that authority be imposed by the British government of George III or the government of the United States after the adoption of the federal Constitution—on that day in 1774, he rose in Carpenters' Hall and declared: "Government is dissolved. . . . We are in a state of nature. . . . The distinctions between Virginians, Pennsylvanians, New Yorkers, and New Englanders are no more. I am not a Virginian, but an American!"[18]

Patrick Henry possessed a genial, outgoing personality that would make him the hero of the ordinary farmers who made up most of the population of the central and western sections of Virginia. And his oratorical gifts, whether unleashed in the courtroom before a jury as he pleaded a case in his role as one of the colony's most successful lawyers or on the stump in a local election campaign or on the floor of the Virginia House of Burgesses, would become legendary. But at thirty-eight years of age at the time of the meeting of the Continental Congress, he had taken a while to get his career launched.

Patrick Henry's father, John Henry, had immigrated to Virginia from Scotland in 1727 and through hard work and a timely marriage had risen to a position of modest prominence within the social and political circles of the still-expanding region of the Virginia Piedmont, the area of the colony that ran westward from the town of Richmond to the base of the Blue Ridge Mountains. Sometime in 1733 or 1734, John Henry married Sarah Winston, the daughter of a prominent Virginia Piedmont family, who had recently been left a widow by the death of her wealthy and politically prominent husband, John Syme. With his newly acquired combination of social connections and wealth, John Henry moved quickly into the lower levels of the gentry of the Virginia Piedmont, gaining appointment as a justice of the Hanover County Court, achieving the rank of major in the county militia and, through his connections in local politics, adding to his wife's inherited landholdings by gaining patents for several thousand acres of western lands. While by no means possessing the wealth or social standing of members of the First Families of Virginia—the Lees, Randolphs, Byrds, Carters or Harrisons—John Henry was in a position to offer his two offspring a solid start in life.

The eldest child, Patrick, was born in 1736, shortly after the marriage between John Henry and Sarah Winston Syme. Patrick's early years hardly foretold a life of achievement. An indifferent student, he apparently abandoned all attempts at formal schooling by the time he was ten, and when, at the age of eighteen he married Sarah Shelton, the daughter of another moderately prominent Piedmont family, it was not at all clear how the young couple would support themselves. The Shelton family had given the newlyweds 300 acres, a modest farmhouse and six slaves as a wedding present, but the farmhouse burned to the ground three years after their marriage. Henry was apparently able to sell a few of his slaves and purchase enough goods to start a country store, but that venture failed within a year. Between 1757 and 1760 Henry and his wife lived at the inn and tavern operated by the Shelton family, with Henry earning his keep by tending bar and entertaining the guests by playing the fiddle.[19]

At that point, after successive failures as a farmer and merchant, and with distinctly unimpressive educational attainments, Patrick Henry made what must have seemed to many an incomprehensible decision: he began legal studies with an eye to becoming a lawyer. His legal education, even by the lax standards of the western regions of Virginia, was exceptionally skimpy. Depending on whose testimony one chooses to believe, Henry spent somewhere between six weeks (Thomas Jefferson's somewhat uncharitable estimate) and nine months preparing for his bar examination. Henry presented himself for his examination before a quartet of the most distinguished lawyers in the colony: Robert Carter Nicholas, a long-time member of the House of Burgesses and soon-to-be treasurer of the colony; John Randolph, Virginia's attorney general; Peyton Randolph, trained at London's Middle Temple and soon to become Speaker of the House of Burgesses; and George Wythe, widely considered to be the most learned lawyer in the colony. Henry's performance before his examiners was by all accounts dismal. John and Peyton Randolph signed Henry's certification to practice law with the greatest reluctance, and, "upon repeated importunity and promises of future reading," Nicholas finally agreed to sign the aspiring lawyer's license as well. All three men, though appalled by Henry's lack of legal knowledge, nevertheless were impressed by his "natural genius," persuading themselves that though he was nearly wholly unprepared to practice law at that moment, he would, in the course of time, "soon qualify himself." George Wythe, the one true legal scholar among the four, simply could not bring himself to concur. He "absolutely refused" to sign Henry's license, but made no attempt to overturn the judgment of his three co-examiners. And, as later events would confirm, the observation of the two Randolphs and Nicholas about Henry's natural genius—his quick wit and charming personality—would prove right on the mark. Although he was relatively poorly educated and, at that moment, poorly disciplined, the force of Henry's personality, combined with the passion of his public performance, would enable him to develop into one of the most successful lawyers in all of Virginia.

After talking his way through his bar exam, Henry immediately set about building a successful law practice, traveling great distances to try cases in the counties of Goochland, Louisa, Hanover, Albemarle, Chesterfield and even distant Cumberland, where disputes among the rapidly growing and litigious Virginia Piedmont population were plentiful and the supply of lawyers was sparse. Henry appears to have been particularly successful in cases involving criminal law, for, it was said, the county justices who heard those cases, like his own father, were often themselves ignorant of the fine points of the law, allowing an ambitious and verbally adept lawyer like Patrick Henry to sway local juries unencumbered by legal guidance from the justices.

By early 1765 Henry had developed a lucrative law practice, as well as a reputation for eloquence and quick-wittedness in the courtroom. In May of that year, William Johnson, the sitting burgess from Louisa County resigned his post to become county coroner. Because of Patrick Henry's growing legal reputation and with Johnson's endorsement, he became the county's new burgess in a special election. Henry set off immediately for Williamsburg to take his seat in the House of Burgesses, and, within nine days of his arrival, on May 29, 1765, he began to carve out his place in history. On that day, the members of the Burgesses learned that Parliament had passed the Stamp Act. The legislature was getting ready to adjourn, and many of the older, more well-established members had already departed. It was at that moment that Patrick Henry presented a set of five resolutions asserting the principle that the free settlers of Virginia possessed all of the same rights as Englishmen living in England, and that among those rights was that taxes could be levied upon them only "by themselves or by persons chosen by themselves to represent them." This assertion of the principle of "no taxation without representation" would become widely accepted by Americans throughout all thirteen colonies, but Henry, in his fifth resolution, was not content merely to assert that principle; he went a step further, announcing that any attempt to deny Americans that right had "a manifest tendency to destroy British, as well as American, freedom."[20]

The combative language of the fifth resolution, widely circulated in other colonies, would escalate the tone of the debate between British and American officials, but it was the language of Henry's speech defending his resolutions that caught the attention of the burgesses that day. Warning his fellow burgesses not only of the danger of the Stamp Tax but also of the consequences suffered by past politicians who had attempted to trample the liberties of the people, Henry thundered: "Tarquin and Caesar each had his Brutus, Charles the First his Cromwell, and George the Third—" At that point his speech was interrupted by cries of "Treason! Treason!" by the Speaker of the House, John Robinson, and several other members of the assembly. According to one burgess, after the interruption, Henry paused dramatically, stared directly into the eyes of the Speaker and finished his sentence with: "—may profit by their example! If this be treason, make the most of it!"

In fact, there are different versions of precisely what Henry said that day, as well as some uncertainty as to how many of Henry's resolutions were eventually adopted by the House of Burgesses. But the precise facts of the event mattered little, for the full text of Henry's five resolutions were circulated and widely adopted throughout the other American colonies, and Henry's reputation as an orator of stunning abilities was immediately established. From that time forward, Henry moved quickly from being a newly elected backbencher to the position of the principal popular spokesman within Virginia for America's constitutional liberties.

By the summer of 1774, Patrick Henry had become a force to be reckoned with in his colony. He had also become the bane of the existence of Virginia's royal governor, John Murray, Earl of Dunmore.

When the Virginia Convention balloted for its seven delegates to represent them at the upcoming Continental Congress, only Peyton Randolph, George Washington and Richard Henry Lee, all of them far wealthier and more experienced than Henry, received more votes. Although later in life Thomas Jefferson would unfairly characterize Henry as "all tongue, without head or heart," it was clear that Henry had established himself as a major player in Virginia politics. And it was no doubt not lost on Henry's fellow Virginians that he was the only delegate to the Congress residing in the rapidly growing back-country rather than from the well-established, tradition-bound Tidewater and Northern Neck sections of the colony.[21]

Henry's rhetoric on that second day of the Congress's proceedings—his assertion that Americans had already entered into a Lockean state of nature, a state of society free of laws and institutions of government, and his embracing of a national, rather than a provincial, identity—suggests a man prepared not only to dissolve the bonds attaching the colonies to the mother country but also to subordinate the distinct character of each of the colonies to a single American entity. In fact, though, Henry's proclamation was entirely consistent with *both* his vigorous defense of Virginia's interests and liberties against British encroachments *and* his subsequent ardent defense of Virginia's sovereign power against the threat of "consolidation" under a newly constituted federal government.

The issue that provoked Henry's outburst was the preference of many delegates that votes in the Congress be apportioned equally among each of the colonies. Mindful that he was representing the oldest and most populous colony in America, Henry believed that "it will be a great injustice if a little Colony should have the same weight in the councils of America as a great one." Henry wished to see each colony's vote in the Congress weighted according to its population— a view obviously at odds with the interests of the smaller colonies and, indeed, one that would present a stumbling block to a durable union for many years to come.

However much Henry's proposal may have appealed to some delegates from the larger colonies, there was another aspect to it that alarmed delegates from a variety of colonies, regardless of their size. John Jay of New York, in answer to Henry's soaring rhetoric, professed himself to be nowhere near ready to endorse the conclusion that "Government is dissolved" or that the colonies were prepared to leap into that dangerous state of nature. Jay cautioned: "I cannot think that all Government is at an End. The Measure of Arbitrary Power is not full, and I think it must run over before We undertake to frame a new Constitution."[22]

Most of the delegates shared Jay's hope that the "measure of arbitrary power" would *not* run over. The delegates had gathered, after all, not to foment revolution but rather, by striking the delicate balance between resoluteness and conciliation, to prevent such an event from occurring. The challenge before the Congress, Jay believed, was to "correct the faults" in England's otherwise admirable constitution, not to create a new American system.[23]

Jay would be among those in the Congress who would consistently attempt to moderate the impulses of the more radical delegates from New England and Virginia. Jay's words and deeds at the Congress commanded attention, for he brought with him to Philadelphia a distinguished résumé. Jay is primarily remembered as one of post-revolutionary America's most important diplomats and as one of the authors of *The Federalist Papers* in 1787–1788, but he had risen to the pinnacle of New York politics well before those events. He was a member of an exceptionally prosperous family. His father, Peter Jay, was of French Huguenot descent and, by the time of John's birth in 1745, had become one of the colony's richest and most influential merchants. His mother, Mary, was a daughter of a fabulously wealthy family of Dutch descent, the Van Cortlandts, owners of a stately manor occupying some 86,000 acres on the Hudson River. John, educated initially by private tutors, was perceived to be "a youth remarkably sedate," with a decidedly bookish tendency. He graduated from King's College in 1764 and then studied for the bar in the busy New York City law offices of Benjamin Kissan. The senior clerk in that office, Lindley Murray, described Jay as "remarkable for strong reasoning powers, comprehensive views, indefatigable application, and uncommon firmness of mind"—all traits that would mark his behavior and personality for the rest of his life.

In 1768, Jay began his own law practice and, in April of 1774, married Sarah Van Brugh Livingston, the daughter of William Livingston, a member of one of the most socially prominent families in New York and later to become the governor of New Jersey. In sum, John Jay enjoyed nearly all of the advantages—by birth, education and marriage—that an aspiring lawyer and politician could hope for.

As a young man Jay presented himself as an individual of effortless, if perhaps somewhat vain, aristocratic grace. He was tall and slender, with fine features and a sharp, straight nose, and his physical appearance was thoroughly in keeping with some of his behavior—self-confident and perhaps a bit self-satisfied—a man who felt quite comfortable in the knowledge that he possessed superior social connections, superior intelligence and, no doubt, superior judgment. Occasionally that pride and self-confidence would lead to excess. Befitting a young man of his social station, Jay was a member of the New York Dancing Assembly and, by 1772, became one of its managers. When another young man, Robert Randall, applied for membership in 1773, Jay recommended his rejection, judging him to be of inferior social standing. Randall objected, accusing Jay of a "stab" at his honor. Jay considered Randall's objection sufficiently insulting that he offered to engage him in a duel to defend his own honor, a challenge that Randall apparently declined.[24]

Beginning in 1773, Jay accepted the first of dozens of appointments to public office—as secretary of a royal commission for settling a boundary dispute between New York and New Jersey. One of the remarkable facts of Jay's political career, which included dozens of posts of high distinction both at the state and national level (including service as the nation's first chief justice of the Supreme Court from 1789 to 1795), was that he rarely had to present himself to the populace for election to any of those offices. Most of the offices he held were either appointive or elected by the legislature, not requiring him to strive for his place in public life. Nor, indeed, would John Jay ever have wished to do so, for throughout his career it was difficult for him to hide his distaste for currying popular favor.[25]

In the aftermath of the 1773 passage of the Tea Act, as the political temper of the colony of New York heated up, Jay was among those who counseled deliberateness and moderation in confronting this new British challenge. Along with this fellow congressional delegate James Duane, he had been successful in persuading New York's

Committee of Fifty-one not only to thwart the effort to adopt Sam Adams's call for all of the colonies to adopt a "Solemn League and Covenant" pledging to boycott all British goods, but also to stack New York's delegation to the Continental Congress with "men of moderation" like himself.

As part of the price for their selection, the New York delegates had grudgingly lent their support to an open letter advocating a non-importation agreement as an "efficacious means to procure a redress of our grievances," but they left for Philadelphia with no specific instructions from the colony's legislature binding them in their actions once the Congress got under way. Free from instructions requiring that he support a radical course of action in opposing the Coercive Acts, Jay had arrived in Philadelphia hoping that reason and deliberation, rather than passion, would prevail in the Congress.[26]

As the debate provoked by Henry on that second day continued, John Rutledge joined Jay in distancing himself from Henry's declamation. The aristocratic and imposingly self-confident South Carolinian was noncommittal on what steps he thought should be taken to counter the Coercive Acts, but responding to Henry's remarks, he gave the assembled delegates a stern lecture about the limits of their authority. The delegates had gathered in Philadelphia, he observed, as agents of their legislatures empowered merely to discuss the present crisis; surely, they had "no legal Authority" to take the sort of sweeping steps implied by Henry's speech.[27]

Rutledge's South Carolina colleague, Thomas Lynch, was less troubled by Patrick Henry's boldness, but he suggested a modification of the Virginian's proposal. The proper object of representation, Lynch argued, was not population alone but the combination of population and *property*. The sort of property that he had in mind, of course, was slave property, and thus for the first but hardly the last time, discussions in the Congress about how to protect American *liberty* were infused with attempts by some delegates to find ways to provide protections for *slavery*. That issue, along with the persistent division of interests between large, populous states and the smaller states over the question of proportional versus equal representation, would stand in the way of a durable and harmonious union for many years to come.[28]

Predictably, the delegates from the smaller colonies disliked Henry's proposal. Samuel Ward of Rhode Island, the colony that along with Delaware had the most to lose if a scheme of proportional representation were adopted, immediately objected. He argued that the common cause would require an equal sacrifice from all of the colonies, large and small, and that if the smaller colonies were prepared to make that sacrifice, they should be given equal weight in the proceedings. He also noted, slyly, that the colony of Virginia, in apportioning representation in its provincial legislature, gave each county, regardless of its population, equal weight of two representatives each.[29]

As the debate continued, it became clear that Patrick Henry had moved too far, too fast. His assertion that "Government is dissolved" was, in the minds of many, not merely premature but at odds with the peace and harmony that most delegates most ardently desired. And his formula for proportional representation, much as it may have made sense in the context of an "American" congress based on the will of the people of America at large, was a non-starter in a congress whose representatives conceived of themselves as mere agents of their colonial legislatures, each of which were themselves representative of widely diverse populations. Quite simply, Henry's proposal was calculated to foment disunity, rather than consensus, among the assembled delegates.

John Adams, though he knew that the interests of Massachusetts would be better served by a system of proportional representation, recognized that it was more important to keep an eye on the main objective of the Congress—a consensus on how best to resist and reverse British policies—than to fight a battle over representation. He pointed out to the delegates that at that moment the individual colonies lacked any reliable means of determining the precise size of their populations, and he concluded that to fight the battle over representation without that knowledge "will lead us into such a field of Controversy as will greatly perplex us." The other Massachusetts delegates, who had already agreed on a strategy of presenting themselves as cooperative and reasonable in order to dispel the prevalent fear that they were a bunch of wild-eyed radicals interested only in their own well-being, joined Adams in opposing Henry's proposal.[30]

But at least a few of the Virginians weren't willing to give up. Henry's colleague Benjamin Harrison, perhaps responding to the condescension with which John Rutledge had dismissed Henry's proposal, complained about the "disrespect" shown his "countryman." But the tide was turning. Christopher Gadsden and Richard Henry Lee—both sympathetic to the radical sentiments of Henry and the New Englanders—nevertheless agreed with John Adams on the impracticality of a system of proportional representation before accurate calculations of the colonies' population could be made. When the colonial delegations finally, and unanimously, agreed to give each state equal weight in voting in the Congress, they took care, probably at Patrick Henry's insistence, to emphasize that the rationale for the decision was the absence of a reliable census that would enable them to determine accurately the population of each colony. Charles Thomson, no doubt unhappy with the decision, made a formal notation in his congressional journal that the decision for equal representation was not intended to signify that the Congress "had been drawn into a precedent."[31]

In spite of the insistence of a few delegates such as Patrick Henry for a system of proportional representation, it is in fact likely that most of the colonial legislatures expected a formula of equal representation when they elected their delegates to the Congress. The size of the various colonial delegations varied enormously, from New York's nine delegates to North Carolina's three to Rhode Island's two. The variations had little to do with population (at that time North Carolina's population of approximately 250,000 inhabitants was slightly larger than that of New York), and most likely had to do with the generosity (or parsimony) of colonial legislatures with respect to paying the expenses of their delegates. As things turned out, the decision for equal representation *did* set a precedent that would last for the full life of the Continental Congress until it was replaced by the Federal Congress under the new United States Constitution in 1789. The Continental Congress would remain just that, a "congress" composed of representatives from autonomous legislative bodies, with the individual identities of delegates being less important than the principle that each delegation, as a collectivity, deserved equal weight in the deliberations of the body. The insistence of delegates from the smaller states that each delegation be given equal weight was of course done in part out of self-interest and self-defense, but, at least prior to independence, it was historically understandable given prevailing understandings of the very purpose of a congress. That insistence on equal representation would, however, prove to be a major impediment to effective legislation in the Congress once independence was declared.

The Rule of Secrecy

The delegates adopted several other rules governing the way they would conduct their business that day, apparently without the controversy accompanying the question of voting. Although they may not have been aware of it at the time, most of their respective legislatures operated under the same basic rules of parliamentary procedure, so agreement on procedures—the method for appointing committees and rules governing debate—in the Congress came rather naturally. And that ready agreement extended to one decision in particular that seems out-of-place to modern observers. The delegates unanimously agreed that "the doors be kept shut during the time of business, and that the members consider themselves under the strongest obligation of honour to keep the proceedings secret, until the Majority shall direct them to be made public."[32]

In enjoining the delegates to secrecy, the Congress was, on the one hand, following a tradition that was commonplace in most of the colonies' provincial houses of assembly. With only a few exceptions, America's colonial legislatures did not provide visitors' galleries and took steps to see to it that the legislators' speeches on the floor of the assemblies were not transcribed or reported in the newspapers. While colonial legislators recognized their obligation as representatives of the people who elected them, in most colonies that responsibility extended only to publishing the final results of their deliberations—as embodied in the formal record of the laws or resolutions passed by that body—and not to the actual substance or tenor of debate.

The meeting of the First Continental Congress differed, however, from meetings of colonial legislatures in at least two important ways. On the one hand, the delegates may have had an even greater reason to enforce secrecy in their proceedings; they were meeting in the midst of a genuine political crisis with imperial authority, and there was a real danger that royal officials in London, should they get wind of speech-making that they considered treasonous, might take punitive action against the offending speakers. Although the delegates no doubt would have insisted that they did not come to Philadelphia to advocate treason, there was every reason to believe that at least some royal officials in London would regard their actions in exactly that light. It was preferable, therefore, that the congressional delegates be free to speak without having to worry about being overheard by suspicious royal officials or royal sympathizers.

On the other hand, the First Continental Congress was, perhaps more than any deliberative body in America that had preceded it, a response to a *popular* and not an *elite* movement. In most of the colonies, the direction of events was being determined by meetings "out of doors," by committees of correspondence and spontaneously called town and county meetings, not by the formal deliberations of political elites within colonial legislatures. Indeed, in many of the American colonies the provincial legislatures were essentially defunct, having been dissolved by their royal governors. Insofar as America's politicians claimed they were leading a *people's movement,* one might think that the delegates would have at least considered opening their deliberations to the public. They did take the step of stipulating that the formal actions of the Congress—which would later appear in a series of resolutions and formal addresses aimed at a wide variety of constituencies ranging from the people of America to King George III—would be published and disseminated. But for the next seven weeks the discussions in the Congress would be shielded from the glare of public scrutiny.

Shielded from public scrutiny perhaps, but not hidden altogether. Thirteen years later, during the Constitutional Convention of 1787, the delegates adopted a similar rule, and scrupulously adhered to it—so much so that barely a word of their proceedings leaked out during that summer and, indeed, for many decades thereafter. But not all of the delegates to the First Continental Congress felt a similar "obligation of honour" on the matter of secrecy. During the proceedings from September 5 to October 26, many delegates wrote letters to friends and family reporting on what was happening inside Carpenters' Hall, but none more so, nor more volubly, than John Adams, who emitted a steady flow of information—passionate, opinionated and often fiercely partisan—in his letters back home. Indeed, some of Adams's reputation as the "Atlas of Independence" owes to his many indiscretions in reporting the events of the Congress, reporting that nearly always placed the Braintree lawyer at the center of the action. Historians writing about the events of the Continental Congress leading to independence have found in Adams a rich source for their accounts of the proceedings. But however much we might admire his passion and commitment to the cause of independence, his large, but delicate ego often led him into reportage that was anything but objective and dispassionate.

But now, on the afternoon of September 6, having chosen the venue for their meetings, selected their officers and agreed on the rules that would govern their proceedings, the delegates were finally ready to confront the substance of the urgent business that had brought them together. The real work of the Congress was about to begin.

SIX

"FIGHT AGAINST THEM
THAT FIGHT AGAINST ME"

A T ABOUT TWO O'CLOCK on the afternoon of September 6, as the delegates were completing their work on the rules governing their deliberations, a horse galloped up to the door of Carpenters' Hall. The express rider, who had begun his ride in New Jersey, was completing the last leg of a relay that had originated in Boston seventy hours earlier. Pushing his way into the East Room, he raced up to the members of the New Jersey delegation and delivered the news that Boston was under a state of siege. British soldiers had seized colonial gunpowder in one of the towns near Boston, and, in response, a party of Bostonians had gone after them. Six of the townspeople had been killed in the skirmish, after which all of Massachusetts and much of Connecticut had taken up arms. Faced with this uprising, the British, according to the report of the express rider, had bombarded the city of Boston all night long. Shocked, the delegates adjourned, scattering throughout the city in the hope that they could learn more. They would reconvene at five in the afternoon to decide how to respond to this alarming threat.[1]

The news spread quickly. Within a few hours church bells were tolling throughout the city, their clappers muffled in a ritual mourning of calamity and crisis. At five, the delegates returned to Carpenters' Hall, and Thomas Cushing of Massachusetts, no doubt hoping to emphasize the gravity of Boston's situation, proposed that the Congress begin its meeting the next morning with a prayer. A few in the Congress—notably, more conservative members such as John Jay and Edward Rutledge, who may have wished to avoid overreacting to the news—objected, suggesting that it was improper to have members of the different religious groups attending the Congress join together in common worship. Sam Adams brushed aside these objections, saying that "he was no bigot, and could hear a Prayer from a Gentleman of Piety and Virtue, who was at the same Time a Friend to his Country." Adams suggested that the Reverend Mr. Jacob Duche, an Anglican minister from Philadelphia, be asked to lead them in prayer, a suggestion readily agreed to. With nothing left to do but wait for further news, they adjourned until the following morning, although we can be sure that their conversations over drink and dinner at the City Tavern were filled with anxious speculation.[2]

The next morning, anxiety about a possible British invasion of Boston soared even higher when another express rider arrived from New York confirming, and most likely exaggerating, the report of the previous afternoon. According to Connecticut delegate Silas Deane, as the delegates began their session, there was an atmosphere of universal indignation, with "every Tongue pronounc[ing] Revenge." It was in that atmosphere that the Reverend Duche appeared before the solemn group of delegates. He opened his sermon with a reading of the thirty-fifth psalm, which exhorted the followers of the Lord to "fight against them that fight against me" and "Take hold of shield and buckler, and stand up for mine help. Draw out also the spear, and stop the way against them that persecute me."

The Reverend Duche followed the reading of scripture with a fiery extemporaneous prayer, resembling more an exhortation from a radical Baptist or New Light Congregationalist than the more sedate rituals associated with the Church of England. John Adams judged it to be as "pertinent, as affectionate, as sublime, as devout, as I have ever heard offered up to Heaven," and Silas Deane, less given to hyperbole than Adams, recalled that it was a prayer "worth riding one hundred miles to hear."[3]

Joseph Reed, a Pennsylvania delegate who sympathized with the New Englanders' radical agenda, would later note the strategic genius of Sam Adams's decision to have Duche give the opening prayer; it was nothing less than "a masterly stroke of policy." In this one symbolic act, Adams made the point that the wild-eyed, puritanical New England fanatics were a good deal more open-minded than many had made them out to be. Moreover, Sam Adams had made a shrewd assessment of local Pennsylvania politics; he knew that the most likely opposition to bold measures in the Congress would come from Pennsylvania Quakers, whereas members of the Church of England, he noted, were among "our warmest friends." Perhaps more important, Duche's sermon, though it was not linked to any of the formal business of the Congress, had an emotional impact that intensified the urgency with which the delegates began their discussion of the issues confronting them.[4]

For the next two days, the city and the delegates remained in a panic. John Adams wrote to Abigail that all of the delegates in the Congress regarded "the Bombardment of Boston, as the Bombardment of the capital of his own Province." "War! War! War! was the cry . . . and it was pronounced in a Tone which could have done honor to the oratory of a Briton or a Roman." Although the delegates moved forward with their formal business during the days of September 7 and 8, their thoughts—and fears—were focused 300 miles to the north, on a city under siege. Boston, which had been an object of suspicion among many of the delegates, had, at least for a moment, become an object of sympathy, and more important, a source of unity.[5]

A few days later, on September 9, the delegates discovered that the earlier reports of a British siege of Boston had been vastly overblown. There had been no gunfire, no bombardment by British naval ships, no killing of Boston residents. British troops, under orders from the Massachusetts Governor, General Thomas Gage, had seized gunpowder from a storehouse in Cambridge and militiamen from Massachusetts and Connecticut had mobilized for a possible confrontation, but no such confrontation occurred. There is no direct evidence that the Bostonians had manufactured the crisis, and, unfortunately, the initial report, which was said to have come from Israel Putnam, a colonel in the Connecticut militia who was in Boston at the time, has not survived. It is perhaps noteworthy that Putnam was one of New England's most energetic political activists, and a strong ally of Sam Adams. Throughout the meeting of the First Continental Congress, Sam Adams seemed always to have a series of couriers prepared to ride to Philadelphia on a moment's notice to apprise the Congress of any new developments in the Massachusetts Bay Colony, and the exaggerated reports emanating from Boston in the so-called Powder Alarm may have been part of his modus operandi, hoping to stir up the Congress and strengthen their resolve. If that was the case, it appeared to succeed, for, at least for those few days, the members of Congress were profoundly affected by the incident.[6]

Not everyone was caught up in the moment. Joseph Galloway, for one, believed that the Powder Alarm had been deliberately manufactured by Sam Adams and his radical faction to "incite the ignorant and vulgar to arms." He was convinced that Adams's use of "continual expresses" between Boston and Philadelphia was part of his plan— really, more of a plot—to incite the otherwise moderate citizens of Philadelphia into "violent opposition" to British rule.[7]

Yet in the wake of the Reverend Mr. Duche's powerful prayer on September 7, the Congress turned to the main business at hand. President Peyton Randolph had moved to appoint two vitally important committees. The first, which would come to be known as the Grand Committee, would draft a statement cataloguing the fundamental rights and liberties of the colonies, listing the instances of British violations of those rights and liberties and, most important, recommending the most appropriate means of obtaining a redress of colonial grievances. The second, the Committee on Parliamentary Statutes, would provide a comprehensive list of the acts of Parliament affecting American trade and commerce, the target of so many of the obnoxious British taxes.

Thomas Lynch of South Carolina proposed that appointments to the committees be made on the basis of who was "Best qualifi'd," a proposal that "occasion'd much debate." Choosing the "Best qualifi'd" was not as easy as it sounded, because once you got past the relatively small number of men who had reputations that extended across all of the colonies, you had a large number—probably more than three-quarters of the delegates assembled—whose qualifications were essentially unknown to one another. The solution, designed primarily to avoid offending delegates from the smaller colonies, was to give each colony equal weight on each of the committees, with the first to be composed of two delegates from each colony, and the second committee one delegate from each colony. This was modified a bit ten days later, when the Grand Committee was expanded slightly to include one additional delegate each from Virginia, Pennsylvania and Massachusetts, an acknowledgment both of the importance of the business the committee was to consider and of the larger populations of those three colonies.[8]

At this stage the Congress was still struggling to find the way to make its deliberations as efficient as possible, while at the same time giving due deference to the "one colony, one vote" policy it had adopted during its previous debate over rules. On committees such as the Grand Committee, there seemed to be a consensus that each colony was entitled to equal representation, with the composition of those committees determined by having each colony's delegation caucus and then recommend a representative from that colony to serve on the committee. But over the course of the next twenty-two months, the Congress would find it necessary to appoint hundreds of ad hoc committees dealing with a myriad of specialized subjects. Delegates serving on those smaller, more select committees were to be elected by all the delegates, each voting as individuals. But as the number of ad hoc committees increased over the course of the months between September 1774 and July 1776, the need to have formal balloting for the composition of each of those committees was likely to slow the business of the Congress to a crawl. It is probable, therefore, that the delegates found more informal ways of composing some of those committees. As the delegates became more familiar with one another, and with their particular talents and weaknesses, they probably found ways to constitute those ad hoc committees without needing to have a formal vote each time one of those committees was appointed.[9]

The selection by each colony's delegation of its representatives to the Grand Committee would portend conflicts still to come. The Massachusetts contingent consisted of John and Sam Adams and Thomas Cushing; with the two Adamses dominating that delegation, it could be relied on to recommend militant steps. The representatives from the other New England colonies—Major John Sullivan and Nathaniel Folsom from New Hampshire, Stephen Hopkins and Samuel Ward from Rhode Island and Eliphalet Dyer and Roger Sherman from Connecticut—could be counted on to support their Massachusetts colleagues. Two militants, Richard Henry Lee and

Patrick Henry, and one moderate, Edmund Pendleton, represented Virginia on the committee. The representatives on the Grand Committee from New York and Pennsylvania were of a different mind. James Duane and John Jay of New York had taken the lead in trying to calm tensions ever since news of the Coercive Acts reached America, and among the Pennsylvanians, Joseph Galloway was the most powerful, visible and vocal of those calling for moderation. Edward Biddle, a lawyer from Berks County, to the north and west of Philadelphia, was an unknown quantity but at that point was thought to be in the Galloway camp. The later addition of Thomas Mifflin to the Pennsylvania delegation provided at least some voice for more militant action, but, overall, the New York and Pennsylvania representatives on the committee would be inclined to seek reconciliation, not confrontation. The meetings of the Grand Committee, behind closed doors, were likely to be contentious, with the Virginians and the New Englanders emphasizing those instances in which the English Parliament had violated America's fundamental liberties, and the delegates from New York and Pennsylvania seeking to moderate those objections.[10]

The Grand Committee met between September 7 and September 24, dividing itself into two subcommittees, one to focus on articulating the colonies' fundamental rights and the other to draw up a list of infringements of those rights. Since the combined membership of both the Grand Committee and the Committee on Parliamentary Statutes was nearly equal to the total number of delegates then present in the Congress, formal meetings of the Congress were suspended for much of the two weeks while the two committees carried out their deliberations.[11]

Massachusetts Shapes the Agenda from Afar

In the aftermath of the Boston Tea Party, Sam Adams had hoped to persuade other colonies in America to adopt his "Solemn League and Covenant," thus striking back at the British forcefully and immediately. Having failed to do that, he was determined to use his presence in the Continental Congress to accomplish the same ends. But all the while he was serving in the Congress, he continued to keep close watch on what was going on in Massachusetts. The Coercive Acts had virtually eliminated the Massachusetts provincial legislature as the governing body of the colony. To fill that void, Sam Adams and the Boston Committee of Correspondence had urged the towns and counties in the colony to form their own "conventions" as a means of maintaining a united front against the British. During the summer of 1774, nine of Massachusetts' twelve counties had called conventions; citizens in several of those counties gathered together to express their solidarity with Boston and their determination to resist the Coercive Acts. The very act of their meeting, in defiance of the provision of the Massachusetts Government Act prohibiting the calling of town meetings, was itself dramatic proof of that determination. Most of the resolutions passed in those extra-legal town and county meetings dealt with matters purely internal to the workings of government in the particular localities—for example, most of the towns and counties were determined not only to protect their own internal governance structures, but also to prevent the meeting of "unconstitutional" British courts in the colony.[12]

But as the delegates made their way to Philadelphia, at least a few of the county conventions had made clear their wish to shape the course of events beyond their own localities. On August 30, the Middlesex County Convention, meeting in Concord, drafted a lengthy set of resolutions directed at the Congress in Philadelphia. While avowing that they were "true and loyal subjects of our gracious sovereign, George the Third," the Middlesex residents went on to lambaste the British Parliament for its attempt to render them "the most abject slaves." The convention adopted eighteen resolutions, among them one expressing scorn for the Massachusetts Government Act as an "artful, deep-laid plan of oppression and despotism." Vowing to disobey all features of the act that affected their fundamental liberties, the Convention boldly proclaimed that "no danger shall affright, no difficulties intimidate us; and, if in support of our rights, we are called to encounter even death, we are yet undaunted, sensible that he can never die too soon who lays down his life in support of the laws and liberties of his country."[13]

The Middlesex Resolutions reached the Continental Congress on September 14, in the midst of the deliberations of the Congress's various committees. According to Sam Adams they were there "read by the several Members of this Body with high Applause." But while Adams was pleased with the sentiments expressed by his Middlesex County neighbors, he was annoyed that the Boston Committee of Correspondence had not taken the lead. Boston was, after all, his home base; he knew that if he had been back home, Boston would have been out front on the issue, and he was disappointed that his political lieutenants in the town had not seized the initiative.[14]

But he would not have to wait long. Two days later, Paul Revere galloped into Philadelphia after a six-day ride, delivering to the delegates in the Congress a set of resolutions from Suffolk County, of which Boston was the principal town. It would be the Suffolk Resolves, not those from Middlesex, that proved to be the catalyst for bold action in the Congress. Though Sam Adams was in Philadelphia when the Suffolk County Convention met on September 9 in Dedham, ten miles west of Boston, he had already set the wheels in motion for the convention before he left for Philadelphia. His hand was easily visible in the resolutions passed that day.[15]

Adams's principal ally in the effort to use the Suffolk Resolves as the means of radicalizing the Continental Congress was Dr. Joseph Warren, a respected Boston physician who, among other things, had the distinction of having inoculated Sam Adams's cousin John against smallpox, the most deadly disease afflicting the residents of America's cities at that time. More important, Warren (who would be killed on June 17, 1775, at Bunker Hill, at the young age of thirty-four), was gaining a reputation as the most dramatic (and, from the British point of view, demagogic) speaker at the gatherings occurring with increasing frequency in Boston. As the conflict between British soldiers and the townspeople of Boston had begun to escalate during the 1770s, Warren devoted at least as much attention to propagandizing against the British as he did to his medical practice. Although not as visibly active in organizing the Boston mob against the British soldiers as Sam Adams, Warren had proven invaluable in publicizing the excesses of the British soldiery. After the Boston Massacre of 1770, Warren delivered a series of commemorative speeches of extraordinary power and vituperation. On March 5, 1772, at the Old South Meeting House on the second anniversary of the melee, Warren declared:

the fatal fifth of March, 1770 can never be forgotten. The horrors of that dreadful night are but too deeply impressed on our hearts. Language is too feeble to paint the emotions of our souls, when our streets were stained with the blood of our brethren, when our ears were wounded by the groans of the dying, and our eyes were tormented with the sight of the mangled bodies of the dead.

When our alarmed imagination presented to our view our houses wrapped in flames, our children subjected to the barbarous caprice of the raging soldiery; our beauteous virgins exposed to all the insolence of unbridled passion; our virtuous wives, endeared to us by every tender tie, falling sacrifice to worse than brutal violence, and, perhaps like the famed Lucretia, distracted with anguish and despair, ending their wretched lives by their own fair hands.

Warren would continue with these orations every year, each more graphic and inflammatory than the one before, until his death. In his final oration, heard by a packed audience in the Old South Meeting House on March 5, 1775, he said:

Approach we then the melancholy walk of death. Hither let me call the gay companion; here let me drop a farewell tear upon that body which so late he saw vigorous and warm with social mirth; hither let me lead the tender mother to weep over her beloved son: come widowed mourner, here satiate they grief; behold thy murdered husband gasping on the ground, and to complete the pompous show of wretchedness, bring in each hand thy infant children to bewail their father's fate: take heed ye orphan babes, lest, whilst your streaming eyes are fixed upon the ghastly corpse, your feet slide on the stones bespattered with your father's brains.

A horrible, vicious massacre indeed! Of course, the Boston mob had done every bit as much to provoke what amounted to a street brawl that had gotten out of hand, and Warren conveniently overlooked the fact that all five of the Bostonians who were killed were bachelors—there were no mourning widows or weeping orphans! Because of his rhetorical gifts, Warren seemed to Sam Adams an ideal substitute in the drafting and presentation of the resolutions at the Suffolk County Convention.[16]

On September 6, a large crowd of men not merely from Boston itself, but also from a wide radius of towns surrounding Boston, convened at the Woodward Tavern in Dedham for the formal opening of the Suffolk Convention. In the minds of both Sam Adams and Warren, the resolves that they hoped to emerge from the Convention had two audiences—the first was General Gage, to whom the resolves were officially, if also undiplomatically, directed, and the second was the delegates in Philadelphia. Warren opened the proceedings by reading a draft of the resolutions. After three days of discussion, the delegates, now meeting in Daniel Vose's tavern in nearby Milton, adopted a revised version of those resolutions, which, largely drafted by Warren, were far more inflammatory in tone. Among the most important items in the resolves were: a vow to refuse to obey either the Massachusetts Government Act or the Boston Port Bill; a declaration that the edicts of any court operating under the terms of the Massachusetts Government Act should be ignored; a call to put the colony's militia in a state of readiness, and, finally, a renewed proposal for a boycott of all British imports, together with an injunction that all citizens "abstain from the consumption of British merchandise and manufactures."

The Suffolk Resolves went further than those of Middlesex in their threat of armed resistance to British policies and actions, but the most striking difference was one of tone. The Suffolk preamble was unusually belligerent, asserting that the Coercive Acts reflected "the power, but not the justice, the vengeance, but not the wisdom of Great Britain." It went on, in language that only Joseph Warren could have crafted, to describe the situation in Boston:

> the streets . . . are thronged with military executioners . . . our coasts are lined and harbours crowded with ships of war . . . the charter of [our] colony, that sacred barrier against the encroachments of tyranny, is mutilated and, in effect, annihilated, . . . a murderous law is framed to shelter villains from the hands of justice . . . and the constitution of Britain, and the privileges warranted to us in the charter of the province, is totally wrecked, annulled, and vacated.[17]

Both Sam and John Adams must have been immensely relieved to see their trusted messenger Paul Revere gallop into town on September 16 with the Suffolk Resolves, and they eagerly presented them to the Congress the following day. John Adams would write in his diary that "this was one of the happiest days of my life," and he was made even happier when he saw the overwhelmingly favorable reception that they received from the assembled delegates. Even Joseph Galloway supported them, and, indeed, Adams facetiously reported, "I saw tears gush in to the eyes of the old grave pacific Quakers of Pennsylvania." On September 18 the delegates unanimously endorsed a resolution approving the "firm and temperate conduct" of the citizens of Suffolk, affirming their deep sympathy over "the suffering of their countrymen in the Massachusetts-Bay, under the operation of the late unjust, cruel and oppressive acts of the British Parliament" and endorsing the "fortitude, with which opposition to these wicked ministerial measures has hitherto been conducted."[18]

Much of the success, both in formulating the Suffolk Resolves and then in gaining their unanimous approval from the Congress, owed to Sam Adams's hard work, mostly behind the scenes in the taverns and boardinghouses of Philadelphia. But beneath the display of united support for Boston, there still lurked, particularly among some of the New York and Pennsylvania delegates, deep concern that Americans were moving too far, too fast and, in the process, dimming the prospects for reconciliation with their mother country. Galloway, though he voted for the expression of support for Boston, did so with gritted teeth, his suspicion of the riotous New Englanders unabated. Moreover, at that point, the Congress had only offered Boston its *moral* support; the delegates would spend the next ten days haggling over how they would back up their expressions of good will with meaningful measures designed to persuade the British to abandon their coercive policies.

From Words to Action

On September 8, ten days before the Congress unanimously endorsed the Suffolk Resolves, the Grand Committee had begun its discussion of the constitutional challenges facing America. New York's James

Duane presented an outline of the task confronting them. It seemed obvious, Duane argued, that they had to define the colonists' rights, then draw up a list of violations of those rights by Parliament and the Ministry and finally agree on how best to persuade Parliament to provide a redress of American grievances. Although Charles Thomson's sloppy record keeping once again makes it difficult to follow what happened next, it appears likely that Duane's outline did shape the general structure of the ensuing debate.[19]

Duane next traced the evolution of America's conception of their rights, from the imposition of internal taxes in the form of the Stamp Act to the imposition of external taxes in the form of the Townshend Duties, to the present threats posed by the Coercive Acts, which, he argued, required that the Congress "place our rights on a broader & firmer Basis." In defining American rights, Duane, known to be among those willing to go the farthest in seeking reconciliation, praised the mother country not only for providing the "Blessings of Protection" but also for the many commercial advantages she had provided, a result, he claimed, of the colonies' "connection and Dependence." Proceeding from his expression of both affection and dependence on his mother country, Duane nevertheless agreed with his more radical congressional counterparts that the principles of English common law and the rights enumerated in the various colonial charters guaranteed to the colonies certain fundamental rights—one of the most important of which being that "it is essential to Liberty that the Subject be bound by no Laws to which he does not assent by himself or his Representative." Read literally, Duane's observations might appear to be a denial of all parliamentary authority, a line of argument that, if carried to its logical conclusion, would have led to a declaration of the colonies' complete independence from the British government. But Duane was no radical; he denied that the colonists were seeking to proclaim themselves exempt from all parliamentary authority, for, he insisted, the colonies owed Parliament some "advantages" in return for the protection provided by the "parent state."[20]

But how could the colonies reconcile what were essentially two different lines of logic—one stressing America's independence of parliamentary authority, the other acknowledging America's dependence? For Duane, the path toward reconciliation required that both sides recognize that the king ultimately possessed sovereign power over all of his subjects and that "Ties of Friendship & Common Interest" required that the colonists acknowledge that superior power. In its essence, Duane's path toward reconciliation depended not on logic, but on hope and affection for the mother country—emotions that would, over the course of the next twenty-two months, be sorely tested.

John Adams had a very different view. He argued that the colonies' claims to their rights were based not only on Duane's rather narrow formulation of the "British Constitution and our American Charters and Grants," but on the "Law of Nature" as well. Richard Henry Lee agreed, arguing that "we should lay our rights on the broadest Bottom, the Ground of Nature." Adams then went further, arguing that the colonists' resort to a reliance on natural rights—which he admitted was a *last* resort—had been driven only by Parliament's intransigent violations of the fundamental principles of the English constitution.

To the more moderate delegates, reliance on the principles of natural law was fraught with danger. Joseph Galloway, James Duane, John Jay and John Rutledge all flatly opposed any reference to that last resort. Far more than their radical opponents, they cherished their connection to the British Empire and to the ideal of a "true British Constitution" by which that Empire was to be governed. And so, in Joseph Galloway's words, they could never find American rights "in a State of Nature, but always in a State of political Society." Galloway, Jay, Duane and Rutledge, still clinging not only to their loyalty to the king but also to their identity as Englishmen, had no desire to give up their status as English subjects. For them, the British constitution was no mere abstraction but a settled body of law and custom to which any disinterested party could turn as an indisputable source for settling all legal and constitutional disputes between the mother country and her colonies.[21]

Many Americans, however—particularly those Bostonians in the firing line facing Great Britain's punitive policies—were beginning to have at least an inkling that the much-vaunted English constitution, seemingly revered by all, was in truth a phantom. It was an *unwritten constitution* based on a jumble of parliamentary statutes, common-law precedent and simple custom. There was in fact no definitive *English constitution* to which opposing parties could turn to settle their differences. Fifteen months later, Tom Paine's *Common Sense* would force Americans to confront that truth directly, but most colonists were not yet prepared to give up either their faith in the protections offered by that unwritten constitution or their loyalty to and affection for the king who was the symbol of the principles embodied in it. The argument between Galloway, Jay, Duane and Rutledge on the one hand, and Richard Henry Lee and John Adams on the other, foreshadowed a fundamental division in the Congress that would last right up until the moment that the delegates voted on Lee's resolution for independence on July 2, 1776.

In the midst of the discussions about the English constitution and natural rights, the Grand Committee had divided itself into two subcommittees, one on "rights" and the other on "infringements," with the former being constituted on September 9 and the latter gathering on September 17, the day before the endorsement of the Suffolk Resolves. Thanks once again to the poor record keeping by Charles Thomson, we do not have a complete list of the members of either subcommittee, although we do know from their own writings that John Adams, Samuel Ward of Rhode Island and John Rutledge all served on the subcommittee on rights. According to the ever-egocentric Adams, it was by far the most important group of men in the Congress, so much so that it was an "Object of Jealousy" to all the other members of Congress who were not serving on it.[22]

John Adams and other militant members serving on the subcommittee on rights were successful in inserting the "Law of Nature" as one of the sources of American rights in the subcommittee's recommendation to the Congress, but the issue of the precise limits of Parliament's authority over the colonies provoked a protracted set of disagreements. The alternatives, as Adams put it, were "whether We should deny the Authority of Parliament in all Cases: whether We should allow any Authority to it, in our Internal Affairs: or whether We should allow it to regulate the Trade of the Empire, with or without any restrictions." At stake in that discussion was the definition of America's place—if it had any place at all—within the British Empire.[23]

In September of 1774, there was no consensus among the delegates, or among people throughout the colonies, on the question of America's place in the empire. As a consequence, the discussion in the rights subcommittee on the alternatives was, in Adams's words, "drawn and spun out to an immeasurable length." Because of all the back and forth, when the subcommittee presented its report to the reconvened Congress on September 22, some of the most important issues about American rights remained unresolved for the next several weeks.[24]

As the subcommittee on rights argued about the limits of parliamentary authority, the committee on parliamentary statutes affecting trade and manufactures and the subcommittee on infringements of American rights went about their work. The Congress met briefly on September 19 to receive the report from the subcommittee on trade and manufactures, which it promptly referred to the subcommittee on rights. At that point, the committee on trade and manufactures effectively ceased to exist, and Thomas Cushing, Patrick Henry and Thomas Mifflin, who had served on that committee, joined the rights subcommittee.[25]

On September 22, the subcommittee on rights, no doubt driven by radicals like John Adams and Samuel Ward, requested that the full Congress assemble in order to adopt a more explicit endorsement of the Suffolk Resolves: in essence, an immediate boycott of all trade with Great Britain.[26]

The twelve delegations in the Congress agreed to endorse the Suffolk Resolves, but they soon discovered that the devil was in the details. On September 26, Richard Henry Lee, acting on the instructions of the Virginia Convention, introduced a motion for a "Non-Importation" to begin on November 1, 1774. Although not mentioned in the congressional journal, Lee's motion apparently extended to American exports to Great Britain as well as imports, with the ban on exports to begin on August 10, 1775.[27]

Some feared that if non-importation were implemented too quickly, it would place too great a burden on those colonists who had ordered goods from British merchants but who, given the uncertainties of ocean transport, might not receive them until after November 1. Thomas Mifflin, one of the few stalwart radicals in the Pennsylvania delegation, supported the November 1 start date, arguing that the colonies' intention to enter into a non-importation agreement had been known to all by late spring and that "no honest orders" would have been placed after that date. The debate continued for another several days, with some worrying that the November 1 date might prove impracticable, but finally, on September 27 the delegates reached what seemed like a fair compromise, unanimously agreeing that beginning December 1, "there be no importation into British America from Great Britain or Ireland, of any goods, wares, or merchandizes whatsoever."[28]

The matter of exports would prove far more contentious than that of imports. Unlike the debate over the start-date for non-importation, which seemed genuinely to be shaped by the delegates' modestly differing opinion about the fairness of the various alternatives, the debate over non-exportation was plainly driven by the delegates' calculations of the economic interests of their respective colonies.

On September 27, Samuel Chase of Maryland rose to argue for a complete and immediate ban on all American exports to Great Britain and the West Indies. He did so in spite of the fact that a ban on tobacco exports would have caused severe economic disruption to his home colony, but, arguing that a ban on American exports to the mother country would produce a "national bankruptcy" in Great Britain in short order, he thought it worth the risk. The tobacco trade alone, he calculated, involved some 225 British ships, which would be idled should the trade cease. In fact, as later events would prove, Chase was overly optimistic in his prediction, but at that moment, he, like others, believed that the Americans could count on the British merchants so affected to rally to the American side. And any delay, he argued, would deprive the colonies of one of their strongest points of leverage.[29]

The two South Carolina radicals, Thomas Lynch and Christopher Gadsden, whose commitment to any and all measures that would increase America's bargaining position vis-à-vis the British government outweighed their desire to protect their colonies' thriving export trade with Great Britain in rice and indigo, also rose in support of an immediate implementation of non-exportation. They were followed by Patrick Henry. The instructions from the Virginia Convention recommended that a ban on exports be delayed until August of the following year, but Henry, risking some disapproval from his constituents back home, spoke in favor of fixing December 1, 1774, as the start-date for non-exportation.[30]

But not all delegates were willing or able to overlook the provincial interests of their colonies. William Hooper of North Carolina had been instructed by his legislature to oppose a ban on exports of naval stores such as tar, pitch and turpentine, for those commodities, he claimed with some exaggeration, amounted to the "whole of the subsistence of People in the Southern Parts." John Sullivan of New Hampshire sought to protect his colony's exported ship masts, boards, plank, fish, oil and potash. Edward Rutledge, parting ways with his colleagues Lynch and Gadsden, reminded the delegates that South Carolina rice was an enumerated commodity—in other words, it was among those products that had enjoyed a special subsidy from British trade legislation on the condition that it be exported only to Great Britain. An immediate ban on exports would effectively put an end to all trade in South Carolina's principal crop; surely it was unfair to expect one colony to bear such a high burden.[31]

Massachusetts' Thomas Cushing closed the day's debate with an impassioned plea for an immediate imposition of non-exportation: "Great Britain has drawn the sword against Us, and nothing prevents her sheathing it in our Bowells but want of sufficient force. . . . I think it absolutely necessary to agree to a Non Importation [and] Non Exportation immediately."[32]

As the day came to a close, it was clear that the tug of war between the particular economic interests of individual colonies and the need for an effective and unified means of gaining the necessary leverage against their British antagonists was still continuing. It was one thing to offer unanimous and enthusiastic rhetorical endorsement of the principles enunciated in the Suffolk Resolves, but it was quite another to persuade at least some of the delegates to offer up the economic interests of their colonies in sacrifice to the common cause.

The delegates had come a long way in the three weeks since they began discussions about American rights, British infringements on those rights and the best means of persuading, or, if necessary, coercing, the British to back off from their current punitive policies. And for the most part, the radicals in the Congress had had their way.

They had gained tentative, though not universal, approval of the principle that American rights were founded not only on the principles of that unwritten English constitution but also on the laws of nature. They had not only gained a unanimous endorsement of the principles articulated in the Suffolk Resolves, but they had, by setting the date of December 1, 1774, as the point at which Americans would cease all importation of British goods, taken an important step in implementing those principles. At least at that moment, however, the Congress had not yet been able to reach a consensus on either the timing or the scope of a similar commitment on the part of the colonies to place a ban on all exports to Great Britain. The debate on that subject had produced the first signs of tension between provincial self-interests and the common cause of protecting American liberty.

With the issue of non-exportation still unresolved, the most resolute conservative in the Congress, would take the floor. And in so doing, he would attempt to put the Congress on an entirely different course.

SEVEN

GALLOWAY'S LAST STAND

FEW PEOPLE EITHER inside or outside Philadelphia really liked Joseph Galloway. His manner—cold, distant, even haughty—did not invite either warmth or ease among those in his company. But whatever his inner demons, there was no denying his worldly success. His father, Peter Bines Galloway, had accumulated substantial wealth as a merchant and farmer in both Maryland and Pennsylvania. Growing up first in Maryland and then Delaware, Joseph apparently had no formal education, relying on family tutors for his early learning. Moving to Philadelphia after the death of his father, Joseph began the study of law, and through a combination of his extensive social connections and acute intellect, he was able to build a lucrative law practice. His rise to prominence was aided by his marriage, in 1753 at the age of twenty-two, to Grace Growden, the daughter of one of the richest men in Pennsylvania. From that time forward Galloway began to expand his economic, intellectual and political activities. He continued his legal practice, acquired a stake in a number of Philadelphia merchant houses and began to speculate in western lands. He also joined Benjamin Franklin's American Philosophical Society, in which he served as vice president for several years.

It was in part through his association with Franklin that Galloway decided to enter politics, becoming a member of the so-called Quaker Party (even though neither Franklin nor Galloway were Quakers) and, with Franklin's support, gaining election to the Pennsylvania Assembly in 1756. Although there was nothing in his personality that endeared him to the voters of Philadelphia, his combination of hard work and shrewd politicking led to his steady ascendancy in Pennsylvania politics, particularly during the years in which Franklin was in London, when Galloway took over some of the duties his political mentor had been performing. From 1766 to 1775, Galloway was elected every year to the speakership of the Pennsylvania legislature. In Pennsylvania, the legislature was by far and away the most powerful institution in the colony, and so Galloway, as Speaker, was the most powerful person in that most powerful body. As the political conflict with Great Britain escalated during the years of his speakership, Galloway was firm in his defense of American rights, but his legalistic instincts always caused him to view that conflict in narrowly constitutional terms and to disapprove of much of the popular opposition to British policies occurring on the streets of Philadelphia. Moreover, Galloway, even more than his legislative colleague and political rival John Dickinson, was a devout believer in the inherent greatness of the British empire. However much he may have disapproved of some of the recent acts of Parliament, his commitment to Pennsylvania's connection to that empire would prove to be unbreakable.[1]

Indeed, Joseph Galloway would eventually throw his lot in with the British, fleeing to England in 1778 and living there until his death in 1803, at the age of 72. But on the morning of day seven of the importation/exportation debate, September 28, Galloway was still a Pennsylvanian, still an American. Undeterred by his opening-day failures to set the venue for the Congress or to keep his political rival Charles Thomson out of the proceedings, Galloway took the floor in what would be his most important attempt to shape America's constitutional relationship with Great Britain. Although there were no doubt some in the Congress who had already decided to oppose almost anything that Galloway proposed, most of the delegates respectfully listened to his proposals with an open mind.

Galloway had most likely been working on his proposals for some time—at least as early as July of 1774 and perhaps even earlier. Why he waited until September 28, in the middle of the fourth week of the Congress's deliberations and well after many of the more radical proposals defining America's relationship with Great Britain were already well under way, is something about which one can only speculate. Perhaps it took him that long to realize that the radical agenda of many of the New England and Southern delegates was already picking up steam, and that he had better interrupt their discussion of non-importation and non-exportation to prevent that particular train from going any further down the tracks. Whatever the case, on that Wednesday morning, in a relatively brief speech, he offered a critique of what had gone on in the Congress up to that time, and then presented his "Plan of a Proposed Union Between Great Britain and the Colonies."[2]

Galloway began his speech that morning with a belated critique of many of the proposals on which the Congress had already agreed. He criticized the demand that Great Britain return the colonies to the state they had been in prior to 1763 as both impractical and intentionally calculated to provoke "further discontent and quarrel." He denounced the proposed ban on imports and exports as wholly illegal, taking particular aim at the proposed ban on exports, claiming that it would have a devastating impact on the economies of nearly all of the colonies, throwing tens of thousands of people out of work and wholly devastating the shipping industry throughout all of America.[3]

After that harsh denunciation of the actions of the Congress to date, Galloway changed his tone, seeking to present a positive alternative to the hostile and provocative course on which the Congress seemed to be setting itself. Although an ardent admirer of all things English, he acknowledged that there was a "manifest Defect" in the much-vaunted English constitution. That defect arose, he explained, because the notion of colonies and colonization had not been anticipated at the time of the origin—dating back to 1215 and the Magna Carta—of the British system of government. That defect notwithstanding, Galloway insisted that it was hardly serious enough to justify sundering ties with England. Indeed, he held, most colonists still retained a deep love of their mother country and had desired to do everything possible to retain that union.

The challenge, Galloway observed, was to find a way to give the American colonies some form of representation within the British system of government. The solution, in his view, was the creation of an American version of the British Parliament charged with setting the rules for the regulation and administration of all activities in which the interests of the mother country and the colonies intersected. This new legislative body was to consist of a president-general appointed by the king, and a Grand Council, whose representatives would be chosen by the legislatures of the several colonies. The Grand Council would meet at least once a year, but could meet more often if circumstances required it. In Galloway's formulation, the council would "hold and exercise all the like rights, liberties, and privileges as are held and exercised by and in the House of Commons in Great Britain."[4]

At first glance, Galloway's Plan of Union held some promise, for it seemed to offer a way in which the colonies could achieve some parity with, and therefore a check upon, the House of Commons in all legislation affecting them. But upon closer analysis, this new legislature's parity was undercut by two other provisions in his plan. The president-general would have a veto over all acts passed by the Grand Council; moreover, Galloway made it clear that the "said President-General and the Grand Council [were] to be an inferior and distinct branch of the British Parliament." Not only would the president-general have a veto over any legislation emerging from the Grand Council, but the Parliament would also have to add its assent to any acts or statutes emerging from the council.[5]

If one puts aside (and one suspects that many of the New Englanders and Virginians would have found it difficult to do so) the harshness of Galloway's critique of the actions of the Congress up to that point, the details of his proposed plan of union had much to recommend it. Although still leaving the colonies ultimately in a state of subordination to the king and Parliament, it did represent a step toward solving the problem of giving the colonies some form of representation within England's parliamentary system. And many delegates, far from dismissing it as just another one of Galloway's attempts at forcing the colonies into submission, took the proposal seriously. Had he proposed his plan a decade earlier, it is possible that a gathering such as that meeting in Carpenters' Hall might have regarded it as a constructive, forward-looking set of suggestions.

But Galloway's fellow delegates, and indeed all Americans, had traveled a good distance along their own constitutional path in the ten years since their first protests against English attempts to tax them. Although not emotionally or psychologically ready to declare their independence in the fall of 1774, most Americans considered themselves sufficiently independent of British authority that they were unlikely to concur with several ingredients of Galloway's formula. The granting of a veto to the president-general, who was, just like the royal governors, sure to be an agent of royal, not provincial, interests, was probably a non-starter. More serious, the fact that the Grand Council would be inferior to the British Parliament—a Parliament that in the past decade had arbitrarily and capriciously sought to impose its will upon the colonies—seemed to many delegates simply unacceptable.

Still, it was a constructive proposal, and it was eagerly seconded by John Jay, James Duane and Edward Rutledge. Indeed, Rutledge praised it as "almost a perfect Plan." Perhaps if it had been presented by a more sympathetic figure, its fate in the Congress might have been different. But, true to form, Galloway, in the debate that followed, did little to try to win over those delegates who might have been wavering on either side of the question. In what must have seemed to many delegates an outrageous misrepresentation of the facts, he reminded the delegates that many colonies, including his own Pennsylvania, failed to provide adequate support for the British war effort during the Seven Years' War. It was those "Delinquencies," he said, that had depleted the British treasury and had resulted in the Stamp Act. Yes, Parliament had been mistaken in its decision to impose the Stamp Tax on Americans without consulting them. But this did not justify a blanket denial of Parliament's constitutional authority over taxation, a move that had eliminated any reasonable grounds for resolving the dispute. And what of the means used to oppose the Stamp Act—rioting, harassment of royal officials and, in some cases, violence against property. With eyes surely turned toward the Massachusetts delegation, Galloway stridently derided those who were still doing everything possible to obstruct reasonable negotiations with Great Britain and to ignore reasonable alternatives to their militant denial of *all* parliamentary authority.[6]

Galloway insisted that Parliament was constitutionally entitled to its claim of supremacy over the colonies. He was lavish in his praise for the way in which the mother country had nurtured her colonies from the time of the earliest settlements forward, providing for those colonies essential protection from hostile adversaries both within and beyond America. It was both illogical and unjust to claim a right to protection from the British government while denying the authority of that government. "Protection and allegiance are reciprocal duties," he proclaimed, "the one cannot exist without the other." Then, in what must have been particularly galling to those who had gathered in Philadelphia seeking to strengthen their sense of common purpose, Galloway reminded the delegates of the "seeds of discord" that had on more than one occasion caused open hostilities between the colonies, as was the case with the recent border wars between New York and New Jersey and between Pennsylvania and Maryland. It was only the gentle intervention of the "Parent State," he claimed, that suppressed the natural tendencies of the colonies toward internecine war. Should the authority of the parent state be weakened or annulled, he predicted, new conflicts would emerge, conflicts that would inevitably degenerate into civil war. Nor did the dangers only come from within. France still coveted territory in America. Disunited and without the protection of the "mother state," with the "weak exposed to the force of the strong," the colonies would in all probability lose much of the land on their western borders to the French. Galloway concluded his defense of "moderation" with a plea to the delegates to pay heed to the

> honour and safety of your country, and, as you wish to avoid a war with Great-Britain, which must terminate, at all events, in the ruin of America, not to rely on a denial of the authority of Parliament, a refusal to be represented, and on a nonimportation agreement; because whatever protestations, in that case, may be made to the contrary, it will prove to the world that we intend to throw off our allegiance to the State, and to involve the two countries in all the horrors of Civil War.[7]

Galloway probably arranged in advance for James Duane to speak in support of his proposal. Now the New Yorker rose with a carefully prepared speech. Duane, the son of a prosperous merchant, was one of New York's most successful lawyers. From the onset of the constitutional conflict between Great Britain and the colonies, Duane had counseled moderation. In November 1765, during the protests over the Stamp Act, a New York mob lashed out at Lieutenant Governor

Cadwallader Colden, breaking into his coach house, destroying his chariot and, later, hanging him in effigy. Duane took the extraordinarily unpopular step of attempting to recruit a group of sailors to counter the actions of the mob. Duane believed that the imposition of the Townshend Duties in 1768 was unwise and half-heartedly supported the informal agreement among merchants in the principal port cities to refuse to import British goods in protest against the act. But, unlike most of the lawyers in most of the colonies, he remained an outspoken critic of anyone or anything he considered disloyal to the Crown. In 1770, he was the lead prosecutor of Alexander McDougall, one of the principal leaders of the New York Sons of Liberty, who had been charged with sedition and libel for writing incendiary pamphlets denouncing Lieutenant Governor Colden and the Tory-leaning De-Lancy family. Writing to his father-in-law, the fabulously wealthy upstate New York manor lord Robert Livingston, Jr., Duane vented his contempt for men like McDougall and the mobs McDougall so frequently employed. "You have once experienced," Duane wrote, "the Rage of the people at your Home. Here we have been terrified with it repeatedly. Every good man wishes to see Order restored, and the government resume its due weight."

The particular "rage" to which Duane referred was a small, ineffectual 1767 riot among tenants and their supporters on Livingston's manor in the Hudson Valley. During it, some 500 "levelers" marched toward the manor house, threatening to "murder the Lord of the Manor and level his house" unless he signed leases more agreeable to them. In that instance too Duane had used his legal skills to lead the effort to prosecute the perpetrators. Indeed, Duane was instrumental in seeing to it that the supposed leader of the abortive uprising, William Prendergast, was convicted of high treason and condemned to death. In the end, George III pardoned Prendergast, but the whole affair made Duane's revulsion toward extra-legal protests all too clear.[8]

Duane's concern was a common theme among many of those who worried about the excesses that sometimes occurred during the popular resistance to British policies. Indeed, although John Adams may have seemed like a fiery radical to Duane, in fact, the Bostonian had also worried about some of those same excesses. But for men like Duane and many of his New York and Pennsylvania colleagues in the

Congress, their concern led them toward distinctly different solutions than those being espoused by Adams.

Duane, Galloway, John Jay and several others in the New York and Pennsylvania delegations had stood by and watched with dismay as the coalition of New Englanders and Virginians moved many of the members of other colonial delegations toward what they considered a dangerously radical course. Galloway's Plan of Union offered them an opportunity to counterattack. In seconding Galloway's proposal, Duane recollected the reasons for calling the Congress in the first place—to discuss measures that might provide relief for Boston and Massachusetts but, equally important, "to lay a Plan for a lasting Accomodation with Great Britain." Alas, Duane commented, up to this point, the Congress had done little to achieve that second goal. Galloway's plan was a step in the right direction, but for it to succeed, Duane insisted, it was essential that "we should expressly ceed to Parliament the Right of regulating Trade."[9]

The New Englanders were infuriated by Galloway's counterattack. They were so close to getting the Congress to agree on a thoroughgoing boycott of all trade with Great Britain—a huge step, they believed, in creating a united opposition to British policies that would have real teeth. In their eyes, Galloway's plan was not only an unacceptable acquiescence to British authority in key areas of taxation and legislation, but also a move designed to persuade the Congress to reverse course altogether. But they bit their tongues, leaving it to the delegates from Virginia to take the lead in opposing the plan. Richard Henry Lee sought to block it by temporizing, remarking that the "plan will make such changes in the Legislatures of the Colonies that I could not agree to it, without consulting my Constituents." Patrick Henry's attack was more direct. Asserting that the colonial legislatures had always enjoyed an independence and autonomy that current British policies were denying them, he noted that Galloway's Grand Council, while "liberat[ing] our Constituents from a corrupt House of Commons," would have the effect of throwing Americans into the "arms of an American Legislature that may be bribed by that Nation which avows in the Face of the World, that Bribery is a Part of her System of Government." For Henry, Galloway's solution was no solution at all: it denied Americans the fundamental right of no taxation without representation and would in the end "lead to war." In Henry's view, if one were to face the prospect of war, it was preferable to do it in the cause of liberty than out of submission to a corrupt English government.[10]

The delegates eventually rejected Galloway's Plan of Union, but the sequence of events leading to that outcome is obscure. At the end of the day on September 28, the delegates declined to take action on the proposal, voting, with six colonies in favor, five opposed, to allow the proposal to "lye upon the table," to be taken up at a later date. Galloway interpreted the action as a positive response to his proposal, and, in fact, at least at that moment, he may have been right. Although he may not have won over a majority of delegations, it does appear that several of them—not only Pennsylvania and New York, but probably New Jersey, South Carolina and either Maryland or Delaware—were sympathetic to his proposal.[11]

More than three weeks later, on October 22, after the Congress had moved forward to adopt more sweeping measures to oppose British policies, the delegates would formally reject a motion to reconsider Galloway's plan. The circumstances of that rejection evoked a wrathful reaction from Galloway. Charles Thomson, the Congress's secretary, did not formally enter Galloway's plan into the minutes on September 28, the day on which he first introduced it, an omission that probably owed less to a deliberate slighting of his political rival's plan than to the general slovenliness that marked his note-taking throughout his service as the Congress's secretary. And on October 22, when Congress declined to take up Galloway's plan again, Thomson made no note of that rejection. The only direct confirmation we have of any action that day is a brief diary entry from Rhode Island delegate Samuel Ward, who simply noted that the Congress "met, [and] dismissed the Plan for a Union." Whether Galloway had over-optimistically misread the decision to table his proposal on September 28, or whether the opponents of the proposal had been successful in mobilizing opposition to it by October 22 is not clear, but by that latter date Galloway could clearly recognize that his Plan of Union had suffered an ignominious defeat.[12] Galloway would be sufficiently enraged by the rejection of his plan that he would later engage in an impassioned pamphlet war both to defend it and to rebuke his adversaries. In a long-winded pamphlet entitled *A Candid Examination of the Mutual Claims of Great Britain and the Colonies; with a Plan of Accommodation, on Constitutional Principles*, published in New York in February 1775, Galloway described the battles that had occurred in the First Continental Congress between "two parties." One, in which he included himself, came to the Congress intending "candidly and clearly" to define American rights and then to humbly petition the king and Parliament for a redress of their grievances. The other party, he claimed, was composed of a group of hotheads whose purpose from the very beginning of their opposition to the Stamp Act had been to "throw off all subordination and connexion" with Great Britain. He accused the other party of using every "fiction, falsehood and fraud" to mislead the people and to "incite the ignorant and vulgar to arms," all with the goal, he claimed, of leading Americans down the dangerous path toward independence. The chief culprit, in Galloway's view, was Sam Adams—"a man, who though by no means remarkable for brilliant abilities, yet is equal to most men in popular intrigue and the management of faction. He eats little, drinks little, sleeps little, thinks much, and is most indefatigable in the pursuit of his objects." It was Sam Adams, Galloway believed, who was at the head of the conspiracy to lead America into revolt against their mother state.[13]

In his "Candid Examination," Galloway claimed that during the debate in Congress on September 28, "all the men of property, and most of the ablest speakers," supported his proposal. He had at that time interpreted the decision to defer a vote on the plan to a later date as a positive sign, and, with that optimistic interpretation in his head, he had not only consented to allow the delegates to resume their discussions of the boycott of trade with Great Britain, but had, in the hopes that some kind of deal could be reached with his more radical congressional adversaries, added his tepid endorsement to the proposal for non-importation of British goods, a measure he had earlier opposed. But, of course, he was to be bitterly disappointed. "The men of *independence* and *sedition* were soon after preferred to those of *harmony* and *liberty*," with the final result being that the plan was not only never again discussed, but was, in his view of things, purposely expunged from the minutes.[14]

Convention secretary Charles Thomson and John Dickinson, who had belatedly been elected by the Pennsylvania Assembly to join the proceedings as a delegate on October 15 (Dickinson officially joined the delegation on October 17), had a decidedly different take on the reception given Galloway's plan. According to them, most of the delegates, when they first heard Galloway's proposal, regarded it "with horror—as an idle, dangerous, whimsical, ministerial plan." Dickinson and Thomson interpreted the vote to table the Galloway's plan as an implicit rejection of it, not, as Galloway claimed, tacit approval of its general principles. Thomson admitted that when he went about the task of revising his minutes in the days immediately preceding the adjournment of the Congress, he omitted the details of Galloway's plan, but not, as a deliberate attempt to prevent others from seeing its merits, as Galloway had charged, but because the "majority were of opinion, that the inserting it on their Journal would be disgraceful and injurious [and that] they unquestionably had a right to reject it."[15]

History has not treated either Joseph Galloway or his Plan of Union kindly. Galloway's biographer, John Ferling, concedes that some of the wounds suffered by Galloway in his own time and in subsequent eras were self-inflicted. His passionate defense of his proposal at the time he introduced it and his intemperate attack on his opponents in the months after its defeat served to diminish, not increase, his support in Congress. And Galloway's personal manner—overbearing, haughty, sometimes arrogant—won him few friends among those delegates who had previously been unacquainted with him. Moreover, unlike such men as John and Sam Adams, who went out of their way to acquaint themselves with delegates from other colonies who may have been initially suspicious of their reputation for radicalism, Galloway remained largely aloof from those social occasions in which he might, by graciousness, tact and diplomacy, have won over skeptical delegates to his side. Indeed, for all of his intellectual attainments, Galloway was nearly altogether lacking in those personal qualities that might have enhanced his influence among the delegates.[16]

One might also fault Galloway for an excessively narrow view of the conflict. By defending parliamentary sovereignty on purely legalistic grounds, he overlooked the highly emotional tone of the debates in the

Congress. The delegates had gathered because Boston was in a state of siege. The circulation of rumors such as that involving the so-called Powder Alarm only heightened the sense of urgency. It's a challenge for any leader to make an appeal to reason at such times, and it's not surprising that the delegates weren't persuaded by Galloway's constitutional abstractions. Of course, it may well have been that, ultimately, Galloway was trying to find a compromise on an issue that was uncompromisable. Even in September of 1774, well before they had embraced, intellectually or psychologically, the idea of independence, the vast majority of delegates in the Congress, and the constituents whom they served, were committed to the principle that Americans needed to enjoy rights of representation on an equal footing with other Englishmen. Anything short of that was likely to be seen as unacceptable.

As one careful historian of the First Continental Congress has concluded, "Galloway stood up in Carpenters' Hall twenty years too late for his compatriots and almost a century too soon for the members of the British Parliament." But Joseph Galloway's Plan of Union nevertheless remains the single most serious effort of the period between the passage of the Stamp Act and the adoption of the Declaration of Independence at finding a means of giving Americans at least a portion of the representation that they were demanding with respect to parliamentary decisions affecting their interests.[17]

With the tabling of Galloway's Plan of Union at the end of the day on September 28, a coalition of radicals and moderates took control of the agenda, never looking back. Although Galloway remained in the Congress until it adjourned on October 26, he increasingly became an obstinately silent, disgruntled delegate. To add insult to injury, on October 14, in a clear sign that he was losing support even in the generally conservative Pennsylvania General Assembly, Galloway was replaced as Speaker of that body by Edward Biddle. Biddle was no revolutionary radical to be sure, but his views on the proper course of American resistance to British policies were closer to John Dickinson's than Galloway's. Galloway's voice would by no means be stilled in the events leading up to Independence, but his political influence would be irretrievably diminished.[18]

EIGHT

GETTING ACQUAINTED
IN THE CITY OF
BROTHERLY LOVE

M OST OF THE delegates from twelve very different colonies didn't know each other when they first came to Philadelphia. They were strangers in a strange city. But during the early weeks in September 1774 they moved slowly toward an identity as "Americans" engaged in common cause. Few, however, would have gone as far as Patrick Henry had in saying that "the distinctions between Virginians, Pennsylvanians, New Yorkers and New Englanders are no more."

The Massachusetts delegates' efforts to cast off their reputation as intemperate militant radicals had been so successful that the earlier suspicions of them began to fade away. Caesar Rodney of Delaware, made note of his changing impression in a letter to his brother, observing that "the Bostonians, who . . . have been Condemned by Many for their Violence, are Moderate men." He felt that the Virginia, South Carolina and Rhode Island delegates appeared more extreme in their views than the men of Massachusetts.[1]

And of all the Bostonians, the one most reputed for his intemperate behavior, Sam Adams, had managed to change impressions most dramatically. Far more than his emotionally volatile younger cousin John, Sam Adams worked self-consciously to build a consensus among all the delegates, even those from Pennsylvania and New York. Drawing on what Joseph Galloway disparagingly termed "Adams's art," he took advantage of the informal sessions among the delegates at the City Tavern and other Philadelphia eating and drinking establishments to cultivate the support of the delegates from the southern and middle colonies.

All the while, Sam Adams never lost sight of his goal, nor ever put aside his primary concern of protecting the safety of his constituents back in Massachusetts. At the same time that he was winning the respect and support of congressional delegates in Philadelphia, he was writing passionate letters to his radical patriot lieutenants in Boston urging them on to ever more militant action. But this was all done out of sight of the delegates in Philadelphia. As he commented to Joseph Warren, to whom he had entrusted the organization of political resistance back home, "it is of the greatest importance that the American opposition should be united," and, at least in his behavior in Philadelphia, he took pains to conduct himself in a manner that would produce that result.[2]

If the congressional delegates were impressed by the moderation of the Bostonians, they were similarly struck by the surprisingly firm and purposeful manner of many of the Southerners who made the trip to Philadelphia. The prevailing view of life on Southern plantations was one of opulent leisure, if not outright laziness and dissipation. For some—in particular some of the delegates from New England—the fact was that much of the opulence so enjoyed by the southerners—whether in their avid consumption of the latest English fashions, their near obsession with fancy dress balls or their patronage of horse races and cockfights—was made possible by the exploitation of slaves from Africa. This realization only heightened the perception that the southern delegates were unlikely to share the values of austerity and virtue that would be necessary if an agreement banning the importation of English goods were to be strictly enforced.

Yet when northern delegates actually met their southern brethren, they were impressed both by their political acumen and their seriousness of purpose. Caesar Rodney, commenting on the Virginia delegation, marveled that "more Sensible, fine fellows you'd Never Wish to See." Connecticut's Silas Deane, writing to his wife, provided descriptions of each of the delegates from Virginia, North Carolina and South Carolina, emphasizing "the ease and eloquence of their speech as well as the gentility of their manners." Most surprising, with a few exceptions such as South Carolina's John Rutledge and his brother Edward, it was the southerners, not the New Englanders, who in their public utterances appeared to be the most militant members of the Congress. As Silas Deane described them to his wife: "I never met, nor scarcely had an Idea of Meeting With Men of such firmness, sensibility, spirit, and Thorough Knowledge of the Interests of America, as the Gentlemen from the Southern Provinces."[3]

This is not to say that cultural and regional differences among the delegates somehow evaporated. If there was one thing the New Englanders might have wished to change about their southern brethren, for example, it was their work habits. Samuel Ward of Rhode Island complained to his son that "The southern Gentlemen have been used to do no Business in afternoon so that We rise about 2 or 3 o'Clock & set no more that Day & as we meet late in a Morning, We shall sett a long while." John Adams voiced a similar complaint about the late start of business in the morning and the early quitting time, noting that it was impossible to persuade the southern delegates to do anything after three in the afternoon.[4]

If there was one thing with which the delegates were most impressed, regardless of the prevalent lifestyles in their home regions, it was the quantity and quality of the parties or "levees" staged by prominent Philadelphians in their honor. Nearly every evening during the seven weeks the Congress was in session, the delegates were hosted at elaborate dinners, teas and dances. John Adams, perhaps because he was a New Englander not used to such displays of conviviality and extravagance, or, perhaps because he was, simply, John Adams, was overwhelmed by the hospitality that he received while in Philadelphia. On September 8, following a dinner at the impressive home of Samuel Powel, then mayor of Philadelphia, he recorded in his diary: "A most sinfull Feast again! Every Thing which could delight the Eye, or allure the Taste, Curds and Creams, jellies, Sweet meats of various sorts, 20 sorts of Tarts, fools, Trifles, floating Islands, whipped Sillabubs &c. Parmesan Cheese, Punch, Wine, Porter, Beer, &c &c." A week later, following a dinner with Benjamin Rush and a number of other Philadelphia notables, Adams marveled that he had attended "a mighty feast again," in which he indulged in the "very best of

Claret, Madeira, and Burgundy." And then, dining with Benjamin Chew, chief justice of Pennsylvania, he once again enjoyed imbibing what was, for him, unusual quantities of alcohol, reporting, perhaps somewhat guiltily, in his diary that he had "found no Inconvenience in it."[5]

Many of the most prominent Philadelphians, meanwhile, though not attending the formal meetings of the Congress, were making their influence felt. Thomas Wharton, for example, one of the wealthiest and most powerful Philadelphia merchants, had dragged his feet in endorsing measures to oppose British policy at every step along the way. In the aftermath of the passage of the Tea Act, Wharton had been one of the last of the Philadelphia merchants to sign a pledge to refuse to accept the East India Company tea. When he finally agreed to sign, the publisher of the *Pennsylvania Chronicle*, William Goddard, noted in his newspaper, acidly, that Wharton was "now despised something less than he used to be." Wharton was also among those Philadelphians who had supported the idea of a general congress only because he thought it might serve as a means of slowing, not escalating, the resistance movement against British policies. As the Congress was carrying out its business, Wharton bragged to a friend that the rule of secrecy would not pose any problems for him, for "my intimacy with the leading members of most of the colonies, gives me an opportunity in conversation of knowing their daily results."[6]

Debate in the full Congress continued amidst the constant rounds of dinners, teas and fancy dress balls. On the final day of September, the delegates agreed, at least in principle, on a comprehensive ban on all exports to Great Britain, Ireland and the West Indies beginning on September 10, 1775. The Congress then elected a committee consisting of Thomas Cushing, Thomas Mifflin, Isaac Low, Richard Henry Lee and Thomas Johnson to devise a more specific plan for implementing the resolution they had just adopted. Among that group, Cushing, Mifflin and Lee were all clearly identified as wanting immediate implementation, Johnson's views were generally not known, and Low, in keeping with the character of his fellow New York delegates, was likely to want to temporize.

The following day, October 1, the Congress agreed to send a petition to King George III "dutifully requesting the royal attention to the grievances that alarm and distress his majesty's faithful subjects in North America" and asking him to intervene to redress those grievances. The committee chosen to draft that petition was a high-powered one—Richard Henry Lee, John Adams, Thomas Johnson, Patrick Henry and John Rutledge. Lee, Adams and Henry were all clearly of one mind, having gone on record repeatedly as desiring bold actions, Johnson was the one moderate and John Rutledge was the one member of the committee who appeared to still be siding with the dwindling number in the Congress trying to apply the brakes to an overly combative approach to the imperial crisis.[7]

As that committee's members went to work, other delegates were closely following their progress. John Jay created a major stir by proposing that the committee be instructed to include in its petition an offer to the king to pay for the tea destroyed in Boston. Isaac Low, James Duane, James Ross (another Galloway sympathizer from the Pennsylvania delegation) and Virginia's Edmund Pendleton supported Jay's proposal, but John Adams, Richard Henry Lee and Patrick Henry resisted it. In a sign that the alliance between South Carolina delegates John and Edward Rutledge and the more conservative New Yorkers and Pennsylvanians might be weakening, both Rutledges gave speeches opposing any move to pay for the East India Company tea. In the end, the Congress decided not to include that offer in the petition, another sign that the conservatives were losing ground.[8]

James Duane introduced a resolution intended to shape the language of the petition to the king, this one emphasizing the colonies' willingness to "cheerfully comply" with royal requests for men and money for defense of the British Empire in America. Although Duane did not explicitly mention taxes, he was, in effect, proposing that Americans make voluntary contributions for the good of the empire, so long as any requests for those contributions did not come in the form of mandatory taxes.

Many delegates thought Duane's language too obsequious. On October 3, Richard Henry Lee proposed that the Congress explicitly reject the need for any "aid" from the British in relation to the defense of the colonies. Lee's proposal asserted that "North America . . . is able, willing and determined to Protect, Defend, and Secure itself" and, following from that logic, recommended that the colonies form a single, well-disciplined and properly armed militia to repel a possible British attack. Lee did not stop there. He included in his proposal language asserting that the Congress itself should be considered the "constitutional, honorable, and compitent support for the purposes of Government and Administration of Justice."[9]

Lee's suggestion of a single North American militia was path-breaking. It was a major step both toward inter-colonial unity and away from dependence on the British military. Equally important, he urged that the Continental Congress assume new powers, transforming itself from a temporary, extra-legal gathering of men carrying out the will of individual provincial legislatures to a legitimate governmental body representing the "united colonies" and armed with the power to raise an inter-colonial militia. American colonial militia companies had in the past cooperated in fighting against French or Indian adversaries on the frontier, but this call for a continental militia, to be used to fight against a British military, was unprecedented.

But Lee was moving too far, too fast. John Rutledge, who had joined the more radical delegates in refusing to offer to pay for the East India Company tea, objected that Lee's language regarding defense could well be interpreted as a "Declaration of Warr," Edmund Pendleton, Benjamin Harrison and Richard Bland of Virginia, Isaac Low of New York, William Hooper of North Carolina and Edward Rutledge all joined John Rutledge in protesting the war-like tone of Lee's language. They all agreed that the creation of a continental militia with the explicit purpose of warding off a British attack, far from frightening the British government into backing off and pursuing a more conciliatory course toward the colonies, was much more likely to make any hope of reconciliation impossible.[10]

Patrick Henry now took the floor, speaking eloquently and at length in support of his Virginia colleague. "A preparation for Warr," he argued, "is Necessary to obtain peace." Returning to the theme that he had raised at the very beginning of the Congress, namely, that Americans now found themselves in a "state of nature," he insisted that the delegates move forward immediately to arm the colonies.[11]

But the delegates were not yet ready to adopt such a belligerent resolution. They would compromise. The first half of the resolution, adopted on October 3, would "assure his Majesty that the colonies have, or will make ample provision for defraying all the necessary expenses of supporting government and due administration of Justice in the respecting colonies." In other words, the colonies would take responsibility for paying their fair share of the costs of administering their own government. The resolution's second half, while not fulfilling Lee's call to arm the colonies, stated the Congress's desire to do whatever was necessary to provide for a militia sufficient to protect the colonies "in time of peace," and, further, that it was prepared to consider additional steps "for raising any further forces" should that prove necessary. A disappointed Lee voted against this watered-down version, but he was in a distinct minority and was outvoted even within his own delegation, and the more weakly worded version passed unanimously.[12]

The delegates continued to debate the substance and tone of their petition to the king for the next three days. On October 5, they wrangled over the language in the petition spelling out the list of actions that the king and Parliament needed to undertake in order for reconciliation to be achieved. It was a long list, including the restoration of the status quo prior to 1763; the repeal of all laws and regulations aimed at raising a revenue in America; an end to attempts to try Americans accused of crimes committed in America in British Courts of Admiralty; and a repeal of all of the punitive laws aimed at Boston and Massachusetts. At first glance this seemed like a pretty substantial list of conditions for the restoration of harmony—indeed, so substantial that it would have been unlikely that King George III would have agreed to it. But in the eyes of many, it did not go far enough. By dating the beginning of America's troubles with Parliament at 1763, it ignored the question of whether that body had the power to pass trade and navigation acts affecting American commerce. Perhaps more important, the argument over whether to limit the statement of American grievances to those actions by Parliament dating after 1763 or to compile a much longer list dating back to the founding of the colonies was propelled by radically different assumptions about the American colonies' historical connection to Great Britain. If England's transgressions on American liberty had only begun in 1763, then, perhaps, a reversal in policy might be sufficient to restore harmony. But if the transgressions had been occurring since the very beginning of colonization, then there might well be some fundamental defect in the colonial relationship that would be much more difficult to remedy.

Silas Deane left a brief record of the debate that day in his diary, and although some of his entries are cryptic, it appears that the delegates were all over the map on the proposed language. Some, including Isaac Low, James Duane, John Jay and probably Edward Rutledge objected on the grounds that the proposed resolution was still too combative. A few others, notably Edward Biddle, Thomas Lynch, Christopher Gadsden, Roger Sherman, Samuel Chase and, most emphatically, Patrick Henry, expressed varying degrees of skepticism about whether the resolution went far enough. Lynch objected that limiting American grievances to the period after 1763 would not deal with some of the "worst acts," especially some of the earlier navigation acts placing restrictions on American trade.[13]

At that point in the debate, two delegates spoke for the extremes. John Jay was taking the role of the most outspoken advocate of conciliatory language in the petition to the king. Patrick Henry, who had already clashed with Jay during the opening days of the Congress, now went after him again, accusing him of pusillanimity. But again, the room leaned toward moderation. Even the two Adamses, as well as Richard Henry Lee, decided to take a middle ground and support the proposed language of the list of American grievances. Recognizing that the question of when to date the beginning of American grievances against Great Britain might create an unbridgeable division in the Congress, they suggested that it "is better for the present to temporize" and not to agitate the question of the pre-1763 trade regulations. In fact, the move here by Lee and the two Adamses was entirely calculated. By agreeing to confine their protests to only those British policies pursued after 1763, they hoped to win the trust of moderates in the Congress whose votes were essential, as Sam Adams had noted a week earlier, to a truly united American opposition. Men like the Adamses and Richard Henry Lee may well have had the thought of independence—at least as a last resort—in their minds even at this early date, but they would have emphatically denied it, and they realized that their best chance of bringing other delegates around to their way of thinking was to move cautiously. Sometime during the day on October 5, the delegates voted on the language of the post-1763 part of the petition, and by a narrow margin, six colonies in favor, five opposed, and Pennsylvania's delegation deadlocked, the Congress reached a fragile consensus. Most of the delegations had members voting on both sides of the question, with some wishing for more pacific and others wishing for stronger language. This was an important moment for the Congress and was in some senses a credit to the strategic vision of men like John and Sam Adams and Richard Henry Lee, for if they had insisted on more strident language, it might have been more difficult to reach agreement on other, ultimately more important, issues down the road.[14]

But the delegates still needed to reach consensus on the difficult details of the non-importation and non-exportation agreements. In spite of their September 30 agreement in principle to impose a ban on all goods imported from Great Britain, Ireland and the West Indies, many colonies still resisted the ban on sugar, coffee and molasses from the West Indies. Further, as everyone in the room knew, many of the goods imported into the mainland colonies from the West Indies were smuggled in, avoiding the payment of British duties altogether. Did the delegates mean to put an end to that trade as well? The issue of whether some items should be exempt from the ban on exports was even more divisive than that relating to the ban on importing sugar, coffee and molasses, for it was here that the specific economic interests of particular colonies, and more generally, the division of interest between the staple-exporting southern colonies and the northern colonies, were brought directly into play. Over the next few weeks the Congress would repeatedly, and unsuccessfully, try to agree on the specifics of the non-exportation policy. On October 6, Isaac Low, whose unhappiness with the Congress's radical turn had continued to grow, used the wrangling over that issue as an excuse to propose that the Congress adjourn for six months, and, after the colonial legislatures had elected new delegates, try once again to reach an accord. In the midst of his speech defending that proposal, Low, in one of the most acrimonious moments in the Congress thus far, went on to rail against the attempt of some of his congressional colleagues to move the colonies toward "Independency." Both John and Sam Adams kept their cool while Low gave his speech, but privately, they worried about whether the colonies would ever be able to unite on common ground. In a letter he wrote but never sent to Abigail because he was worried about his correspondence being intercepted, John Adams complained that "fifty strangers" in the Congress, overcome by fear and jealousy, would stand in the way of any decisive action to protect the afflicted citizens of Boston. Sam Adams echoed his cousin's fears and frustration. Writing to his Boston confidant Joseph Warren, he worried that in spite of all of the Massachusetts delegation's efforts to appear "cool and judicious," men like Low were seeking to depict them as intemperate and rash advocates of independence.[15]

In the midst of the debates over the precise details of non-importation and non-exportation, Paul Revere appeared on October 6 with another of his "expresses" from Boston, alerting the delegates that General Gage had deployed more British troops, effectively turning Boston into a military garrison, with its residents "to be treated by the soldiery as declared enemies." Drafted by the Boston Committee of Correspondence on September 28, this was not a mere strategic ploy devised by Sam Adams. In fact, Gage was escalating his efforts to assert military control over Boston, and the committee was genuinely concerned that Boston was in danger of imminent devastation. But arriving as it did in the midst of the debates over the petition to the king over non-importation and non-exportation, some of the more conservative delegates were quick to conclude that it was all part of a radical plan to push Americans into "Independency."

Revere's message from Boston came in the form of a petition. It ostensibly sought the advice of the Congress as to whether, in the face of Gage's display of military force, the residents should evacuate the town altogether. Alternatively, and this appeared to be the more serious proposal contained in the message, the residents might, "by maintaining their ground . . . better serve the public cause." The Boston petitioners must have realized that outright warfare between the British troops and the townspeople was the likely consequence of this latter strategy, and they vowed not to "shrink from hardship and danger" should this be the course chosen. They noted too that the suspension of civil government in Massachusetts had "made it impossible that there should be a due administration of justice." Although the petition concluded with a request to Congress for "advice" on how to respond to the vacuum in governmental authority in the colony, Massachusetts' political leaders—and in particular the leaders of the Boston Committee of Correspondence—were prepared to take matters into their own hands.[16]

As the committee drafting the petition to the king met, the remaining members of Congress spent most of the next week discussing a response to the Boston petition and to General Gage. This probably infuriated the conservatives in Carpenters' Hall, for not only did it seem to be a diversion from the Congress's main business, but to some, among them Galloway, Duane and Low, it was clearly a ruse planned by the likes of Sam Adams to "throw a veil" over their plans to provoke a military confrontation and hasten the move toward independence.[17]

The Adamses, for their part, tried to keep themselves "out of sight" on the question of aid to Boston. But they both recorded their views on how far the Congress should go in confronting General Gage. Sam Adams, far more radical on this point, composed an inflammatory draft of a letter to Gage for Congress's consideration. Describing the closing of Boston Harbor as "unjust and cruel" and the suspension of provincial government as a deliberate effort to destroy the liberty of all British subjects, Adams warned Gage that the resistance that he faced in Boston was not confined to a small faction, but, in fact, was supported by "the united voice and Efforts of all of America." Adams took particular aim at the continuing efforts of the British to fortify Boston, an action that, if it did not cease, would send all of America and Great Britain into the "Horrors of a Civil War!"[18]

The draft response composed by John Adams was more conciliatory in tone than his cousin's. The younger Adams repeated the assertion that the people of the "whole of the Continent" were determined to resist enforcement of the Massachusetts Government Act, and while he too denounced the increased British fortification of Boston as likely only to excite "the Jealousies and Apprehensions of the People," he ended with a more humbly worded entreaty that General Gage reverse course and "desist from further Fortifications."[19]

Richard Henry Lee offered yet another alternative, as combative as Sam Adams's, but which led in a different direction. Asserting that it was "inconsistent with the honor and safety of a free people to live within the Controul and exposed to the injuries of a Military force not under government of the Civil Power" and citing the increased danger to Boston's residents from Gage's military garrison, Lee proposed that the Bostonians "quit their Town and find a safe asylum among their hospitable countrymen." While it's unclear whether Lee's draft of the letter to Gage was ever put to a vote, it is likely that both the Massachusetts delegates and the more conservative middle-colony delegates opposed it. John Adams acknowledged that the mass departure of Boston's residents would produce a dramatic effect, but he did not think that it was practicable—"how 20,000 people can go out," taking with them all their necessary personal property, "I know not," Adams averred.[20]

More generally, Adams voiced frustration at the Boston Committee of Correspondence's failure to provide the Continental Congress with clear directions on how best to respond to the heightened military threat posed by General Gage's actions. He complained that the enigmatic quality of the committee's petition to the Congress had left the delegates to "Guess at its meaning." In a letter to William Tudor, a member of the Boston Committee, he cautioned his colleague not to be under any delusion that the Congress would support "offensive Measures" against the British troops. Indeed, Adams wrote, he had "clear evidence that the Congress would "not vote to raise Men or Money for Arms or Ammunitions."[21]

The final version of the Congress's letter to General Gage, agreed to on October 10, was toned down even further from John Adams's already toned-down version of his cousin's more belligerent response. It protested the increased fortification of the city but merely expressed the hope that "you will discontinue the fortifications in and about Boston." And, in a separate resolution intended to give Boston advice on how to proceed in the future, the Congress advised Boston's residents "still to conduct themselves peaceably toward his excellency General Gage and his majesty['s] troops now stationed in the town of Boston, as far as can possibly be consistent with their immediate safety and the security of the town." The townspeople were to avoid any unprovoked attacks "on his Majesty's property" or any insult to his troops and were advised to "peaceably and firmly persevere in the line they are now conducting themselves, *on the defensive.*" Clearly the Congress wished to avoid doing anything to cause the strained relationship between General Gage and Boston's citizens to become even worse. In agreeing to the more conciliatory version of the letter to Gage, the Congress preserved a fragile unity among the delegates, but they had yet to make progress on some of the most difficult issues still confronting them.[22]

Amid the confused and occasionally acrimonious debates over the situation in Boston and enforcement of the boycott on all trade with Great Britain, John Adams's mercurial temperament swung from ebullience to despair. His weary letter of October 9 to Abigail bemoaned the difficulty of getting things accomplished in a room full of natural politicians.

> The Business of the Congress is tedious, beyond Expression. This Assembly is like no other that ever existed. Every Man is a great Man—an orator, a Critick, a statesman, and therefore every Man upon every Question must show his oratory, his criticism, and his Political Abilities. The Consequence of this is; that Business is drawn and spun out to an immeasurable Length. I believe if it was moved and seconded that We should come to a Resolution that Three and two make five We should be entertained with Logick and Rhetorick, Law, History, Politics and Mathematicks, concerning the Subject for two whole Days, and then We should pass the Resolution unanimously in the Affirmative.[23]

Adams's sour mood carried over to other aspects of his stay in Philadelphia. "Phyladelphia," he confided to his diary, "with all its trade and Wealth, and Regularity, is not Boston. The Morals of our People are much better, their Manners are more polite, and agreeable—they are purer English. Our Language is better, our Persons are handsomer, our Spirit is greater, our Laws are wiser, our Religion is superior, our Education is better. We exceed them in everything, but in a Markett, and in charitable public foundations."[24]

Just as John Adams the provincial Puritan had felt guilty pleasure at the lavishness of the feasts on his many social outings among Philadelphia's gentry, so too was he finding it difficult not to be carried away by the magnificence of the trappings, and even some of the ritual, of the Catholic Church. He disapproved of the Catholic faith—it was aimed, as he wrote, at seducing the "simple and ignorant"—but he was not immune to its attractions. He confessed to his diary that its "Scenery and the Musick is so callculated to take in Mankind, that I wonder, the Reformation ever succeeded. The Paintings, the Bells, the Candles, the Gold and Silver. Our Saviour on the Cross, over the Altar, at full Length, and all his Wounds a bleeding. The Chanting is exquisitely soft and sweet."[25]

In elections to the Pennsylvania colonial legislature, John Dickinson, Thomas Mifflin and Charles Thomson, all "warm in the cause of liberty," won over the opposition of the Quakers, "the Broadbrims," as they were called for the hats the men wore. Those results would, Adams predicted, "change the Balance in the Legislature here against Mr. Galloway." And some of the consequences of that shift in power were felt immediately. For example, on October 15 the Pennsylvania legislature elected John Dickinson to join that colony's delegation to the Continental Congress. In the short term, Adams was correct, for Dickinson's presence in the Congress would help him move some of his agenda forward. But in the longer term, there would be no member of Congress more exasperating to the Braintree lawyer than the distinguished "Farmer in Pennsylvania."[26]

NINE

POWER TO THE PEOPLE

Slow but Steady Progress

From October 12 to its adjournment on October 26, the Congress labored over six documents: the statement of American rights and grievances, final drafts of the much-debated plans for the imposition of economic sanctions on British trade, an address to the people of Great Britain, an address to the people of Quebec, another new message to "the inhabitants of British North America" and the petition to the king. Discussions of these documents occurred more or less simultaneously, both in committees and on the floor of the Congress. It was a busy, confusing time, for there was considerable overlap among the six documents, and there was still substantial disagreement among the delegates not only on the content of each of them, but also on the overall message that should emerge from the Congress once its business had been completed.

On October 12, the delegates returned to the essential—but still unresolved—question of American rights. On that day, John Dickinson presented a draft report on that subject. In fact, Dickinson had not yet officially joined the Congress as a member, but such was his influence that this technicality did not prevent him from taking the lead in working with other delegates—most notably John Adams—in crafting the language of the report.[1]

Many of the items in the report on rights were familiar and non-controversial. Those involving the right of representation in all cases relating to taxation and the colonies' internal governance had been accepted by Americans as constitutional orthodoxy beginning with the resolutions of the Stamp Act Congress in 1765 and further elaborated by Dickinson himself in his *Letters from a Farmer* in 1767–1768. That orthodoxy included a willingness of the colonies to submit to some regulation of trade in order to "secure commercial advantages" for the "whole empire." But one phrase in the report, probably written by John Adams, drew the delegates' attention. It acknowledged that the colonists would "cheerfully consent" to some forms of the regulation of their trade, implying that the colonists had the right to withdraw that consent should they find it against their interests. Along with the specific denials of Parliament's right to impose taxation for revenue purposes or to pass legislation without the colonists' consent, this voluntary concession to allow Parliament to regulate the trade of the empire—a concession that they might presumably withdraw—came very close to a complete denial of parliamentary authority.

For the next three days, the delegates would debate, occasionally acrimoniously, the report on rights, with Adams's phrase of "cheerfully consent" being the focus of much of that acrimony. James Duane, on guard as usual for any hint of language that might widen the breach between England and her colonies, insisted that parliamentary authority to regulate American trade was a fundamental part of the colonists' "compact"—meaning, for Duane and others, a fundamental principle in the unwritten English constitution—with their mother country and could not be withdrawn at the whim of any colony. Duane warned that Great Britain would quite justifiably defend her right to such regulation "at the expense of the last drop of her blood and the last farthing of her treasure." Focusing on the distinction between Adams's "consent" and Parliament's "right," Duane insisted that "there must be some supreme controlling power over our trade, and that this can only rest with Parliament."[2]

Samuel Ward, a stalwart member of the radical New England coalition from Rhode Island, rose and delivered an impassioned speech asserting that the question before the Congress was one on which "the Happiness or Misery not only in the present Generation of Americans, but of Millions yet unborn," might well depend. Basing his argument both on his interpretation of the constitutional compact between the Crown and its colonies *and* on the higher principles of the "Society of Nature," he was in effect denying that Parliament had any right whatsoever to regulate American trade. Skirting very close to advocating outright independence, Ward asserted that "one kingdom should not be governed by another." He then went on to impugn the character of the British nation as a whole. The Parliament was now irredeemably corrupt, "subject to the Frowns, Flatteries & Bribes" of a venal and self-serving ministry. "The people of England, formerly a sober frugal industrious & brave People" had, he observed, become "immersed in Luxury, Riot & Dissipation." Indeed, the nation at large, once "wholly free from debt," was now mired in debt, all the result of bribery and corruption. "Would you," he asked, "put your all into such hands?"[3]

As the debate moved forward, it became clear that in the choice between a few words—"cheerfully consent" versus "right by compact"—the very nature of America's relationship with her mother country hung in the balance. Although Charles Thomson failed to make a formal entry in the congressional journal on October 13, it appears that at some point on that day the draft report, containing Adams's language, was put to a vote, with the tally standing at five colonies in favor, five opposed, and two, Massachusetts and Rhode Island, divided. Although John and Sam Adams and Samuel Ward had voted to include the language implying that Parliament did not have an unqualified authority to regulate trade, their New England colleagues Thomas Cushing and Robert Treat Paine from Massachusetts and Stephen Hopkins from Rhode Island were apparently not prepared to go that far. By the rules of the Congress, it appeared that the body had rejected Adam's more militant statement of American rights.[4]

On the evening of October 13 John Dickinson hosted a dinner including John Adams, Samuel Chase, William Paca, Isaac Low, Thomas Mifflin, Richard Penn and Charles Lee, representing a range of views on Adams's language, and the discussion that evening may have had the effect of winning over some to support the more radical verbiage. The following day, Charles Thomson recorded in the congressional journal the approval of a Declaration of Rights and Grievances that included Adams's phrase "cheerfully consent." Thomson's horrible record keeping makes it unlikely that we will ever know what caused the discussion over the Declaration of Rights to move from a deadlock to a narrow endorsement of the more radical position, but, in fact, in spite of Thomson's journal entry, the debate over the limits of British authority over the colonies did not end with that fragile agreement. Some delegates continued to spar over the language respecting Parliament's right to regulate trade for some time thereafter. Joseph Galloway later recalled that the debate continued on for "better than a fortnight," with the "violent party" eventually getting its way.[5]

Accompanying the enumeration of American "rights" was a catalogue of American grievances, which were all packaged into the eleventh resolution in the Declaration of Rights and Grievances. The committee charged with listing American grievances had uncovered many infringements on American rights that occurred prior to 1763, but, "from an ardent desire that harmony and mutual intercourse of affection and interest may be restored," they agreed to pass over the pre-1763 grievances "for the present." For the most part, the list was a familiar one to anyone who had followed the deteriorating state of America's relations with Great Britain since 1763—all of the various acts of taxation "for the purpose of raising a revenue in America"; the establishing of an American board of customs commissioners; the act requiring Americans to quarter British soldiers in their homes; orders increasing the size and presence of a British standing army in the colonial seaport cities; and, of course, the package of punitive acts including the Boston Port Bill and the Massachusetts Government Act that Parliament had passed in the aftermath of the Boston Tea Party.

The one new, and to twenty-first-century eyes, jarring addition to the American grievances was the condemnation of the Quebec Act, which Parliament had passed two months after the Coercive Acts in 1774. The condemnation of the Quebec Act, though phrased in terms of fundamental American rights and liberties, was infected with anti-Catholic sentiments. The act itself was aimed both at bringing some of the Indian territory in what is now the upper Midwest of the United States under firmer British control and at winning the allegiance of the settlers of what had previously been the French colony in Canada, now a British colonial possession. The principal means of winning the allegiance of the settlers of that region was to guarantee some continuity in the legal structure of the former French colony and to guarantee to those settlers the freedom to continue to practice their Catholic religion. But the delegates chose to view the Quebec Act as an attempt to abolish the English system of laws altogether and, worse, to establish the "Roman Catholick Religion in the province of Quebec." Both of these charges were unfair. The Quebec Act merely assured toleration for Catholics in the province who wished to practice their religion. Similarly, the guarantees that French, not English civil law would be used in some legal proceedings between individuals was yet another attempt at a conciliatory gesture to the French residents of Quebec. In all public matters, including all criminal proceedings, English common law was to be supreme.[6]

The debate in the Congress over the Quebec Act suggests that those who most stridently denounced it were motivated by a combination of anti-Catholic prejudice and a desire to find any excuse that they could to add to their list of grievances against the British. John Jay, joined by James Duane, pointed this out to some of their more radical opponents. Why, Jay asked, should Americans who had complained of British interference with their own legislatures feel compelled to pass judgment on "the police of other governments?" Indeed, the particular form of government proposed for the former French Canada was one to which the majority of residents of that province had given their consent. On the matter of the grant of toleration to Catholics, Jay noted that this was a principle explicitly guaranteed to the French in that province by the terms of the treaty of peace ending the Seven Years' War eleven years earlier.

Virginia's Richard Henry Lee, his anti-Catholic bias in full flower, would have none of it. Invoking the Saint Bartholomew's Day massacre of French Huguenot Protestants in Paris in 1572, he wanted no part of Catholicism in any British province. John Adams and Patrick Henry, as well as Thomas McKean of Delaware, shared Lee's views. Adams's speech in favor of including the Quebec Act among the American grievances was replete with references to "Romish Superstition, the Knights of Malta, the Orders of the military Monks" and, indeed, the "Goths and Vandals." And Henry believed that the denunciation of the Quebec Act was an essential element in the Americans' statement of grievances. Ethnocentrism won the day, and on October 17 the Congress affirmed by unanimous vote its intention of keeping the denunciation of the Quebec Act as one of the grievances.[7] If the comprehensiveness of the American list of grievances made it highly unlikely that the British would receive the American Declaration of Rights and Grievances with any sympathy, the tone of the document—particularly the charge that the various measures enacted by Parliament since 1763 were intended to "enslave America"—made an open-minded reception of it even less likely.

As the delegates moved toward a reluctant consensus on the content of the Declaration of Rights and Grievances, they continued to jostle for position on the specific contents of the non-exportation agreement. When it had first been voted on as a general statement of intent on September 30, the delegates from the southern colonies, whose economies were most dependent upon exports, had extracted a compromise from the Congress delaying implementation of the measure until September 1775. But as the Congress continued to debate the specifics of implementation, they pushed their northern colleagues even harder. On October 16 or 17, four of the five delegates from South Carolina—John and Edward Rutledge, Thomas Lynch and Henry Middleton—essentially brought debate on non-exportation to a halt by declaring that unless rice and indigo, the principal export crops of their colony, were exempted from the non-exportation agreement, they would leave the Congress altogether. John Rutledge, defending the exception, noted that only about five percent of New England's exports were shipped to Great Britain, whereas in South Carolina's case, sixty-five percent of the rice and one hundred percent of the indigo went there. According to Rutledge's biographer, Richard Barry, Rutledge elaborated on these statistics in a speech that could have done little to ease the tensions in the hall that day. The statistics, Rutledge argued, "will reveal to you that if this association is perfected the northern colonies will suffer very little, for they can still carry on their trade with Europe and pay indirectly their debts in England, while if South Carolina enters into it her chief businesses are ruined. . . . I have not consulted my constituents, and am speaking only for myself, but I can never consent to the people of South Carolina becoming the dupes of the people of the North, or in the least, to yield to their unreasonable expectations." Nor did the South Carolinians confine their opposition to the inclusion of rice and indigo to speech-making alone. Sometime around October 16 or 17, the two Rutledges, Lynch and Middleton walked out of the Congress altogether in protest.[8]

The South Carolinians' obstinacy paid off. Realizing that the defection of a colony so important to America's export trade as South Carolina would have a disastrous impact on the effectiveness of the non-exportation agreement, Sam Adams reluctantly helped broker a compromise by which indigo was to be included in the embargoed items, but rice exempted. On October 18, Charles Thomson persuaded the four South Carolina delegates to return to Carpenters' Hall, and the final details of the non-importation and non-exportation agreements, including the concession to the South Carolinians, were officially agreed to. Christopher Gadsden, the one South Carolinian who had been steadfast in desiring an embargo on all exported items, was dismayed by what he saw as the selfishness of his colleagues. "Take care," he was reported to have said, "or your liberties will be traded away."[9]

At that moment on October 18 when the delegates grudgingly gave in to South Carolina's demands and adopted what many considered an imperfect agreement on non-importation and non-exportation, many delegates were awakening to the reality of just how difficult it might be to achieve a genuinely united effort in their opposition to coercive British policies. It would provide an even more troubling glimpse of the greater challenges that lay ahead, as the "united colonies" began to consider the possibility of independence from their mother country.

The Association

On October 20, the Congress made what would prove to be a momentous decision, approving the non-importation and non-exportation agreements, which had by then come to be known as the Association. It was a term that was probably inspired by an earlier Virginia Association, formed in that colony to resist enforcement of the Townshend Duties. This was the first act of the Congress that bound the people of the American colonies to specific actions—not only that of enforcing a trade boycott against the British, but also overseeing the actions of local merchants and public officials. With the endorsement of the Association, the Continental Congress truly became a governing body, rather than a mere debating society.[10]

Although the Continental Congress's adoption of the Association has been most closely linked to the efforts of Boston radicals like Sam Adams, the genteel and deliberative George Washington had earlier helped set in motion a similar plan in his home county of Fairfax, Virginia. In early July of 1774, Washington's close friend and neighbor, George Mason, drafted a set of resolutions in response to the Coercive Acts. Not only did these resolutions deny the right of Parliament to tax or legislate for the colonies but they also warned that if Parliament persisted in its punitive treatment of the Bostonians, such behavior would "establish the most grievous and intolerable species of tyranny and oppression that was ever inflicted on mankind." The resolutions were not a mere exercise in rhetoric. They issued a call to all the American colonies for a united ban on British imports.

On July 17, Mason traveled to Washington's plantation at Mount Vernon where the two men polished the language of the twenty-four resolutions that Mason had carried with him. They agreed to present them to the Fairfax County Committee of Correspondence in nearby Alexandria, at the county courthouse, the following day. Washington felt honor-bound to share the content of the resolutions with his close friend and patron, Bryan Fairfax, a member of the powerful, proprietary family of the Northern Neck of Virginia and a loyal supporter of the king. Fairfax urged him to tone the language down, but Washington politely, but firmly, declined. On July 18 Washington chaired the meeting of the Fairfax County Committee of Correspondence, at which Mason's resolutions were overwhelmingly adopted. In August of 1774, Washington carried the Fairfax County resolutions to the Virginia Convention in Williamsburg, which strongly endorsed a similar set of resolutions and then forwarded them to the Continental Congress in Philadelphia.[11]

The Association began with the customary assertion that the delegates considered themselves to be "his majesty's most loyal subjects . . . , avowing our allegiance to his majesty, our affection and regard for our fellow subjects in Great Britain and elsewhere." Following that obligatory nicety, the Association, like the Declaration of

Rights and Grievances, enumerated the grievances against Parliament and a "wicked ministry" that necessitated the action the Congress was about to take. The list was not as comprehensive as that contained in the Declaration of Rights and Grievances, but the very existence of that document made such an enumeration unnecessary. And the document creating the Association had a very different purpose; it was concerned primarily with action, not exhortation or verbal persuasion.

The document then spelled out the specific terms of the non-importation and non-exportation provisions, stipulating the precise dates on which importation and exportation of items would cease and, in a nod to the South Carolinians, exempting rice from the list of items not to be exported. Although the debate on those specifics had revealed some important cleavages among the delegates with respect to the varying interests of the colonies they were representing, the fact that the agreement was as comprehensive as it was, and that, ultimately, the delegates were able to come together unanimously in their endorsement, was no small accomplishment.[12]

The Association and Slavery

One significant item not mentioned in previous drafts and resolutions appeared in the final draft of the Articles of Association. The delegates pledged to "neither import nor purchase any slave imported after the first day of December next; after which time we will wholly discontinue the slave trade, and will neither hire our vessels nor sell our commodities or manufactures to those who are concerned in it." This was not primarily a humanitarian gesture. It was an economic one. That particular "commodity" provided a significant amount of income for merchants on both sides of the Atlantic; if the primary purpose of the embargo was to make British merchants feel some of the consequences of Parliament's actions, then the ban on slave imports made perfect sense. But the emphatic language of the provision suggests that at least some of the delegates felt qualms about the slave trade in its own right. As Americans began to resort to language in which they described their condition as one of "enslavement" by an unjust Parliament, it was becoming more difficult for at least some to ignore the moral hypocrisy of continuing the traffic in human beings.[13]

The unease that at least some delegates felt about the moral un-
derpinnings of slavery was given particularly explicit expression in the
resolutions of the July 18, 1774, Fairfax County meeting. There the
delegates endorsed a resolution drafted by George Mason not only
urging that the slave trade be suspended "during our present difficulties and distress," but also going one step further, declaring that "We
take this opportunity of declaring our most earnest wishes to see an
entire stop forever put to such a wicked, cruel, and unnatural trade."[14]

We should not leap to the conclusion that the adoption of that particular article in the Association signaled anything resembling a more
general assault on the institution of slavery. In 1774, slavery was legally
protected in every one of the British North American colonies. Not
surprisingly, its demographic, economic and social importance varied
enormously across those colonies. In most of New England, slaves
were a tiny portion of the total population, and the institution of slavery, as a means of mobilizing a labor force, was economically insignificant. The ownership of slaves was a modest "convenience," not an
economic necessity, for those few New Englanders who were willing
to make the investment. The one exception was Rhode Island, where
slaves constituted five percent of the overall population of about
60,000, a reflection of the fact that Rhode Island merchants were actively involved in the international slave trade. In the middle colonies
slavery remained a reasonably significant, if not economically vital, institution. Slaves constituted ten percent and 7.5 percent, respectively,
of the populations of New York and New Jersey; in Pennsylvania,
where Quakers consistently voiced their opposition to slavery, slaves
were only 2.4 percent of the population. Although Delaware may
technically have been a southern colony, slave ownership there was
similar to that of the middle colonies, at 6.6 percent. But as one moved
south—Maryland had 32.8 percent, Virginia, 41 percent, North Carolina, 33.7 percent and South Carolina, 53.9 percent—the importance
of slaves and slavery to the economies and social structures of those
colonies rose dramatically.[15]

The pattern of slaveholdings among the delegates themselves mir-
rored the overall patterns of slave ownership within the colonies, but
the delegates, drawn from the upper ranks of their societies, tended to
own even larger numbers of slaves. Although the records on slave

ownership among the delegates to the First Continental Congress are incomplete, it seems likely that every delegate from South Carolina, North Carolina, Virginia and Maryland owned slaves. Indeed, most of those individuals owned large numbers. The slaveholdings of each of the South Carolina delegates except for Christopher Gadsden numbered in the hundreds, with Henry Middleton topping the list with his 800 slaves. Among the Virginians, Peyton Randolph, Benjamin Harrison, Richard Henry Lee and George Washington each owned at least 200 slaves. Even the upstart lawyer Patrick Henry had acquired upwards of thirty slaves by 1774, a number that would grow to nearly 100 over the course of his life. Whereas slaves served as a vital component of the economic interests and well-being of the delegates from the South, those northern delegates who owned slaves tended to own only a few, using them primarily as house servants. Among the delegates from the middle colonies, John Dickinson had a substantial number of slaves working on his multiple property holdings, although by 1774 he had gone on record opposing the institution and was in the process of freeing his slaves. Among the New Yorkers, James Duane owned at least three house slaves, and Philip Livingston most likely had at least a few slaves living on his upstate manor. William Livingston, being a Livingston, no doubt also had a few slaves working on his substantial properties in New Jersey. There is no evidence that any of the New England delegates owned slaves, including the two delegates from Rhode Island, even though merchants in that colony had played an active role in the international slave trade.[16]

It is difficult to disentangle the American colonists' occasionally moralistic pronouncements against the slave trade from their more pragmatic aim of inflicting economic punishment on Great Britain, but it seems likely that the primary motivation behind the suspension of the slave trade was political, not moral. However, if the delegates could cloak the resolution temporarily suspending the slave trade with a high-sounding moralism, all the better.

Enforcing the Association

The Association was not the first American attempt to use a boycott to persuade Parliament to change its policies. But unlike the boycotts in opposition to the Stamp Act in 1765–1766 and the resistance to the Townshend Duties during the period from 1768 to 1770, the Association committed all of the people of the "united colonies," not just a small group of merchants in a few seaport cities, to abide by the terms of the embargo. In the case of the Townshend Duties in particular, merchants in New York, Boston and Philadelphia had fallen to bickering over who was or was not faithfully adhering to the terms of the agreement. By contrast, Articles Five and Six of the Association made it clear that *all* American merchants were responsible for adhering to the terms of the embargo, and that anyone found to be in violation was to be held accountable to the public. Similarly, any owner of a vessel or captain of a ship who was caught with any of the prohibited goods on his ship would face "immediate dismission from their service." By the terms of Article Nine, any merchant or vendor who took advantage of any scarcity of goods by selling an item at a higher-than-usual price was to be dealt with severely—"no person ought, nor will any of us deal with any such person . . . at any time thereafter, for any commodity whatever."[17]

Whereas enforcement of the boycotts during the protest over the Townshend duties was left in the hands of the merchants themselves, Article Eleven of the Association stipulated that every county, city and town elect committees "to observe the conduct of all persons touching this association," and, in the case of violations, to publish the names of the offenders, in order that "all such foes of the rights of British America may be publicly known, and universally condemned as the enemies of American liberty." The decision to lodge enforcement of the Association in the hands of local committees was a clear sign of distrust toward at least some American merchants (particularly those in New York and Philadelphia who were suspected of violating previous non-importation agreements), but, equally important, it signified the extent to which America's resistance to British policies was becoming a broadly based, grassroots movement—a feature that would prove essential to any ultimate revolution against British rule.[18]

Although the primary aim of the Association was punitive and coercive—aimed at effecting a change in British policy toward America—it also served as an exhortation to all American colonists to live more virtuous lives, reflecting some of the Puritan moralism that infused the rhetoric of its most enthusiastic New England advocates. Article Seven spoke of the need to "use our utmost endeavours to improve the breed of sheep, and increase their number to the greatest extent; and to that end, we will kill them as seldom as may be." Moreover, those who found themselves "overstocked" with sheep were encouraged, rather than killing them, to give them "to our neighbours, especially to the poorer sort, on moderate terms." Article Eight encouraged "frugality, economy, and industry" and discouraged "every species of extravagance and dissipation, especially all horse-racing and all kinds of gaming, cock-fighting, exhibitions of shews, plays, and other expensive diversions and entertainments." It went so far as to recommend that, "on the death of any relation or friend, none of us . . . will go into any further mourning-dress, than a black crape or ribbon on the arm or hat for gentlemen, and a black ribbon and necklace for ladies, and we will discontinue the giving of gloves and scarves at funerals." Clearly, this part of the Association went far beyond resistance to England laws. It suggested that America's cause was no longer merely economic or constitutional, it was in some important senses a reformation of manners and morals.[19]

The final article in the Association was directed not at merchants or vendors but at the political leaders of all thirteen colonies. The delegates agreed to cut off all relations with any colony found to be in violation of the terms of the Association, publicizing the offending colony "as unworthy of the rights of freemen, and as inimical to the liberties of their country." Strictly speaking, the Congress had no formal constitutional power, nor any of the requisite institutional structures, to bind any colony to do anything that it did not wish to do, but this final article, at least rhetorically, was yet another step toward creating a Congress with real governing power, a Congress prepared to speak in the name of the people of the "united colonies."[20]

In both its economic and political contexts, the Association was a genuinely radical document. It asked the American people, and American merchants in particular, to make significant sacrifices. At the same time it asked the American colonies—including Georgia, which remained absent from the Congress—to submit themselves to the authority of a superior entity. Isaac Low, one of the New York delegates most uneasy, if not downright unhappy, about the direction in which the first Congress was moving, asked: "Well, Can the People bear a to-tal interruption of the West India trade? Can [they] live without Rum, Sugar, and Molasses? Will not their Impatience, and Vexation defeat the Measure?"[21]

In spite of misgivings like these, all of the delegates, including Low, endorsed the Association. Each of those present on October 20 was asked to sign his name to the Association—an act not merely of *affirmation,* but of *commitment* to uphold its provisions. And, apparently, everyone in the hall, with the exception of Samuel Rhoads, who had resigned from the Congress when he was elected mayor of Philadelphia, and Robert Goldsborough of Maryland, who had already departed for home, did so. Even Joseph Galloway, albeit reluctantly, stepped forward to sign. He later claimed that he did so only to prevent even "more violent measures" from being proposed by the Congress. He also reported around this time that he was fearful for his safety, having received a halter as a "present" from an anonymous political enemy, which Galloway interpreted as a threat on his life.[22]

That evening the delegates relaxed at a grand feast, staged in their honor by the Pennsylvania Assembly. The delegates gave toasts to the work of the Congress and to the spirit of American liberty. One toast expressed a more pacific sentiment: "May the Sword of the Parent never be Stain'd with the Blood of her Children." John Adams enjoyed himself that evening, but unable to repress his Puritan distrust of Quakerism, and of Pennsylvania's Quaker political leaders in particular, added, "Two or 3 broad-brims, over against me at Table—one of them said this is not a Toast but a Prayer, come let us join in it—and they took their glasses accordingly." Adams would never let go of his distrust of the "broad-brims" and rarely missed an opportunity to say something disparaging about members of the Quaker sect, but even he must have felt great satisfaction over how far the Congress had come.[23]

TEN

THE FIRST CONGRESS
COMPLETES ITS BUSINESS

The SIGNING OF the Association—the *unanimous signing*—was a momentous event. It had not come easily—with nearly all of the delegates calculating the self-interest of their respective colonies, the obstinacy of the South Carolinians in insisting that rice be exempted from the ban on exports to Great Britain and the grumbling of at least a few delegates from New York and Pennsylvania. But amidst all the grumbling and jostling, the delegates had achieved unity on what would prove to be the most important action that the Congress would take that fall. The adoption and implementation of the Association would set in motion a series of events involving local enforcement officers, American merchants and royal officials in London that would have profound consequences for relations among American colonists and between American colonial officials and the royal government in London. It also marked the first occasion in which the Congress asserted genuine legislative, as opposed to purely rhetorical, power, to speak and act in the name of the people of the American colonies.

The Congress's next item of business was to compose messages to two large groups, neither of whom were present in Philadelphia in a physical sense, but whose interests in the outcome of their deliberations were always in the back of the delegates' minds. Richard Henry Lee, John Jay and William Livingston would be charged with drafting both of these addresses. The first was directed at the people of Great

Britain. In October of 1774, the delegates were still thinking of themselves as loyal subjects of the king and proud members of the British empire. Although their anger with Parliament and with many of the king's ministers was steadily rising, their sense of common identity with their fellow subjects back in England was undiminished. John Jay would take the lead in drafting the address to their fellow subjects in Great Britain, still seeking to cloak the Congress's fairly radical moves in a tone of moderation. Addressed to "Friends and Fellow Subjects," its purpose was, in effect, to go over the heads of the members of Parliament, seeking to persuade the voters who elected them to force a change in their behavior. Jay acknowledged England's glorious heritage, "a nation led to greatness by the hand of Liberty," but then went on to observe a lamentable trend in which, by the actions of a few, corrupt ministers in Parliament, the government had descended "to the ungrateful task of forging chains for her Friends and Children, and instead of giving support to freedom, turns advocate for Slavery and Oppression." Then followed a litany of the familiar American grievances, from unconstitutional taxes to the suspension of trial by jury to the patent injustices of the Coercive Acts. Jay reserved particular scorn for the Quebec Act. Appealing to the instinctive ethnocentrism and anti-Catholicism of his fellow subjects in England, he raised the specter of an ever-increasing papist influence in both America and England. Jay concluded with a passionate plea that the inherent virtue, sense of justice and public spirit of the British people would carry the day. He asked his fellow British subjects to ignore the false accusations about the seditious behavior of the colonists, assuring them that the Americans had no desire for independence, that if permitted "to be as free as yourselves . . . we shall ever esteem a union with you . . . we shall ever be ready to contribute all in our power to the welfare of the Empire." That happy state could only be achieved, however, if the British people elected a Parliament capable of seeing the error of its ways and repudiated the "wicked ministers and evil counsellors" responsible for the present crisis.[1]

When it came to their fellow colonists, the delegates had a different task. The "Address to the Inhabitants of the American Colonies" reveals a body aware that it needed to legitimize its actions and its own ability to speak for and act on behalf of the people of the colonies. Although the committee consisting of Lee, Livingston and Jay was supposedly responsible for drafting this address as well, it appears that John Dickinson, who had only the day before taken his seat in the Congress, was the author. Its moderate, measured tone was very much in Dickinson's style, and, more important, the substance of the writing reflected the delegates' realization that many Americans living away from the center of the conflict with England needed to be persuaded that the increasingly radical steps being taken by the Congress were justified.[2]

As they put the finishing touches to the two addresses on the afternoon of Friday, October 21, now forty-seven days into the Congress, many of the delegates were becoming restless, anxious to get about their business back home. Peyton Randolph, the President of the Congress, left for Williamsburg on October 22 to take up his duties as Speaker of the House of Burgesses. And when Randolph left, most of the Virginia delegation—Patrick Henry, Richard Bland, Edmund Pendleton and Benjamin Harrison—went with him.[3]

The departure of the Virginians was an early warning sign of an absenteeism that would plague the Continental Congress for nearly the whole of its existence—right up to its extinction in March 1789. The Congress would always struggle not only with differences of opinion within its ranks on key policy issues, but also with the continuing tug and pull of the real work to be done back in the delegates home colonies. Those provincial interests were themselves a cause of differences of opinion on policy issues (for example, with South Carolina's insistence that rice be exempted from the non-exportation agreement), but they were also persistent sources of distraction and inattention. The fact that five of Virginia's seven delegates departed on October 23 (only Richard Henry Lee and the ever responsible George Washington remained) was a telling sign of the way in which provincial loyalties and affairs of a single colony often trumped the business of the "united colonies."

The Address to the King of Great Britain

In spite of the departure of most of the Virginia delegation, there was still important business to be done. In drafting their Declaration of Rights and Grievances, the delegates had essentially denied that Parliament had any authority over the colonies. The only entity to which it continued to pledge loyalty and obedience was the institution of the monarchy, and therefore the only person to whom they could turn for a redress of their grievances was King George III.

The delegates had elected a committee consisting of Richard Henry Lee, John Adams, Thomas Johnson, Patrick Henry and John Rutledge to draft a petition to the king way back on October 1. The men elected were not only among the most prestigious and outspoken members of the Congress but also represented a rough geographical balance north to south. Sometime before October 21, Patrick Henry tried his hand at writing a draft of the petition. But whatever Henry's oratorical skills, he was a failure, both on this and subsequent occasions, as a writer. Although there is no written record of the fact, it appears that the committee rejected Henry's version and asked Richard Henry Lee to try his hand at composing another draft. John Dickinson, writing long after the fact, noted Henry's "language of asperity" as the cause of its rejection, and though this is consistent with Henry's reputation as a fiery and passionate advocate of resistance, the actual text of Henry's draft was if anything milder than the final version adopted by Congress. The more likely explanation was its flat, passionless prose. Whether Henry's departure from Congress on October 23 was the result of pique at having his attempt summarily rejected we do not know, but it is clear that Henry's concern about provincial affairs back in Virginia had taken precedence over his interest in the formal proceedings of the Congress.[4]

Compared to Henry, Richard Henry Lee was shorter and more pointed in his criticism of Parliament. He singled out specific ministers—Lord North, the king's chief minister; Lord Mansfield, the chief justice; and Lord Bute, the king's (and, more important, the king's mother's) close confidant—as the men most responsible for the "unwise and destructive" policies being pursued by the British government. In so doing, it made what was supposed to be a conciliatory message to the king into something far more combative, for Bute, Mansfield and North were, after all, the *king's* ministers, appointed by him and serving at his pleasure.[5]

Whereas Henry's draft was rejected outright by his fellow committee members, Lee's was used as a basis for a final draft. That version, as was the case with the address to the inhabitants of the American colonies, was almost certainly written by the newly arrived John Dickinson. Dickinson put a lot of time and ego into his effort, writing three separate drafts, each long and self-consciously learned. Consistent with Dickinson's own personal loyalty to the king, his final attempt was fulsome in its expressions of affection for George III. His version, like that of Richard Henry Lee, was inclined to place most of the blame on the king's ministers, "those designing and dangerous Men, who for several Years past incessantly employed to dissolve the Bonds of Society by prosecuting the most desperate and irritating projects of Oppression." Unlike the Declaration of Rights and Grievances, which explicitly denied parliamentary authority in nearly all matters of taxation and legislation, the petition to the king did not even mention Parliament. Instead, in its conclusion, the petition made clear that the Americans not only owed their allegiance to the king but, in so doing, depended upon him to intercede and to restore those rights they had so long enjoyed.[6]

John Adams, writing in his diary two days after Dickinson presented his draft to the Congress, described the Pennsylvania delegate as "delicate and timid," suggesting that he found the draft overly submissive. This moment saw the beginning of what would come to be a persistently adversarial relationship between the two. In fact, Dickinson's petition was a nearly pitch-perfect reflection of the divided state of mind of the vast majority of American colonists in the fall of 1774. On the one hand, it would have been hard for any royal official back in England to ignore the fact that the American Congress—not just a few hotheads in Boston but, apparently, nearly all of the representatives of the American colonies—had reached the point where they were denying Parliament's authority in nearly every aspect of the colonies' relationship with the mother country. And the language used to describe American grievances in every document emanating from the Congress, including Dickinson's draft of the petition to the king, was highly emotional, even hyperbolic. "Evil," "designing" ministers in Parliament, systematic plots among members of Parliament to "enslave"

Americans—this was not the language of conciliation. But while the language and tone of the American protests against imperial policies would seem to be leading straight to the "independency" that some moderates and conservatives in the colonies so dreaded, the expressions of loyalty and affection for the king and the empire he ruled were extravagantly phrased. "Your majesty's most faithful Subjects," "your loyal people in America," hearts that would "willingly bleed in your majesty's service"—nearly all of the members of the Congress embraced those words not merely as a rhetorical ploy to flatter the king into a more sympathetic view of their cause, but also out of a genuine attachment to His Majesty and the empire he ruled.[7]

The Congress gave its official approval of the petition to the king on the morning of October 25. Although all sorts of British subjects had for at least two centuries sent petitions to the king *and* Parliament asking for a redress of grievances, Congress's decision to deliberately separate the two was an unprecedented act whose significance would not be overlooked by either the king or members of Parliament. The Congress chose Richard Henry Lee to write to the colonial agents in London requesting that they present the petition to the king. One of the most important of those agents—in terms of both his international prestige as a scientist and his experience as a diplomat—was Benjamin Franklin, who spent most of the years between 1757 and 1775 living in London, acting as the agent—in effect, a paid lobbyist—for the colonies of Massachusetts, New Jersey and Pennsylvania. The other truly notable colonial agent serving at that time was Edmund Burke, the prominent Anglo-Irish politician and political philosopher who, while he was serving as a member of Parliament was also serving as the lobbyist for the colony of New York. Lee's letter asked the agents to "call in the aid of such Noblemen and Gentlemen [in London] as are esteemed firm friends to American liberty," the hope being that by mobilizing the support of London's most prominent citizens, especially those with close connections to the king and his circle, the king might be inclined to view the Americans' petition more favorably.[8]

With the sending of the petition, the Congress had but one last substantive piece of business to dispatch before it could consider its mission complete. On October 26, its final day in session, the Congress approved an address to the people of Quebec. That document had the tricky task of winning the support of the people of that province while avoiding saying anything that Quebec's Catholic residents, whom the delegates had already disparaged in their condemnation of the Quebec Act, would find offensive. With Dickinson once again the primary writer, the address emphasized the virtues of English principles of law and liberty and invited the residents of Quebec to send delegates to the Continental Congress when it next met—an invitation that must have seemed more than a little tardy and probably condescending in the bargain. When the Congress next convened in May of 1775, it was perhaps not surprising to anyone that the province of Quebec would choose not to send delegates.[9]

The Congress's final act, though ceremonial, was nevertheless one of great consequence. The forty-seven of the fifty-six delegates still in attendance lined up at the table at the front of the room to sign the Address to the King. The signatories even included those delegates who had been the most outspoken critics of the radical direction in which Congress had been moving, men like Joseph Galloway, James Duane, John Jay, Edward Rutledge and Connecticut's Eliphalet Dyer. However much John Adams may have been inclined to criticize John Dickinson, the principal author of the petition, for his timidity, the fact that the Congress was able to achieve unanimity in its petition to the king owed at least in part to the ability of men like Dickinson to reach across the spectrum of political opinion in Carpenters' Hall and forge a consensus. And with that significant achievement behind it, the Congress adjourned.[10]

Parting Impressions

By the time Henry Middleton, who had stepped in to serve as president after Peyton Randolph's departure, raised the gavel to adjourn, the delegates were all eager to head home. Indeed, within a few days, the boardinghouses that had housed them for the past seven weeks would be empty. Almost all of the delegates, as they mounted their horses or climbed into their carriages, felt a sense not only of accomplishment but of camaraderie as well.

Thomas Lynch of South Carolina, who had allied himself with the more militant delegates from Virginia and New England from the moment he arrived in Philadelphia, wrote to a friend of his positive impression of the New England delegates. In spite of their reputation as hotheads, they had proceeded "without rashness," advocating "a steady, manly, cool and regular conduct" throughout the whole of the Congress's meeting. Lynch concluded that "America, though sincerely attached to England and desirous of perpetual union, will, by force only, be brought to admit of domination."[11]

John Dickinson, though a late addition, had contributed impressively to the Congress's proceedings. Assessing the situation as the Congress adjourned, he concluded that "Great Britain must relax, or inevitably involve herself in a Civil War." While fully supporting America's resistance to British policies of the past several years, he remained convinced—or perhaps was laboring mightily to convince himself—that the source of the conflict with England was all the fault of a few misguided or designing men. He cited the king's ministers and the two most obnoxious of the royal governors of Massachusetts, "the Butes, Mansfields, Norths, Bernards & Hutchinsons &c whose Falsehoods and Misrepresentations have enflamed the People." Dickinson continued to hold out the hope that if only those individuals could be removed from power and replaced by more virtuous leaders who would abide by the true principles of the English constitution, then the crisis would pass. "I wish for peace ardently," he wrote to Arthur Lee of Virginia, "but must say, delightful as it is, it will come more grateful by being unexpected."[12]

If peace was his wish, then his more realistic expectation was that any further outbreaks of violence, or any attempt by the British to send military reinforcements to General Gage in Boston, would "put the whole Continent in arms from Nova Scotia to Georgia." Dickinson, like most of the departing delegates, was torn between hope and fear. "May God in his infinite Mercy," he wrote, "grant a happy Event to these afflicting agitations."[13]

Joseph Galloway, not surprisingly, left the Congress in a decidedly foul mood. Writing to his brother-in-law Thomas Nickleson, he complained that he had done everything possible to moderate the "Violent Temper of the Warm & indiscreet People here," but to no avail. Although Galloway had grudgingly signed the various addresses and petitions passed by the Congress, he insisted that he did not approve of them: "They are too warm & indiscreet and in my Opinion have not pursued the right Path to Accommodation."[14]

Sam Adams, who had been so instrumental in bringing many of the events of the previous year to pass, left Philadelphia almost immediately after the Congress adjourned. During his time in Philadelphia, Adams had always had one eye turned toward Boston; his correspondence with friends and family was nearly wholly preoccupied with the fate of his hometown. But he had, through forceful lobbying rather than public speaking, been as influential a presence in the Congress as any man there. He had not gotten all that he wanted. He had chafed when the Congress admonished Boston to resort to arms only for "defensive" purposes. He feared that the British military might overpower his town and his colony before the Congress had even completed its deliberations. He lamented that the Congress had limited its list of grievances to only those British violations of American rights beginning in 1763, and he would probably have preferred an even bolder denial of British authority in America. But by keeping his cool and letting others do most of the talking, he had helped to forge a rough consensus among the delegates that would pay off in a big way in the months to come.

Sam Adam's cousin John had, as we have seen, gone through many mood swings during his seven weeks in Philadelphia. The delegates who gathered in Carpenters' Hall beginning on September 5 may not have been, as John claimed, as contentious in their dealings with one another as "Ambassadors from a dozen belligerent Powers of Europe," but upon their arrival in Philadelphia, the potential sources of difference among them might have operated as powerfully to divide them as their common grievances over the provisions of the Coercive Acts to unite them. With only a few exceptions, however, they understood that the suppression of individual egos and provincial interests was important if they were to achieve the sorts of compromises that would make common cause possible. Even Adams himself, though he may have indulged himself in private rants to his diary or to Abigail, restrained himself in his public utterances.

Looking back on the events of that first Congress, in fact John Adams found much to be pleased with. In his autobiography, which he began writing more than a quarter of a century later, he gave himself primary credit for the drafting of the Declaration of Rights and Grievances and, summing up his work that fall, he noted that while he had entered Philadelphia as an unknown Massachusetts lawyer, by the time he left Philadelphia on October 28, he had established a "reputation much higher than ever I enjoyed before or since." As was often the case, Adams elevated excessively both his contributions to the Congress and the reputation he had gained from his contributions. But there is no doubt that he would never again enter the town of Philadelphia merely as an obscure Massachusetts lawyer.[15]

As the delegates took their leave of Philadelphia, none of them could with any confidence predict what the future would hold. Most probably occupied the same intellectual and emotional ground as John Dickinson—outraged at British infringements of their rights and deeply suspicious of the "designing" and "misguided" royal officials and members of Parliament who were, in their overwrought state of mind, intent on "enslaving" the king's loyal subjects in America. But at the same time, they remained just that—loyal subjects— and for that reason they had, in addition to signing on to strong measures aimed at resisting British policies and practices, signed on as well to humble supplications to King George III.

A few, like Galloway, still opposed militant resistance. With 20/20 hindsight we can see that those like Galloway who wished to avoid independence at any cost were justified in their opposition to the course the Congress had adopted, for it was a course that would make it more difficult, not easier, to achieve any sort of accommodation. There were a few, but only a few—Sam Adams, Patrick Henry and Richard Henry Lee—who might have wished for even bolder action. In Sam Adams's case, that desire was borne less out of a commitment to independence per se than it was out of the fear that British military power, directed at Boston, was not likely to be restrained by mere words, or even by economic boycotts. Henry's and Lee's positions were probably shaped more by temperament than by any sense of immediate danger to their colony, for in spite of Lord Dunmore's increasing hostility toward Henry in particular, the threats to Virginia's economy and polity were nothing like that confronted by the Bostonians.

The Evolution of a "Congress"

However much individual delegates to the First Continental Congress may have differed in their diagnoses of and prescriptions for Boston's and America's plight, the Congress, as a collective body, had made remarkable strides during the seven weeks that it had been in session. The delegates had come together as a group of strangers, vaguely in agreement on the need to respond in some way to the Coercive Acts, but also with a clear sense that they were coming to Philadelphia at least as much to defend the provincial interests of their individual colonies as they were to act in the name of a continental entity called "America." But, gradually, most of the delegates began to think in continental, rather than provincial terms. The seven weeks that they had spent together inside Carpenters' Hall hammering out the language of their various resolves, addresses and petitions helped create some of that cohesion. But equally important, the convivial experience of dining together in the city's taverns, of being royally entertained almost nightly in the homes of Philadelphia's most prominent and affluent citizens and even the discomfort of being crammed together in the tiny bedrooms of the city's boardinghouses, acted in powerful ways to promote mutual respect and, in most cases, affection and friendship.

The First Continental Congress operated on two levels—as America's first response to an immediate economic and political crisis, and gradually, as the duly constituted government of the "united colonies" of America. Equally important, first in endorsing the Suffolk Resolves and subsequently in the specific prescriptions for resistance embodied in the Association, the First Continental Congress began to act like a government. The Association not only prescribed a specific course of action, dictating even the specifics of which items would or would not be included in the embargo on trade with Great Britain, but it also vested authority in specific institutions—most notably, the local committees—in the enforcement of American intentions. By empowering the local agencies to carry out its agenda, the Congress was able to increase its authority and its credibility as a body dedicated to serving the common good of the people of the colonies as a whole. As we will see in subsequent chapters, there would be occasions on which local committees would show excessive zeal in carrying out their enforcement obligations, but on the whole, congressional sanction tended to moderate, not agitate, the actions of local committees. The local committee of Hanover, New Jersey, for example, vowed to end "all unlawful, tumultuous and disorderly meetings of the people," and in York County, Maine, the committee labeled "Riots, Disorders, or Tumults" as "subversive of all civil government [and] destructive to the present plan proposed and recommended by the Continental Congress for our deliverance."[16]

On October 22 the delegates agreed that another session of the Congress would be convened on May 10, 1775, "unless the Redress of grievances, which we have desired be obtained before that time." John Adams, as he was leaving Philadelphia on October 28, recorded in his diary that "it is not very likely that I shall ever see this Part of the World again." It is not clear whether Adams genuinely believed this or whether it was simply an expression of wishful thinking, but of course, he would be mistaken. That redress of grievances would not be forthcoming. Indeed, by the time the Second Continental Congress convened, America would find itself at war with England. John Adams, along with many of those delegates who had spent that fall in Philadelphia, would find that their residence in that city would be of far longer duration than they had ever imagined.[17]

ELEVEN

ESCALATION

A S THE MASSACHUSETTS delegation to the Second Continental Congress prepared to set out for Philadelphia in late April of
1775, they knew already that their trip would be different from that
of the previous year. There would be no leisurely pace, no relaxed and
convivial evenings with local politicians along the way. Outright warfare had erupted in the Massachusetts towns of Lexington and Concord on April 19. One of the sparks that ignited the military conflict
in those towns was a widespread rumor that the British army had
mobilized to arrest Sam Adams and another, new addition to the
Massachusetts delegation, the wealthy Boston merchant and fire-
brand John Hancock.

Adams and Hancock, who had been meeting in the Lexington
home of one of Hancock's relatives, had intended to return to Boston
in order to pack and prepare for their trip to Philadelphia. But with
British soldiers actively seeking their arrest, they were now on the
lam. They holed up in Woburn, a town a few miles from Lexington
and Concord, for a few days, and then on April 24 made their way to
Worcester, where they managed to stay out of sight until they were
joined five days later by the other three Massachusetts delegates—
John Adams, Thomas Cushing and Robert Treat Paine.

How had the climate of opinion, and the pace of events, changed
so quickly in less than six months? The answer to that question lies in
the behaviors of a wide swath of people—from King George III to his
subjects in England, from provincial American leaders in the colonies'
legislatures to the people of the colonies at large. Events on both sides

of the Atlantic after the adjournment of the First Continental Congress served only to widen the breach between, on the one hand, the king and his British subjects and, on the other, Americans of all social classes. With the benefit of hindsight, we find it hard to imagine how outright hostilities between British army regulars and American militiamen could have been avoided. But no one at the time possessed that acuity of vision, and the events of late October 1774 to early May 1775 unfolded in often chaotic and unpredictable ways.

The British React to America's Plea for Peace and Harmony

The First Continental Congress had labored long and hard on its Address to the King. The closing lines of John Dickinson's final draft, endorsed and signed by the delegates on October 26, wished "your majesty . . . every felicity through a long and glorious reign over loyal and happy subjects," emphasizing that the delegates' most "sincere and fervent prayer" was that "your descendants may inherit your prosperity and dominions 'till time shall be no more.'"[1]

John Adams argued at the time that Dickinson went too far in his expressions of love and affection for the British sovereign, but, as later events would make clear, King George III felt otherwise. Three of America's colonial agents in London—Benjamin Franklin, Arthur Lee and William Bollan—presented Congress's Address to the King to the British secretary of state, Lord Dartmouth, on December 21. Dartmouth, seeing "nothing in it improper," agreed to send it along to the king, and later reported back to Franklin that the king had received the petition "graciously" and would present it to both Houses of Parliament when they next convened. In fact, Dartmouth was being wholly disingenuous. He had heard no such thing from the king and had no expectation that the king would receive the Congress's petition favorably. Indeed, on January 24, 1775, he had sent a message to the royal governors of the American colonies ordering them to "use your utmost endeavours to prevent" the appointment of delegates to the Second Continental Congress and to "exhort all persons to desist from such unjustifiable proceedings, which cannot but be highly displeasing to the King."[2]

George III eventually transmitted the Congress's Address to the House of Commons on January 19, along with a large packet of 148 other documents relating to the growing crisis in America, but aside from that nominal gesture, the king, far from responding "graciously" to the petition, refused to acknowledge that he had read it or even seen it. And most members of Parliament either ignored the Address or regarded it as treasonous. When Franklin, Lee and Bollan petitioned Parliament on January 26 asking for permission to speak before the body in support of the Address to the King, one indication of Britain's mood was that their request was overwhelmingly rejected, by a vote of 218 to 68.[3]

Although few then or now have been inclined to attribute to King George impressive powers of intellect, he was neither stupid nor illiterate. Not only was he able to read beyond the words in the Continental Congress's petition praising him and to understand the seriousness of the petition's denial of parliamentary authority, but his eyes were focused even more sharply on another document that represented an even greater, and more concrete, threat to royal authority in America. When he read the language of the Association, he declared: "The New England governments are now in a state of rebellion; blows must decide whether they are to be subject to this country or independent."[4]

Not surprisingly, members of the British Parliament who had been the direct target of the Congress's wrath fully agreed with their king. Not only had their authority over the colonies been brazenly challenged, but, even more insulting, their motives and personal characters were being described with terms like "wicked," "designing" and "dangerous." During the previous disputes over the Stamp Tax and the Townshend Duties, Americans could count on at least a few influential friends in and out of Parliament. Men like William Pitt the Elder, who during the Seven Years' War had been chief minister (an office that later would be called prime minister) and Edmund Burke, warned the king and his ministers about the dangers of abandoning a policy of salutary neglect. But although Pitt and Burke still sought to soften the harsher punishments laid down in the Coercive Acts, their efforts at persuading their fellow members of Parliament to adopt a more conciliatory policy toward the colonies were undercut by the language of the addresses and resolutions coming from the American Congress. When Pitt, the First Earl of Chatham, introduced a motion into the House of Lords asking the king to order General Gage to remove his troops from Boston in the hopes of easing tensions, his proposal was treated with contempt and overwhelmingly defeated. He also introduced legislation that would have restored some of the power to provincial juries taken away by the Coercive Acts, but accompanying that proposal was a statement asserting Parliament's supremacy over the American colonies, a clear refutation of the central argument of all of the Congress's addresses and petitions. Even that was too lenient for Chatham's colleagues, and they rejected that attempt at conciliation as well.[5]

Frederick, Lord North, who would over the course of the next year become the object of intense hatred among nearly all Americans, had the dubious distinction of serving as the king's chief minister during the years leading up to the American Revolution. Thus, it fell on his shoulders to respond to all of the Congress's various addresses and petitions. His exceptionally poorly named "Peace Plan," adopted by both houses of Parliament in mid-March of 1775, declared Massachusetts in a state of rebellion and imposed additional sanctions on American commerce, sparing only Georgia, which had not participated in the First Continental Congress, and New York and North Carolina, which North mistakenly believed to be on the Crown's side. North later proposed that if a colony agreed to contribute its fair share for the "common defense and general government," by which he meant that if the colonies were willing to voluntarily tax themselves in an amount equal to those taxes being imposed by the British government, the government would, upon the approval of the king and Parliament, not exercise its right to levy taxes directly on that colony. One of the few parliamentary critics of North's proposal, David Hartley, a close friend of Benjamin Franklin, noted that North's plan was "not free but compulsory"; its essence was to proclaim: "give us as much money as I wish, till I say enough, or I will take it from you." Far from being the effort at "conciliation" that North claimed it to be, it further indicated how far the two parties on each side of the Atlantic were from one another.[6]

If there was any man in England who understood the folly of attempting to bring America to its knees through punishment, rather than through meaningful conciliation, it was Edmund Burke, the Anglo-Irish member of Parliament, political theorist, orator and, not at all coincidentally, paid lobbyist for the colony of New York. On March 22, 1775, after listening to the barrage of denunciation of the rebellious American colonies from his parliamentary colleagues, Burke rose in Parliament and pleaded with his colleagues to adopt a more conciliatory approach. It was a remarkable speech, both for its profound understanding of the unique character of the American colonies and for its repudiation of nearly all of the logic of current British policies toward America. Although Burke had never been to America, he began by observing that "a love of freedom is the predominating feature which marks and distinguishes" the people of the American colonies. And, he noted, "as an ardent is always a jealous affection, your colonies become suspicious, restive, and intractable, whenever they see the least attempt to wrest from them by force, or shuffle from them by chicane, what they think the only advantage worth living for. This fierce spirit of liberty is stronger in the English colonies probably than in any other people of the earth; and this from a variety of powerful causes."

Burke then proceeded to enumerate the reasons why Americans were so attached to and jealous of their freedom, the foremost of which was that "the people of the colonies are descendants of Englishmen." He reminded his listeners, that England "is a nation, which still I hope respects, and formerly adored, her freedom." He went on to present an extraordinarily perceptive catalogue of those aspects of life that were peculiar to America. He noted the exceedingly "popular" character of the American governments, in which representatives directly elected by their neighbors in local constituencies were esteemed as "the most weighty." He called attention to the effect in the colonies of dissenting Protestant religions, which further nurtured a jealous regard for the preservation of liberty. Anticipating the objection that the Church of England was the dominant religion in most of the southern colonies, he observed, with astonishing astuteness, that free white residents owned "vast multitudes of slaves. Where this is the case in any part of the world," he noted, "those who are free are by far most proud and jealous of their freedom. Freedom is to them not only an enjoyment, but a kind of rank and privilege. Not seeing there, that freedom, as in countries where it is a common blessing, and as broad and general as the air, may be united with much abject toil, with great misery, with all the exterior of servitude, liberty looks, amongst them, like something that is more noble and liberal." In that single piece of his analysis, Burke had captured the essence of why so many of the slaveholding gentry of the South were every bit as fiery in their defense of American rights as were their dissenting Protestant New England brethren.

Burke also pointed to patterns of education in America, which leaned particularly to the study of the law, a profession that made the Americans all the more attentive to their legal and constitutional rights as Englishmen. And finally, he noted the fundamental, geographic fact that may have acted more powerfully than all the rest:

> Three thousand miles of ocean lie between you and them. No contrivance can prevent the effect of this distance in weakening government. Seas roll, and months pass, between the order and the execution; and the want of a speedy explanation of a single point is enough to defeat a whole system. You have, indeed, winged ministers of vengeance who carry your bolts in their pounces to the remotest verges of the sea. But there a power steps in that limits the arrogance of raging passions and furious elements, and says, "So far shalt thou go, and no farther."

Having stated the causes of the Americans' extreme attachment to freedom, he pointed to the utter folly of attempting to coerce their submission by further punishment, by the very denial of freedom. "In order to prove that the Americans have no right to their liberties," Burke admonished, "we are every day endeavouring to subvert the maxims which preserve the whole spirit of our own. To prove that the Americans ought not to be free, we are obliged to depreciate the value of freedom itself." Such an effort, Burke insisted, was not only self-defeating, for Americans, far from submitting, would only grow more rebellious. But, equally serious, it was an effort that violated those very things "for which our ancestors have shed their blood."[7]

Burke's analysis and admonishment fell on deaf ears in Parliament, as, indeed, he knew it would. He would later note that he and the few others who opposed North's so-called peace plan did so "more for the acquittal of their own honour and discharge of their own consciences" than from any realistic hope that a majority of his colleagues would agree with him. Nevertheless, he accompanied his speech with a set of eleven resolutions, including a statement that Parliament would refrain from taxing the colonies, as well as proposals for the outright repeal of the Townshend Duties, the Boston Port Bill and the Massachusetts Government Act. These steps were, he argued, essential if the British government hoped to head off the secession of the colonies from the British Empire. In fact, in spite of Burke's vastly more sympathetic and realistic view of a path toward reconciliation between the colonies and the British government, most Americans would have found at least some of his proposals unacceptable. For example, Burke's proposals contained the necessary assertion—necessary, at least, from the perspective of any member of the British Parliament—of Parliament's superior power over any and all of the colonial legislatures. But it didn't matter, because the vast majority of the members of Parliament would have none of it. They emphatically rejected Burke's proposals by a vote of 270 to 78.[8]

It was not merely Parliament and the king who were unpersuaded of the justice of America's cause. Most members of Parliament, occupying safe seats that did not require that they expend any effort to win the voters' favor on election day, did not pay much attention to the opinions of their constituents. In this case, however, it appears that most of those constituents would have agreed with their parliamentary representatives. The Address to the People of Great Britain adopted by the First Continental Congress on October 21, 1774, may or may not have been widely circulated on the other side of the Atlantic, but either way, the English people seemed largely unmoved by the colonists' plea for their support. Even British merchants, the one group that had in the past tended to side with the Americans because of the ill effects that a boycott might have on their businesses, were at best divided on whether to make any concessions to the Americans.[9]

Strengthened Resolve at Home

And so in the several months after the conclusion of the First Continental Congress, it became clear that that body's efforts to reach some sort of accommodation—largely on American terms—had failed miserably. Yet the Congress's actions, and the British government's hostile reactions to those actions, would prove strikingly successful in strengthening the resolve of Americans and their leaders. In spite of Lord Dartmouth's stern instructions to royal governors to clamp down on the opposition in their colonies, all of the colonial legislatures, with the exceptions of those of New York and Georgia, had within a month of the Congress's adjournment endorsed the addresses, petitions and, most important, the call for the creation of the Association to enforce the boycott on all trade with the British. At the same time that they endorsed the Congress's proceedings, most colonial legislatures moved quickly to elect delegates to the Second Continental Congress to meet in May, a clear sign that many of them were already pessimistic about the prospect of their grievances being satisfactorily addressed in London. Somewhat tardily, on April 7, 1775, North Carolina, which, along with New York and Georgia had been excepted from Lord North's order for punitive actions against American commerce, disappointed the British chief minister by announcing its support of the Second Continental Congress and selecting its delegates. On that same date, North Carolina's royal governor, Josiah Martin, dissolved the legislature.[10]

The royal governors did indeed have the power to dissolve recalcitrant provincial assemblies, but by now that act was nearly useless. If dissolved, the assemblies simply continued to meet as extra-legal conventions or congresses in taverns and churches. In the face of increasingly united resistance from the colonies' provincial political leaders, and lacking the military power to coerce them into submission, the royal governors all watched any semblance of authority over the colonies they were supposed to be governing slip away. In Virginia, the royal governor, Lord Murray, the Earl of Dunmore, who had taken up his position only in 1771, in the midst of deteriorating relations between royal officials and provincial leaders, found himself unable to enforce his will on an implacably hostile Virginia "convention." Challenged by Lord Dartmouth to put a stop to such rebellious behavior, Dunmore assured his superior that he was doing everything in his power to bring the Virginians to heel, but, he confessed, every effort to "counteract the dangerous measures pursuing here . . . is entirely disregarded, if not wholly overturned." The particular bane of Dunmore's existence was Patrick Henry, who, when the Virginia Convention met in St. John's Church in Richmond on March 23, 1775, to select its delegates to the Second Congress, resoundingly rejected efforts at accommodation with Great Britain. Henry immortally proclaimed,

> It is in vain, sir, to extenuate the matter. Gentlemen may cry, Peace, Peace, but there is no peace. The war is actually begun! The next gale that sweeps from the north will bring to our ears the clash of resounding arms! Our brethren are already in the field! Why stand we here idle? What is it that the gentlemen wish? What would they have? Is life so dear, or peace so sweet, as to be purchased at the price of chains and slavery? Forbid it, Almighty God! I know not what course others may take; but as for me, give me liberty or give me death![11]

The New York provincial assembly, still operating under the strong influence of conservatives like James Duane and John Jay, refused even to recognize the resolutions and petitions of the First Continental Congress as binding on their colony. Although Jay, Duane and other New York delegates to the First Congress had reluctantly signed on to the decisions of that body, their support of actions such as the Declaration of Rights and the Association was tepid at best. Moreover, when they returned home to their own provincial legislature—a body dominated by wealthy upstate manor lords and conservative New York City merchants—they discovered that the mood among those legislators was actually hostile to the initiatives proposed by the Congress. Indeed, on February 17, 1775, the legislature refused even to give a vote of thanks to the New York delegates who had served in the Congress; on February 21 it refused to endorse the Association; and on February 23 it refused to appoint a delegation to the Second Continental Congress. In March, the legislature approved its own petitions to the king and Parliament, the language of which included a general statement of colonial subordination to Parliament and was notably milder than that of the petitions from Congress. Once again, however, the gulf between British political opinion and even the most moderate American opinion proved unbreachable. Both Houses of Parliament refused even to consider the New York petition, and although George III received the petition with a "gracious expression of regard," according to Lord Dartmouth, he was nevertheless not moved to act on it.[12]

In January of 1775, a provincial "Convention" replaced New York's provincial assembly, which had been prorogued by the governor. On April 21, that Provincial Convention appointed delegates to the Second Continental Congress. Their delegation would be a large one, including all of the members of the First Congress except for Isaac Low. New delegates were Lewis Morris, Philip Schuyler, George Clinton, Francis Lewis and Robert Livingston.[13]

One colony of the thirteen was absent from the first months of the Second Congress. Georgia, which in 1774 had a population of about 40,000 people, nearly evenly divided between free whites and black slaves, was the youngest of the English colonies in America. For the most part, it had been relatively uninvolved in the protests against British attempts to tax the colonies in the previous decade. Preoccupied with purely local concerns—in particular an ongoing conflict with American Indians on its western frontier—Georgia had not sent a delegation to the First Continental Congress and would continue, at least for the first part of the Second Congress, to remain absent. But at least some of the residents of the colony were beginning to awaken to the fact that a threat to the liberties of neighboring colonies might be a threat to their own. On July 4, 1775, nearly two months after the Second Continental Congress began its meetings, the Georgia legislature formally approved the actions of the First Continental Congress and elected members to join the delegates already serving in the Second Continental Congress. Finally, all thirteen North American mainland colonies had joined together to delegate at least some measure of authority to a Congress that could now claim to represent the "united colonies of America." And with the endorsement of its previous actions by all of the colonial legislatures except for that of the stubbornly cautious New York, it had gained yet another important measure of legitimacy in its effort to speak for those united colonies.[14]

The People's Resistance

Revolutions do not happen by accident, nor are they affected simply through the will of a small cadre of political leaders. They can only be successful if they gain the broad, active support of the people at large. For such support to happen, an organizational structure is needed that mobilizes and channels the popular will. Among the most important actions of the First Continental Congress had been the creation of the Association, which by November 1774, began to show results. The Association would pave the way for the creation of a multitude of grassroots organizations unprecedented in America's colonial history.

Beginning in November and continuing through and beyond the battles at Lexington and Concord on April 19, 1775, popularly elected local committees effectively took control of local government in nearly all of the American colonies. Even in New York, where the provincial legislature had explicitly refused to endorse the Association, local committees nevertheless sprang up, seizing the initiative and radicalizing the American resistance beyond anything that most of New York's political leaders would have desired.[15]

Americans had used the device of the economic boycott as a way of protesting British policies on previous occasions—most notably during the Stamp Act crisis in 1765 and as a way of forcing repeal of the Townshend Duties a few years later. But those boycotts were loosely organized and relied on voluntary compliance, which in some colonies proved only partially effective. The great task facing the local committees charged with carrying out the provisions of the Association was *enforcement*. Article Eleven of the Association stipulated that these popularly elected local committees would closely "observe the conduct" of the communities' residents, and if a majority of the members of the committee found that any member of a community was violating the boycott of British goods, the committee would "forthwith cause the truth of the case to be published in the gazette; to the end that all such foes to the rights of British Americans may be publickly known, and universally condemned as the enemies of American liberty; and thenceforth we respectively will break off all dealings with him or her."[16]

The essence of the enforcement mechanism of the Association was, then, not to be physical violence against the offenders, but, rather, *shame and ostracism*, which were, apparently, great motivators. During the first year in which the committees' efforts took hold, the value of commercial imports from Great Britain to America decreased from £3,000,000 in 1774 to £220,000 in 1775.[17]

One of the most striking features of the Association was the vagueness with which the small group of men in the First Continental Congress had delegated authority to these local committees. They made no attempt to keep the enforcement of the economic boycott in their own hands, nor did they spell out what they thought the size or composition of the local committees should be. Aside from a provision that restricted voting in the selection of committee members to those eligible to vote for representatives to their legislatures—in most colonies free, white males who owned at least a modest amount of property—residents of each locality were free to form their committees as they saw fit. By delegating such important authority to local committees, the Congress had, either wittingly or unwittingly, extended political authority to some 7,000 Americans, most of whom had never before exercised political leadership in their communities. And they interpreted the grant of authority given to them liberally. Not only did the size and composition of the hundreds of local committees that sprung up across America vary considerably, but, equally important, some committees felt free to exercise their authority across an area that extended well beyond commercial regulation.[18]

As time went on, many of the committees began to operate as extra-legal governments themselves. Drawing their authority as much from the people in the local communities who had elected them as from the Congress that had created them, many of the committees began to operate as de facto governments themselves. In so doing, they were, simultaneously strengthening the legitimacy and authority of the Congress and at the same time staking out their claim as independent entities, sharing power with that Congress. The mutually supportive roles of both the Congress and the people of America at large would prove to be of greater and greater importance as Americans across all of the colonies began to debate in earnest the possibility of declaring America's independence from Great Britain.[19]

Most of the new Association committees were scrupulous in adhering to the mandate laid out for them by Congress, taking care, in the words of the Richmond, Virginia, committee, "to "confine ourselves literally within the line of duty marked out to us by the Continental Congress." But that did not mean that there were not significant variations in the way in which the committees did their business within their local communities. In Sutton, Massachusetts, for example, the Association committee reflected the Puritan heritage of that community. On the one hand, the Sutton committee members were reluctant to take precipitous action in publicly shaming those who had violated the boycott. "What," the Sutton committee asked, "if there should appear any symptoms of sorrow and hopes of repentance" among the violator? The Sutton committee members concluded that those who publicly apologized might be restored "to fellowship" without having to endure being publicly rebuked. On the other hand, the Sutton committee offered little leniency to those who refused to cooperate in giving information about possible violations, including heads of families who refused to "use his or her parental authority in obliging all under them strictly to observe said Association."[20]

On occasion, though, other committees were not so scrupulous in discussing and implementing enforcement and punishment procedures that conformed to the guidelines issued by Congress or to the wishes of the local community. In Connecticut, Simon Deane, brother of congressional delegate Silas Deane, lamented that the committee's work was often marked by "so much petty mobbing and disorder." And in Anne Arundel County, Maryland, a committee that learned that the owners of a ship had imported tea in violation of the terms of the Association, ordered that the tea be removed from the ship and burned; but that was not enough for some in the community, who threatened to tear down the house of one of the owners of the vessel and who were successful in coercing local merchants not only to burn the tea, but the ship as well.[21]

There was at least one occasion in which local enforcement of the Association had a direct impact on the Continental Congress itself. In November of 1775, when Martha Washington was scheduled to pass through Philadelphia on her way to join her husband at his encampment in Boston, a number of Philadelphia's most prominent residents, including some of the members of Congress, arranged to stage a fancy dress ball at City Tavern in her honor. As some of the town's residents became aware of the elaborate arrangements for the event being made at City Tavern, they began to express their anger at a festivity that would be in such obvious violation of the austere directives of the Association. On the day of the ball, Christopher Marshall, a Quaker member of Philadelphia high society, was told that if the ball were held that evening, City Tavern "would cut but a poor figure tomorrow morning." Marshall first tried to find John Hancock, who was by then serving as president of the Congress, to warn him. Unable to find Hancock, he managed to track down Sam Adams and asked him if he could intervene and arrange to call off the ball. Adams, whose strict Puritan lifestyle made him especially sensitive to the ways in which a fancy dress ball might be perceived by the residents of the city, called together a meeting at the American Philosophical Society of the event's organizers, and they agreed call it off. A few members of the organizing committee, perhaps joined by Hancock, then paid a visit to Martha Washington to explain to her that out of respect for "our worthy and brave General, now exposed in the field of battle, in defense of our rights and liberties," it would be best if she did not attend the ball, a request to which she agreed. Later that evening, congressional delegate Benjamin Harrison, a wealthy Virginia planter who was used to fancy affairs of the sort planned in honor of Mrs. Washington, lambasted Sam Adams for his role in canceling the event. Harrison declared that it was not only a "legal," but a "laudable" tribute to both the general and his wife. Martha Washington never recorded her feelings about the sudden cancellation of the event, but in the eyes of many Philadelphians, the decision may well have saved the Continental Congress's principal after-hours meeting place from total destruction![22]

If the committees overseeing the implementation of the Association were, on the whole, restrained in their enforcement of the boycott, British officials hardly saw it that way. Virginia's Lord Dunmore compiled a catalogue of their abuses, including their "illegal searches," their surveillance of "every inhabitant without distinction" suspected of wrongdoing, their harsh interrogations and their efforts to stigmatize anyone they suspected of violating what he derisively referred to as "the Laws of Congress." This last, disparaging reference to the laws of Congress was, much as Dunmore would have been loath to admit it, yet another proof of the legitimacy the Congress had gained through its decision to authorize the creation of the local committees. The net effect of all of this, Dunmore grudgingly acknowledged, was devastating to his power and authority. Lawful government, he wrote to his superiors back in London, had effectively ended. Nor was Dunmore the only royal official in America complaining about the challenges to his authority. In North Carolina, Governor Josiah Martin complained of evil demagogues who were manipulating the passions of the people in much the manner of a puppeteer pulling the "magic wires" of puppets. Even in Georgia, where things had been relatively calm for most of the decade, the royal governor there, Sir James Wright, wrote to officials back in London that "the licentious spirit . . . has now gone to great a length" so that there was little he could do to control it.[23]

More than any previous American action, the creation of the Association brought the conflict with England down to the local level, with an effect that was felt in people's daily lives. Not surprisingly, there were at least some Americans who shared Lord Dunmore's distaste for the committees. A conservative New Yorker, Samuel Seabury, later to become a Tory, complained that the committees, which relied on "mobs and riots," were imposing a "tyranny, not only over the actions, but over the words, thoughts, and wills of the good people of this province." And one Philadelphian, obviously voicing the views of the increasingly pro-British Joseph Galloway, claimed that the committees "aimed at a general revolution, and were promoting every measure to overthrow our excellent Constitution;—drunk with the power they had usurped, and elated with their own importance, they were determined on nothing so much as to increase discord and confusion." There were no doubt others, in New York, Philadelphia and elsewhere, who may have felt unease at, or perhaps even opposed, the actions of the local committees of the Association, and it is likely that the charge given to the committees to use shame and ostracism as a means of enforcing the terms of the boycott may also have served to coerce into silence many of those who felt that unease. But on the whole, what is striking about the implementation of the Association was the extent to which all elements of society—artisans and mechanics as well as merchants and lawyers, radical activists as well as individuals inclined to a more moderate stance—came together in common cause in enforcing the boycott. Even in Philadelphia, where there was no shortage of British sympathizers, some of the town's most conservative merchants, such as Thomas Wharton, chose to join radicals like Charles Thomson, Joseph Reed and Thomas Mifflin on that city's committee in hopes of tempering some of its actions.[24]

The First Continental Congress had never been conceived by any of its members as a revolutionary body. Indeed, many of the politicians from New York and Pennsylvania who had first proposed it hoped that it would be just the opposite—a gathering of thoughtful and deliberative men who would work to moderate the behavior of some of the more radical New Englanders and find a peaceful path toward reconciliation with their mother country. But in creating the umbrella organization of the Association, the Congress had taken an important step toward transforming American resistance to British policies from one consisting of isolated acts of protest emanating from a few commercial cities and colonial capitals of government to a grassroots movement affecting nearly every town and county in America. In so doing, the Congress had taken a huge step in rendering British institutions of government in America virtually powerless, while at the same time granting authority to altogether new American institutions of government—from the elite body of the Continental Congress to the popularly elected local committees charged with enforcing the Association. It was the beginning of a truly revolutionary transformation in American government. But it was, of course, only the beginning. With the outbreak of war on April 19, 1775, that revolutionary transformation would accelerate. The committees of the Association, working with newly formed "committees of safety," would become the agents of revolution.

General Gage's Dilemma

By the winter and early spring of 1775, Massachusetts' military governor, General Thomas Gage, found himself in an unenviable position—thoroughly detested by the residents of Massachusetts and nearly wholly disrespected by royal officials back in London. He was receiving increasingly strident orders from London to crack down on the Massachusetts resistance. Lord Dartmouth had told Gage's predecessor, Thomas Hutchinson, that all those who signed the Association should be considered guilty of treason, and Dartmouth meant for Gage to begin treating them as traitors. But given the relatively modest military force at his disposal—probably fewer than 3,500 troops—Gage knew he could never contain the escalation of resistance occurring not only in Boston but throughout the Bay Colony. As he wrote to Lord Dartmouth, the people of the colony were "numerous, worked up to a fury, and not a Boston rabble but the freeholders and farmers of the country." He estimated that it would take at least 20,000 troops, about seven times as many as he had at his disposal, to subdue the rebellious spirit in the colony. By January of 1776, he had already sensed the size and spirit of the rebellion: "if you would get the better of America in all your disputes, you must conquer her."

But his masters back in London would have none of it. Ignoring his call for additional troops, Gage's superiors in London sent back angry missives denouncing him as "devoid both of sense and spirit." Disputing Gage's claim that the opposition was numerous and that it had the support of the great majority of the people of the colony, Lord Dartmouth, who had never set foot there, characterized the Massachusetts opposition as a "rude rabble without plan, without concert, and without conduct." He considered Gage's request for 20,000 troops ridiculous. All Gage needed to do was to arrest the "principal actors and abettors in the provincial congress" and punish them swiftly and, Dartmouth predicted, the opposition would cower into submission. If Gage were not up to the task, many of his critics in London complained, then he should be replaced by someone of greater "spirit."[25]

Gage had been bombarded with these petulant messages from his superiors in London all of the winter and early spring of 1775, but in mid-April of 1775, he received a more formal directive from Dartmouth. The letter was actually dated January 27, but because of further tinkering with its language and then a particularly slow passage across the Atlantic, it did not reach him until April 14. It ordered him to arrest the leaders of the Massachusetts resistance and to seize any munitions the rebels had been storing. Whether through wearied resignation or through a sudden jolt of pent-up anger and frustration over the king's subjects whom he was supposed to be overseeing, Gage swung into action. His sudden gathering of all the British troops at his disposal was impossible to hide from Bostonians, who had already been fearing such action. In that sense, the course of events of April 19, if not their precise timing, had been long anticipated.[26]

On that day, as the Massachusetts' delegates to the Second Continental Congress readied themselves to leave the following week for Philadelphia, the shots heard round the world were fired, first at Lexington, and then, in a far bloodier confrontation, in Concord. The evening before, the fiery Boston orator Dr. Joseph Warren, who was himself the target of possible arrest by the British army, met with Paul Revere. He asked Revere to ride to Lexington and warn Sam Adams and John Hancock that a company of British soldiers was traveling to Lexington to arrest them and then to move to Concord to seize the guns and ammunition that the Boston patriots had stored there. In fact, Gage's orders from Lord Dartmouth placed top priority on the seizing of the arms and ammunition in Concord, but if Gage were able to capture Boston's two most dangerous rebels in the process, all the better.[27]

Fearing that someone might tip off the Bostonians to his plan to march British troops on Concord, Gage issued an order prohibiting anyone from leaving the city. But Revere, leaving his home on North Square, a few blocks from the North Church about 10:15 p.m., quickly mounted his horse and rode to a wharf on the waterfront of the Charles River in the North End of Boston just before Gage's troops received the order. There he met two friends, Joshua Bentley and Thomas Richardson, who would help him row a small boat across the river. They were nearly spotted by a British warship on the river, but Revere's vessel, shrouded in a dark shadow of an unusually bright moon, managed to sneak by and reach the other side of the river by about eleven p.m. Meeting with a group of patriot sympathizers, he announced, "I want to git me a horse." His patriot greeters were well-prepared: they furnished him with one of the fastest horses in town, Brown Beauty, a mare belonging to John Larkin, deacon of the local Congregational church. Revere then set out, on his famous midnight ride, heading north across Charleston Neck and then turning west on the road to Lexington, hoping to find Adams and Hancock in time to warn them of their impending arrest. Eluding British troops along the way, Revere rode toward Lexington, warning people along the road of a possible British attack. He arrived in Lexington around midnight, and was joined there about a half hour later by another rider, William Dawes, who had taken a different route across the dangerous and heavily patrolled Boston Neck. The two men met with Adams and Hancock in the home of one of Hancock's relatives, warned them to get out of town and then continued to Concord, sounding the alarm of the British attack along the way. At about 5:30, just as the sun was rising, a shot was fired in Lexington—we will never know which soldier from which side pulled the trigger first—and then a volley of fire erupted from each side. It was a brief skirmish, but eight Lexington townspeople were killed and nine wounded. At the moment those shots were fired, Adams and Hancock were hiding in the fields, "near the scene of the action." They made their way to the parsonage in the town of Woburn, northwest of Lexington. Later in the day, at Concord, the Massachusetts militiamen and the British regulars would engage in sustained combat; at the end of the day, the toll of dead and wounded among the militiamen stood at around ninety, and among the British regulars some 250. The American Revolutionary War had begun.[28]

Adams and Hancock had avoided arrest, or some more terrible fate, by leaving the scene of battle before it had actually begun. But even after the fighting at Lexington and Concord had ended, and with the British soldiers now actively seeking their arrest, they had no choice but to hole up in Woburn for a few more days. On April 24 they made their way to Worcester, about forty-seven miles west of Boston, where they stayed out of sight until they were joined by Thomas Cushing and Robert Treat Paine. Ever concerned about his appearance, Hancock had managed in the immediate aftermath of the battles to get some proper outfits of clothing, probably brought to him in Worcester by his wife, Dolly, and his Aunt Lydia. Adams, who had escaped from the British with nothing more than the typically soiled and tattered clothes on his back, had to rely on Hancock's generosity to purchase a new suit of clothes for his journey to Philadelphia.[29]

The four Massachusetts delegates left Worcester on April 28, riding toward Hartford, where on April 29 they met up with the fifth, John Adams, who had been delayed due to illness. They banded together with members of the Connecticut delegation somewhere around Stamford. From that point on, the two delegations were accompanied by armed guards, and, as news of the battles of Lexington and Concord spread, they were greeted in every town through which they passed by frenzied crowds cheering their progress and denouncing their British foes. In New York City, it seemed as if every man, woman and child turned out to celebrate their arrival. John Hancock's description of their welcome in New York is vivid if also egocentric:

> When we Arriv'd within three Miles of the City we were Met by the Grenadier Company and Regiment of the City Militia under Arms, Gentlemen in Carriages and on Horseback, and many Thousand of Persons on Foot, the Roads fill'd with people and the greatest Cloud of Dust I ever saw. In this Scituation we Entered the City, and passing thro' the Principal Streets of New York amidst the Acclamations of Thousands . . . the Numbers of Spectators increas'd to perhaps Seven Thousand or more . . . no Person could possibly be more notic'd than myself.[30]

Sam Adams, already becoming thoroughly weary of Hancock's penchant for self-promotion, would later describe him as behaving as if he were an "oriental prince," and this tension would continue during their time together in Congress. But that bit of personal rivalry aside, the Massachusetts and Connecticut delegations, now joined by the delegates from New York, moved together toward Philadelphia. As they made their way into the city on the morning of May 10, escorted by some 200 militiamen with their swords drawn, the streets were lined with people jubilantly shouting their welcome.[31]

A profound shift in the popular mood had taken place between the adjournment of the First Continental Congress in late October of 1774 and the convening of the Second Congress in May of 1775. The First Continental Congress had been a closed affair in which leading politicians and intellectuals sought simultaneously to defend what they esteemed to be their constitutional liberties while at the same time seeking a path toward reconciliation with their mother country. By May, in the aftermath of Lexington and Concord, the delegates would begin their deliberations in Congress amidst an aroused and engaged American population—a population that was prepared to cheer their efforts on behalf of American liberty, but which might also be prepared to turn wrathful if the delegates appeared out of step with the fast-evolving state of popular opinion. In the fall of 1774, the delegates might have been able to convince themselves that they were leading public opinion, but by May of 1775 many of those delegates would find themselves in a struggle to keep up with the popular mood.

TWELVE

A NEW CONGRESS,
CHANGED CIRCUMSTANCES

W HEN THE "GREENE country towne" of Philadelphia was first settled in 1681 by the English Quaker William Penn, the tenets of the Society of Friends, including religious tolerance and nonviolence, were central to the daily life of the town. By 1775 only fifteen percent of Philadelphians were members of the Society of Friends, but the city was still widely known as a Quaker town, and the adherents to that sect continued to dominate the politics and the economy of the city. In spite of the Quakers' commitment to pacifism, more than a few delegates were struck by the martial atmosphere of Philadelphia's public spaces as they arrived for the Second Continental Congress in May of 1775. Thousands marched to the sounds of fifes and drums. "All Ranks and Degrees of men are in Arms," reported North Carolina's Joseph Hewes, and "all the Quakers, except a few of the old Rigid ones, had joined in." Such was the military fervor in the city that supplies of drums, flags and "Colours" were running low.[1]

The Delegates Re-assemble

Fifty of the sixty-five delegates to the Second Continental Congress had served in the First as well. Well-acquainted and for the most part bound in common purpose, they were ready to take on the work at hand. Some of the new additions, in particular, John Hancock and

Benjamin Franklin, would add considerably to the prestige and political clout of the gathering. Philadelphia lawyer James Wilson, still a relatively obscure political figure within his colony, would contribute significant intellectual depth to the discussions about to get under way. And Robert Morris, Philadelphia's wealthiest resident, would prove to be an important representative—for better and for worse—of the city's powerful merchant community.

Two colonies would send significantly bigger delegations than the others. New York, which had already sent a large, if largely skeptical, delegation to the First Continental Congress, sent five additional delegates—George Clinton, Francis Lewis, Robert R. Livingston, Lewis Morris and Philip Schuyler. All five wielded substantial political power within their colony, and most would use that power to buttress their colony's resistance to any radical steps toward escalating the conflict with England. Virginia's delegation, already one of the strongest in the Congress, would be augmented six weeks into the session by the still relatively little-known Thomas Jefferson—who would join his colony's delegation when Peyton Randolph, once again having to withdraw due to the press of business back home, departed from Philadelphia after only two weeks on the job.[2]

And even Georgia would finally get into the act, though at first it was through unusual means. Lyman Hall of St. John's parish in Georgia timidly knocked on the door of the Assembly Room of the State House on May 13. He asked if he might be admitted to the Congress as a representative of his parish, which, he told them, had unsuccessfully sought to induce the remaining parishes in the colony to join the gathering. Deciding that it was better to have representation from a part of Georgia than none at all, the delegates admitted him. It would take another two months for the Georgia provincial legislature to get its act together and send a full delegation.[3]

Joseph Galloway had spent the early months of 1775 unleashing a stream of vitriol at the key members of the First Continental Congress. The leaders of that Congress, Galloway wrote, were nothing more than "wretches" whose minds were "fraught with dark and sinister designs." He was convinced that the Congress had as its objective that "ill-shapen, diminutive brat, INDEPENDENCY." Though selected by the legislature to serve, Galloway declined, deciding that he could have more impact on the course of events by using his influence in the Pennsylvania provincial legislature to keep his colony on a moderate course. Although there remained in the New York and Pennsylvania delegations members who shared at least some of Galloway's views, his absence would be felt, for there was no one in the Second Continental Congress who possessed his combination of political clout and determination to avoid independence at all costs.[4]

The Pennsylvania Assembly again offered the Assembly Room of the State House for use by the delegates. This time they would accept with alacrity. With Galloway's influence in decline, the leaders of the Congress apparently felt no need to assert their independence from the marginalized Pennsylvania legislator. And with ten additional delegates, it's likely that the elegance of Carpenters' Hall no longer compensated for its cramped rooms. On May 10 the delegates formally convened. Although there was probably a good deal of informality and fluidity in the seating arrangements inside the Assembly Room, it appears that the delegates from each colony gathered together, arranging themselves in a circular pattern, with those from the southern colonies sitting on the south side of the room, the delegates from the mid-Atlantic region arranging themselves in a semi-circle on the west side of the room and the New England delegates on the north side of the room.

In their first act, they unanimously re-elected Peyton Randolph as their presiding officer and Charles Thomson their secretary. The delegates later agreed that "the rules of conduct in debating and determining questions laid down by the last Congress be adopted and observed by the present Congress." They also reiterated their commitment to the rule of secrecy, but this time underscored its importance, enjoining the delegates to abide by the rule "under the strongest obligations of honor." This more emphatic reaffirmation of the rule of secrecy may have been occasioned by an awareness that some had not been entirely scrupulous in observing the rule during the First Continental Congress, but a more likely explanation is that the delegates knew they were now involved in a *war* in which lives might be put at risk by an impolitic sharing of the Congress's deliberations.[5]

Following the selection of officers, and no doubt moved by their powerful memories of the electrifying sermon he delivered during the opening days of the First Congress, the delegates asked the Reverend Jacob Duche to open the proceedings the next day with prayers. He did so apparently to a similar effect, delivering "a most pathetic and pertinent prayer." The delegates spent the remainder of that second day reading and discussing a report from America's colonial agents in London describing the unfavorable reception of the First Congress's petitions by the English Parliament. They also received depositions from towns in and around Lexington and Concord describing the events of April 19. The peace-loving residents of Lexington and Concord, deposition after deposition reported, had not provoked the conflict. On the contrary, the onset of armed hostilities owed entirely to the aggression of the British soldiers, who, in addition to taking innocent lives, "plundered," "ravaged" and "destroyed" everything in their path. By inserting both the agents' report and the depositions into the minutes of the Congress, the delegates clearly intended to reinforce their contention that their peaceful petitions to Parliament and the king had been ignored, and that, in spite of the call from the First Continental Congress to put the colonies in a state of defense, the violence that erupted on April 19 had been wholly unprovoked.[6]

The delegates next agreed to operate as a committee of the whole, rather than as a formal legislative body bound by parliamentary rules of procedure, as with the First Continental Congress. The "committee of the whole" was a fairly common practice, used for more than a century in both Parliament and by many colonial legislatures, and it would allow the Congress to proceed more informally, with flexible rules of debate and with the opportunity to reconsider any decisions upon which they had agreed earlier. And indeed, the sessions of the Congress during the next several weeks were of a very different character from those of the First Continental Congress. The primary cause of that difference, however, was not merely the procedural device of operating as a committee of the whole. Rather, the fundamental character of the Congress's business had changed dramatically from the First to the Second. During their earlier gathering, the delegates had earnestly debated the nature of America's constitutional relationship with the mother country, the extent of Great Britain's transgressions on American liberty and the best means of obtaining a redress of American grievances. By May of 1775, with issues relating to the limits of British power largely settled, and with at least one of the American colonies already at war with Great Britain, the task confronting the Congress was very different. In the fall of 1774, the Congress had begun to act like a legislative body, passing resolutions, such as that creating the Association, that would have a binding effect on the colonies represented there. By the spring of 1775, the Congress, while by no means abandoning its legislative function, began to assume an executive function as well, attempting to manage the mobilization of America's military efforts against the British.[7]

Beginning on Tuesday, May 16, the delegates would start to confront the full range of issues before them. First and foremost, the outbreak of hostilities at Lexington and Concord required that they take immediate steps to bolster the military forces not only in Massachusetts but in surrounding colonies. This task was given greater urgency by the news, which reached Philadelphia the following evening, that a small group of American militiamen led by Ethan Allen had made a successful raid on the British fort at Ticonderoga on Lake Champlain. In addition to the escalating military situation, the members of the Congress would need to deal with the response—or nonresponse—of the king and Parliament to the various petitions and addresses sent by the First Continental Congress.

Richard Henry Lee opened the debate by putting before the Congress a bold plan for raising an army. It would not be a rag-tag collection of individual colonial militias, but a truly "continental" army. Although he did not speak on the subject, Colonel George Washington strongly supported Lee's proposals and, indeed, had most likely discussed them with Lee before and during their trip together from Virginia's Northern Neck to Philadelphia.[8]

But there was dissent in the ranks. South Carolina's John Rutledge, though ostensibly supporting Lee's proposal, began to equivocate. He insisted that before moving to organize an army, "some other points must be settled." The most important of these was the question of whether "we aim at Independency" or, as he obviously preferred, whether it would be prudent to make further requests to England "for a Restoration of rights & putting of Us on Our old footing." New York's Robert Livingston, new to the Congress, sided with Rutledge. At that point, John Adams rose, and in a lengthy speech that almost certainly irritated some in the room, complained that Rutledge and Livingston were merely rehashing old business. He reminded the delegates that the First Congress had already agreed that the principles of the English constitution guaranteed to the colonies an absolute independence from *Parliament*. Any talk of "independency" beyond that purely constitutional relationship between the colonies and Parliament was, Adams argued, simply unnecessary. But of course the question was not that simple. It would prove all but impossible to avoid a discussion of next steps—both political and military—in light of the king's contemptuous response to the petition drafted by Adams and others at the conclusion of the First Congress.[9]

John Dickinson Takes the Floor

In the midst of the discussion of Lee's proposal on May 16, John Dickinson rose to his feet and embarked on an extended presentation of his own plan for confronting the present crisis. At that moment, Dickinson probably had a greater claim to representing the views of the vast majority of members of Congress than any other delegate. Although he had made his entrance into the First Continental Congress late in the game, he had immediately enhanced his standing among his fellow delegates by his key role in drafting the language of many of the petitions and addresses that were eventually sent to London. Men like Charles Thomson, who had worked so hard to persuade Dickinson to cooperate in the mobilization of opposition to the Coercive Acts in Philadelphia, while having no doubt about the strength of Dickinson's commitment to defending American liberty, knew also that his cautious and deliberative cast of mind would likely make him an advocate of restraint, not revolution. But at the moment he spoke, there was no one in the Assembly Room who was more likely to gain the attention of his fellow delegates than John Dickinson.

His address to the delegates was classic Dickinson—thoughtful, logical but, ultimately, cautious in its approach to solving the problems confronting the Congress. He joined Richard Henry Lee in supporting "Vigorous preparation for Warr," and, if the war should persist, "a Vigourous prosecution of it." But the bulk of his speech, lasting nearly an hour, amounted to a plea for continuing efforts at "a reconciliation if it is possible." However much he might have hoped for a good result from the First Congress's petitions to the king, Parliament and people of Great Britain, Dickinson had been shocked when he heard news of Lexington and Concord. He would describe those events in a letter to Arthur Lee as an "inexpressibly cruel War began with the butchery of unarm'd Americans." He now had to face the fact that the British had not been swayed either by the righteousness of the Americans' cause or the logic of their petitions. "The Rescript to our petition," he concluded "is written in Blood. The impious War of Tyranny against Innocence has commenc'd in the neighbourhood of Boston." And yet, at least initially, Dickinson told Lee that the repressive actions of the British were an aberration. He continued to tell himself that they were the work of a "few worthless persons," "fools and knaves," who had somehow come to dominate the British ministry. And he saw reason for hope. As the Second Continental Congress was preparing to meet, Dickinson found cause for optimism in the news that nearly 400 London merchants had petitioned Parliament to ease up on their coercive policies toward the Americans. (He seemed to ignore evidence that at least an equal number of London merchants sided with the government's punitive policies.) By Dickinson's reasoning, if Congress remained firm, but at the same time resisted the temptation to act rashly, a sufficient number of the members of Parliament would see the error of their ways.[10]

In his May 16 speech Dickinson suggested that while the colonies should vigorously resist any British attempt to tax them for the purposes of raising a revenue, they should cede to Parliament the right to regulate America's trade for the good of the whole empire. Silas Deane recorded his "disgust" with the spirit of timidity underlying Dickinson's speech, acknowledging that Dickinson had argued his points "smoothly," but, ultimately, "sophistically."[11]

Dickinson continued to argue for further attempts at reconciliation in subsequent weeks. In a lengthy and elaborately constructed speech, which he delivered on May 23, he laid out what he believed to be the three alternatives facing the Congress. America could, he began, move forward with preparations for war without making any effort either to petition the king or to send agents to England in search of an accommodation. While this might have the effect of "encourag[ing] our friends and terrify[ing] our enemies," it also ran the risk, if the British did not back down, of having "the War brought down upon Us with greater Fury before We are properly Prepared." Dickinson believed—and he was no doubt correct—that the king and his ministers would not stand down in the face of American preparations for war. In his analysis of the mood of Parliament and the ministry, he displayed a sophisticated understanding not only of the workings of the English government but also of the balance of power within Parliament and the ministry. And the picture he painted was a gloomy one. While acknowledging that America had a few friends in Parliament—men like Lord Chatham and Edmund Burke—he noted, acerbically and accurately, that those very men were deemed to be "personally odious to the King." And, lest Americans fool themselves that there was some hidden reservoir of support for them in the Parliament at large, he correctly observed that a clear majority of the members of Parliament believed that Great Britain was "contesting for her very existence in this Dispute with America." As long as the majority held that view, a satisfactory resolution of the conflict would be impossible. To make matters worse, there was every indication that the people of England, at least in their present, ill-informed state of mind, fully supported the belligerent views of their parliamentary representatives. The result, he predicted, would be almost certain war, with "many valuable lives lost that might be saved & much other Destruction that might perhaps be prevented."[12]

Dickinson's description of the likely war that would ensue may have struck many of his listeners as excessively pessimistic, but as things turned out it was also prescient. The popular outrage following Lexington and Concord may have led to a sense of self-righteous exhilaration within America—that Americans could, because their cause was *just*, win a quick and speedy victory over their adversary. But, Dickinson warned, "we have not yet tasted deeply of that bitter Cup called the Fortunes of War."

The Multitude thrown out of Employ by the loss of their Fisheries and the stoppage of their Trade—Disease breaking out among their Troops unaccustomed to the Confinement of an Encampment—Divisions in any one province which might interrupt provisions or Relief going to their Aid by Land—the Enemies superiority forbidding it by Sea—the Difficulties from Distance if no other Objections—The danger of insurrection by Negroes in Southern Colonies—incursions of Canadians & Indians upon the Northern Colonies.

And perhaps even more to be feared: the "false hopes—selfish designs" and "Civil Discords" that inevitably accompanied the "tedium" of a long and bloody war. It was imperative, Dickinson insisted, that Americans exhaust every possibility before plunging themselves into such a struggle.[13]

But what alternatives remained? In defiance of all of the evidence that he had previously laid out with respect to the state of opinion among members of Parliament, the king's ministers and the people of England, Dickinson clung to the belief that if the colonies persisted, peacefully and with "Unanimity & Firmness," they could win over a majority in Parliament and "within 12 months dethrone the ministry."[14]

The second option proposed by Dickinson—to continue preparations for war but simultaneously to petition the king and Parliament for relief—was in his view better than the first. But given the failure of their past petitions, Dickinson admitted that this too was unlikely to be successful. So Dickinson championed a third option—the dispatching of American agents to England to negotiate a settlement.

Dickinson spoke at some length on this third option. He wove back and forth between pessimism over the state of Anglo-American relations and optimism that American concessions on the matter of Parliament's authority to regulate trade for the benefit of the whole empire, along with a concerted diplomatic effort, might swing English public opinion to their side. Dickinson hoped that a careful negotiation between capable and flexible American agents (although he had in the past clashed with Benjamin Franklin in the local politics of Pennsylvania, he must have had the good doctor in mind here) and the British king, might result in a form of treaty spelling out a limited set of American obligations to the mother country while at the same time providing explicit protections from encroachments on fundamental American liberties.

He also anticipated criticism that his position was excessively timid and subservient to English interests. Far from being an indication of

American timidity, Dickinson argued, such an approach might be seen as an evidence of American strength. After all, when the king and Parliament first received the petitions from the Continental Congress, England had not yet "lost a battle," but Lexington and Concord had changed all that. Moreover, Americans were now "more united & and more determined beyond all Comparison" than they had been just six months earlier, a fact, he claimed, not lost on the British.[15]

The author of the famed *Letters from a Farmer in Pennsylvania* was an eminently rational man, a systematic thinker and writer. But his long, rambling speech to the Congress on May 23 was filled with contradictory logic and contradictory evidence. A thoroughly detached listener—and there may have been none of those in the chamber that day—might have been able to see that Dickinson was engaged not only in an argument with those "extremists" advocating more radical action, but also in an argument with himself—between his head, which could easily see the gravity of the situation, and his heart, which still insisted on allegiance to the king and the empire.

Dickinson predicted that his speech would not be pleasing to many of the delegates, and he was correct. Patrick Henry rose to his feet that same day and in a lengthy retort hotly disputed Dickinson's proposal to offer trade concessions to the British. In doing so, he argued, the body would be repudiating the very position it had taken six months earlier in its Declaration of Rights and Grievances. Even more odious to Henry, Dickinson had left the impression that he was prepared to backtrack even further, going so far as to volunteer to repay the East India Company for the tea destroyed in Boston. Richard Henry Lee and Thomas Mifflin would quickly side with Henry against Dickinson, but that was predictable. More tellingly, South Carolina's John Rutledge, who had often been on the fence in the fall of 1774, stepped forward to denounce Dickinson's plea for reconciliation. Silas Deane, recording a few details of the debate in his diary, recollected that Rutledge had treated Dickinson's plan "with the utmost Contempt," opposing "any Concession whatever" to Lord North and the British ministry.[16]

Uncharacteristically, John Adams appears not to have spoken during this particular debate, although in the coming weeks he would make clear his contempt for Dickinson's point of view. Dickinson, he later commented, was attempting the impossible by holding "the sword in one hand and the olive branch in the other." Adams ridiculed the notion that American agents could somehow succeed in "the education of the sovereign, . . . the Lords, the Commons, the electors, the army, the navy, the officers of the exercise, customs, &c, &c, &c," when all of those individuals and agencies had proven themselves so irretrievably corrupted. For Adams, "powder and artillery are the most efficacious, sure, and infallible conciliatory measures we can adopt." But Adams, at least temporarily, kept his peace, for even he realized that provoking discord among the delegates at that moment would be counterproductive.[17]

Adams knew too that Dickinson had his supporters, some of whom, especially the delegates from New York, genuinely agreed with him. Others, although they held out little hope that further petitions and negotiations would do much good, nevertheless saw no harm in going the extra mile to seek a reconciliation—so long as that reconciliation occurred on American terms.

Over the course of the days between May 23 and May 26 a variety of delegates proposed resolutions aimed at charting America's next steps. Late in the day on May 26, the delegates reached tentative agreement. The first three of the four resolutions adopted that day passed unanimously. The first was purely rhetorical, stating the obvious fact that "his Majesty's most faithful subjects" had been placed in a "dangerous and critical situation" by the concatenation of events culminating in the battles of Lexington and Concord. The second, making specific reference to the warfare in Massachusetts, vowed to put all of the colonies in a state of defense in support of the residents of that colony. The third, again an exercise in rhetoric and not action, offered a perfunctory plea for "a restoration of harmony between our Mother Country and these colonies." The fourth resolution, which passed only narrowly, agreed to open negotiations with the British "in order to accommodate the unhappy disputes subsisting between Great Britain and these colonies." That request for negotiations was to be included in a petition to the king, a petition of the sort envisioned all along by John Dickinson.[18]

Dickinson had, at least for the moment, gotten his way. But all of the resolutions passed on May 26 were exceedingly vague. They did not specify the means by which the colonies would defend themselves, nor did they spell out the precise language of the petition to the king or the method by which negotiations might be carried out. Although satisfying those like Dickinson who wanted to go the extra mile to seek reconciliation, they did not yield any ground on the subject of Parliament's authority over the colonies. Although Dickinson may have seen the resolutions as a form of olive branch to the British, they did not include a concession about the right of Parliament to regulate trade. And, consistent with the position taken by both sides in the debate in Congress, the resolutions made it clear that the Americans were not only prepared to defend themselves but, indeed, that they were already taking steps to do so.

To fail to include the commitment to a determined military defense of the colonies would have run the risk of alienating another, even more important group in the country. Outside the walls of the Assembly Room of the Pennsylvania State House, the people of America, in town and county meetings across the country, had expressed *their* determination to resist British military advances. Although the delegates to the Congress had vowed to carry out *their* deliberations in secret, the growing militancy of Americans out of doors was becoming readily apparent to all. However much the delegates to the Congress may have believed in the efficacy of their strategy of secrecy, at some level they realized that they could not—should not—insulate themselves entirely from those people whose fates and whose freedom were at stake.

THIRTEEN

JOHN HANCOCK
ENTERS THE DRAMA

MOST AMERICANS KNOW at least one thing about John Hancock—he was the man who put his "John Hancock" at the very top of the list of signers of the Declaration of Independence, in a handwriting that was at least half again as large as that of any other signer. It was an outsized signature from a man with an outsized ego. During the decade leading up to independence, he had, depending on the direction in which the political winds were blowing, been at times one of the most visible and flamboyant opponents of British attempts to tax the merchants of Boston, and at others, a man who seemed wholly comfortable with some of the perks that royal officials were pleased to bestow upon him. Larger than life in many ways, John Hancock would play no small role in the Continental Congress during the year leading to independence.

As we have seen, when John Hancock and his fellow delegates from Massachusetts, Connecticut and New York rode into Philadelphia together on May 10, they received a heroes' welcome. Never a man to undervalue his own worth and standing among his fellow citizens, Hancock claimed that the focus of the public's attention was the most illustrious hero of them all—the bold, courageous leader of the fight for liberty in Massachusetts—none other than himself. Although a recent biographer has claimed that Hancock, "more than anyone else there, made enormous sacrifices and deserved [the] public acclaim," it is likely that at least two of Hancock's traveling companions—John and Sam Adams—would have had a different view of who deserved to be the objects of the public's affection that day.[1]

John Hancock came from a long line of Massachusetts ministers. His father, the Reverend John Hancock, was the Congregational minister in Braintree and probably the most respected man in town. The younger John Hancock was born in January 1737. The other Braintree lad, John Adams, a year older than Hancock, remembered the Reverend Hancock as "one of the most amiable and beloved of men" but described the son as having "a peevishness that sometimes disgusted and afflicted his friends."[2]

Adams's youthful acquaintance with John Hancock did not last long. In the spring of 1744, Reverend Hancock died of a sudden illness, leaving the family in relative poverty. But young John Hancock was not destined to live a life of deprivation. His uncle, Thomas Hancock, owner of the House of Hancock, Boston's most powerful and profitable merchant house, but childless after thirteen years of marriage, promised Reverend Hancock's widow that he would support her and her children for life if she allowed her oldest son John to come to Boston and live with him as his adopted son. And so, from the age of seven, John Hancock was raised in one of the wealthiest and most opulent households in all of Boston.

John Hancock's life on Beacon Hill was altogether different from his early childhood in Braintree. Where he had once dressed in the plain clothes suitable to a young son of a Puritan minister and had gone to a small, local elementary school, he now wore the clothes of a young gentleman and attended Boston Latin, the town's most prestigious private school. At the age of thirteen and a half—an early age even at a time when it was not unusual for boys to enter college in their middle teens—he was admitted to Harvard, where he was ranked fifth in his class of twenty, purely as a result of his social standing. Because of his youth, Hancock resided during his freshman year at the home of a congregational minister in Cambridge, but in his sophomore year he moved into Harvard's oldest building, Massachusetts Hall, which then served as the dormitory for all Harvard students (today it houses Harvard's president and other university officials). In spite of the college's injunction to students to lead "sober, righteous, & Godly lives," Hancock used a portion of his newfound independence to indulge in frequent bouts of drinking. During one binge, he and his friends made a slave owned by former Harvard President Edward Holyoke drink to "such a degree as greatly endangered his life." That particular episode caused the ruling elders at Harvard to "degrade" his class rank down to ninth, an unusually severe punishment.[3]

Whereas both Sam and John Adams had been diligent students at Harvard, Hancock did not allow either intellectual ambition or diligence to get in the way of having a good time. He continued merrily in his partying, drinking ways. When he graduated in 1754, his academic record was wholly undistinguished, but he wasn't concerned, because he had always had his eye on mercantile success, not academic honors. He immediately went to work for the House of Hancock, where he began to learn not only the business but also how to emulate the affluent style of his uncle and adoptive father, Thomas. Still only eighteen, he began to dress in the most elegant clothing styles from London, outdoing even Uncle Thomas, wearing fancily ruffled shirts, silver-buckled shoes, gilt-edged jackets and one particularly stunning red velvet outfit. There were frills not only on his cuffs, but on his shirt front. He was every inch a dandy from his bob wig down to his fancy-buckled shoes. Fully comfortable with the flamboyance of his attire and of his personality, he began to socialize with other members of Boston's mercantile elite, continuing to indulge his taste for fine food and wine.[4]

But John also became serious about learning the business of being a merchant. He mastered not only the finances of what had become Boston's largest and most successful mercantile firm but also how to negotiate with the full range of people with whom a successful merchant had to deal—sellers, buyers, ship owners, captains and, perhaps most important, the ordinary seamen who manned the ships. In John Adams's recollection, Hancock "became an example to all the young men of the town. Wholly devoted to business, he was as regular and punctual at his store as the sun in its course."[5]

In 1760, John's uncle sent him to London. He spent a year there not only making the necessary connections with the city's leading merchants, but also raising his standard of living still further, spending a small fortune on an even more up-to-date English wardrobe, dining in the city's finest restaurants and, in general, taking advantage of the considerably higher standard of living available to a London gentleman. His expenses during that year were so high that they earned him a rebuke from his uncle. John responded that he had felt out of place by "the Plainess of my Dress," so, "to appear in Character I am obliged to be pretty Expensive."[6]

Whatever friction there may have been between John and his uncle quickly disappeared. When John returned to Boston in the fall of 1761 he was welcomed back into the firm. Indeed, he was quite obviously being groomed to take over the business. Thomas Hancock had been sick for some time, and when he finally succumbed to apoplexy in 1764, John, now twenty-seven, found himself the head of the House of Hancock, proprietor of a business with a large warehouse, several stores and a fleet of six ships, as well as contracts with dozens of other ship owners who helped the firm build its transatlantic trade.

Hancock would prove an excellent steward of the company, and an even more ostentatious symbol of its wealth. He spent even more money on clothes and fine food, and took particular pleasure in being driven around town in a coach made of gold. Hancock's conspicuous consumption and his obvious delight in displaying his wealth seems more appropriate to the twenty-first-century New York of Donald Trump than it does to eighteenth-century Puritan Boston, but most of the residents of the town—the Adamses perhaps excepted—seemed to enjoy sharing vicariously in his opulent lifestyle.[7]

Like most Boston mercantile firms, the House of Hancock had always managed to avoid paying at least some of the customs duties levied on goods imported into the port of Boston. To put it more simply, some degree of smuggling was a part of their business. In fact, John Hancock, as proprietor of one of Boston's largest firms, probably found it less necessary to smuggle than some of smaller merchants operating with only one ship. But it is likely that, prior to the enactment of the Molasses Act of 1764, which was aimed at tightening up on the enforcement of customs duties on that product, ships sailing under the banner of the House of Hancock may have smuggled in as much as a half a million gallons of molasses each year from the West Indies without paying the obligatory customs duties. When Parliament initiated its first serious attempts to enforce existing customs laws in 1764, and then followed up by imposing new taxes with the Stamp Act in 1765 and the Townshend duties in 1767, British customs officers, both suspicious and perhaps jealous of Hancock's lavish lifestyle, seemed particularly eager to make an example of him.[8]

This would all come to a head on April 9, 1768, when British customs officers boarded his ship *Lydia,* moored in Boston Harbor, suspecting that the cargo contained smuggled tea, paper and possibly other illicit goods. Hancock quickly mobilized a bunch of seamen who blocked the customs officials' access to the ship's hold. That evening, a customs agent without a search warrant tried to sneak into the hold of the ship to inspect the contents, but Hancock and a small mob captured him, brought him above-deck and dangled him over the side of the ship until the agent agreed he had no business aboard the *Lydia* that evening. British officials were forced to sit by and watch while Hancock's mob humiliated their agent. Part of the reason for their passivity owed to the fact that the agent had not gone through the proper legal channels in seeking to search the ship, but an even more important reason was that the size and passion of the mob was far greater than anything the royal officials could muster.[9]

The royal officials in Boston hardly forgot that moment of humiliation. A month later they sought revenge. This time they prepared a proper warrant to search another of Hancock's ships, the *Liberty.* Hancock's ship entered Boston Harbor with what was likely a full cargo of "the best sterling Madeira," most of it unreported on the ship's bill of lading. But Hancock was prepared for the customs officers. He managed to unload the illegal cargo in the dark of night. Later, finding cargo that only took up one quarter of the ship's capacity, the customs officials collected the required duty on that small cargo—about twenty-five casks of wine—but they knew they had been duped. Frustrated by their inability to prosecute Hancock for the wine they knew he had smuggled, they decided instead to lay in wait to find another excuse to get back at their nemesis. On June 10, after Hancock had reloaded the *Liberty* with what was most likely a legal cargo of whale oil and tar bound for England, the customs officers, aided by a detachment of sailors from the fifty-gun British man-of-war *Romney,* seized the *Liberty* on the trumped-up charges that customs documents had not been filled out properly. Hancock had not in fact posted bond on the cargo before it was loaded on board as he was technically required to do, but the common practice was to do so before the ship actually sailed for its destination. The customs officers then proceeded to tow the *Liberty* out into the harbor and to anchor it under the "protection" of the *Romney*. As the sailors were carrying out their orders, they were greeted by a hail of rocks and garbage thrown by a mob of "sturdy boys & negroes."

The story of the *Liberty* affair gained in the telling on both sides of the Atlantic. Sam Adams and the Sons of Liberty quickly put out the word that the seizure of the *Liberty* was a prelude to a full-scale British naval invasion of Boston. Royal Governor Francis Bernard, reporting on the event to his superiors back in London, made the mob action that night seem like the beginning of full-scale rebellion—a "trained mob," he claimed, was now in control of the town of Boston.[10]

In the aftermath of the seizure of the *Liberty*, the British attempted to prosecute Hancock for the alleged customs violations. Though Hancock no doubt was guilty of *some* customs violations, the evidence in this particular case was so flimsy that Hancock's defense attorney, none other than John Adams, was able to have it thrown out of court. Nevertheless, Hancock did suffer a considerable loss as a consequence of the *Liberty* affair, for the British permanently confiscated the ship, converting it to a coast guard cruiser charged with the task of patrolling the waters of New England in search of—surprise!—smugglers![11]

The *Liberty* would ultimately come to an unhappy end—burned to cinders and ignominiously sunk in Newport, Rhode Island, by a mob of protesters in July of 1769. But there would be one happy consequence of the *Liberty's* role in the coming of the American Revolution: it would propel John Hancock into even greater public prominence, not merely as the merchant prince of Boston, but, increasingly, as a political figure to be reckoned with. Hancock had begun to serve in the Massachusetts General Court, the colony's lower house of assembly, but in his elections to that body in the aftermath of the *Liberty* affair, his popularity soared, so much so that he was now receiving as many votes as his fellow legislator Sam Adams.[12]

In fact, the year 1768 would prove to be one that marked the beginning of an uneasy and highly competitive alliance between Hancock and Sam Adams. By 1768 Adams had already honed his skills as a provincial politician and as the principal organizer of opposition to British policy in the streets of Boston, and he had much to teach his younger colleague about the give-and-take of popular politics. The often shabbily dressed Adams was capable of putting his writing skills to work and crafting a sophisticated argument about America's constitutional liberties on one day and of printing an incendiary broadside aimed at mobilizing a mob the next. He served as an ideal intermediary between the affluent and socially prominent politicians who served in the Massachusetts provincial assembly and the artisans, mechanics, merchant seamen and unskilled laborers who made up the Boston mob. The fashionably dressed John Hancock, riding around Boston in his gold coach, seemed an unlikely candidate to become a favorite of that mob, but his spirited defense of his own economic self-interest in his battles with English customs officials was seen by the men who made up the bulk of the workforce for the House of Hancock—the merchant seamen of Boston—as a defense of their interests too. At Harvard, Hancock had shown much more interest in living the good life than in studying, and it's likely that he was much more interested in promoting his own interests than in philosophical concepts like the cause of liberty. Indeed, during the *Liberty* affair, the British had offered Hancock the return of his ship and, possibly, the dropping of all smuggling charges, if he posted the requisite bond and made appropriate gestures of obeisance to British authority. It was only after an angry confrontation with Adams, who intimated that Hancock would no longer be welcome in the Long Room Club and the Boston Caucus—the two radical organizations that essentially controlled the street politics of Boston—that Hancock turned down the offer.[13]

Adams would again have reason to challenge Hancock's patriotism in the latter half of 1770, in the wake of the Boston Massacre and after news of the repeal of the Townshend duties, the very taxes that had gotten Hancock in trouble in the first place, reached America. When Hancock heard reports of the confrontation between the Boston mob and Captain Thomas Preston and his British soldiers, he did everything he could to distance himself from the event, holing up in his Beacon Hill mansion until the furor died down. With the re-peal of the Townshend Duties, Hancock's motivation to be out front in his opposition to British policies began to wane.[14]

Between the summer of 1770 and the passage of the Tea Act in 1773, Hancock seemed to reach a rapprochement with Governor Thomas Hutchinson. In the spring of 1772, the governor went so far as to honor Hancock with an appointment as commander of the Company of Cadets, a "gentleman's militia" of eighty men that served as the governor's honor guard. Sam Adams was furious—both that Hancock had been given the honor and that he had accepted it. He grumbled that the governor had exceeded his power in offering the commission to Hancock in the first place. But even more annoying, it appeared to Adams that Hancock truly had gone over to the other side. Rumors had been circulating that the Crown, in its attempt to quash the rebellious spirit in Boston, was thinking about conferring a formal title of nobility on Hancock. Had King George III been craftier, he would have followed through and awarded the title, for, given Hancock's vanity, that might well have ended his association with the radical opposition in Boston.[15]

In the fall of 1772, it still made sense for Hancock to distance himself from the radicals. In spite of his past conflicts with British customs officers, Hancock's thoughts were still primarily about how to further the interests of John Hancock. Rapprochement, not further combat, seemed the best path toward that end. Certainly the idea of independence was nowhere in Hancock's mind. Thus when Sam Adams persuaded a Boston town meeting to create a Committee of Correspondence in November 1772, designed to inform the people of British infringements of their rights, Hancock declined an invitation to join. Not wishing to become alienated from Boston's radical politi-cal elite altogether, however, Hancock did agree, grudgingly, to sign an incendiary letter sent out to every town in Massachusetts contain-ing a long list of America's grievances against Parliament.[16]

At this point, the tensions between Sam Adams and Hancock were becoming obvious enough that Thomas Hutchinson began to think more actively about ways to drive a wedge between the two. He wrote to friends noting that "Hancock and Adams are at great variance," bragging that "I think we have so divided the [patriot] faction that it must be something very unfortunate which can unite them again." That "something very unfortunate" happened, and it proved to be two unrelated events. The first was the passage by Parliament of the Tea Act, which would revive popular opposition to British trade policies all over America and make it impossible for merchants like Hancock to remain on the sidelines any longer. The second, occurring quite unexpectedly, was the controversy over the stolen letters written by Governor Hutchinson and Lieutenant Governor Andrew Oliver to a former English treasury official, Thomas Whately, the very same letters that had landed Benjamin Franklin in the cockpit in his confrontation with Lord Wedderburn.[17]

Governor Hutchinson often wrote to his friend Thomas Whately back in England describing his travail in governing the obstreperous New Englanders. Those letters, meant only for his friend's eyes, were written with the candor and informality typical of purely private communications not intended to be read by the public. Though much of what Hutchinson wrote was unexceptionable, he did not hide his contempt for his radical opponents in Boston, and at one point averred that in order to quell that opposition, "there must be an abridgement of what are called English liberties." How Franklin came into possession of the letters remains a mystery to the present day. We do know, however, that it was Franklin's decision to send the letters to Sam Adams that landed the good doctor in the cockpit in London. When Sam Adams received them, he was unable to resist the temptation, in spite of Franklin's desire that they be kept confidential, to use them to stir up patriot opposition to the much-detested royal governor. In spite of his uneasy relationship with Hancock, he realized that their release might have more impact if his more conservative rival took the lead role. Sharing the contents of the letters with Hancock, he asked him to make an announcement to the Massachusetts General Court revealing the letters' controversial contents. Hancock, realizing that the explosive content of the letters could never be kept secret and that to fail to make an open break with Governor Hutchinson at this stage would be disastrous, agreed to do so. Two days later, Adams, with Hancock's full concurrence, recited passages from the letters to the assembly, after which

it voted by a margin of 101 to 5 to condemn the governor and his letters as having a "design and tendency . . . to subvert the constitution
and introduce arbitrary power into the province."[18]

From that time forward, Adams and Hancock, whatever the differences in their personal and sartorial styles, whatever their differences in ideology and temperament, were destined—or doomed—to
be partners in the fight against arbitrary British power in the colony
of Massachusetts.

By the time Hancock took his seat in the Second Continental
Congress on May 10, he was by no means unknown to those outside
of the Massachusetts delegation. The *Liberty* affair had become a *cause
célèbre* throughout the American colonies, and, as the story of Lexington and Concord gained in the telling, the roles played by Hancock
and Sam Adams were further inflated. Among the Massachusetts
delegates, Sam Adams was still most widely known as the wily activist
politician, and his cousin John as the most loquacious, and, to some,
the most obnoxious, member of the delegation. Hancock, though
initially known for his extravagant clothes and egocentric manner,
would, as time passed, be thrust into a more prominent role.

Neither Hancock nor Sam Adams could have predicted the circumstances that would put the flamboyant Massachusetts merchant into
that role. Sometime around May 21, the Congress's president, Virginia's Peyton Randolph, announced that he had to return home to attend to his duties as leader of the Virginia provincial assembly, now
meeting as the Virginia Convention. After considerable backstage maneuvering, John and Sam Adams, wrongly believing that Randolph
would return quickly, proposed that Hancock assume the chair. They
enlisted George Washington and his Virginia colleague Benjamin
Harrison to support the nomination. When the delegates unanimously
endorsed Hancock's appointment, Harrison escorted him to the front
of the room, reportedly commenting to the new president: "We will
show Great Britain how much we value her proscriptions."[19]

When Peyton Randolph returned to the Congress in September of
1775, both he and most of the other delegates assumed that Hancock
would step down and that Randolph would resume his position as
president of the Congress. But Randolph's "temporary" replacement
had no intention of stepping down. And the delegates, having no past

precedents either with respect to parliamentary procedure or simple, civil etiquette, sat passively by as Hancock continued in his role as president of the Congress. Randolph himself sat "very humbly in his seat," while "our new one," as John Adams caustically commented, "continues in the Chair, without Seeming to feel the Impropriety." Hancock would continue to sit in the armchair on the raised dais in the front of the Assembly Room for the next ten months, until the time when the delegates finally reached their final, epochal decision on the relationship of the American colonies with their mother country.[20]

FOURTEEN

CONGRESS ASSUMES
COMMAND OF A WAR

O N MAY 24, 1775, after John Hancock walked up to the table on the raised dais in the front of the Assembly Room in the Pennsylvania State house for the first time, the Congress began a discussion of "the state of America." Virtually everyone in the Congress would have agreed that America was in a perilous state indeed. Hancock and the Congress would quickly face a series of dramatic challenges. Their overtures to the king, Parliament and British people having been rebuffed, and facing renewed efforts at repression from royal governors throughout America, the members of Congress knew that they would have to respond on multiple fronts.

The previous week's news of the capture of Fort Ticonderoga raised Americans' hopes that they might be able not only to defend themselves within their own colonies but also to "liberate" Canada in the bargain. But the news also raised new questions about the Congress's role in overseeing an ever-expanding military conflict. As the militiamen commanded by Ethan Allen and Benedict Arnold stormed Ticonderoga (which at the moment of the attack was guarded by only two sentries; the other forty-two British soldiers at the fort were sound asleep), they cried out that they were taking the fort "in the name of the great Jehovah and the Continental Congress." While there is no record of what the great Jehovah thought of the raid, there is an abundance of evidence indicating that the Continental Congress knew nothing about the operation and, moreover, had no idea what to do with Fort Ticonderoga now that it was supposedly in their possession.[1]

It was one thing to agree on high-sounding resolutions about American rights and liberties, but quite another to take responsibility for managing the conduct of an expanding military operation. The Continental Congress, which had initially convened as an extra-legal assembly of representatives from individual colonies who owed their allegiance not to a "continental" legislature but to the British Crown, was evolving into a body that was not only assuming legislative powers binding on all of the British mainland colonies, but also making decisions about the prosecution of the war—an activity more commonly associated with the executive branch of a sovereign government.

The "success" at Ticonderoga, and, later, at the neighboring British fort at Crown Point, twelve miles to the north, raised other questions. The raids on Ticonderoga and Crown Point had been carried out in the name of the Continental Congress. But, in fact, they had been orchestrated by extra-legal committees of safety in Massachusetts and Connecticut, with the acquiescence of the rebellious provincial governments of those colonies, without the Congress's authorization. And the raids themselves had taken place on New York soil. New York's political leaders, who had never been enthusiastic supporters of any kind of militant resistance against the British, could hardly have been pleased by this escalation of warfare in their own territory. In the eyes of many New Yorkers, the so-called victory at Fort Ticonderoga was just another example of the way in which the Continental Congress was pushing their colony into a war they ardently wished to avoid.[2]

In fact, it had become clear as early as May 15 that, like it or not, New York's fate would be inextricably linked with that of Massachusetts. In the wake of Lexington and Concord, royal officials in London began to lay plans to send additional troops to America, and it was widely believed that New York, with its strategically important port and a population more likely to be friendly to British troops than the fanatics of Boston, would be a destination for many of those troops. On May 15, the New York provincial legislature formally requested advice from the Congress on how it should proceed if the British troops arrived in the colony. The Congress responded immediately, albeit incompletely: the colony should act only defensively, and with restraint, but, "defend themselves and their property and repel force by force." What it failed to do, at least at that juncture, was to give the

New Yorkers any guidance, or support, on just how their colony might raise the necessary armies to repel an attack by the British.[3]

Massachusetts and Connecticut were not the only colonies taking matters into their own hands. On May 23, the New Hampshire provincial assembly notified the Congress that it had gone ahead and ordered the raising of a militia force of 2,000 men—a step, the New Hampshire assembly explained, that was "too urgent to be delayed" until the Continental Congress came up with a coherent overall plan for the colonies' defense. Pointedly, the New Hampshire legislators also made clear that they had no idea how they were going to pay the costs of raising that force, suggesting that the Congress should take at least some responsibility in that effort. By contrast, New York, less eager than its neighbor to the north, had to be prodded by the Continental Congress to prepare itself for the rapidly escalating conflict. On May 23, the Congress instructed New York's militia to "be armed and trained and in constant readiness to act at a moment warning" and then issued more explicit instructions as to how and where they should plan for a possible British attack. And on May 31 the Congress took the further step of asking both New York and Connecticut to send reinforcements to the garrisons of Crown Point and Ticonderoga in order to defend those forts against a rumored British counterattack.[4]

All of these developments—the unauthorized initiatives of Massachusetts, Connecticut and New Hampshire, as well as the far less enthusiastic support of the war effort in New York—caused Congress to realize that it had to take a coordinated approach to what was likely to be a rapidly escalating military conflict. The most significant step in causing Congress to take that step occurred on June 9, 1775, when it received a lengthy letter from the Massachusetts Provincial Convention asking for advice on two important matters.

Ever since Parliament had passed the Massachusetts Government Act in early May of 1774 dissolving the Massachusetts General Court and putting the colony under the control of a military governor, the colony's legislature, even though it continued to meet, was doing so wholly in defiance of the law. Faced with the increasingly burdensome task of both raising an army and paying for the cost of an ever-expanding military campaign, the members of the legislature were eager to acquire for themselves a greater sense of legitimacy among those Massachusetts residents from whom they were asking ever greater sacrifices. Although they knew that their colony was in a state of outright rebellion against British authority, their commitment to an orderly, civilian government was, if anything, greater than it had ever been in the past. In the words of the Massachusetts petitioners, "the sword should in all states be subservient to the civil powers," and for that reason they believed it imperative that the civil power in Massachusetts be put on a firm legal basis. In asking the Continental Congress—itself an extra-legal body—to give them that legal sanction, they were, in effect, asking the Congress to acknowledge that their government was an entity entirely independent of royal authority.

The second request, though more straightforward, had equally momentous consequences. Noting that several colonies were now organizing their own militia forces, the Massachusetts legislators asked the Continental Congress to take formal responsibility for the "regulation and general direction" of the army, by which they meant, to create a "continental army."[5]

The Congress received the Massachusetts letter on June 2. Following their usual procedure, the delegates elected a committee the following day to consider the requests. That committee, consisting of John Rutledge, Thomas Johnson, John Jay, James Wilson and Richard Henry Lee, fairly represented the spectrum of opinion in the Congress concerning the most appropriate next steps to be taken to deal with the rapidly escalating crisis. Lee and Johnson were on the militant side, Jay and Wilson urged caution and John Rutledge, as was often the case, tried to occupy both sides. In this case, however, all of the committee members seemed to come together, and their recommendation, made on June 9, was promptly approved. The members of the Congress concurred in the logic of the Massachusetts provincial assembly's letter: by altering the charter of the colony, dissolving its legislature and virtually eliminating the offices of governor and lieutenant governor, the British Parliament had acted unlawfully. Therefore, the Congress recommended that the colony's extra-legal legislature write formal letters to the inhabitants of all of those towns entitled to representation in the assembly, requesting them to elect new representatives to a legislative body that would, under the terms of the Massachusetts

Charter of 1691, have a claim to be the duly constituted assembly of the colony. The new assembly would then elect "councillers" (meaning, members of the Governor's Council, which itself had become virtually defunct in the wake of the Massachusetts Government Act), and together the assembly and council would exercise the powers of government. The offices of governor and lieutenant governor were to be considered as vacant "until a Governor of his Majesty's appointment will consent to govern the colony according to its charter." In essence, the Congress had encouraged the political leaders of Massachusetts to go forward with the forming of a new government, based on the consent of the people of that colony, and not on that of the king or Parliament. While nowhere was the word "independence" mentioned, the practical implications of authorizing the creation of institutions based on a source of authority other than those of the king or Parliament, certainly led in that direction.[6]

While some in the colony would have preferred the stronger step of drafting a new constitution, thus declaring Massachusetts an independent state, members of Congress, in addition to being wary of any move that might be interpreted as an outright endorsement of independence, realized that the time and disputation involved in replacing the old colonial charter with a new constitution would result in an unacceptable delay in putting Massachusetts government on a solid footing. Of the Massachusetts delegates, the two Adamses are the only ones who recorded their opinions. John was reasonably content with the outcome. He grumbled a bit that "this continent is a vast, unwieldy machine," making it impossible to "force events," but he nevertheless believed that the Congress's recommendation was a step in the right direction. Sam Adams, although he continued to keep a low profile, acknowledged the frustration that "Business must go slower than one would wish."[7]

The decision on how Massachusetts should organize its government was the easy part. Massachusetts's request that the Continental Congress take over the command and control of the armies of the several colonies already involved in combat with the British proved much more difficult. Clearly, the direction of events on the battlefield was making it harder for the members of Congress to evade that responsibility, but still they hesitated. Writing to the members of the Massachusetts provincial convention notifying them of their recommendation respecting the colony's government on June 10, John Hancock equivocated, telling them that the Congress was so busy that it had been prevented from "Determining upon the other matters mention'd in your Letters to them."[8]

In fact, Hancock probably knew the direction in which the Congress was heading. John Adams, once again violating his oath of secrecy, wrote Abigail, telling her, strictly confidentially, that plans were in the works to field an army of 10,000 men in Massachusetts and 5,000 in New York "at the Continental Expence." That phrase would prove to be of crucial importance, both at that moment and in subsequent months, even years, for it meant that the Congress would take its first step not only in raising an army but also in seeking to find some way—as yet unknown—to pay for it.[9]

On June 14 the Congress moved in precisely the direction that Adams had suggested it would, agreeing to support 10,000 militiamen from Massachusetts and 5,000 from New York. More important, recognizing that the military conflict was not likely to be confined to Massachusetts and New York, the Congress unanimously agreed to raise ten companies of riflemen, six from Pennsylvania and two each from Maryland and Virginia. Notably, each rifleman to be enlisted in this new army was to sign a statement acknowledging that he was "voluntarily enlisted . . . as a soldier in the American continental army."[10]

With that, seemingly casual phrase, "American continental army," the Congress created the first, truly *American* army. It would prove to be a momentous step. At the time of its creation, the army was still viewed by many, perhaps most of the delegates, as a *defensive* force, not as the vehicle by which the American colonies would be the first political entities in the history of the world to fight for their independence from an imperial power. Few could have imagined that that defensive force would remain in the field for eight years of extraordinarily hardship and sacrifice. And few could have imagined that at the end of that time the existence and persistence of that army would, perhaps even more than the act of declaring independence, help forge a truly *American* national identity.

The next day, June 15, the Congress initiated what was probably the most important step in ensuring the success of its newly created "continental army." Secretary Charles Thomson's typically spare prose did not do the moment justice. The Congress first "Resolved: That a General be appointed to command all the continental forces, raised, or to be raised, for the defence of American liberty," with the sum of $500 per month allotted "for his pay and expences." Following that entry, Thomson wrote: "the Congress then proceeded to the choice of a general, by ballot, when George Washington, Esq. was unanimously elected."[11]

George Washington, Commander-in-Chief

The decision to select George Washington as commander-in-chief of the Continental Army would be one of momentous consequence, not only for the future of the American struggle for independence, but for the very future of the colonies as a unified nation. Washington, forty-three years old at the time and a colonel in the Fairfax County, Virginia, militia, was the only man in America who could claim to have a military reputation that went beyond not merely the borders of a single colony, but, indeed, all the way across the Atlantic. During the French and Indian War, first as a lieutenant colonel and then a commander of the Virginia militia, he had proved himself a leader of uncommon bravery and coolness under fire. Although the battles in which he was engaged just as often ended in defeat as in victory, Washington always managed to come away from them with his reputation enhanced. In one of those engagements, a battle with the French near Fort Duquesne in the Ohio Country in 1754, he recorded his impression: "I heard Bullets whistle and believe me there was something charming in the sound." That observation, which circulated widely both in America and abroad, caused even King George II to take notice of the brave and self-confident American.[12]

When on May 4, 1775, Washington set out for Philadelphia in his impressive chariot, guided by a coachman and a postilion (and accompanied once again by his servant Billy Lee), he had already heard news of the Battles of Lexington and Concord—he knew that

America—or at least Massachusetts—was now at war. Washington had packed the blue and buff uniform of the Fairfax County, Virginia, militia in his luggage, and beginning sometime in late May he began to wear the uniform to sessions of the Congress. Had any other delegate to the Congress—a civilian body—turned up in full dress military uniform, his fellow delegates would have regarded it as not a merely inappropriate, but a pathetic attempt to electioneer among the delegates for the appointment of commander of a continental army that had not even yet been created. But Washington? He no doubt appeared to the delegates as entirely in character—possessing what Philadelphia physician Benjamin Rush described as "so much martial dignity in his deportment that you would distinguish him to be a general and a soldier from among ten thousand people."[13]

During the month between its opening session on May 10 and June 15, as the Congress transformed itself from a debating society concerned primarily with defining the limits of British power to a wartime legislature, Washington began to play a much more active role in the Congress's business. Though he continued to remain relatively silent as a speaker in the Congress, his military experience made him an invaluable member of a large number of committees charged with the task of mobilizing American defenses.

Much has been written about the behind-the-scenes politicking that led up to the decision to select Washington as commander of the army. That there is still a perception—or misperception—that Washington faced significant competition for the post of commander of the Continental Army can be credited (or blamed) on the always voluble John Adams, who went to great lengths in his own recollections to put himself at the center of the decision-making process. If we are to believe Adams, the selection of Washington was not only not inevitable, but unlikely, and indeed, that the ultimate outcome of the decision to select Washington owed largely to Adams's efforts.

As John Adams recollected the events of the days leading up to Washington's selection, the effort to have Washington appointed to the post began a few days before June 15 while he and his cousin Sam were walking in the State House Yard. As they walked John unloaded all of his worries about the dire state of affairs upon his cousin, and then informed him that he intended that day to stand up in the Congress and propose the creation of a continental army with Colonel Washington in command. But, Adams further recalled, there was considerable sentiment in the Congress for appointing someone from New England to the post, for, after all, that region was bearing the brunt of the fighting. Adams also claimed that there were many delegates, both from Virginia and elsewhere, who opposed Washington's appointment on other grounds.[14]

The most likely candidate from New England was Artemas Ward, who had been serving admirably as commander in chief of the Massachusetts militiamen currently fighting the British in Boston. Another candidate was a Virginian, the forty-four-year-old Charles Lee. Born in England, he had spent nearly his entire adult life as a professional soldier, or, more accurately, as a soldier of fortune. He had fought for the British army in the French and Indian War in America and had a brief stint in Portugal, but he had also fought for both the Polish and Russian armies in such faraway places as Poland and Turkey. He returned to the American colonies in 1773 and in early 1775 settled in Berkeley County, in the northwestern portion of Virginia, in what is today West Virginia. Upon hearing of the conflict at Lexington and Concord, Lee rushed to the Bay Colony to offer his services, immediately demonstrating his abilities as a brave and experienced officer.

Although Horatio Gates's military career was perhaps not as colorful as that of Charles Lee, in other respects their lives went down similar paths. Gates had also lived most of his life in England and, like Lee, had fought valiantly in the French and Indian War wearing the British uniform. In the early 1770s, realizing that his upward advancement in the British army was being thwarted by his lack of sufficiently prestigious connections, he moved to America, and, like Lee, settled in Berkeley County. In the aftermath of Lexington and Concord, he too volunteered his services to the American cause, and, owing in part to a warm recommendation from George Washington, who had come to know him during the French and Indian War, established himself as an invaluable officer in the military conflict that was escalating in Massachusetts.

Finally, there was the president of the Congress, John Hancock, who, though his actual military experience was nonexistent, fancied himself a natural leader more than capable of carrying out the tasks of commander-in-chief. In his autobiography, John Adams expressed some doubt as to whether Hancock would actually have accepted the appointment had he been offered it, but he left no doubt that Hancock wished to be offered the appointment, if only "to have the honor of declining it."[15]

Adams was convinced that it was his championing of Washington, overcoming the objections of the New Englanders and even those of a few of Washington's fellow Virginians, that swung the balance toward Washington. In his account:

> I rose in my place and in as short a Speech as the Subject would admit, represented the State of the Colonies, the Uncertainty in the Minds of the People, their great Expectations and Anxiety, the distresses of the Army, the danger of its dissolution, the difficulty of collecting another, and the probability that the British Army would take Advantage of our delays, march out of Boston, and spread desolation as far as they could go. I concluded with a Motion . . . that Congress would Adopt the Army at Cambridge and appoint a General [and] that though this was not the proper time to nominate a General, yet I had reason to believe this was a point of the greatest difficulty, [and] I had no hesitation to declare that I had but one Gentleman in my Mind for that important command, and that was a Gentleman from Virginia who was among Us, and very well known to all of Us, a Gentleman whose Skill and Experience as an Officer, whose independent fortune, great Talents, and excellent universal Character would command the Approbation of All America and unite the cordial Exertions of all the Colonies better than any other person in the Union.

Adams went on to recollect that at that point, Washington, hearing his name mentioned, discreetly slipped out of his seat in the Virginia delegation and "darted into the Library Room" in order to allow the debate to proceed freely without his presence. John Hancock's reaction, according to Adams, was quite different: "Mortification and resentment were expressed as forcibly as his Face could exhibit them." Adams then reported that a lengthy and acrimonious debate followed. It was only after extensive consultations "out of doors," that those dissenting from Washington's appointment withdrew their opposition. At that point, Thomas Johnson of Maryland formally nominated Washington, after which the Virginian was unanimously elected. The *only* portion of Adams's recollection substantiated by other accounts is the last: Thomas Johnson did indeed nominate Washington, and the Virginia colonel was indeed then unanimously elected.[16]

If one pieces together the other accounts of the maneuverings behind Washington's appointment, the picture that emerges is of a decision that was less acrimonious than the one described by John Adams and certainly less dependent on Adams's politicking. While it is true that some of the New Englanders favored the appointment of Artemas Ward, they were also aware that Ward's health was in a precarious state. They were certainly open to other candidates, though they may have continued to prefer an individual from their own region. Other New Englanders, however, realized that the appointment of someone from outside their region would help counter the still-prevalent feeling that the actions of Massachusetts alone had gotten the American colonies into the fix they were in in the first place. And though there was support in some quarters for the appointment of Charles Lee, the fact that Lee had not been born in America and seemed willing to fight for anyone who would pay him appeared to some a disadvantage.

Whatever maneuvering there may have actually been surrounding Washington's appointment, the delegates' reaction to the Congress's decision was uniformly positive. Silas Deane, writing to his wife on the day of Washington's appointment, was unrestrained in his praise of the new commander: "Our youth look up to THIS Man as a pattern to form themselves by, who Unites the bravery of the Soldier, with the most consummate Modesty & Virtue." Connecticut's Eliphalet Dyer, who was one of those who not only wished to slow the progress toward independence but also would have preferred "one of our own" (which is to say a northerner) as commanding general, nevertheless acknowledged that Washington was "discreet & Virtuous" and "Sober, steady, and Calm." And Robert Treat Paine, writing to break the news to Artemas Ward, whom he had favored for the post, assured Ward that Washington was "heroic & amiable," and, as a bit of consolation, notified Ward that he had been appointed second in command.[17]

This sense of Washington as a man who somehow stood—literally and symbolically—above all the rest, had begun to take shape among the delegates from nearly the first day they encountered him during the First Continental Congress. The delegates immediately began to repeat the story—possibly apocryphal—that Washington had, in the weeks following passage of the Coercive Acts, volunteered to raise and support an army of 10,000 men at his own expense and march them to Boston for the defense of the people there. And although there is no record of his ever having given a significant speech in either the First or Second Continental Congresses, he had earned a reputation as a man whose actions spoke louder than words; he had supported all of the boldest recommendations in the two congresses, and his influence on other delegates out of doors—in the informal meetings of delegates in the taverns and private homes of Philadelphia—was almost certainly profound.[18]

Washington never revealed whether he wanted the job. There were certainly reasons why he wouldn't have, among them his pride of ownership of his highly successful plantation of over 8,000 acres looking majestically over the Potomac River. Although he had more than 100 slaves helping him with the cultivation of wheat and tobacco, the raising of livestock and running a small fishing enterprise, the task of keeping all of the many parts of his self-contained empire at his beloved Mount Vernon was time-consuming, and, according to Washington, immensely satisfying. Indeed, one of the most striking characteristics of nearly all of the Washington's letters back home during the many years when he found himself away from Mount Vernon is the extent to which they focus on every detail of the operations of his plantation, from the amount of manure to be used in fertilizing his crops to the precise placement of fences on the property.

John Adams's recollection that Washington immediately absented himself from the Assembly Room of the Pennsylvania State House when the delegates began to discuss the matter of the commander of the army is probably accurate, for Washington, in one of his very few comments at the time of his appointment, made it clear that he had never desired the position nor made any effort in his behalf to obtain it. In letters both to his wife, Martha, and to his Virginia neighbor Burwell Bassett, he insisted that the appointment was "an honour I by no means aspired to." Indeed, he claimed it was "an honour I wished to avoid," both because of his "unwillingness to quit the peaceful enjoyment of my Family [and] from a through conviction of my own Incapacity & want of Experience in the conduct of so momentous a concern." He went even further in a comment he apparently made to Patrick Henry, in which he asked his fellow Virginia delegate to "Remember what I now tell you: from the day I enter upon the command of the American armies, I date my fall and the ruin of my reputation."[19]

Washington persisted in these expressions of humility in his acceptance speech to the Congress, a speech in which at the same time he expressed his gratitude at the "high honour" accorded him, he confessed his "great distress, from a consciousness that my abilities and military experience may not be equal to the extensive and important Trust." Washington would repeat a version of this self-deprecation in virtually every important address he would give from that time forward—in countless speeches to gatherings of his officers over the course of the war, in his speech accepting the post of President of the Constitutional Convention of 1787, and in both his First and Second Presidential Inaugural Addresses. At some point in his career, Washington's consistent displays of humility assumed a ritualistic quality, an expected part of the behavior of a man whose reputation for selfless virtue and unquestioned integrity was known by all. But on this occasion, Washington's first decisive moment on the continental stage, it was probably all the more heartfelt, and, therefore, all the more impressive to those who heard him speak.[20]

Organizing and Financing the Continental Army

In the two days following Washington's appointment as commanding general, the Congress dealt with a plethora of issues relating to the further organization of the army. The delegates agreed on a pay scale for all of the officers and enlisted men in the army (a scale, which, according to the parsimonious John Adams, seemed a bit on the high side). They also recognized the man who had led the Massachusetts militia forces in resisting British assaults, appointing Artemas Ward as first major general, effectively Washington's second in command. They also appointed Charles Lee as second major general, and Horatio Gates as brigadier and adjutant general, thus finding suitable subordinate positions for the other principal candidates for the position to which Washington had been appointed. If Washington's appointment had been relatively noncontroversial, the decision about the rank order of his principal subordinate generals provoked considerable argument among the delegates, with both regional and purely personal jealousies getting in the way of a speedy decision. John Adams, once again ignoring the vow of secrecy, reported to Elbridge Gerry back in Massachusetts that "the natural prejudices and virtuous attachment of our countrymen to their own officers" made the decision on the rank order an especially contentious one. Adams, in spite of his New England attachments, would have preferred to see Lee appointed second in command, but such "dismal bugbears were raised," presumably relating to Lee's reputation as a soldier of fortune with no strong allegiances to the patriot cause, that Ward was given preference over him, an outcome that Adams reluctantly endorsed.[21]

Within several days of those decisions the members of Congress would decide that four generals—Washington, the ailing Artemas Ward and the two recent arrivals to Virginia—were not sufficient. Whatever the military soundness of their reasoning, the political imperative of defending the interests of their own colonies or regions caused the delegates to increase the number of major generals from two to four and of brigadier generals from four to eight. By this action, New York (Philip Schuyler) and Connecticut (Israel Putnam) could each claim a major general, Massachusetts was given three brigadier generals, Connecticut two, and New Hampshire, Rhode Island and New York each one. Although the provincial motives behind this expansion of the officers' corps may have been dubious, the practical effect was probably beneficial, for among three original appointees, Ward would soon retire from the field due to illness, Lee would flame out in a series of controversies and Gates, though he would serve for the duration of the war, would develop a bitter rivalry with his Virginia neighbor and former patron, General Washington.[22]

Over the course of what would be an excruciatingly longer war than either side could have imagined, many of the subordinate officers in the Continental Army would become embroiled in predictable rivalries and quarrels. But Washington's steadfast refusal to engage in self-promotion or self-aggrandizement would give to the army a stability and camaraderie that it might otherwise have lacked. The officer corps of the Continental Army would never be free of competition and intrigue, but Washington's leadership certainly helped keep it under control.

The principal problems faced by the army were rooted not in the character of its leadership, but in the pathetic weakness of its finances. It was one thing to constitute an army and designate its officer corps. It was quite another to find the means of paying and equipping the army—officers and enlisted men alike—as it confronted the most powerful military force on earth.

On June 17, New York's James Duane wrote to the provincial congress of his colony observing that since the colony "had made no progress" raising the 5,000 soldiers mandated by the Congress, troops from Connecticut would be employed in their stead. He also agreed that the provincial congress's complaint about the "want of money" to pay troops was a valid one, and promised that the Continental Congress would soon come forward with a remedy. In fact, the Congress was already actively considering the remedy. On June 22 it announced that it was prepared to issue bills of credit in the amount of up to "two million Spanish milled dollars" to help support the escalating military effort. These bills of credit were essentially IOUs, and indeed, IOUs issued by a Congress that had no formal legal authority and no means of raising the revenue to make good on them. The second part of the Congress's announcement revealed the source of the money—the "twelve confederated colonies" (Georgia had still not formally joined the Congress at that time) would all pledge to chip in to make sure that the bills of credit were eventually redeemed at their face value. Of course, none of those colonies had made such a pledge, and, as future events would prove, few of them would step up to meet their obligations in any way that could be considered adequate. As the historian of the Continental Congress, Edmund Cody Burnett, has written: "Congress had launched the vessel of its hope upon the uncertain sea of paper money; but through what storms the ship would pass, at what far port it would find land and in what condition, no man could foretell." In fact, the storms would be of hurricane proportions, and their duration—seven arduous, spirit-sapping years of warfare marked by constantly shifting momentum—would extend far beyond anything anyone could have imagined at the time.[23]

Washington Departs Amidst an Escalating War

George Washington, now General Washington, stayed in Philadelphia for another week before departing for the scene of battle in New England. Never an expansive letter-writer, he spent a good deal of time during that week writing to friends and family sharing the news of his appointment and, in what was a constantly recurring theme, expressing great uncertainty about what lay ahead of him on the "tempestuous ocean" on which he would now voyage. And, with thoughts of the dangers that he would face on that tempestuous ocean very much on his mind, he sent to his wife Martha a copy of a new will.[24]

There had been a good deal of business to be settled before his departure. Although he had been appointed chief general, his duties, his authority and his relationship with the raft of other generals that the Congress had appointed in the days after his own appointment still needed to be worked out. He scarcely knew the four major generals and eight brigadier generals whom the Congress had appointed in the aftermath of his own appointment. Astute observer of politics that he was, he could see that much of the rationale behind those appointments had more to do with minimizing provincial rivalries and achieving sectional balance than it did with assembling the most effective possible officer corps. Moreover, although the formal instructions issued to him by Congress on June 20 gave him authority to recruit additional soldiers "not exceeding double that of the enemy," the Congress also made it clear that he was expected to consult with the large corps of adjutant, major and brigadier generals, forming themselves in a council of war, before making any strategic decisions about the conduct of the war. Reporting to a Congress riven by myriad regional and ideological divisions and working with a group of generals who were themselves riven by those same divisions, Washington knew that the challenges he was about to face would not be solely those on the field of battle.[25]

the time this lithograph was completed in 1846, the destruction of the 90,000 pounds of tea in Boston
arbor by the "Mohawk Indians" on the night of December 16, 1773, had become a part of American
gend. (National Archives)

This portrait of Samuel Adams by John Singleton
Copley displays a respectable-looking gentleman,
rather than the "New England fanatic" so thoroughly
detested by British officials both in Boston and
London. (Library of Congress)

London it was not, but the skyline of Philadelphia, as seen from the Delaware River, was unquestionably the most impressive of any city in America. (Library of Congress)

Benjamin Franklin's confrontation with Lord Wedderburn in the "Cockpit" may have been the moment in which the American scientist and diplomat ceased to consider himself a loyal subject of the British Empire and embraced an identity as a defender of American liberty. (Courtesy of the Huntington Library, Art Collections, and Botanical Gardens, San Marino, California)

City Tavern

The unofficial after-hours meeting place for the delegates to the Continental Congress, Smith's City Tavern, may have been the site of as much important business relating to America's relationship with Great Britain as the Assembly Room of Independence Hall. (Library of Congress)

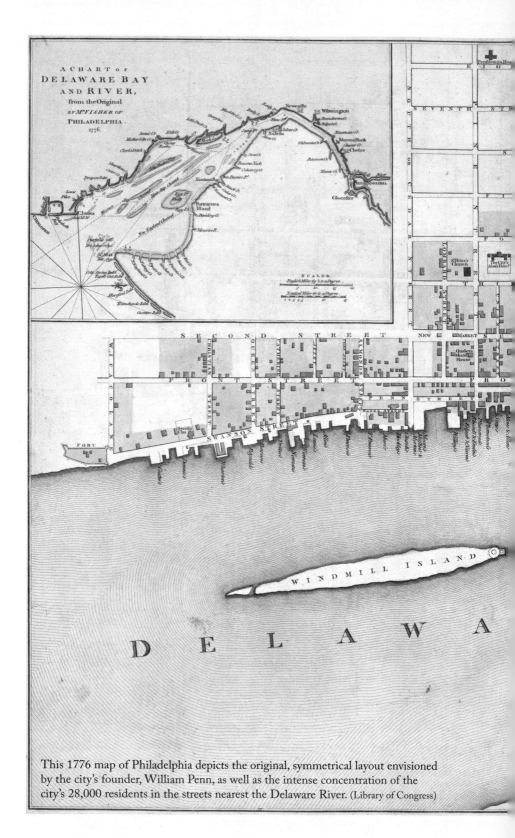

This 1776 map of Philadelphia depicts the original, symmetrical layout envisioned by the city's founder, William Penn, as well as the intense concentration of the city's 28,000 residents in the streets nearest the Delaware River. (Library of Congress)

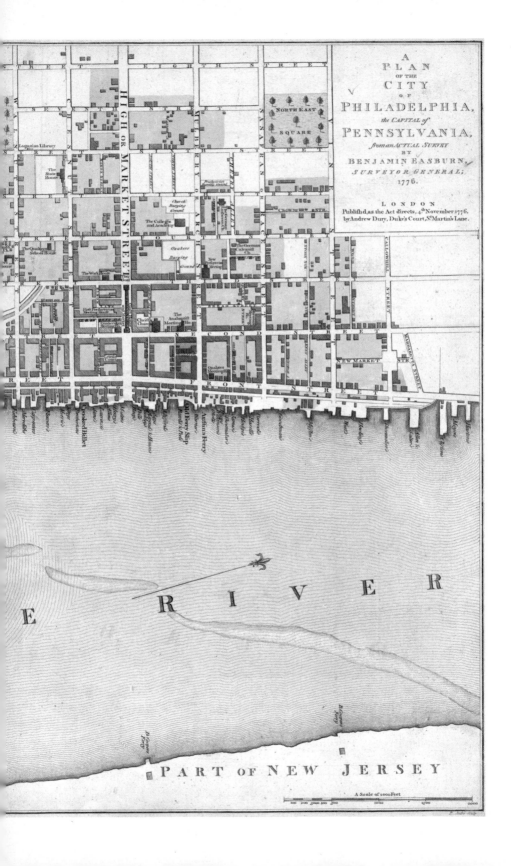

A
PLAN
OF THE
CITY
OF
PHILADELPHIA,
the CAPITAL of
PENNSYLVANIA,
from an ACTUAL SURVEY
BY
BENJAMIN EASBURN,
SURVEYOR GENERAL;
1776.

LONDON
Publish'd, as the Act directs, 4th November 1776,
by Andrew Dury, Duke's Court, St Martin's Lane.

NORTH EAST
SQUARE

E   RIVER

PART OF NEW JERSEY

A Scale of 2000 Feet

Portly, prematurely balding, John Adams admitted that "By my Physical Constitution I am but an ordinary man." But his intelligence and his passion for defending American liberty were anything but ordinary. (Independence National Historic Park)

Tall, slender, John Dickinson was, in his physical appearance and cool emotional demeanor, the polar opposite of his frequent rival, John Adams. But he was at least Adams's equal both in intelligence and in his commitment to defending American liberty. (Independence National Historic Park)

This "backyard view" of the Pennsylvania State House, eventually to become America's iconic Independence Hall, was in fact seen by most Philadelphians at the time as the front entrance to the building. (Library of Congress)

CARPENTERS' HALL.[1]

Philadelphia's Carpenters' Guild Hall would serve as the meeting place for the First Continental Congress. (Courtesy University of Pennsylvania Library, Volume 2 of Benson John Lossing's *The Pictorial Field-Book of the Revolution* (New York: 1851–1852))

The Speaker of the Virginia House of Burgesses and the most respected member of one of his colony's most prestigious families, Peyton Randolph was unanimously elected by his fellow delegates as president of the First Continental Congress. (Library of Congress, Prints and Photographs Division [LC-USZ6-834])

Charles Thomson would serve as Secretary of the Continental Congress from its inception in September of 1774 until its replacement by the First Congress of the United States in 1789. His fervent patriotism was unquestioned; his miserable secretarial skills were perhaps equally well-recognized. (Independence National Historic Park)

When Patrick Henry arrived at the
First Continental Congress he was
dressed modestly in a simple gray suit
of country clothing. This elegant
portrait of Henry painted by Thomas
Sully portrays the fiery Virginia patriot
in more aristocratic garb. (Independence
National Historic Park)

This sketch of Joseph
Galloway perhaps unfairly
depicts him as a rather sour
and ill-natured fellow, but,
in fact, Galloway won few
friends or allies among his
fellow delegates to the First
Continental Congress. (Library
of Congress, Prints and Photographs
Division [LC-USZ62-47131])

Lord Frederick North, the king's chief minister during the six years leading to America's independence, no doubt thought of himself as a "peacemaker," a British statesman trying to find a way of keeping the North American colonies in the British Empire. The American people, on the other hand, tended to view him as the embodiment of all that was evil about the much-detested British ministry.
(Library of Congress)

John Hancock, never lacking in self-confidence or in pride in his personal appearance, was no doubt pleased by this portrait by the artist John Singleton Copely.
(Library of Congress)

This portrait of George Washington by Charles Willson Peale was painted in 1779, during the Revolutionary War. It depicts Washington at the Battle of Princeton, which took place two years earlier. (Library of Congress)

This highly stylized, and wholly mythical, depiction of a battle scene at Bunker Hill, painted in 1786 by the artist John Trumbull, is nevertheless an accurate reflection of the way in which that bloody battle was perceived in the minds of the American colonists. (Library of Congress)

The Scottish aristocrat, John Murray, the Fourth Earl of Dunmore, royal governor of Virginia and perhaps the most detested man in the colony. (Virginia Historical Society)

Perhaps no British sovereign, no matter how wise or politically astute, could have prevent the secession of the American colonies from the British Empire. King George III, thoug neither the devil nor the tyrant the America believed him to be, certainly did not possess either the wisdom or the political skill to av that outcome. (Library of Congress)

Tom Paine, armed simply with his pen, would do as much as any man in America to move the "united colonies" toward independence. (Independence National Historic Park)

Charles Willson Peale painted this portrait of Thomas Jefferson in 1791 when Jefferson was Secretary of State. Peale then hung the portrait in his museum with other portraits of notable Americans. It is one of the few portraits that shows Jefferson's natural red hair. (Independence National Historic Park)

An outspoken advocate of bold opposition to British policies from the moment he began his service in the First Continental Congress, Virginia's Richard Henry Lee would introduce into the Congress the resolution for American independence on June 7, 1776. (Independence National Historic Park)

John Trumbull's 1817 painting of the signing of the Declaration of Independence on July 4, 1776, takes many liberties with the actual events of that day. But perhaps more than any painting in American history, it has shaped the image that most Americans have of their nation's founding. (Library of Congress)

George Washington was not pleased with the lack of discipline shown by his troops when, on the even of July 9, 1776, they pulled down the equestrian statue of King George III. But some practical good resulted from the effort, for the 4,000 pounds of lead in the statue were subsequently melted down to make 42,000 bullets! (Library of Congress)

Washington also tended to his personal and professional needs. He purchased five new horses and a new four-wheeled phaeton that would carry him and some in his party when he did not wish to ride on horseback. He ordered a new uniform. There being no official uniform of the Continental Army at that time, he used the design of the Fairfax Independent Company, his militia company in his home county of Fairfax, Virginia. The uniform, with its blue coat, yellow buttons, and gold epaulettes, would be featured in countless portraits of Washington from that time forward.[26]

Just a few minutes before his departure from Philadelphia on June 23, Washington scribbled one more quick note to Martha, mindful of the fact that time and circumstances might not permit him to communicate with her very frequently in the coming months. He expressed his "full confidence of a happy meeting with you sometime in the Fall"—a hugely overoptimistic prediction—and ended by repeating his "unalterable affection" for her—perhaps not a passionate and uninhibited expression of love and devotion, but, for the ever self-controlled Washington, perhaps as close to that as he was likely to come.[27]

The delegates to the Continental Congress assembled outside the State House on the morning of June 22 to bid Washington farewell and Godspeed. As Washington began to mount one of five new horses, Thomas Mifflin, a prominent member of Congress but now Washington's new aide-de-camp, rushed out to help the general place his foot in the stirrup, an act of devotion that elicited a round of applause from the assembled crowd. Accompanied by Generals Charles Lee and Philip Schuyler, as well as Philadelphia's City Light Horse Troop, outfitted in dress uniforms and on horseback, they rode northward, out of town. The entire Massachusetts delegation, which had the most at stake, was not content merely to bid Washington farewell outside the State House. They, along with members of the Connecticut delegation and several other members of Congress, piled themselves into carriages and accompanied Washington for the first few miles of his journey.[28]

John Adams, who was among those who accompanied Washington for a few miles, was moved by the display of martial pomp and ceremony, but at the same time, could not hide his feelings of inferiority and self-pity. As he described the glorious scene to Abigail, he couldn't resist adding: "Such is the pomp of War. I, poor Creature, worn out with scribbling for my Bread and my Liberty, low in Spirits and weak in Health, must leave others to wear the Lawrells which I have sown; others, to eat the Bread which I have earned."[29]

John Adams always stood at the center of the world of John Adams, but Washington, as he was taking his leave, had another, more ominous, and potentially momentous, subject on his mind. The previous evening an express rider from Boston had arrived in the city to deliver the news that yet another battle—far bloodier and perhaps more consequential than those at Lexington and Concord—had been fought on the outskirts of Boston, at Bunker Hill on the Charlestown Peninsula. As Washington made his way toward Boston, he knew that his new responsibilities would be far more taxing than his relatively leisurely schedule as a delegate to the Continental Congress.

FIFTEEN

DESPERATE EFFORTS AT RECONCILIATION AMIDST AN ESCALATING WAR

Bunker Hill

In the days before George Washington was chosen commander of the Continental Army, his British counterpart, General Thomas Gage, set in motion a plan to win a decisive victory over the insurgents in Boston. Gage ordered his troops to begin to make preparations to occupy the hills around Dorchester, which commanded a strategic position above Boston. The Massachusetts Committee of Safety, learning of the plan on June 13, 1775, ordered the New England militia, still under the command of Artemas Ward, to pre-emptively take up a position on Bunker Hill on the Charlestown peninsula. Lying to the north of Boston, and with its southern tip separated by only about 1,000 feet of water from the port of Boston, the Charlestown peninsula actually had two strategically important hills. The now immortal Bunker Hill, with an elevation of about 110 feet, was at the northern end. Breed's Hill, with a height of a little over 60 feet, was 600 yards closer to the southern tip of the peninsula, and therefore nearer to Boston. Both hills could potentially be a useful bastion for artillery, which could then be used to bombard the town of Boston.

Ward was not at all confident of the soundness of the plan, fearing it was too risky, but urged on by Brigadier Israel Putnam—a grizzled veteran of many battles in the French and Indian War—as well as by General Seth Pomeroy of Connecticut and the Boston physician and president of the Massachusetts provincial congress, Joseph Warren, he moved forward with a plan to place some 1,200 troops there.

On the evening of June 16, the militiamen, most of them without uniforms and carrying their own muskets, occupied Bunker Hill, stopping short of Breed's Hill. Once they reached Bunker Hill, the commanding generals decided to leave a small detachment there, and then to push on to Breed's Hill with the bulk of the force in order to take advantage of its better location. Once on Breed's Hill, the militiamen began frantically to fortify their position, digging deep trenches and then erecting six-foot-high walls with the earth they had dug for the trenches. Over the course of the next twelve hours, sometimes in the face of British cannon fire from ships anchored in Boston Harbor, the New England troops fortified both Breed's Hill and Bunker Hill.

General Gage awoke on the morning of June 17 to find that he had been beaten to the punch by the patriot militia. He immediately gave orders for British ships to fire on the patriot fortifications from the sea as well as to mobilize 1,500 British soldiers to mount a direct attack on the encampment from all sides. Waiting for them were the 1,200 patriot militiamen, only scantily protected by the dirt walls they had so hurriedly erected. The Americans repelled two British attacks that day, inflicting significant casualties on their adversaries. By the time of the third assault, coming at the end of the day on June 17, the Americans had nearly run out of gunpowder and were forced to retreat. As they did, the British forces, reinforced by additional troops, rained massive fire down on them. Unable to reply, the patriot forces would suffer most of their casualties during that retreat at Bunker Hill. Although the British gained control of both of those hills that day, they paid an extraordinarily heavy price for their victory—226 soldiers killed and 828 wounded, with a particularly heavy toll among the British officer corps—a toll that would have a dramatic effect on British military leadership for the duration of the Revolutionary War. The patriot militiamen had not escaped easily—with 450 casualties, of whom 140 died in the battle. Among those killed in the retreat across Bunker Hill was Joseph Warren, who, though he had been given the formal title of general, had volunteered to fight as a private in the ranks of the militiamen.[1]

General Washington received the first detailed reports of the battles at Bunker and Breed's Hill in New York City, while en route to Boston. He was both distressed and angry that the shortage of gunpowder had been a major factor in the patriot army's retreat—a retreat during which they had suffered most of their casualties. He immediately sent word to Congress pressing them to expedite the shipment of munitions to Boston—a request that would become a persistent refrain throughout the remainder of a long war in which the shortage of munitions and of the funds to pay for them would be a constant source of frustration for the general. Back in Philadelphia, the delegates reacted with a combination of alarm and pride. On the one hand, the patriot army had been forced to yield valuable ground, and the shortage of ammunition was a harbinger of many more supply problems to come. But the casualty reports were a cause for hope: the early reports suggested that the Americans had suffered fewer than 200 casualties, with between forty and seventy killed, with the British army suffering some 500 casualties. As more details of the battle became known, the delegates came to understand better the full magnitude of the British losses, but also of their own.[2]

The Massachusetts delegates were especially devastated by news of the loss of their compatriot Joseph Warren. Only thirty-four at his death, a medical doctor and patriot, Warren, as we have seen, was an orator famed for his fiery and poetic annual remembrances of the Boston Massacre. In his last such oration, he might be said to have foreseen his own end with the lines "Approach we then the melancholy walk of death." At the same time, the Massachusetts as well as the other delegates celebrated what Sam Adams referred to as the "tried Bravery" of the Massachusetts militiamen who had fought at Bunker Hill. Such bravery suggested that the inherent virtue of the patriot cause would in the end prove triumphant. Indeed, most Americans would draw a similar conclusion. This perhaps made it all that much more difficult in the months and years to come, when the toll of hardship, bloodshed and defeat inflicted on the patriot army would be greater than anyone had imagined.[3]

On June 23, the day that Washington left Philadelphia to begin his journey to Boston, the Congress appointed a committee—John Rutledge, William Livingston, John Jay, Thomas Johnson and a notable newcomer, Benjamin Franklin—to draw up a Declaration to be published and read by the general upon his arrival in Boston. The purpose of the document was twofold—to rally the continental troops as they were readying themselves for further battles, and to explain the military conflict to the American people at large. Although the mood in Congress and across America was growing more militant in the aftermath of Bunker Hill, the composition of the committee was anything but that. There were no New Englanders on the committee and all of the members, with the exception of Franklin, a recent arrival who up to that point had seldom spoken in the Assembly Room in the State House, were advocates of moderation. John Rutledge composed a first draft the following day, but Congress sent the declaration back to the committee for further consideration. Secretary Thomson, true to form, seems to have lost the Rutledge draft, so we can only speculate as to whether the members of Congress thought it too mild, too militant or simply poorly composed.[4]

Obviously some new approach was needed. On Monday, June 26, the Congress, after debating another version of the declaration and still finding it wanting, not only sent it back to the committee, but also added two other members: another newcomer, Thomas Jefferson, and the distinguished and experienced John Dickinson. According to members of the Virginia delegation, the addition of Jefferson to the committee owed to the fact that he had already established "a reputation for literature." In fact, the committee would ask Jefferson to write the next draft of the declaration, a move that would help propel the newly arrived Virginian into a position of prominence in the Congress.[5]

The Two Newcomers: Franklin and Jefferson

Though Benjamin Franklin had just returned to Philadelphia, he was well known personally by many, and by reputation to everyone there. By that time in his life, in his seventieth year, Franklin had already achieved international acclaim as a scientist and widespread respect in

America as a shrewd and effective lobbyist for the colonies' interests in London. And virtually everyone in the Congress, upon their first encounter with him, would be bowled over by his charm and his sense of humor.

Franklin had spent more than a decade in London as a colonial agent representing Pennsylvania, New Jersey, Georgia and, eventually, Massachusetts. He had loved his time in London, and, indeed, at that stage in his life may have considered himself as much a Londoner as a Pennsylvanian. He enjoyed the high life of London politics and took pride in his close relationship with some of the most important royal officials in the empire. But as we have seen, in the wake of the Boston Tea Party and the scandal involving the publication of the letters from Massachusetts Governor Thomas Hutchinson, Franklin's relationship with royal officials, and, indeed, his very identity as an Englishman, underwent a dramatic transformation. His confrontation with Lord Wedderburn in the cockpit in late January of 1774 would change the course of Franklin's life, and, in some senses, the course of American history. Franklin would remain in London for more than a year after his confrontation with Wedderburn, and, in spite of his humiliation that day, he would continue in his efforts to persuade British officials to relax their coercive policies up until the final hours before his departure back home to America.[6]

Franklin was elected to a seat in the Continental Congress on May 6, 1775, one day after he got back to Philadelphia, and, simply by an accident of timing, he was able to be present when the Congress began its business on May 10. For the most part, he remained uncharacteristically silent during the first few months of the Congress's deliberations. Silas Deane, writing to his wife, observed that "Docr. Franklin is with Us, but he is not a Speaker." Deane went on to note that though Franklin had added his approval to all of the measures adopted by the Congress, he had hoped for more from the illustrious American scientist and diplomat: "Times like these," Deane noted, "call up Genius," and thus far Franklin, so well-known for his genius, had remained largely passive. John Adams observed the same passivity, telling Abigail that thus far "he has had but little share farther than to cooperate and assist."[7]

Franklin's outward demeanor notwithstanding, John Adams, at least in his early interactions with the most famous man in America, praised the good doctor for his support of even "our boldest Measures." Indeed, Adams believed that, should the Americans be "driven to the disagreeable Necessity of assuming a total Independency," Franklin would support the decision. Even at this early stage though, Adams could not resist complaining that most people in England were wrongfully attributing the American resistance to imperial policies to Franklin's influence. Adams noted that "there cannot be a greater Mistake," for, of course in his mind, that principled opposition owed primarily to brave, outspoken sorts like John Adams. Adams's jealousy of Franklin's fame would continue to grow during the months leading to independence. Adams expressed his wonder that Franklin, "from day to day sitting in silence, a great part of the time fast asleep in his chair," was being appointed to many of the most important committees, while he himself was unaccountably passed over. It was hardly a fair assessment. Franklin may indeed have been relatively silent in the public arena of the Assembly Room, but his deep knowledge of the intricacies of British politics across the Atlantic, combined with his shrewd abilities as a convivial dinner and drinking companion— both in City Tavern and in his spacious townhouse near Fourth and Market Streets—would prove invaluable in forging the consensus among the delegates that would eventually result in independence.[8]

Sometime around the end of June, Benjamin Franklin wrote a lengthy "Vindication" of the colonists' resistance to British policies. Drawing on his vast experience as an observer and participant in the politics of Anglo-American relations, he refuted the notion that the American colonies had been settled at the "expense of Britain," and that, by their present behavior, were displaying their ingratitude toward Great Britain's benevolence. Franklin produced a long catalogue of facts to prove, at least to his satisfaction, that from their infancy the colonies had done far more *for* the British Empire than the empire had done for the colonies. Anticipating some of the arguments that would shake the world in Thomas Paine's *Common Sense*, Franklin rejected the notion that anything done by the British for the colonies in their infancy could possibly justify the systematic violation of American liberties now that the colonies had reached a state of maturity.

Since Franklin's "Vindication" was never formally presented to the Congress nor published, the audience for whom it was intended remains unclear. It is likely, however, that it did circulate privately among many members of Congress. Franklin wrote it with Lord North and his ministers in mind. Having so recently returned from England and still smarting from the humiliation he had suffered in the cockpit and up until the day of his departure, he clearly felt some need to vindicate his own behavior during that trying moment in his diplomatic career.[9]

The arrival of thirty-two-year-old Thomas Jefferson in Philadelphia on June 20, coinciding as it did with Bunker Hill and General Washington's impending departure, received little notice. As we have seen, although Jefferson had begun to earn a reputation for his literary and intellectual skills through the publication of his *Summary View of the Rights of British America,* he was not yet a major player on the continental scene. He had traveled to Philadelphia on a brief trip nine years earlier in order to be inoculated against smallpox, but his journey there in 1775 would mark his first meaningful stay outside of Virginia.

When the Virginia Convention had balloted for delegates to attend the Second Congress, Jefferson's name had not been included on the list of seven Virginians selected. But on the final day of its session, the Convention selected Jefferson as an alternate in case Peyton Randolph should be forced to return to his duties as president of the Convention. Although he may not have ranked even among the top ten politicians in Virginia at the time (there were more than a dozen members of the legislature whose service in that body was more extensive), he was beginning to acquire a reputation for intellectual acuity that transcended the provincial boundaries of Virginia.[10]

Jefferson's relatively modest family background would not have predicted an influential political career. His father, Peter Jefferson, was a surveyor and planter of some means. But to the extent that Jefferson could rely on social clout to advance his standing in Virginia, it was through his mother, Jane Randolph, a somewhat marginal member of one of the most powerful families in Virginia (her father was a distant cousin of the man Jefferson was replacing in the Continental Congress, Peyton Randolph). Unlike many sons of the Virginia gentry, Jefferson did not travel to England, or even to Princeton, for his education, instead riding the 120 miles eastward from his home in Shadwell (a few miles east of what is today Charlottesville) to Williamsburg to enter the College of William and Mary at the age of sixteen.[11]

Jefferson's intellectual and social skills had blossomed during his time at William and Mary. His principal mentor at the college, the professor of natural philosophy William Small, taught him mathematics, metaphysics and philosophy, introducing Jefferson for the first time to the work of the English political philosopher John Locke. After his graduation in 1762, Jefferson stayed in Williamsburg to take up the study of law with George Wythe, the most respected lawyer in Virginia, an experience that would profoundly affect the future course of Jefferson's life. Wythe recognized genius when he saw it, and he would enthusiastically not only serve as Jefferson's legal mentor but also nurture Jefferson's education in philosophy and classical literature. He would also introduce Jefferson to people at the highest level of Virginia society. Although never accomplished as an orator or public performer, at an early age Jefferson displayed an ability to charm and impress company in more intimate settings. Beginning in 1764, Jefferson became part of a regular dinner party with his two mentors, Wythe and Small, and the royal governor of Virginia, Francis Faquier. Looking back on those evenings fifty years later, Jefferson recalled that he had heard "more good sense, more rational and philosophical conversations" during those dinners than at any other time in his life. The combination of talents and experiences in that group—a learned, but practical-minded lawyer; a deeply intellectual professor; and a worldly, but also highly intelligent royal governor—must have made a deep impression on young Jefferson, just graduated from college.[12]

Jefferson was admitted to the bar in 1767, and, after a brief period practicing law, he was elected to the House of Burgesses in 1769. He was a relatively quiet member of that body, but in 1774, in the aftermath of the passage of the Coercive Acts, he drafted a lengthy address intended as a set of instructions to Virginia's delegates to the Continental Congress. Jefferson's draft wasn't chosen, at least in part because some thought it too emphatic in its denial of British authority. But it was published as a pamphlet, *A Summary View of the Rights of British America*. It not only buttressed the increasingly popular notion that the

American colonial legislatures were independent of Parliament's authority but also began to establish Jefferson's reputation beyond Virginia as both an elegant stylist and a persuasive defender of America's constitutional liberties. Indeed, Jefferson's visibility following the publication of his *Summary View*, which was read by people all across America, may have been higher outside of Virginia than inside. In his home colony, he was seen as just another member of the House of Burgesses; but for those outside Virginia, his authorship of *A Summary View of the Rights of British America* spoke loudly of a keen intellect that might prove useful in the coming conflict with Great Britain.[13]

When Jefferson set off for Philadelphia, he traveled in an ornate phaeton, accompanied by two slaves—Jesse, who rode as postilion; Richard, a body servant who rode with him in the carriage; and Jupiter, Jefferson's longtime personal servant and companion who traveled behind the phaeton with two extra horses. No doubt eager to display his own status as a Virginia gentryman, Jefferson outfitted his slaves in formal attire. His trip to Philadelphia took ten days—an unusually long time to cover the 325 miles from Williamsburg—the result, in part, of getting lost somewhere outside of Wilmington, Delaware, but also the consequence of his intellectual curiosity about the natural sights along the way. Upon arriving in Philadelphia on June 20, he took up lodgings in a room in a house on Chestnut Street belonging to one of Philadelphia's premier cabinetmakers, Benjamin Randolph. He set up an account at City Tavern to take his dinner and late evening suppers there. Taking the place of Peyton Randolph and the now-departed George Washington, he most likely joined his fellow delegates Richard Henry Lee, Benjamin Harrison and several others as a member of a "club" that dined together around a common table at the tavern. He was already personally known and generally admired by his fellow Virginia delegates, but, still, he knew that he was taking his place on a stage far larger and far more consequential than he ever could have imagined.[14]

"The Declaration on the Causes and Necessity for Taking Up Arms"

The invitation to write a revised draft of the declaration to be read by General Washington to his troops would give Jefferson his first opportunity to appear on that larger stage. Jefferson probably began work on his draft immediately after he was added to the committee charged with writing it—sometime around June 26. In the meantime, John Dickinson headed a committee created in the aftermath of the May 26 vote to attempt one more approach to the king. They drafted a formal petition based on the four propositions Dickinson had so arduously put before the Congress in late May. And yet another committee, composed of Richard Henry Lee, Robert Livingston and Edmund Pendleton, wrote another Address to the Inhabitants of Great Britain justifying America's rejection of Lord North's proposal and seeking to solicit the sympathy and aid of their "Friends, Countrymen, and Brethren" across the Atlantic. All of these political manifestos would come before the Congress toward the end of the first week in July, and all of them would generate a fair amount of criticism and controversy.[15]

First up was the declaration to be read by Washington to his troops. As soon as he was added to the committee charged with drafting the document, Jefferson set to work on the project, formally titled "The Declaration on the Causes and Necessity for Taking Up Arms," but more commonly referred to by the delegates as the "Declaration on Taking Arms." He prepared at least two different drafts over a ten-day period, settling on a final version in the first week of July. Although much of the argument in Jefferson's final draft was less emphatic in its denunciation of British violations of American rights than in his *Summary View*, at least some of the committee members found it too strident. In particular, New Jersey's William Livingston, who remained in the camp of those committed to conciliation and was becoming extremely cranky in the bargain, thought that Jefferson's draft "had the faults common to our Southern gentlemen." He criticized it for lacking a "sense of dignity," complaining that the radicals in the Congress, in whose number he now counted Jefferson, seemed to think that "a reiteration of tyranny, despotism, bloody &c [is] all that is needed to unite us at home and to convince the bribed voters of the North of the justice of our cause." The sheer nastiness of Livingston's comment suggests that, however much the delegates may have shared a common concern for the militiamen in Boston, there was still major disagreement—even acrimony—among them with respect to the most appropriate "next steps." Livingston's contention that Jefferson's draft reflected a difference of style and opinion between North and South was in fact misleading, for there were no doubt many delegates from southern colonies—for example, Maryland, Delaware and South Carolina—who may also have had reservations about Jefferson's draft, and in the North, there were significant differences of opinion between the New England delegates, on the one hand, and those from New York, New Jersey and Pennsylvania on the other.[16]

John Dickinson also thought that Jefferson's draft was "too strong," but unlike Livingston, he played a constructive role in improving it. According to Jefferson's later recollection, Dickinson, like Livingston, still retained the hope of reconciliation with the mother country and feared that the effectiveness of Jefferson's draft might be weakened "by offensive statements." When confronted by Dickinson's criticisms, and because he continued to view the Pennsylvania congressman as "so honest a man, and so able a one," Jefferson agreed to allow Dickinson to take his draft and "put it into a form he could approve." When Dickinson took on that task, he did not confine himself to minor editing. In fact, he significantly rewrote it, leaving in place only four and a half paragraphs of a thirteen-paragraph document.[17]

A few of Dickinson's changes to Jefferson's draft were stylistic. He toned down some of the harshness of Jefferson's language and emphasized that "We have not raised Armies with ambitious Designs of separating from Great-Britain, and establishing Independent States." The more important changes were substantive—he included a recitation of the Congress's previous efforts (many of them coming at his own instigation) at conciliation, and he softened Jefferson's absolute denial of parliamentary authority, suggesting that the original charters issued to each of the colonies did not give the legislatures of those colonies the degree of autonomy from Parliament that Jefferson had claimed. Even with Dickinson's changes, the finished product was decidedly muscular. Although "the farmer in Pennsylvania" continued to cherish the American allegiance to the king, he did not pull any punches when speaking of "Ministerial rapacity" or the "pernicious project" and "insidious maneuver" of the British Parliament. And, taking some phrases from Jefferson's draft but reworking them into an even more stirring conclusion, Dickinson proclaimed:

> Our cause is just. Our union is perfect. Our internal resources are great, and, if necessary, foreign assistance is undoubtedly attainable. We gratefully acknowledge, as signal Instances of the Divine Favour toward us, that his Providence would not permit us to be called into this severe Controversy, until we were grown up to our present strength, had been previously exercised in warlike operation, and possessed of the means of defending ourselves. With hearts fortified with these animating reflections, we most solemnly, before God and the World, declare that . . . the arms we have been compelled by our enemies to assume, we will, in defiance of every hazard, with unabating firmness and perseverance, employ for the preservation of our liberties; being with one mind resolved to dye Free-men rather than live Slaves.[18]

The final version of the Declaration on Taking Arms was, as the eminent Jefferson scholar Julian Boyd concluded, the result of a true "collaboration on the part of the two men, however unwilling each was to accept the work of the other." Whatever differences of opinion delegates may have had about the prospects of reconciliation, and whatever personal rivalries or clash of egos may have conditioned their behavior toward one another, the final draft of the Declaration on Taking Arms was unanimously and enthusiastically adopted by the Congress on July 6. Even John Adams, who by this time had developed a hearty dislike of Dickinson and who was beginning to complain that most of the Congress's literary efforts were a waste of time, grudgingly acknowledged that it was a "spirited manifesto."[19]

Somewhat anticlimactically, on July 8 the delegates approved a final draft of the Address to the Inhabitants of Great Britain. Mindful that their earlier effort in this regard eight months before had failed to rally the British people to their cause, the drafting committee spent less time focusing on the fine points of America's constitutional argument and more on a recitation of the atrocities committed by the British military in the subsequent months. It is likely that few in the Congress had much hope that the address would have much effect.

John Adams caustically commented to James Warren, a distant kin of the recently killed Joseph Warren, that the address "will find many Admirers among the Ladies and fine Gentlemen; but it is not to my Taste. Prettynesses, Juvenilities, much less Puerilities, become not a great Assembly like this the Representative of the people." He sarcastically predicted that all of the various petitions, declarations and addresses on which the Congress was spending so much time would result only in further "Bills of Attainder and other such like Expressions of Esteem and Kindness." Adams anger and sarcasm were, typically, a bit over the top, but they were also reflections of the tensions continuing to build in the Congress—tensions between, at one extreme, many of the New Englanders and perhaps most of the Virginians and, at the other, the more conservative delegates from the mid-Atlantic colonies, with many other delegates still struggling with their feelings about how best to resolve what was looking more and more like an irreconcilable crisis.[20]

The Olive Branch Petition and John Adams's Wrath

If John Adams was skeptical about the Address to the Inhabitants of Great Britain, he was downright indignant over the eventual passage and transmittal of yet another conciliatory petition to the king. The committee that had been working on that petition since early June presented its final draft to the Congress for its approval on July 5. The prestigious drafting committee—John Dickinson, Thomas Johnson, John Rutledge, John Jay and Benjamin Franklin—notably contained no New Englanders or Virginians. Dickinson and Jay had been outspoken about the need to go the extra mile to seek reconciliation, Rutledge had tended to waver back and forth between militancy and moderation and Franklin had been mostly silent; only Thomas Johnson of Maryland had been outspoken in his support of the New Englanders and the Virginians. Most importantly, it was primarily Dickinson—both because he was the most earnest champion of yet another petition to the king and because of his superior writing abilities—who shaped the final product.

The petition was, as its author intended it, extraordinarily pacific in tone, if not in its logic and substance. It was a "humble" petition from his "Majesty's faithful Subjects." It acknowledged that the union existing between "our Mother country" and the colonies had "produced benefits so remarkably important" to both sides that it had become "the wonder and envy of other Nations." And although it castigated the "British ministry" for its "delusive pretences, fruitless terrors, and unavailing severities," it differed from the petition sent by the First Continental Congress to the King in that it did not go into a lengthy recitation of American grievances. It closed by beseeching "your Majesty, that your royal authority and influence may be graciously interposed to procure us relief" from the afflictions from which the colonies had been suffering.[21]

According to John Adams's later account, the debate over the final draft of the petition lasted two days and was filled with acrimony. Placing himself at center stage, he took credit for leading the opposition to Dickinson's petition, an opposition, Adams claimed, that made Dickinson begin to "tremble for his Cause." At one point in the debate, Adams left the Assembly Room and went out into the State House Yard. As Adams remembered it, Dickinson, observing his departure, "darted out after me. He broke out upon me in a most abrupt and extraordinary manner. In as violent a passion as he was capable of feeling, and with an Air, Countenance and Gestures as rough and haught as if I had been a School Boy and he the Master, he vociferated out: 'What is the Reason, Mr. Adams, that you New England men oppose our Measures of Reconciliation?'" Adams claimed that Dickinson then threatened to lead other colonies in a move to "break off from you in New England" if that region's members continued to oppose his petition to the king.

In Adams's account, Dickinson, who had always been known for his cool, even cold, demeanor, was the hothead, his emotions out of control. By contrast, Adams, known by virtually every member of Congress to oscillate between emotional peaks and valleys of jubilation and despair, and whatever his mood, to wear his heart on his sleeve, presented himself as having dealt with Dickinson's threats "cooly" and in a "very happy temper." However cool or happy his temper may have been during that encounter, Adams admitted that his "Friendship and Acquaintance" with Dickinson ended at that moment. The two would never again exchange a word with one another except in the formal setting of the Congress. Adams concluded: "The more I reflected on Mr. Dickinson's rude Lecture in the State House Yard, the more I was vexed with it, and the determination of Congress, in favour of the Petition, did not allay the irritation."[22]

However vehemently John Adams and a few others—his cousin Sam, Richard Henry Lee and Patrick Henry—may have opposed what the delegates came to refer to as the Olive Branch Petition, even Adams was resigned to the fact that it was bound to be endorsed by virtually all of the members of the Congress. As Adams acknowledged in a letter to James Warren, "We must have a Petition to the King and a delicate Proposal of Negociation." He could not resist adding: "This Negociation I dread like Death." His greatest fear, he confided, was that the king and his ministers might agree to the petition but would then proceed to ignore it. His greatest hope, he confessed, was that the king and his ministers would reject it.[23]

Congress formally passed the petition sometime during the day on July 5. It was then written out and signed on July 8 "by the several members." All of the delegates present that day signed it, including John Adams, although he must have done so with gritted teeth. Thomas Jefferson, for his part, was more polite. He was in the midst of developing a cordial and constructive relationship with Dickinson in the writing of the Declaration on Taking Arms, and though he probably held out little hope that Dickinson's Olive Branch Petition would do much good, he merely commented that "Congress gave a signal proof of their indulgence to Mr. Dickinson, and of their great desire not to go too fast for any respectable part of our body, in permitting him to draw their . . . petition to the King according to his own ideas, and passing it with scarcely any amendment." Jefferson's more temperate view of both Dickinson and his petition was representative of the mainstream of opinion in the Congress at that moment. Though he and many other delegates were not optimistic about the prospect of it doing much good, they also believed that it could do little harm. And Jefferson, far more than John Adams, understood the need to continue to strive for consensus among the delegates.[24]

Consensus or no consensus, John Adams continued to fume, both about the petition itself—which he derided as a "measure of imbecility"—and about what he saw as Dickinson's pernicious influence on the body. In a letter to James Warren on July 24 he railed against "A certain great Fortune and piddling Genius" whose high reputation was wholly undeserved and who "has given a silly Cast to our whole Doings." Instead of wasting its time on frivolous petitions and addresses, Adams wrote, the Congress should have "completely moddelled a Constitution," creating a comprehensive legislative, executive and judicial structure to govern the "whole continent." In other words, the Congress should have been taking purposeful steps towards independence.[25]

Alas, the letter never made it to James Warren. Intercepted by a British sympathizer as it was being carried to Boston, it was published in the *Massachusetts Gazette*, a paper widely suspected of Tory sympathies, with the aim of discrediting Adams by making public his disdain for one of the most respected men in all of America and of revealing his aggressive advocacy of independence. Upon reading Adams's description of him, Dickinson was obviously not pleased but made no public mention of it other than to write in the margins of his copy of the newspaper reprinting Adams's outburst: "Letter from John Adams of Massachusetts Bay in which he abuses me for opposing the violent measures of himself and others in Congress." A more dispassionate observer of the contretemps, the firm patriot Benjamin Rush of Philadelphia, noted that Adams was regarded with "nearly universal detestation" for his rude behavior toward Dickinson.[26]

For the first time since Joseph Galloway's rebuff in the First Continental Congress, a mood of personal animus crept into what had been a mostly civilized body. The months to come would see a more general decline in cordiality, which, along with the heat of the Philadelphia summer, would make the crucial deliberations of the late summer and early fall even more trying.

Benjamin Franklin's Articles of Confederation

In spite of their occasional disagreements over the tone and substance of their responses to the events of the previous months, the delegates had accomplished a great deal: creating an army; appointing a commanding general and an extensive staff of subordinate officers; devising a temporary, and, as things would turn out, highly dubious, plan for financing the military effort against Great Britain;

and churning out an array of additional petitions, addresses and declarations aimed simultaneously at justifying American resistance and bolstering the morale of American troops, while at the same time continuing to issue calls for reconciliation and resisting the desire of a radical few to move toward independence.

As the month of July was drawing to a close, many of the delegates were showing signs of exhaustion. The Congress had already been in session longer than most of them had expected. And their work hours—in session for six hours a day, six days a week, not to mention their after-hours discussions and negotiations at convivial meeting places like City Tavern—were, at least by the standards of these eighteenth-century gentlemen, grueling. But the delegates still had a few pieces of business with which to deal before they could adjourn.

Since 1754, Benjamin Franklin had sought to promote greater cooperation among the colonies. In those early days, with most colonies feeling a stronger connection to the imperial government in London than to one another, Franklin's "Albany Plan of Union"—so named because he presented it at a meeting of representatives from the colonies in Albany, New York, to discuss ways of cooperating during the impending French and Indian War—went nowhere. But he never let go of the idea. On July 21, he circulated a plan for an Articles of Confederation and Perpetual Union to the delegates. It called for the creation of an entity called "The United Colonies of North America." Its aim and substance were not altogether different from the document of the same name that was eventually adopted by the independent American states in 1783. Franklin's plan was intended as a "league of friendship" among the colonies, with the goal of promoting their general defense, safety and "mutual and general welfare." The plan would, in essence, have converted the extra-legal Continental Congress into a duly constituted body, and, going even further than the eventual Articles of Confederation, it called for each colony to contribute revenues to a "common Treasury" in proportion to their populations.[27]

Franklin's proposal is a testament to his wisdom and foresight. As perhaps the most cosmopolitan member of the Congress, he realized that some more formal union among the colonies—or, perhaps, eventually, the independent states—was essential to the common good. But he also had the foresight to realize that he was probably ahead of the game, and that Congress was not yet prepared to embrace his plan. Rather than formally proposing it to Congress, he simply asked Charles Thomson to circulate it among the delegates, believing it would at least get the delegates started in "turn[ing] the subject in their minds."[28]

The final article of Franklin's plan stipulated that the "Union thereby establish'd is to continue firm till the Terms of Reconciliation proposed in the Petition of the last Congress to the King are agreed to." Franklin probably hoped that this article would deflect any fears among the delegates that the act of entering into a confederation of "United Colonies" would imply that independence from Great Britain was somehow inevitable. Whether or not he actually believed that that was the case, he did not reveal. Whatever he believed, Franklin was correct in his prediction that many of the delegates—indeed, probably a majority of them—were simply not ready to move forward in creating a formal union among their colonies.

Thomas Jefferson agreed with the plan's general thrust, but he noted that "others were revolted by it." As a consequence, both Franklin and Jefferson, realizing that the plan would not likely be adopted by the Congress, and not wishing to "startle many members so much that they would suspect we had lost sight of reconciliation with Great Britain," were content merely to circulate it without asking the delegates to vote on it.[29]

A Final "NO!" to Lord North

Way back in February of 1775, Parliament had passed a set of resolutions endorsing Lord North's plan of "reconciliation." It was a plan so obviously unacceptable to the colonies that the Continental Congress had never gotten around to formally rejecting it. In late May, the New Jersey and Pennsylvania legislatures, still hoping to find some common ground with the British ministry, had asked the Congress to consider North's resolutions. But the intervening events—especially the Battle of Bunker Hill and the firmly worded Declaration on Taking Arms—made the whole subject seem moot.

But the matter did not die. In late April of 1775, Virginia's governor, Lord Dunmore, in a move that would prove disastrously misguided, insisted that the colony's provincial legislature take North's proposals under consideration. On June 12, the House of Burgesses responded, in the form of a committee report drafted by Thomas Jefferson, who had not yet left for Philadelphia. Jefferson, backed unanimously by his Virginia colleagues, could not have been more emphatic: North's proposals, when "viewed in every point of light," brought nothing but "pain and disappointment." The offer to forbear taxing the colonies if the colonies agreed, to Parliament's satisfaction, to tax themselves, "only change[d] the form of oppression without lightening its burden." Although Jefferson had already left for Philadelphia by the time his report was adopted by the Virginia Convention, it eventually found its way to the Continental Congress, prompting the Congress on July 22 to appoint a committee consisting of Jefferson, Franklin, John Adams and Richard Henry Lee to consider Lord North's proposals. Jefferson would again be tasked with drafting a response.[30]

The committee's report, presented to the Congress on July 31, reiterated the colonies' longstanding commitment to the notion that they and they alone had the "sole and exclusive privilege of giving and granting their own money," itself a flat-out rejection of the premise of Lord North's proposal. Not content merely to reject the logic of North's proposal, the report branded it as "unreasonable and insidious," and then proceeded to a recitation of Great Britain's evil deeds since North's offer was first tendered. The report concluded with a determined assertion of intent: "nothing but our own exertions may defeat the ministerial sentence of death or abject submission."[31]

Whatever their differences on the tone and substance of the Olive Branch Petition, there was no disagreement among the delegates on what virtually everyone considered to be Lord North's insulting response to the American statement of grievances. Jefferson's draft of the response to Lord North and Parliament, although toned down ever so slightly, was unanimously endorsed by the Congress on the day it was introduced, July 31. While somewhat anticlimactic, the passage did signify that the Congress, in spite of its conciliatory gesture with the sending of the Olive Branch Petition, was emphatic in its rejection of Lord North's insulting "peace proposal."

By this point, the Congress was truly exhausted. Many of the New York and North Carolina delegates had begun to leave by mid-July, the Maryland delegates had all left for home by July 23 and Richard Henry Lee was the only Virginia delegate who stayed around until the Congress officially adjourned on August 2. Connecticut's Eliphalet Dyer confided to Joseph Trumbull, the son of his colony's governor, Jonathan Trumbull: "We are all exhausted sitting so long in this place and being so long confined together that we feel pretty much as a Number of passengers confined together on board ship in a long Voyage."[32]

On August 2, meeting at the unusually early time of eight in the morning, the Congress rushed through its remaining business— relating primarily to the details of financing the activities of the Continental Army—and then adjourned until September 5. Although many of the delegates scurried home with relief and anticipation, a significant number, particularly those from the deep South, chose to venture northward to Cambridge, Massachusetts, to see for themselves how the war with the army of their not-so-maternal mother country was faring.

The delegates had been in session for less than three months since the Congress reconvened on May 10, but to most of the delegates, as they headed home, it no doubt seemed much longer. It had been a grueling session, involving multiple decisions. Some of those decisions, the most important of which was the creation of an *American* army—would have the effect of moving the colonies closer to independence. But others—most notably the crafting and transmission of the Olive Branch Petition—were signs that many in America were a long way from abandoning their identity as subjects of the king to which that petition was sent. Although their recess was relatively short—only a month—the delegates would need their rest. Eleven months had passed since the First Continental Congress had convened in September of 1774. The next eleven months would prove even more trying.

SIXTEEN

MANAGING A WAR
WHILE SEEKING PEACE

A LTHOUGH THE CONGRESS was supposed to reconvene on
September 5, another week passed before enough delegates had
managed to straggle back into Philadelphia to constitute a quorum.
The Congress was then forced to delay its meeting because President
John Hancock was suffering from "a Touch of the Gout." Hancock
had recovered by the following day, September 13, and when the delegates assembled they discovered that among those present were
three newly appointed delegates from the colony of Georgia, which
had finally admitted that the critical state of affairs had "roused the
attention of this Province." This was a significant turn of events, for,
from this time forward, the Congress would be in a position to speak
with greater authority for "the united colonies" of mainland British
North America.[1]

We have only John Adams's impression of those Georgia delegates.
The Reverend Dr. John Zubly, a native of Switzerland, was a "Clergy-
man of the Independent Perswasion." Adams judged him to be "a man
of warm and zealous spirit," one who spoke several languages—
English, Dutch, French and Latin—in the bargain. The thirty-one-
year-old John Houstounn was, in Adams's view "sensible and spirited,
but rather inexperienced." Adams's only comment about the third
Georgia delegate to appear that day, Archibald Bullock, was to note
approvingly that he was "cloathed in American Manufacture."[2] None
of those delegates would play a significant role in the debates in the

coming months, and, in fact, none would be present ten months later when it came to vote on the crucial subject of independence.

The compositions of one of the colonial delegations had changed significantly. Benjamin Harrison, Thomas Jefferson, Richard Henry Lee and Peyton Randolph returned as delegates from Virginia, but Patrick Henry, who had been an outspoken, but relatively ineffective member of the two sessions of the congress, had traded his place in the Virginia delegation for the position of colonel and leader of Virginia's patriot militia. Although the extra-legal Virginia Convention had re-elected Richard Bland as a delegate, he declined to serve on account of his advanced age and illness. He was replaced by yet another Lee, Francis Lightfoot Lee. Also added to the delegation were Jefferson's legal mentor, George Wythe, and Thomas Nelson, another member of one of Virginia's longtime ruling families. There were a few other substitutions. New Hampshire elected Josiah Bartlett to replace John Sullivan, who had left the Congress in July to serve alongside George Washington in the Continental Army, and North Carolina sent John Penn to take the place of Richard Caswell. Most of the remaining delegations stayed the same, and the tenor and temper of the body remained pretty much unchanged—which is to say, divided among militants, moderates and those still sitting on the fence.[3]

One of the most prominent delegates to the Congress had arrived in a somewhat altered condition. Sam Adams, a city boy all of his life, had steadfastly refused to learn to ride long distances on horseback. On his trip back to Philadelphia from Boston with John Adams, he had, as usual, chosen to travel in a small carriage. But soon after they left Boston, John persuaded him to try riding on horseback. According to John, Sam was "persuaded to put my Servant with his" into the carriage, and then to mount John's horse, "a very genteel and easy little Creature." Sam surprised everyone in the party by the "easy, genteel Figure" that he cut upon the horse, and he ended up riding 300 miles all the way to Philadelphia. But although he may have looked good upon the horse, apparently his bottom was not doing so well. When they stopped in Woodstock, New York for the night they saw that he "could not Sit So erect in his Chair as he had Sat upon his Horse," a problem they remedied by making for him a heavy set of flannel drawers, which, apparently, not only "defended [him] from further Injury, but entirely healed the little Breach which had been begun."[4]

The agenda of the Congress had not appreciably changed during the six-week adjournment. The delegates would spend most of their time dealing with the pressing business of financing and managing an ever-expanding war—a war that seemed at many times to be moving in a distinctly unfavorable direction from the patriot point of view. And, of course, the delegates were still awaiting the response of the king to what they believed to be their conciliatory petition. The contradictory tone and substance of the Declaration on Taking Arms on the one hand and the Olive Branch Petition on the other revealed their own divisions and uncertainty about the message they wished to convey, and while they would continue to wrangle about the most effective rhetorical strategy for dealing with the king and his ministers, there was little they could do until they had received the king's response to the Olive Branch Petition.

Governing the American War Effort

It had been a little less than three months since George Washington departed to take command of the American military campaign. In June, when the Congress had taken its hasty first steps to create an army in response to the outbreak of armed warfare, it hadn't had the time to deliberate with any care on the proper means of governing that army. Since the army itself was composed almost entirely of members of the Massachusetts militia, the Congress simply adopted the articles of war formulated by the extra-legal governments of the New England colonies. When Washington had arrived in Cambridge to take command of his Continental Army, he was appalled by the lack of discipline he found. In part his impression came from the cultural differences between Virginians and New Englanders. The militias of every American colony tended, by the standards of the British regular army, to be ragtag gatherings of relatively poorly trained civilians. In Virginia, notions of subordination and deference to officers of superior social standing encouraged at least a bare minimum of military discipline, but this seemed not to be the case in New England, where a more egalitarian ethic permeated the culture not only of the society, but of the militia as well. A New York physician, after observing the absence of any social or military distinctions between officers and enlisted men in the Connecticut militia, commented: "The popular form of Government & equality of condition" had created such a "level of sentiment and familiarity, that little or no discipline or subordination . . . exists among them."[5]

This lack of hierarchy would have its costs. Washington's general orders to his troops, which he felt compelled to issue with some frequency, give a hint of the behaviors he confronted: one requested that the militiamen refrain from the practice of wasting valuable ammunition by firing their muskets in the air "to no Purpose"; another ordered the men to cease urinating in public places; and yet another sought to put an end to bathing near the bridge in Cambridge, "where it has been observed and complained of, that many Men, lost to all sense of decency and common modesty, are running about naked upon the Bridge, whilst Passengers, and even Ladies of the first fashion in the neighbourhood, are passing over it, as if they meant to glory in their shame." More serious, many of Washington's troops seemed to regard the term of their enlistments exceedingly casually, taking off for a week or two to visit their families, and then strolling back into camp as if such behavior were perfectly permissible.[6]

Washington, who perhaps more than any man in America was used to being honored with the respect and deference of those under his command, was simply appalled. In a letter to a distant cousin, Lund Washington, he complained that the New England militiamen were "an exceedingly dirty & nasty people." His official reports from Cambridge insistently repeated the need for "exact discipline" and "due Subordination" throughout the whole army. But achieving that discipline was no easy matter. As much as American patriots extolled the virtues of a "citizens' militia" as opposed to Great Britain's "mercenary army," Washington understood that an army composed of short-term volunteers, no matter how good their intentions, would be at a disadvantage in combat with a well-trained and well-armed regular British army. "To expect . . . the same service from Raw, and undisciplined Recruits as from Veteran soldiers," he wrote plaintively to John Hancock, "is to expect what never did, and perhaps never will happen."[7]

The other recurring theme in his reports to the Congress was his frustration at the obstacles to achieving discipline and "due Subordination." Washington pronounced the New England articles of war as "Relaxed, and unfit . . . for the Government of an Army." It would take nearly a year before the Congress discarded the New England articles of war and replaced them with a system much more closely modeled on a virtually exact replication of the rules of war used by America's British adversaries.[8]

More generally, a congress composed of delegations of varying size spread widely across the expanse of mainland North America was hardly the ideal governmental structure to oversee a military enterprise of the scale soon to engulf America. But in the absence of a legitimate "continental government" and lacking even an extra-legal governmental structure that included a proper chief executive, the Continental Congress was the only body in America remotely capable of taking on the job. During the course of the year 1775, the Congress appointed no fewer than fifty-nine committees focusing on military issues, some charged with the tasks of drafting addresses and petitions, but increasingly, to manage the practical affairs of carrying out an undeclared war and managing the day-to-day business of keeping an informal continental union among the colonies together. In the very first few days of its meeting in September 1775 alone, the delegates would elect more than a dozen committees to manage the war, among them a committee of accounts to pay the bills; a committee to manage the office of the commissary general, which was responsible for supplying provisions to the army; a committee to study the state of trade within America; a committee to purchase woolen goods for the army; and perhaps most important, a committee charged with answering General Washington's countless letters filled with requests and complaints about the state of the American army!

Government by committee would prove to be a messy and often inefficient way of accomplishing the business of the "united colonies." Over time the delegates would become more knowledgeable in their voting for the members of these committees, gradually developing a better understanding of the skills and experience of their colleagues in making their choices for committee assignments. But the committees were too often shaped by concerns about regional balance or personal rivalries. For better or for worse, this would remain the way the Congress carried out its business until well after the colonies formally declared their independence. Eventually, the Congress would begin to create more permanent structures of continental governance, but even then, influenced by their legacy of distrust of executive power as embodied in their former king, both the Congress and the people at large would resist granting power to a chief executive. In the absence of a strong chief executive, congressional committees would continue, often ineffectively, to carry out most of the tasks of governance. By 1776 the number of committees created by Congress had increased to 233, and over the course if its existence, until it expired with the initiation of operations of the new federal government in 1789, it created a grand total of 3,249 committees. The Americans' experience with royal government had given them a healthy suspicion of concentrations of power in the hands of a few, but the practical consequences of dispersing that power to thousands of committees had their own disadvantages.[9]

That September the delegates took small steps to regularize oversight of the army. They appointed a few standing committees such as that on "Accounts" and on supervising the office of the commissary general, staffed by individuals who might over time develop some expertise in overseeing the conduct of the war, although the relatively frequent rotation of delegates in and out of the Congress undercut some of the stability of these standing committees. The Congress elected one of the most important of those, the so-called Secret Committee, on September 19, to take responsibility for the purchase and distribution of arms and ammunition. That committee, so named because of the importance of keeping strategic military decisions secret from their British adversaries, would eventually function as an informal Department of War. But standing committees making decisions from afar were only slight improvements over their predecessors.[10]

Washington continued to bombard the Congress with requests and complaints about poor discipline, poor supplies and the chaotic organization of the officer corps. On September 29, responding to those complaints, the Congress decided to appoint a three-person committee to travel to Washington's headquarters at Cambridge and, after conferring with Washington and officials from Massachusetts, New Hampshire, Rhode Island and Connecticut, to make recommendations on "the most effectual method of continuing, supporting, and regulating a continental army." The following day the delegates, voting by ballot, elected Benjamin Franklin, Thomas Lynch and Benjamin Harrison to serve on the committee. On that same day the Congress appointed yet another committee to draw up instructions for the three-person committee, and on October 2, the delegates agreed to a set of instructions that limited the committee's authority to making "inquiries" and then reporting back to the Congress. This method of oversight, ultimately involving the entire membership of Congress in the details of the prosecution of the war, was an archetypical example of congressional governance in action. In the case of this particular committee, the results would be positive ones, for when the three men traveled to Cambridge, their interactions with General Washington were supportive and helpful. But over the course of a long war, such harmony would not always be the norm.[11]

John Adams was not at all sure that the three men—particularly the southerners Harrison and Lynch—would be sufficiently supportive of the urgent need to do everything possible to support military action in his home colony. In a letter to James Warren that he sent via a courier traveling with the committee of three to Cambridge, he expressed his fear that the two southerners had formed "some unfavourable Impressions from Misrepresentations concerning our Province." Cousin Sam was more sanguine. Also writing to Warren, he had nothing but good things to say about the trio of emissaries and expressed his confidence that "this embassy . . . will be attended with great and good Consequences." The tone of both of the Adamses' letters suggested, however, that provincial, rather than continental, concerns were uppermost in their minds.[12]

The three committee members arrived at Washington's headquarters on October 15. Washington was no doubt uneasy, perhaps unhappy, about the prospect of the committee's arrival. He was already faced with the conflicting ambitions and egos of an excessive number of congressionally appointed generals—and frustration, bordering on outrage, at the poor discipline of the militiamen whom he had inherited and the difficult but vitally important task of appointing subordinate officers. Now he had to greet a committee charged with assessing not only the military situation, but also, no doubt, *his performance.*

But whatever Washington's reservations, he impressed his visitors. When Franklin, Lynch and Harrison returned to Philadelphia on November 2, they advocated everything that Washington had asked of them. When the Congress acted on their report on November 4 and November 7, it agreed to every one of the committee's recommendations. In addition to strengthening the army in Boston, Congress ordered three battalions to be sent to South Carolina and one to Georgia in anticipation of British military campaigns in the South and voted for additional arms, ammunition and supplies for the army. And it included both carrots and sticks to improve the discipline and morale of the army. It promised pay raises for officers and enlisted men, which Washington had sought in an effort to keep them from leaving the army after their initial, short-term enlistments had expired. And it approved a lengthy set of new rules and regulations for the army, including severe punishments for soldiers found guilty of violating them, even going so far as to stipulate that any soldier or officer who left his post in search of plunder during an engagement with the enemy—apparently a frequent occurrence—would not only be "drummed out of the army with infamy," but also whipped with no fewer than twenty nor more than thirty-nine lashes. Thomas Lynch conveyed the news of Congress's actions to Washington. Referring to the congressional agreement to pay raises for the officers—raises that went beyond even what Washington had requested—Lynch commented, "Being now paid, [the soldiers] must do their Duty & look as well as act like Gentlemen."[13]

Of course, voting for additional troops and stricter rules of discipline was not the same as actually providing those troops or enforcing that discipline, and Washington would continue to struggle to fill the ranks of his army; to feed, clothe and equip it; and to enforce the new rules of discipline. However much America's political leaders would boast about the ideological virtues of a "citizens' army," as opposed to England's professional "mercenary" army, the reality of short-term enlistments, combined with the natural instincts of obstreperous young men who were unused to subordinating their desires to a superior authority, would prove a constant source of frustration to General Washington. His complaints about poor discipline would continue to the end of the war.

But for all his complaining in private, his public behavior, reserved and formal, was always in the service of the well-being of his men. By his self-conscious and public support of his troops, he came to be seen by nearly all of his officers and enlisted men, as not only their leader, but their *champion*. Quite extraordinarily, soon after he took command of the army, he began to be referred to both in official correspondence and by those addressing him as "His Excellency." As historian Joseph Ellis has observed, "His Excellency" was perhaps one notch lower than "His Majesty," but it was a designation that nevertheless placed Washington head and shoulders above any other man in America.[14]

The Creation of an American Navy

Once warfare with the British had erupted, the American colonies found themselves confronted not only by a powerful, professional army, but, perhaps even more unsettling, by what was possibly the most formidable naval force in the world. It was a force capable of blockading all of America's principal ports, virtually putting an end to all American commerce, as well as bombarding American residents from the sea. On October 5, the Congress appointed a committee of three—John Langdon of New Hampshire, Silas Deane of Connecticut and John Adams—to prepare a plan for intercepting two British ships known to be carrying arms and ammunition. Without a navy, such actions would require arming American merchant ships to carry out any such attacks. In the coming weeks, the Congress appointed additional committees dealing with naval affairs and, by October 30, was moving forward with the idea of arming American merchant ships to defend the American coastline. But by now, many in Congress and in the individual colonies believed they needed to create an American navy capable of protecting American commerce and of thwarting British naval attacks on New England coastal towns.[15]

The New England colonies, because of their jagged coastlines, which presented a nearly infinite number of opportunities for British naval incursions, would lead the push for an American navy. While the Congress was in recess, the Rhode Island legislature had formally requested that it take the necessary steps for "building and equipping an American fleet." On October 5, the delegates began to debate the wisdom of the Rhode Island recommendation. Samuel Chase of Maryland was adamantly opposed, calling the proposal the "maddest idea in the World," one which neither the colonial nor continental governments could ever afford. The South Carolina delegates, whose port of Charleston was extremely vulnerable to British attack, generally supported the Rhode Islanders. Christopher Gadsden, the one South Carolinian who consistently favored militant measures to oppose the British in almost any context, argued that some form of naval defense was "absolutely necessary," and his South Carolina colleague John Rutledge, taking something of a middle ground, argued that the Congress needed at least to take stock of how many ships would be required and what the cost of building them would be. The majority of the delegates probably agreed with Rutledge, and for that reason the Congress deferred action on creating a navy for the moment. But they would soon be compelled by the exigencies of war to take at least incremental steps in that direction.[16]

On October 13, the Congress authorized the purchase and arming of two ships, the *Andrea Doria* and the *Cabot*, to be used against British merchant ships that were attacking American merchant vessels on the high seas. A few weeks later it commissioned another ship, the USS *Alfred*, and a week later passed a resolution calling for the raising of two battalions of marines to serve with those ships. But these were seen as only temporary measures in response to specific threats. Each time the delegates debated whether to arm a ship, not to mention the innumerable other strategic military decisions with which they were faced, made glaringly obvious the inefficiency of leaving such decisions to a body of fifty or more delegates, with widely varying knowledge of military operations and tactics but with each possessing strong opinions about military strategy. Indeed, if General Washington had been present to hear some of the armchair military strategizing occurring in the Congress during those months, he might well have given up in despair.[17]

By the end of November of 1775, the Continental Congress had made enough ad hoc decisions strengthening the colonies' naval defenses that it had, even without formally acknowledging it, effectively created an American Navy. On November 28, the delegates unanimously adopted an elaborate set of rules for the Regulation of the Navy of the United Colonies, and on December 13 they authorized the fitting out of thirteen additional ships with naval armaments to defend the coasts and harbors of New Hampshire, Massachusetts, Rhode Island, Connecticut, New York, Pennsylvania and Maryland. It was a navy pathetically weak in comparison to the formidable and intimidating character of the British naval forces, but it represented at least the beginning of an attempt to coordinate American military efforts on land with modest efforts on the seas.[18]

The challenges of organizing a military response to a vastly superior British force would not only strengthen the position of those who were arguing against a precipitous American move toward independence, but they would also reveal once again the significant limitations of the governing structure of the Congress itself. Although no doubt some in the Congress enjoyed their time micromanaging the details of the escalating military conflict with the British, many others were gaining appreciation of the importance of a continental, as opposed to a purely provincial, vision of how the government needed to be organized and empowered if the "united colonies" were to be eventually successful in becoming the "United States." Not surprisingly, many of those same men would be in the forefront of the movement in 1787 to create a governmental structure vastly more effective—and significantly more powerful—than the ad hoc structure of a Continental Congress.

SEVENTEEN

WAITING FOR
KING GEORGE III

THE AMERICANS WERE not the only ones confronting difficult challenges as the conflict between the colonies and their mother country expanded. In London, the British ministry and King George III were wrestling with the same two tasks occupying the attentions of the American Continental Congress. On the political front, the king and Parliament were being forced to confront the fact that their various pronouncements asserting the principle of parliamentary supremacy over the colonies were having the effect of only strengthening the Americans' resolve to deny that supremacy. On the military front, as it became clear that the colonists would rather fight than submit to Parliament's attempts to tax and punish them, Britain's political leaders were being forced to take further steps to bolster their effort to forcibly suppress what was becoming a widespread colonial rebellion. Achieving these twin challenges would have been a formidable task for even the most able and farsighted British politicians, but the crew confronting those challenges in London in the fall of 1775, while neither hopelessly stupid nor deliberately evil, was obviously not up to that task.

Although Lord North was the primary object of the American patriots' scorn, George III had been anything but a passive bystander. In his refusal even to read the petition from the First Continental Congress, he had given a pretty clear signal that he was hardly a sympathetic supporter of the colonists' cause. And as the situation in America deteriorated, he became even more actively involved in the discussions among his ministers about how to deal with what was rapidly escalating from a minor rebellion to outright war.

Our images of King George III are distorted by the lenses of history. In particular, the fact that in his later years he suffered bouts of "madness" ensured that the retrospective view of this king would be anything but charitable. But during the period of Great Britain's imperial crisis with her North American colonies, George III was neither a tyrannical despot nor insane. Although it is easy in retrospect to point to some of the weaknesses in his character and intellect that made him far from the ideal British sovereign to deal with the American imperial crisis, these failings may not have been so obvious at the time.

George was the third in a line of Hanoverian British kings, members of the royal family in Hanover, in what is today Germany. They had gained their right to rule in Britain by a complicated Act of Settlement following the death of Queen Anne, who had died childless. George's great-grandfather and grandfather were born in Germany, and both spoke English only haltingly. As a consequence, neither played an active role in the governance of England, letting British ministers such as Sir Robert Walpole and Thomas Pelham, the First Duke of Newcastle, do much of the day-to-day work of running the empire.

George was the first Hanoverian king to be born in England, to speak English as his first language and, most important, to attempt to play an independent role in leading his empire rather than merely delegating all power to his ministers. He had been greatly influenced by Henry, Viscount Bolingbroke, and his 1749 work *The Idea of a Patriot King*. In that essay, Bolingbroke exalted the concept of a virtuous and impartial monarch capable of transcending the quarrels and intrigues that had marked the behavior of members of Parliament and the king's ministers. But George would not find it easy to turn Bolingbroke's theory into practice. And though George was by no means the dullard some of his critics made him out to be, neither was he the brightest candle in the chandelier, and his studious nature, which helped him keep informed about the issues facing his empire while he was monarch, was at time undermined by his lack of self-confidence and judgment.[1]

If there was any trait upon which George III's contemporaries most commented, it was his seriousness. George's grandfather, George II, would reign from 1727 until his death in 1760. But George III's father, Frederick, Prince of Wales, the next in succession, died suddenly after a brief illness in 1751, when George was thirteen. And so from that young age onward, George knew that the responsibilities of serving as the King of England awaited him. With the death of his grandfather in 1760, the full weight of those responsibilities fell on the shoulders of the twenty-two-year-old grandson. Once he had ascended to the throne, however, he showed every indication of being fully prepared to serve in his new role. In addition to his seriousness of mind, we might add conscientiousness and commitment to our description of him, for George III, unlike his grandfather and his great-grandfather, was determined to be a responsible and active sovereign.[2]

For most of the first fifteen years of his reign—until the conflict between Crown and colonies reached a state of genuine crisis in the winter and spring of 1775—most Americans carried with them a reverence and love not only for the idea of the monarchy but also for the very person of the king himself. Yet as the military conflict escalated, Americans began to change their view, increasingly referring to him as a devil and a tyrant intent on enslaving them. Even the rigorously rational Thomas Jefferson, in the Declaration of Independence, attributed to him such characteristics as "cruelty" and "perfidy," charging him with having "plundered our seas, ravaged our Coasts, burnt our towns, and destroyed the lives of our people." Toward the end of George's extraordinarily long sixty-year reign as King of England, the onset of what came to be called the "madness" of George III—whether the result of a longstanding tendency toward manic depression or perhaps a psychological reaction to the painful disease of porphyria—led subsequent generations of Americans, incorrectly, to attribute his "tyrannical" behavior at the time of the Revolution to simple insanity.

George was determined to exercise all of the powers of the sovereign of his nation, but in the fall of 1775, he found himself depending upon his chief ministers when it came to the American situation. However much he may have wished to act as an independent sovereign, he was working within a system in which ministerial power within both Parliament and his own royal circle was deeply entrenched. Moreover, the array of issues with which he was confronted required that he rely on the expertise of others. Like his ministers, he was no doubt dumbfounded about how the posturing of a few radicals in Boston had escalated into warfare and, in the bargain, had spread to nearly the whole of North America. Ignoring the wise counsel of men like Edmund Burke, whose speeches arguing for conciliation George came to regard with contempt, he was more inclined to agree with Lord Sandwich, who in a speech in the House of Lords in the spring of 1775 had dismissed the American colonists as a bunch of "raw, undisciplined, cowardly men." But the king did not need to depend on the disparaging remarks of a British lord to bolster his sense of rectitude. He had ample evidence both from members of Parliament and from most of the leading members of the merchant class in London that the people of England, in spite of the carefully crafted addresses from the Continental Congress trying to convince them otherwise, were thoroughly in his corner.[3]

But what to do? It was one thing to be convinced of the correctness of his position, but quite another to decide on a course of action that would bring the Americans to their senses. Clearly, what the king had initially perceived as a ragtag rebellion was rapidly becoming something else entirely. Reports of the Battle of Bunker Hill reached London on July 25. General Gage had attempted to put the best face on things, informing chief minister Lord North and secretary of state Lord Dartmouth that the British forces had won an important "victory" at Bunker and Breed's Hills, but as news of the extent of British casualties became widely known, undersecretary of state William Eden quite accurately summed up the situation: "If we have eight more such victories," he observed, "there will be nobody left to bring news of them."[4]

Lord North, though still hoping to find some path toward reconciliation, admitted to the king after Bunker Hill that the war had indeed "grown to such a height that it must be treated as a foreign war, and that every expedience which would be used in the latter case should be applied in the former." The king's response was even more belligerent. "I am clear," he said, "that we must persist and not be dismayed by any difficulties that may arise on either side of the Atlantic. I know that I am doing my duty and therefore can never wish to retract." As the events of the next eight years would demonstrate, his emphatic determination to defend royal authority may have been driven more by ego than by a realistic calculation of the costs and benefits of a protracted, and ultimately unsuccessful, war. But the king would not be the first, or the last, monarch to be so driven.[5]

At an emergency cabinet meeting on July 26, the king's ministers debated what to do in the aftermath of Bunker Hill. The secretary of war, Viscount Barrington, argued that British forces would always be at a disadvantage in a land war and proposed that the king use Great Britain's naval superiority to blockade all American ports and starve the colonists into submission. Lord Dartmouth, whose days as secretary of state were numbered, and the Duke of Grafton, the king's former chief minister who by 1775 was serving as Lord Privy Seal, one of the king's personal advisers, argued for further negotiations with the Americans. Both were prepared to make at least modest concessions in order that America's and Great Britain's political leaders could "shake hands at last." But they were in the minority. The ministers, with the king's support, decided to send another 20,000 men to America, including five regiments of British troops currently in Ireland. Their hope was that by winning a decisive victory in New England, and perhaps in New York, other colonies would see the light and give up the fight. It was also becoming clear that General Gage, who had long ago lost the king's confidence, would have to go. On July 28, two days after the ministers' meeting, George III instructed Lord Dartmouth to recall Gage for "consultations."[6]

In fact, General Gage's persistently pessimistic reports about the state of the rebellion in Boston and its vicinity had been consistently accurate. His advice to the ministers during the summer and early fall of 1775—to evacuate British troops from Boston and to establish a more powerful base of operations in the colony of New York, whose population was considered to be friendlier to the British cause—would prove to be the most sensible course of action. It was, in fact, the strategy his successors eventually adopted. But most of the ministers in London, and, in particular, King George III, had run out of patience with him. As one of the king's ministers commented, "I shall never cease to wonder, that a disciplined army, small as yours was at the beginning of the campaign, could ever suffer an undisciplined rabble to collect themselves, to train and form themselves into an army, and to besiege you in the manner they have done during the whole summer. . . . General Gage must account for this." And account for it he did. On September 26, 1775, he received the news that he had been relieved of his responsibilities as the military governor of Massachusetts.[7]

General Gage was not the only person to whom the king would be unforgiving. Contrary to whatever expectations John Dickinson may have had, George III reacted with pure contempt to the Pennsylvanian's Olive Branch Petition. Indeed, in the context of the long, bloody war that would follow, the story of the delivery—or non-delivery—of the petition might be viewed as the stuff from which tragedy is made.

Richard Penn, the son of Pennsylvania's proprietary governor John Penn, had been specially dispatched to London to deliver the petition to America's colonial agents, Arthur Lee, William Bollan, Charles Garth and Edmund Burke. Penn landed in Bristol on August 13, but since he had been instructed not to break the seal on the document until after he had delivered it to the colonial agents, another week went by before he or anyone else in England knew its contents. In fact, Bollan, Garth and, most interestingly, Edmund Burke wanted no part in the actual delivery of the petition, so it was left to Penn and Arthur Lee to deliver it to Lord Dartmouth, a delivery that was supposed to take place on August 24 but, for reasons unknown, did not occur until the first of September.

Alas, by that time King George III had already made his opinions about the state of the American colonies public. On August 23 the king issued his Proclamation for Suppressing Rebellion and Sedition, which had been in the works for at least a few weeks. Lord Dartmouth hoped to delay issuing the king's proclamation until the content of the colonists' petition was known, but because his influence with the king and within the ministry was fast fading, he was unable to slow things down.

Lord North, though he may have had similar feelings, was not of a mind to stand up to the king, who was becoming steadily more exasperated by the Americans. In the proclamation the king repeated the common, but mistaken, belief that the crisis had been caused because "many of our subjects in divers Parts of Our Colonies" had been "misled by dangerous and ill-designing Men." Those same designing men were to be blamed for the "disorderly Acts," the "obstruction of lawful Commerce, and . . . the Oppression of Our loyal Subjects." But no matter who was to blame, it was now evident that the colonies were in a state of "open and avowed rebellion," in which the rebels were "traitorously preparing, ordering, and levying War against US." Given the state of war existing between the mother country and her colonies, the king had no choice but to order the forceful suppression of any and all acts that might serve to undermine the authority of the king and his empire. The king no doubt hoped that his subjects in America would come to their senses, and he probably did not intend his words to be the equivalent of a declaration of war. The king's misreadings were yet more evidence of the wide gulf in attitude and emotion between the king and his subjects in America.

By the time that Lord Dartmouth got around to presenting the colonists' Olive Branch Petition to the king, sometime after September 1, George III was in no mood even to look at it. Arthur Lee and Richard Penn, in their report back to Congress, averred that though "we thought it our duty to press his Lordship to obtain an answer . . . we were told, as his Majesty did not receive it on the throne, no answer would be given." The Duke of Grafton, looking back on that moment after the final separation between king and colonies had occurred, believed that this failure of communication may well have doomed any hope for reconciliation. Grafton was aware that John Dickinson "and his party" had worked hard, against the wishes of many, to persuade the delegates in the Continental Congress to give their unanimous support to the Olive Branch Petition, but that it was commonly understood among the delegates that "in the case of a rejection of this final application," the next step would be a "declaration of Independency."[8]

Grafton was himself fast losing favor with the king. He was probably as out of touch about the mood of the British ministry as he was about the possibility that the Americans in Congress could ever have viewed the Olive Branch Petition as a satisfactory basis for compromise. And he was certainly incorrect in his conjecture that some sort of deal had been made in the Continental Congress by which the delegates had agreed in advance that a "Declaration of Independency" would somehow automatically follow should the petition be rejected. Clearly though, the king's insistence on going forward with his Proclamation for Suppressing Rebellion and Sedition before even looking at the Olive Branch Petition did not advance the cause of reconciliation.

Nor did belligerent words from the king stop with his August proclamation. October 26 was the date of the king's annual address at the opening session of Parliament, normally a merely ritualistic affair. But on this occasion the king would devote the whole of his speech to the situation in America. There had been a good deal of jockeying and negotiation among the king's ministers between his August 23 proclamation and his speech to Parliament, with some advocating decisive, punitive action against the colonies, and others arguing for further negotiations. Lord North and Lord Dartmouth continued to hope for some path to reconciliation. They had hoped to insert into the king's speech some language about the creation of a peace commission. Such a body might perhaps have the authority to negotiate a settlement with individual colonies, if not with the Continental Congress, which most of the ministers assumed had set itself too implacably against any form of reconciliation that would be acceptable to the king. In the end, however, the king's speech contained no mention of a peace commission. Its tone was essentially similar to that of the August 23 proclamation. It laid blame for the crisis on deranged, self-interested rabble-rousers in the colonies who had duped "my people in America" to "openly avow their revolt, hostility, and rebellion." Their ultimate desire, an "independent empire" in America, would, he warned, be crushed by "decisive exertions" of force by the British army and navy. Indeed, if the colonists deceived themselves into thinking that the British forces would be insufficient to put down the revolt, the British military had "received the most friendly offers of foreign assistance" should that prove necessary—a clear sign that the king was prepared to use mercenaries from Russia and Germany to augment their forces.[9]

In the midst of this belligerent rhetoric, however, there was one small ray of hope—a hope no doubt inserted by the dwindling number of individuals who, like Lord North and the soon-to-be-replaced

Lords Dartmouth and Grafton, wished to leave the door to peaceful negotiations at least slightly ajar. The king declared:

> I shall give authority to certain persons upon the spot to grant general or particular pardons and indemnities, in such manner, and to such persons as they shall think fit; and to receive the submission of any province or colony, which shall be disposed to return to its allegiance. It may also be proper to authorize the persons so commissioned to resort such province or colony so returning to its allegiance, to the free exercise of its trade and commerce, and to the same protection and security, as if such province or colony had never revolted.[10]

Those words amounted to an offer of amnesty—on the king's terms—to those colonists or colonies willing to submit to the his authority. They were almost certainly not intended, at least in the mind of the king, as an open-ended offer to carry out peace negotiations. But they would have the effect of further complicating the decision-making process back in America, for they offered to men like John Dickinson a glimmer of hope that somehow, someway, peace with the mother country might still be achieved.

It is difficult to find even that glimmer of hope in the king's speech. Indeed, all of the evidence suggests that virtually all of the avenues of reconciliation had been closed. The king himself—ever more confident of his abilities and his authority—was becoming more belligerent toward the American rebels by the day. One by one, those among the king's ministers who were inclined toward reconciliation—Lords Dartmouth and Grafton the most prominent among them—were ousted from their positions of power. The members of Parliament who heard the king's speech generally supported it. Indeed, with the exception of a few outliers like Edmund Burke and Lord Chatham, most members of Parliament were more hawkish about the need to use massive military force to crush the American revolt than Lord North. Finally, those members advocating a hard line with the Americans could be confident that they had the support of their constituents. When the Continental Congress agreed on the Association, many of the delegates believed that the boycott of British goods would bring the British economy to its knees. In fact, in the fall of 1775, at which point the effects of the American boycott of all trade with Great Britain were not yet being felt, the British economy was booming. As Henry Cruger, a Bristol merchant, reported to his uncle in New York: "Strange to tell, but a melancholy truth it is, this country apparently enjoys the most perfect repose. And were it not for the newspapers, the people at large would hardly know there was a civil war in America. The poor are industrious, and the manufacturers have full employment." Cruger went on to report that the king was "enraged beyond measure at the defiance" of the Continental Congress, and that the people of the country at large shared in that rage. "Believe me," he wrote, the "bulk of the people will support [the king and his ministers] with their men, and money; and America by the end of next summer will be in a bad plight, unless a peace is made."[11]

Given the apparent solidarity of the British government and its people on the need to crush the rebellion in America, it is in some senses surprising that the imperial crisis between the mother country and her colonies did not explode into a full-scale revolution for independence in America by the late summer or early fall of 1775. One reason for the Americans' vacillation has a simple explanation: the slow progress of news across the Atlantic once again produced a delayed reaction within America to the bad news coming from the palace of King George III. Members of Congress did not hear news of the king's refusal to read the Olive Branch Petition or of his Proclamation for Suppressing Rebellion and Sedition until the second week of November; and it was not until early January 1776 that the text of the king's speech to Parliament reached American shores. The more important reason for the vacillation, though, was that there remained in the Continental Congress a substantial number of delegates—perhaps a higher percentage in Congress than among the people of the colonies at large—whose attachment to king and empire, even if shaken, was not broken. And there would be many more months of vacillation and acrimony among the delegates before that attachment would finally be severed.[12]

EIGHTEEN

SMALL STEPS TOWARD
INDEPENDENCE

A S THE CONGRESS awaited the king's response to the Olive Branch Petition and struggled to manage an undeclared and increasingly destructive war, it also sought to build a common ground on which the delegates of thirteen colonies—all of whom were committed to obeying the instructions of their respective legislatures—could find some basis for unified action. This was no small task, for the story of America's agonizing decision for independence is not a single story, but rather, at least thirteen separate stories, involving differing conditions and differing responses in each of the mainland North American colonies.

In late October, the delegates lost one of their most widely admired colleagues, the man whom they had originally elected president of the Congress, Peyton Randolph. On the evening of October 22, Randolph and his wife Elizabeth, accompanied by Thomas Jefferson, were dining at the country home of Henry Hill, about three miles outside of town. Shortly after the meal, Randolph began to choke, and then was seized by what observers called "an apoplectic fit," most likely a stroke. He died a few hours later. Genuinely saddened, the delegates arranged for a state funeral, which was held on October 24, presided over by the man who had become their on-call preacher, the Reverend Jacob Duche. Not only could they count on Duche to deliver a consoling and inspiring sermon, but he shared Randolph's Anglican faith.[1]

The Move for Political Autonomy in
New Hampshire and South Carolina

Although the Congress was steadily accumulating power and respon-sibility, the delegates from each of the colonies were well aware that they were just that—*delegates*. They were bound by each of their colo-nial legislatures to represent the particular interests and opinions of those bodies. And the mood of those legislatures often varied consid-erably. Not surprisingly, the New England colonies were in the radical vanguard with respect to their relationship with royal authority. Mas-sachusetts had already organized itself as a quasi-independent gov-ernment in the summer of 1775. Rhode Island and Connecticut, because their corporate charters had allowed them to act more inde-pendently of royal authority from their very beginning in the seven-teenth century, were able to finesse the issue of their relationship with the mother country.

The remaining New England colony, New Hampshire, was char-tered as a royal province in 1680. Its governor, the American-born John Wentworth, had spent most of his adult life in the service of the Crown and felt duty bound to uphold all of the directives of the king and his ministry. But New Hampshirites, perhaps even more than their neighbors in Boston, showed little respect for royal authority. By the summer of 1774 Wentworth had alienated most of the political leaders of the colony by dissolving the colonial legislature, and as early as December of 1774, well before the battles of Lexington and Concord, a group of some 350 armed New Hampshire militiamen stormed Fort William and Mary in Portsmouth, briefly imprisoning the British commander of the fort, John Cochran, and, according to Cochran, with a round of huzzas, "hauled down the King's colors." The following day the assault escalated. Some 2,000 New Hampshire colonists marched on the fort, stripping it of all of its armaments and virtually destroying it.[2]

Wentworth, watching helplessly as Fort William and Mary was de-stroyed, was furious. He demanded that the colony's attorney general, Samuel Livermore, arrest those responsible for the "many treasonable Insults & Outrages." Livermore, realizing that the royal forces of law and order were vastly outnumbered by those who had attacked the fort, replied that "a prosecution at this time would be altogether useless both for the impossibility of apprehending and securing the offenders and for the getting of them convicted in case they should be brought to a trial." Livermore went on to observe, sagaciously, that "whenever civil power attempts things hazardous and fails in the execution, it becomes a miserable example of its own weakness."[3]

Wentworth stayed on as royal governor for another seven months, but he was a governor in name only. As his orders were consistently ignored by the residents of his colony, he found himself living in virtual exile in his governor's mansion. By the middle of June 1775, with his mansion surrounded by a patriot mob, he was forced to take refuge in a British fort in the Portsmouth, New Hampshire, harbor and two months later sailed for England. From that time on, New Hampshire's legal and political status was wholly unclear. The residents of provincial New Hampshire—a colony that was still composed of a collection of scattered, frontier communities—possessed the individualistic "Live Free or Die" attitude that has characterized the political culture of the state down to the present day. Thus it was difficult to persuade the people to cede much power to *any* government authority, be that a royal governor or a provincial assembly. But with the royal governor in exile, and a provincial legislature meeting on a purely ad hoc basis, the challenges to exercising any sort of government authority, including the collection of taxes, were even greater. To make matters worse, now that New Hampshire was actively involved in a war that required the raising and supplying of troops, it became necessary for the extra-legal provincial legislature to increase its demands on a reluctant and obstreperous population.[4]

On September 1, 1775, the New Hampshire provincial congress, the extra-legal successor to the colonial legislature, instructed the colony's two delegates to the Continental Congress, John Sullivan and John Langdon, to ask the Congress for its "advice & Direction . . . with respect to a Method for our Administering Justice and regulating our civil Police." The New Hampshire provincial congress was, in effect, asking the Continental Congress to allow it to create a government independent of British authority, much as the Continental Congress had earlier done when Massachusetts made a similar request. After some delay, on October 18 the New Hampshire delegates

(Josiah Bartlett had by that time replaced Sullivan) presented their colony's request to the Continental Congress, setting off a heated debate in the Assembly Room of the Pennsylvania State House. "The arguments on this matter," the New Hampshire delegates reported to one of their colleagues back home, "were Truly Ciceronial." It was one thing to grant Massachusetts, which was already in a state of war with the British, the authority to organize its own government. Many of the delegates, however, felt that New Hampshire's situation—marked by vigilante violence to be sure, but not outright warfare—did not warrant the step of authorizing still another colony to declare its independence from royal authority. Facing down those who opposed New Hampshire's request to form its own government, John Adams urged the Congress to direct all of the "states . . . to call Conventions and institute regular Governments." His use of the word "states" was intentional, for by that time, as he later recalled, he "mortally hated the Words 'Province, Colony, and Mother Country'," and sought to "erase [them] out of our language."

On October 26, Adams, along with John Rutledge, Samuel Ward, Richard Henry Lee and Roger Sherman, was chosen by the Congress to serve on a committee to draft a response to the New Hampshire request. On November 3, the committee recommended, and the Congress approved, a resolution encouraging the New Hampshire provincial convention to move forward to "establish such a form of government as, in their judgment, will best produce the happiness of the people, and most effectively secure peace and good order in the province," although they stopped short of embracing Adams's use of the term "state" to describe the government that was to be created."[5]

The New Hampshire resolution was a critically important step in the process by which the American colonies began to establish governments independent of royal authority. The structures and methods of operation of the Massachusetts colonial government had been explicitly laid out in that colony's charter of 1691, and the Congress had been equally explicit in laying out the terms under which the Bay Colony could form its own government. New Hampshire lacked a royal charter, and the Congress gave to the colony's political leaders an open-ended endorsement to establish whatever form of government would best serve the needs of the people of the colony. It would be a government without any vestige of royal influence or authority.

The following day, November 4, the Congress received a similar petition from South Carolina. In one sense South Carolina's situation was like that of New Hampshire: the circumstances that paved the way for the request to form a new government were brought about by the forced departure of each colony's royal governor—in South Carolina's case, the unexpectedly speedy exit of Lord William Campbell, who had only assumed the governorship in mid-June of 1775 and initially attempted to work with the provincial leadership of the colony. But two sets of circumstances worked against those efforts. Although up to that point there had been no armed conflicts within South Carolina between British troops and South Carolina militiamen, virtually all of the residents of the colony's principal port city of Charleston were painfully aware of the vulnerability of that port to British naval attack. The growing presence of British warships in Charleston harbor was visible to all.

Another, more complex set of events was occurring on South Carolina's frontier. It did even more to undermine the relationship between the governor and the provincial leadership of the colony. Those events had little to do with America's imperial crisis with Great Britain. It was a purely internal affair brought on by resentment among many of the ordinary settlers of the South Carolina backcountry. They were angry over what they believed to be the unresponsive, and in many cases outright corrupt, behavior of their local judges and political officials. The fact that many of those local officials were politically connected to the ruling political elite was not lost on the backcountry settlers. As tensions between royal and provincial officials increased, Governor Campbell attempted to win the backcountry settlers over to his side. By mid-July, rival military forces, some loyal to the governor and others to the patriot cause, began to jostle for position in the South Carolina backcountry, and in mid-September, those tensions exploded into brief, but bloody warfare. At that point, relations between the ruling provincial elite in Charleston went rapidly downhill, and Governor Campbell dissolved the South Carolina provincial assembly in Charleston and, with a small cadre of royal officials, fled the city, relocating their government to a British warship, HMS *Tamar,* in the Charleston harbor.[6]

The conflict was sufficiently unsettling to South Carolina's delegation to the Continental Congress that the rival factions in that delegation—the radicals Christopher Gadsden and Thomas Lynch on the one hand and the two Rutledges on the other—came on November 4, 1775, to support a petition from the South Carolina Provincial Convention asking permission to organize a government of their own.[7]

John Adams, who had often bristled at what he saw as the Rutledges' timidity, was exultant that John Rutledge "was now completely with Us, in our desire of revolutionizing all the Governments." In fact, John Rutledge probably did not consider the move to reorganize South Carolina's government as quite the revolutionary step that Adams believed it to be, nor did he believe that it was a step that should necessarily be imitated by other colonies. Indeed, Rutledge's concerns were more parochial, relating to his commitment to remaining the most powerful politician in South Carolina. As soon as Congress passed the resolution authorizing South Carolina to organize its own government, Rutledge set sail for Charleston so that he could fend off any of his political rivals as his colony embarked on the process of creating a government independent of royal authority. But however much the actions of South Carolina's provincial leaders both inside the colony and within the Congress may have been motivated by their desire to maintain their oligarchic power in their colony, the practical effect of those actions was to move the colony much closer to a position of virtual autonomy from royal authority.[8]

John Adams saw in the resolutions authorizing New Hampshire and South Carolina to reorganize their governments an opportunity to encourage other colonies to follow suit. Indeed, during the debate on those resolutions Adams argued that the Congress should "expunge the Word Colony and Colonies," from the congressional journal altogether, substituting the words "State and States." He also wanted the Congress to refer to the conflict with England as a "War" rather than a "Dispute." During that same debate, he even tried, unsuccessfully, to persuade the Congress to pass an additional resolution urging the people of all the "states" to create new governments. Had he been successful in these efforts, the Congress truly would have taken a giant step toward revolution. But, Adams lamented, "the Child was not yet weaned," and the Congress refused to take that step.[9]

New Jersey Bucks the Tide

Whatever the differences between the conditions and motives surrounding the decisions by New Hampshire and South Carolina, they had nevertheless moved in the same direction. But not all states were inclined to follow them. Indeed, New Jersey—whose royal governor was William Franklin, Benjamin Franklin's illegitimate son and a man who had for most of his life had a problematic relationship with his father—seemed to be moving in the opposite direction. On November 27, the New Jersey provincial assembly went so far as to draft its own olive branch petition to the king, "humbly beseeching him to use his interposition to prevent the effusion of blood; and to express the great desire this House hath to a restoration of peace and harmony with the Parent State." The following day, the assembly passed another resolution explicitly disavowing any desire for "Independency," a sentiment echoed by Governor Franklin in a letter to the British secretary of state, Lord Dartmouth, in which he assured Dartmouth that most of the people in New Jersey, as well as those in Pennsylvania, were opposed to independence.[10]

Although a majority of delegates to the Congress were still not ready to advocate independence in the late fall of 1775, most frowned upon New Jersey's actions, which seemed a deliberate attempt to undermine congressional authority. New Jersey's determination to disavow any sentiments leading toward independence was in some senses merely an echo of an earlier action by Pennsylvania's assembly, where a prevailing conservative majority had on November 8 instructed its delegates to the Continental Congress to "dissent from and utterly reject, any Propositions . . . that may cause or lead to a Separation from the Mother Country or a Change of the Form of this Government." But New Jersey's actions were particularly annoying, for by the second week in November, the delegates to the Congress had learned of the king's refusal even to read the Olive Branch Petition and of his Proclamation for Suppressing Rebellion and Sedition. And so, on December 4, the Congress unanimously passed a resolution rebuking that colony for even thinking about separately petitioning either the king or Parliament. The fact that the New Jersey congressional delegates joined in voting for that position was just one of many indications of the tensions that sometimes existed between those serving in the Congress and the colonial legislatures that had elected them. The Congress then dispatched a committee of three influential members—John Dickinson, George Wythe and John Jay—to the colonial capital in Burlington to persuade the New Jersey assembly to reverse course.[11]

John Dickinson's Disappointment

John Dickinson had only rarely taken part in the proceedings of the Congress during the month of November. The Pennsylvania provincial assembly, of which he was also a member, had been meeting upstairs in the Long Room of the Pennsylvania State House while the Continental Congress remained in session and occupied the Assembly Room. But by the end of November, having received the news of the king's cavalier dismissal of the petition on which he had labored so diligently and on which he had staked so much of his personal reputation, Dickinson was every bit as unhappy with New Jersey's actions as were his fellow congressional delegates.

Although Dickinson left no record of his reaction upon receiving the news of the king's refusal to read his petition, he was certainly acutely aware of the "I told you so's" that were being uttered by those who had so strenuously opposed sending the petition in the first place. Rhode Island's Samuel Ward, writing to his wife, Deborah, expressed relief that the king had spurned the Congress's overtures, for it had the "Happy effect," he said, of causing "those who hoped for Redress from our Petitions now [to] give them up & heartily join with us in carrying on the War vigorously." The following day, in a long letter to his brother Henry, Samuel was even more ebullient, noting that "One of the Gentlemen"—most likely Samuel Chase of Maryland—"who has been most sanguine for pacific measures & very jealous of the N.E. Colonies, addressing me in the stile of Brother Rebel, told me he was now ready to join Us heartily. We have got says He, a sufficient Answer to our Petition." As for Ward himself: "I want nothing more but am ready to declare Ourselves independent." In a letter to his Massachusetts comrade-in-arms James Warren, Sam Adams could not contain either his relief or his pleasure at hearing the news of the king's rejection. He had been more patient and restrained in his utterances than his younger cousin throughout the deliberations of both the First and Second Congresses. And feeling a constraint imposed by the rule of secrecy, he gave Warren no specifics of the king's response to the Olive Branch Petition, but he nevertheless reported, exultantly, that the king and his ministers, by their actions, would "necessarily produce the grandest Revolutions the World have ever yet seen." It is worth noting that Adams referred to the "grandest Revolutions" in the plural, indicative of the fact that he was thinking about the revolt against Great Britain as one of multiple revolutions carried out in individual colonies, rather than a single effort among the "united colonies."[12]

Surprisingly, Sam's cousin John did not comment on the king's cavalier rejection of the Olive Branch Petition, even though his correspondence during the days and weeks following news of the rejection was filled with detailed information about the secret business of the Congress. And given his now-open contempt for John Dickinson's timidity, it is also surprising that he did not use the occasion of the arrival of the news as yet another opportunity to disparage his Pennsylvania rival. One possible reason for his reticence may have been the adoption by Congress of a much more explicitly stringent rule regarding secrecy on November 9. Although there is no record of the debate that preceded the Congress's decision, there is no mistaking that body's heightened concern on the subject. The resolution, which every member of Congress was required to sign, not only reiterated the sentiment that "ties of virtue, honor, and love of his Country" obligated all members of Congress to abide by the rule of secrecy, but it went further, stipulating "that if any member shall violate this agreement he shall be expelled [from] this Congress and deemed an enemy to the liberties of America." Certainly one reason for adopting the more stringent rule of secrecy was the fact that America was involved in an ever-expanding war, and the members of Congress were daily discussing and making both tactical and administrative decisions about how that war should be fought. As a consequence, the risks now posed by indiscretion among the delegates were no longer limited to minor embarrassments; the lives of soldiers were on the line, and any bit of indiscretion that might further endanger the lives of those soldiers was simply not tolerable.[13]

And the new secrecy rules seem to have accomplished their purpose. As one reads the letters back home from members of the Congress after the adoption of the stricter rule of secrecy, it is apparent that the delegates were more careful in what they reported. Even John Adams, though on occasion he continued to violate—or at least severely strain—the revised and more stringent rule of secrecy, seems to have been more constrained in his reporting to his wife and friends back home.[14]

John Dickinson was never as active or voluble a correspondent as his Massachusetts rival, but given the disappointment he must have felt over the news of the king's rejection of his petition, it is not surprising that he kept his feelings to himself. When he made the trip to Burlington, New Jersey, with his fellow committee members John Jay and George Wythe, he was motivated not only by the determination to enforce a united front among the colonies but also to demonstrate that his zeal for defending America's liberties had not diminished. In his speech to the New Jersey legislature Dickinson tried to walk the line that he had been walking in the Congress itself. He made it clear that the Congress had gone the extra mile in once again petitioning the king in the hope of achieving a peaceful solution to the conflict. But in the wake of the king's rejection, the Congress had, Dickinson proclaimed, "drawn the sword and thrown away the scabbard." It was imperative therefore that the British realize the strength of the Americans' resolve to persevere in their military defense of their liberties. The New Jersey petition, he warned, might be misinterpreted as a sign of American weakness. Dickinson concluded his speech to the legislature with a comment that might have surprised critics like John Adams, for far from being naïve about British intentions, he told the New Jersey legislators that "neither Mercy nor Justice was to be expected from Great Britain." Those words, coming from a man as respected for his moderation as for his political acumen, had their effect, and the New Jersey legislature decided not to send their petition to the king.[15]

Virginia Moves into Open Rebellion

Virginia's provincial leaders had in past decades enjoyed unusually cordial relations with their royal governors, but as we have seen, their relations with their new royal governor, John Murray, Earl of Dunmore, had been going steadily downhill since his arrival in 1771. Dunmore's relationship with the most outspokenly radical and popular politician in Virginia, Patrick Henry, had deteriorated even further. By May of 1775, Dunmore had proclaimed Henry a rebel and subject to arrest, accusing him and "a number of deluded followers" of having "taken up arms, chosen their officers, and styling themselves an independent company . . . put themselves in a posture of war . . . to the great terror of his majesty's faithful subjects, and in open defiance of law and government." In fact, the opposition to Dunmore's policies was hardly confined to a small cadre of "deluded followers." Inspired by the leadership of Patrick Henry, Richard Henry Lee and, perhaps most important, General George Washington, the tide of opinion in Virginia was turning decisively toward the patriot cause.[16]

When Henry departed from the Continental Congress in September of 1775 to return to Virginia in a new role—colonel and commander of Virginia's provincial militia—he became even more of a thorn in Dunmore's side. On November 7, finding himself totally isolated from Virginia's ruling elite and his military forces outnumbered by those who had enlisted in the provincial militia under Henry's command, Dunmore took the one step that he hoped would change the balance of military power and allow him to impose his authority on the rebellious Virginians once and for all. Instead, it would do more than any other action to propel all Virginians—or at least all white Virginians—into revolution.

On that date, Dunmore issued yet another proclamation—this one aimed at Virginia's slave population. Resorting in desperation to what he admitted was a "most disagreeable but absolutely necessary step," Dunmore announced that all indentured servants and slaves "able and willing to bear arms" who deserted their masters to fight on the side of "his Majesty" would be granted their freedom. It is one of the great ironies of America's revolutionary history that the one act, more than any other, that convinced Virginians, and, no doubt, many other southerners, that the British king and his minions were out to enslave them, was Lord Dunmore's offer of freedom to slaves willing to desert their masters and fight for their own freedom on the side of the British. There was no act more threatening—not taxes or trade embargoes or dissolutions of colonial legislatures—to the "freedom" of America's slaveowners than the promise of freedom to those ensnared in the Americans' peculiar institution.[17]

Patrick Henry immediately denounced Dunmore's offer to the slaves as "fatal to the public safety," a warning that needed no explanation to any white resident—slaveowners and non-slaveowners alike—in the colony. At the same time, he ordered the Virginia militia to mobilize for war.[18]

By early December of 1775 more than 800 slaves, motivated by the prospect of freedom, had fled from their masters' plantations and enlisted in Dunmore's army. On December 9, Dunmore ordered a force of some 280 soldiers, including a significant number of "Volunteers and Blacks" to attack a small patriot militia force of seventy or eighty men led by Colonel William Woodford at Great Bridge, near Norfolk. It would prove to be a precipitous, and disastrous, military decision. The patriot forces held their ground, and in part because of the hasty and inadequate training of his new "volunteers," Dunmore's army suffered devastating losses, with sixty-seven soldiers killed or wounded and another fifteen captured. "Dunmore's War," as it came to be called, had lasted less than thirty minutes, ending in a British retreat.[19]

Americans had won a small military victory, but it was the psychological effect of the event that would have the greatest impact. Virginians (and other southerners) would never again rest easy in the assumption that their slaves could always be counted upon to be their "faithful servants."[20]

One of the Virginians most powerfully affected by Dunmore's Proclamation was residing 575 miles to the north, in Boston, at the time of the battle. In October of 1775, General George Washington, influenced in part by his fury at the lack of discipline among his troops in Massachusetts and in part by the prejudices and fears of a man who himself held more than 100 men in bondage, had issued an order explicitly excluding "Negroes"—slave and free—from service in the Continental Army. Upon hearing of Dunmore's Proclamation, Washington railed against Dunmore as "an arch traitor to the rights of humanity"—a denunciation, which, to our twenty-first century sensibilities, seems to contain a combination of irony and hypocrisy. But whatever Washington's moral blindness on that subject, he was coming to understand some of the consequences of ceding this valuable source of manpower. On December 31, 1775, he wrote to John Hancock reversing his previous position, acknowledging that "the free Negroes who have served in this army are very much dissatisfied at being discarded," and admitted the possibility that that dissatisfaction might well cause them to "seek employ in the ministerial army." Washington informed Hancock that he had "given license" for those free blacks to be enlisted in the Continental Army, a decision endorsed by the Continental Congress two weeks later. It was a decision that would have enormous consequences, for during the course of the revolutionary war, free blacks would constitute at varying times between six and twelve percent of Washington's army. That this reversal of policy owed at least in part to the actions of the "arch traitor" Lord Dunmore is just one of the many ironies surrounding the complicated history of slaveholding, liberty-loving white Americans as they found themselves engaged in conflict with their British adversaries.[21]

On December 4, even before "Dunmore's War," members of the Continental Congress began to think about the political consequences of the deteriorating political situation in Virginia. On that date the Congress recommended to the extra-legal Virginia Convention that they begin to take steps to organize a new government. Although it would be another six months before the Convention acted on Congress's resolution, they had, by that time, in the wake of the battle near Norfolk and with the retreat of Lord Dunmore to one of the British naval ships in Norfolk harbor, effectively eliminated royal control over the governance of their colony.[22]

It might seem that in those closing months of 1775, Americans were being drawn inexorably, perhaps inevitably, toward independence. From Lexington and Concord to Bunker Hill to expanded military conflict in New England, Canada and, by the end of the year, in Virginia—more and more Americans found themselves at war. The consistent, emphatic refusal of the British king and Parliament to give even the most conciliatory American petitions a sympathetic review, or, indeed, any review at all, left the advocates of "moderation" in Congress with precious little ground on which to stand. And at least a few colonies—beginning with Massachusetts, then New Hampshire and then South Carolina—began to form their own governments, essentially independent of any authority from the Crown. Through it all, the Congress itself was acquiring increasing legitimacy as the political representative of the "united colonies."

But no one in December of 1775 was gifted with the wisdom that hindsight affords, and many of America's political leaders, both within the Congress and in the various colonial legislatures, were doing everything they could to avoid the last resort of independence. No colonial legislature had come out explicitly favoring independence, and, indeed, most of them had issued formal disavowals of any desire for independence. Some of those disavowals may have been perfunctory, but several—from Pennsylvania, New Jersey, New York and Maryland among them—were both emphatic and sincere.

And the delegates were getting tired. Although the Congress never formally adjourned for the remainder of its existence, as November dragged into December, attendance flagged—so much so that the Congress passed a resolution on November 16 stipulating that any member desiring to leave the Congress had to ask for formal permission before doing so. Going further, the Congress issued a statement to delinquent delegates that it "expect[ed] their immediate attendance." In some senses the decrease in attendance was a consequence of the decision to adopt a system of voting in which each colony had a single vote, with the consequence being that many delegates felt no compunction to be present so long as at least one of their fellow delegates was on the floor. But by this time the business of the Congress involved much more than voting. The Congress had, in effect, asserted its authority as a "continental *government*," and a huge part of that authority involved overseeing an increasingly expanding war through the device of a multitude of committees. It was essential therefore that there be a sufficient supply of committee members to allow the Congress to carry out its responsibilities.[23]

Although attendance at the Congress continued to wane during the month of December—among those departing were John Adams and Thomas Jefferson—most of the delegates kept at their task, working right through the end of the year. The delegates put in a long day on Saturday, December 23, and then took Sunday the 24th and Christmas day off. But they were back at it December 26, dealing with a host of military and financial issues relating to the war effort. It is of course unimaginable that our present Congress would return to work the day after Christmas, but the apparent diligence of their predecessors in the Continental Congress is more easily explicable, for Christmas was not viewed as such an important day of celebration in the eighteenth century. The delegates worked straight through to the end of the year, taking Sunday, December 31, off, but then went right back to work on the first of January.

NINETEEN

THE YEAR 1776 DAWNS

THE FIRST FEW weeks of the momentous year of 1776 brought nothing but bad news for the Americans. On January 7, an express rider from Baltimore brought word that Lord Dunmore had launched a major naval counterattack on Norfolk, Virginia, bombarding the city and burning it to the ground. In fact, those reports were only half-true. Although Dunmore's forces did initiate the setting of fires in the town, it soon became apparent that Dunmore and his men were not solely to blame. Other reports indicated that members of the patriot militia seeking revenge, but also rioters and looters taking advantage of the chaos in the town, may have been primarily responsible for the destruction of Norfolk. It was not clear what was worse—the counteroffensive by Dunmore or the virtual anarchy that had been unleashed in the town.[1]

Worse news was still to come—this time from the north. When a coalition of Massachusetts and Connecticut militiamen captured Fort Ticonderoga in May of 1775, many delegates to the Continental Congress hoped that that victory might mark the beginning of American control of the Canadian provinces that had been acquired by the British in 1763 at the conclusion of the French and Indian War. Beginning in July of 1775, the Congress began to plan an invasion of Montreal and Quebec, the two principal population centers and the strongest of the British military garrisons in the Canadian provinces. General Richard Montgomery, a former officer in the British army who settled in New York in 1771 and now thoroughly committed to the patriot cause, was to command the attack on

Montreal. The young, exceptionally talented Benedict Arnold—a favorite of General Washington—was to lead the assault on Quebec, some 140 miles away.

In late October, Montgomery and a force of 350 troops launched a successful assault on Fort Chambly, a gateway to Montreal. After a difficult march through water, snow and ice, his poorly equipped troops secured the surrender of the British forces guarding Montreal on November 13. They then boarded ships captured from the British and sailed up the Saint Lawrence River to meet Arnold's forces outside of Quebec.[2]

Benedict Arnold and his men had trekked more than 400 miles from Boston and then through the Maine and Canadian wilderness. Confronting stormy, icy weather, an uncertain route involving upriver travel on largely uncharted waters and perilous portages through the heavily forested land, the only thing more disastrous than the toll on Arnold's wrecked boats and the supplies they carried was that suffered by the men in his army—nearly half of his original force of 1,100 men either died or deserted en route to Quebec City. They arrived at the city in rags, their clothes and coats in tatters, boots so waterlogged that they simply fell apart. Moreover, they were ridiculously underequipped. They had no heavy artillery, and many of the soldiers' rifles had been rendered useless either by the horrendous weather conditions or by lack of ammunition. In spite of their pitiable condition, Arnold and his men approached the city's walls and demanded its surrender. His demand being met by British cannon fire, Arnold retreated twenty miles downriver to Pointe-aux-Trembles to await the arrival of General Montgomery's troops [3]

The two men, with their badly depleted armies, joined forces at Pointe-aux-Trembles on December 2. They set out for Quebec four days later, arriving at the city's walls on December 6. The Americans again demanded that the governor of the province and commander of the British forces, General Guy Carleton, surrender the city to them. Carleton, unimpressed by the ragged state of the patriot forces, would refuse not only on that occasion but several other times over the course of the month.

Finally, at about four a.m. on December 31, in the midst of a blizzard, the two American commanders attacked, hoping that the poor weather conditions would offer them cover. Their plan was for Mont-gomery's and Arnold's two sets of forces to converge in the lower part of the city and then to move over the walls protecting Quebec's upper part. The plan failed miserably. General Montgomery was killed early in the battle in the lower part of the town, his head literally blown off by a fusillade of grapeshot fire. Arnold's troops managed to breach the outer gates of the northern end of the lower part of the town, but as they reached the walls of the upper part of town they encountered a devastating assault from the British from above. Arnold himself was shot in the ankle and had to pass command of his forces to his subor-dinate, Daniel Morgan.

The battle was effectively over by seven that morning, with sixty American soldiers killed, as many as 100 wounded and over 300 captured—more than a third of their combined forces. The British casualties numbered only nineteen. Although Arnold would refuse to retreat, staying on the outskirts of Quebec until the spring in an unsuccessful attempt to lay siege to the city, the end result was an ut-ter failure on the part of the Americans to capture Quebec.[4]

News of the devastating defeat at Quebec reached Congress on January 17, 1776. As details trickled into Philadelphia in the next few days, the full magnitude of the defeat began to sink in. Americans, in spite of their anti-French and anti-Catholic biases, had genuinely hoped to recruit the English settlers of Quebec to join their common cause against the British army. Not only had the crushing defeat suf-fered by Montgomery's and Arnold's forces put a dent in that hope, but the behavior of many of Montgomery's and Arnold's soldiers, whose loyalty to the "patriot" cause was so weak that they deserted the army in droves, was anything but encouraging.[5]

In spite of the decisiveness of the American defeat, a substantial majority in the Congress wished to persevere, voting within just days of receiving the news to send reinforcements to the remains of a badly depleted American army camped outside of Quebec. Their determi-nation to do this may at this point have been based more on a purely defensive desire to fortify the northern border of the American colo-nies from British attack from Canada than from an expectation that they could be successful in "liberating" Canada. Whatever the case, however, over the course of the next few months the Congress would send substantial resources—both human and material—to bolster what would prove to be an absolutely futile effort. On January 19, the Congress ordered General Washington to detach one of his battalions in Cambridge and send it to "with the greatest expedition possible to Canada." At the same time it sent out requests to the colonies of New Hampshire, Connecticut, New York and Pennsylvania to send additional troops to the Canadian front.[6]

George Washington found himself in a quandary. He shared the common fear that British control of Canada would constitute a grave military threat to America's northern border, and he had great confidence in Benedict Arnold, who, at least for the time being, remained in charge of the American troops encamped outside of Quebec. But he already faced desperate shortages of troops in Cambridge and could ill afford to divert any of those troops to Canada. Immediately after hearing the news of the debacle in Quebec, and without consulting the Continental Congress, he sent out a direct request of his own to the governments of Massachusetts, Connecticut and New Hampshire to supply troops to reinforce the depleted forces in Quebec. Perhaps wary of having done this without authorization by Congress, he wrote to John Hancock, the president of the Congress, the same day explaining that he had acted only after considering "the fatal consequences of delay."[7]

When Washington received from Hancock a congressional order that he supply a battalion of troops from his own meager supply, he emphatically rejected the request. He wrote Hancock on January 30 that as much as he might like to contribute to "the relief of our friends" in Canada, he simply could not, and would not, deplete his own forces in Cambridge any further. Washington's relationship with Hancock, and through Hancock, with the entire Congress, was on balance a cordial and constructive one, but this would not be the last occasion during this critical period of the war that he would resist the efforts of the politicians in Philadelphia to tell him how to run his military operations.[8]

Bad News in the New Year: The Political Front

On January 8, nine days before receiving the news of the disastrous defeat at Quebec, the delegates to Congress had learned of King

George III's October 26 speech to Parliament emphatically rejecting their various overtures. Most of the delegates were not surprised. Virginia delegate Francis Lightfoot Lee, writing to Richard Henry Lee, interpreted the speech as proof positive of "the bloody intentions of the "King & ministry," and Samuel Ward railed against the king as a "savage" who "ever meant to make himself an absolute despotic Tyrant." He predicted that "every Idea of Peace is now over," and urged his countrymen to begin preparations for all-out war.[9]

John Dickinson, perhaps more than any man in Congress, was powerfully affected by the news of the king's intemperate denunciation of the colonies. He had put himself far out on the limb in persuading the Congress to send the Olive Branch Petition in the first place, and now he could see the king and his ministry busily sawing that limb. But still looking for bright spots, he read the king's intimations of clemency for those colonists who ceased their rebellious behavior as an opening for possible peace negotiations. And perhaps he saw one glimmer of hope in the arrival in Philadelphia of Thomas Lundin, Lord Drummond.

Drummond, a Scotsman who had settled in New Jersey, enjoyed cordial relationships with at least a few royal officials in London. He went to London in late 1774 and sometime in the spring of 1775 gained an audience with Lord North to share with the British chief minister his ideas about achieving a reconciliation with the American colonies. North was still hoping to find some way to peel off "moderate" Americans from those "riotous" New Englanders whom he still believed to be responsible for the mess that they were in. He asked Drummond to serve as his unofficial envoy in America. Drummond's own views about the best means of reconciliation were not all that different from North's, which is to say, they were likely to be unacceptable to the vast majority of Americans. When Drummond arrived in Philadelphia in late December, he began meeting with delegates from those colonies that he and Lord North thought might be most amenable to some sort of peace plan.[10]

Not everyone was pleased with Drummond's activities, and there was a move, possibly led by Sam Adams, to have him arrested as a British spy. In late December of 1775 and early January of 1776, Drummond held a series of informal discussions with James Duane and John

Jay of New York, Thomas Lynch of South Carolina and James Wilson of Pennsylvania. Drummond reported on January 14 that his private conversations with the delegates had left him confident that at least seven of the thirteen colonies were prepared to accept the compromise proposal that he and Lord North had discussed. But however sincere Drummond may have been in trying to achieve some sort of reconciliation, his confidence was based more on wishful thinking than on a definitive head count of delegates within the Congress.[11]

James Wilson, and perhaps his Pennsylvania colleague John Dickinson, may have been among those members of Congress trying to move Drummond's still vaguely formulated peace plan forward. Wilson had significantly enhanced his reputation as an insightful analyst of America's relationship with Great Britain with the publication in 1774 of his *Considerations on the Nature and Extent of the Legislative Authority of the British Parliament*, a pamphlet that stood alongside Thomas Jefferson's *Summary View* as the most sophisticated defense of the autonomy of America's colonial legislatures. But Wilson, far more than Jefferson, remained committed to going the extra mile to seek reconciliation with Great Britain. On January 9, he proposed to Congress that they draft a response to the king's speech announcing "to their Constituents and the World their present Intentions respecting an Independency." By that Wilson meant an explicit *denial* of any intentions to seek independence unless absolutely compelled by British intransigence to do so. Discussion of Wilson's proposal was deferred several times and, obviously finding no favor among the delegates, it was eventually tabled permanently. Wilson also prepared a lengthy "Address," which according to Richard Smith, a delegate from New Jersey, was "very long, badly written, and full against Independency." Wilson soon realized, however, that like his proposed resolution, it had no chance of finding favor with a majority of delegates, so he quickly withdrew it.[12]

John Dickinson, his spirits somewhat buoyed by the appearance of Lord Drummond, and, no doubt seeking to put a more favorable spin on the king's October 26 speech, prepared a lengthy draft of "Proposed Resolutions for Negotiating with Great Britain." The essence of his resolutions, which he apparently never presented, was that a small group of delegates to the Congress be sent immediately to Great Britain to give personal assurance to the king that the colonies were not seeking independence and, once those assurances were given, to use the king's offer of clemency as an opportunity to place before him "the humble supplications of his faithful Colonists" to begin negotiations that would result in a "perfect and lasting Accommodation."[13]

Dickinson also drafted a set of instructions to be issued to these peace commissioners. But they, like his proposed resolutions, were never formally presented to or discussed by the Congress. The preface to the instructions reiterated the commitment of Congress (although at this point it was perhaps more an expression of Dickinson's views than those of the Congress as a whole) to reconciliation and emphasized the humble character of the colonists' supplications to the king. Then followed a lengthy set of instructions that the proposed American peace commissioners were to follow in their quest for a restoration of colonial governments, a return to the *status quo ante* 1763 and, it was hoped, a cessation of the armed conflict. Dickinson's literary efforts, like Wilson's, went nowhere. They were never presented to the Congress for discussion, and by mid-January, the efforts at reconciliation from both sides—from Lord Drummond and by men like Jay, Duane, Lynch, Wilson and Dickinson—had faded out of sight.[14]

The news reaching Philadelphia during those first weeks of 1776 had been truly dispiriting. Lord Dunmore's assault on Norfolk; the horrendous losses suffered by the patriot forces in Quebec; the unyielding tone of the king's speech to Parliament, together with the mounting evidence that "peace negotiations" were likely to prove chimerical—all of these developments suggested not only that reconciliation with Great Britain was very much a long shot but also that a successful military solution to the colonies' differences with their mother country was by no means a sure thing.

Those most disappointed by these developments were moderates like Dickinson and James Wilson—men who were prepared to fight a war if necessary, but who still desperately sought some accommodation short of all-out war. Some of the militants in the Congress—men like Sam Adams and Samuel Ward—although no doubt disappointed by American military setbacks, channeled their disappointment into *anger* and a heightened determination to mobilize the American people into a full-scale effort aimed both at military victory *and* independence. That combination of anger and the increasing realization that there was no alternative to fighting for independence, no matter how difficult that battle might be, would, in those same few weeks in early January, find exquisite expression in the pen of an obscure, recently arrived immigrant from England. The first rounds of artillery fire at Lexington and Concord may have been shots heard round the world, but the verbal fusillade unleashed by Thomas Paine would have at least an equal, if not greater effect, in quite literally changing the world in which the Americans lived.

TWENTY

"THE SCALES HAVE FALLEN FROM OUR EYES"

O N JANUARY 17, 1776, the president of the Continental Congress, John Hancock, writing to Thomas Cushing in Massachusetts, enclosed "a pamphlet which makes much Talk here, said to be wrote by an English Gentleman Resident here by the name of Paine. . . . I send it for your and Friends' Amusement." Thomas Paine's *Common Sense* had appeared in Philadelphia seven days earlier. The greater part of Hancock's letter was aimed at providing solace to his Boston neighbor, who had been replaced by a more fervent advocate of independence, Elbridge Gerry, probably at the instigation of Hancock's more radical rival, Sam Adams, as a member of the Massachusetts delegation to the Congress.[1]

Hancock's reference to *Common Sense* was almost an afterthought. But, in fact, by the time Hancock wrote to Cushing, the work was already having an explosive impact. "Its effects," Benjamin Rush recalled, "were sudden and extensive upon the American mind. It was read by public men, repeated in clubs, spouted in Schools, and in one instance, delivered from the pulpit instead of a sermon."[2]

A Most Angry Englishman

Thomas Pain (he did not add the "e" to his last name until the second edition of *Common Sense* appeared) was born in the small village of Thetford, in the eastern lowland county of Norfolk, on January 29,

1737. His Quaker father, Joseph Pain, earned his living making corsets, those contraptions that, with their ribs of steel or whalebone and laced together on the sides with ribbon, enabled (or constrained) the women of eighteenth-century England to present themselves as narrow-waisted and amply bosomed. Pain's Anglican mother, Frances, was the daughter of one of the town's most successful lawyers. An odd pairing it was—Quakers, a tiny percentage of the English population, were viewed as highly suspect dissenters by the established Anglicans, and Joseph Pain's profession placed him permanently in the working class, whereas Frances came from a family comfortably situated in England's upper middle class.[3]

The marriage of Joseph and Frances was a formula for downward mobility, and the only way the family could send young Tom to grammar school from the ages of six to thirteen was by borrowing money from Joseph's sister-in-law. At the age of thirteen Tom left school to begin his apprenticeship in what was so often the fate of the son of a poor man—following, or being dragged, in his father's footsteps. Although he would spend twelve years making corsets, he appears to have hated every minute of it. Indeed, at the age of sixteen he ran away from home and enlisted to serve as a buccaneer aboard the English privateer *Terrible,* under the command of a certain William Death. Pain's father Joseph scurried to London and was able to talk his son out of his impulsive career change, which was fortunate, as the *Terrible* soon fell prey to the French privateer *Vengeance*; and more than 150 of the 175-man crew went down with the ship, including the appropriately named Captain Death.

Pain had escaped death, but after a brief return to his father's trade, he again signed on as a crewman on a privateer, the *King of Prussia.* He would make the voyage this time, serving for six months and earning thirty pounds—a substantial sum in those days—in commissions. But the money didn't last long—perhaps this was the time in which Pain began to develop his attraction to alcohol—and by 1758 he was back working as a journeyman staymaker in the southeastern town of Dover.[4]

The next several years of Pain's life would be filled with disappointment, and even heartache. For much of that time he moved from town to town in southeastern England, plying his trade first as a journeyman staymaker and then attempting, unsuccessfully, to set up his own business. During that time he met and soon after married Mary Lambert, a maid to a local shopkeeper's wife. Though it was a marriage made of love, only unhappiness and trauma followed. During her first pregnancy, Mary went into an early labor, which ended with her own death and that of her child. Tom Pain was genuinely grief-stricken and, with no wife, no money and few prospects, he slunk back to Thetford to live with his parents.

While living with his parents, Pain studied for an exam to qualify for a position as collector of the excise taxes, a profession described by Samuel Johnson as a low-paying and generally despised profession. He passed his exam in December of 1762, and for the next few years worked as a low-level collector in Lincolnshire. Bad luck, or poor judgment, struck once again, however, and in 1765 he was dismissed from the excise service for "stamping his ride"—the not uncommon practice of reporting that he had examined goods he had not in fact actually examined. It was back to stay-making for a while, and then, for a few years, he managed to eke out a living by teaching part-time at a local academy in London. In 1768, after sending a petition to the board of excise in which he "confess[ed] the justice of your honors' displeasure" and "humbly begged" forgiveness, Pain was given another chance, this time as an inspector in the port of Lewes. During his four years in Lewes, Pain lodged at the home of Samuel Ollive, and when Ollive died in 1771, Pain married his daughter Elizabeth and helped to run Ollive's tobacconist shop on top of his duties as an exciseman. Pain's marriage to Elizabeth was a disaster. The union was never consummated, for reasons that Pain never revealed, and after a few years, the two separated for good. One of the benefits of his marriage to Elizabeth was that he became the owner of her deceased father's tobacconist shop. And though Pain continued to perform his duties as an exciseman, he was becoming increasingly vocal in his discontent about the low wages and demeaning status associated with the position.[5]

Pain sought solace for his woes in the taverns and coffeehouses of Lewes, where he not only indulged his fondness for drink, but also his fondness for *words*. He began to discover his one true talent—his skill at debate—and he spent nearly every night engaged in argument over both local and national political affairs. It was that skill which caused many of Pain's fellow excisemen to ask him in 1772 to draft a petition to Parliament demanding an increase in their unspeakably low salaries. *The Case of the Officers of Excise*, Pain's first polemical effort, gives us some hint of what was to come. Its structure was logical, its style simple and plain-spoken and its tone passionate, angry. In some passages, it went beyond the matter of the unfortunate situation of the excisemen to address larger issues of poverty and inequality. For example:

> Poverty, in defiance of principle, begets a degree of meanness that will stoop to almost anything. . . . He who never was an hungered [man] may argue finely on the subjection of his appetite; and he who never was distressed may harangue as beautifully on the power of principle. But poverty, like grief, has an incurable deafness, which never hears; the oration loses all its edge; and *"To be or not to be"* becomes the only question.[6]

After completing his petition, Pain traveled to London, where he would spend the better part of a year, without leave from the excise service, lobbying members of Parliament to pay heed to the plight of the excisemen. During that time his marriage was disintegrating, the business he had inherited from his father-in-law was collapsing and, not surprisingly, his employers were growing increasingly displeased by his absence. Although King George III was granted a raise in salary of 100,000 pounds that year, the excisemen would get nothing. Pain's petition was not only ignored but considered incendiary and subversive, and on April 8, 1774, the Board of Excise, citing his absence from his post without leave, fired him, suggesting at the same time that he might be subject to arrest on account of his failure to collect the required excises that had accumulated in his absence. No wife, no job, facing the threat of imprisonment—Pain was by this time nurturing a deep-seated anger about the unfairness of life in the kingdom ruled by King George III.[7]

A New Beginning

Shortly after these disasters had befallen upon him, Tom Pain paid a visit to 36 Craven Street, around the corner from Covent Garden, in search of a fresh start. One of the men whom he had met in his campaign for the excisemen, George Lewis Scott, had provided him with an introduction to the American colonial agent and, by that time, renowned experimental scientist Benjamin Franklin. Pain's visit with Franklin would mark the beginning of a long and close friendship. Equally important, when he took his leave of Franklin that day, Pain carried with him a letter from the widely esteemed Philadelphian. The letter was specifically addressed to Franklin's son-in-law, Richard Bache, but it was intended as a general introduction to the community of merchants and artisans of Philadelphia:

> The bearer Mr Thomas Pain is very well recommended to me as an ingenious worthy young man. He goes to Pennsylvania with a view of settling there. If you can put him in a way of obtaining employment as clerk, or assistant tutor in a school, or assistant surveyor, of all of which I think him very capable, so that he may procure a substance at least, till he can make acquaintance and obtain a knowledge of the country, you will do well, and much oblige your affectionate father.[8]

We don't know when Pain made the decision to leave England for Philadelphia. But it is clear that he would not have had the means to purchase a ship's passage to that city had it not been for a settlement he received from his wife and her family upon their separation sometime in the late spring or early summer of 1774. In return for his agreeing not to lodge a claim for any part of their house and possessions in Lewes, Pain was given a sum of thirty-five pounds, enough to enable him to make a new—and, as things turned out, earthshaking—start in life.

The seven-week voyage to America across often-rough seas in the North Atlantic was never an easy one in those days, but for Pain it was a good deal worse. He spent most of the voyage below decks, suffering from a combination of seasickness and what may have been a case of typhus, which killed five other passengers on that voyage. When the ship finally docked at the port of Philadelphia on November 30, 1774, Pain had to be carried off on a stretcher.[9]

His note from Dr. Franklin would help him more quickly than he imagined, as it gained him access to a doctor who would treat him for the next six weeks. After regaining his strength, he paid his call, letter of introduction in hand, to Richard Bache, who arranged a few, short-term private tutoring jobs for him—enough to replenish at least some of his fast-dwindling supply of money.

On January 10, 1775, Pain made contact with a man who, perhaps more than anyone other than Franklin, helped him change his life. Visiting the print shop and bookstore next to his boardinghouse, he fell into conversation with Robert Aitken, a recent Scottish immigrant who was starting a new magazine, *The Pennsylvania Magazine; or American Monthly Museum.* It was, like many eighteenth-century journals, a compilation of miscellany, featuring snippets of information on topics ranging from natural science to mathematics to new practical inventions, as well as essays on politics, literature and culture. Whatever Pain's failings as a staymaker or an exciseman, he unquestionably had a way with words, and he managed to talk Aitken into appointing him editor of the new magazine. And a wise decision it proved to be, for the magazine's circulation soon increased from 600 subscribers to 1,500. Readers responded to Pain's essays, which ranged remarkably widely, from lighthearted pieces on marriage and on "Cupid and Hymen" to serious topics such as the iniquity of the institution of slavery. His attack on slavery must have struck a nerve even in a city like Philadelphia, where antislavery sentiments were relatively common. Pain was at that time living across the street from a slave market, and he was appalled both by the "wickedness" of the trade in human commodities and by the brutality of the institution itself, which he described as "inhumane" and "barbarous."[10]

Although he did not write any essays on the escalating conflict between Great Britain and American during his early days as editor of *The Pennsylvania Magazine,* it is clear that the newly arrived Englishman was following those events. In a brief piece entitled "Reflections on Titles," Pain expressed his general disapproval of the bestowing of titles on mere mortals, but then made an exception:

> Modesty forbids men, separately or collectively, to assume titles. But as all honours, even that of Kings, originated from the public, the public may justly be called the fountain of true honour. And it is with much pleasure I have heard the title of Honourable applied to a body of men,

who nobly disregarding private ease and interest for public welfare, have justly merited the address of The Honourable Continental Congress.[11]

Reading Pain's essays in *The Pennsylvania Magazine* even from the distance of nearly two and a half centuries, one can see the emergence of a marvelous mix of genuine literary and polemical talents. Although he had begun to find his voice when he wrote *The Case of the Officers of Excise,* in his position at *The Pennsylvania Magazine* he had found a platform from which to develop and broadcast that voice. Although all of his essays were written under a variety of pseudonyms, among those knowledgeable about the cultural and political life of Philadelphia, he would acquire—in less than a year's time and after two decades of hardship, disappointment, frustration and anger—something of a reputation.

But sometime in the fall of 1775, Pain's cantankerous, argumentative nature put him into bitter conflict with his employer. Robert Aitken was unhappy with the slow speed with which Pain was turning out essays, and perhaps also by the impression, as Aitken later recounted it, that Pain's pen could only produce prose when well-lubricated by the decanter of brandy always at his side. Pain, for his part, was unhappy both with Aitken's badgering of him and with his salary. Although friends of the two tried to intercede and broker some sort of rapprochement, the breach was irreconcilable, and Pain stopped writing for the *Pennsylvania Magazine.*[12]

Pain's cantankerous nature almost certainly played a role in the termination of his relationship with Robert Aitken, and his temporary unemployment could not have been good for his already precarious financial situation. But he now had the time to begin the writings that would make him famous. Unencumbered by his editorial responsibilities, Pain began work on an extended essay on the conflict between the American colonies and Great Britain. Although we don't know if the idea to undertake such a project was first proposed by the Pennsylvania physician and political activist Benjamin Rush or whether Rush merely encouraged Pain to go forward with a project that Pain had already conceived, we do know that Rush was an active collaborator. According to Rush's later recollection, he had himself considered writing such an essay, but fearing that his reputation and medical practice might be damaged by the "popular odium to which such a pamphlet might expose him" among the conservative political elite in Philadelphia, he persuaded Pain, who at that point had few ties to Philadelphia, to undertake the task.

Pain would seize the opportunity enthusiastically, devoting himself to the writing of the pamphlet beginning sometime in late October, and continuing through December of 1775. According to Rush, Pain shared with him every chapter of his treatise as he was composing it. When Pain finished the pamphlet, Rush also suggested that he show it to Benjamin Franklin (who was now back in Philadelphia), the astronomer David Rittenhouse and Sam Adams, "all of whom I knew were decided friends of independence." Pain had intended to call his treatise "Plain Truth," but at Rush's suggestion, he changed the title to "Common Sense." Rush, possibly with some help from Franklin as well, helped arrange for Robert Bell, a Scottish-born bookseller in Philadelphia who was an avid advocate of independence, to publish it. When the pamphlet made its first appearance on the streets of Philadelphia on January 10, 1776, its author was described only as "an Englishman," but it would not take long for Philadelphians, and soon after the rest of the world, to become aware of the identity of the real author, who, beginning with a second edition, which he himself arranged to be printed on February 14, revealed himself as Thomas Paine, with an "e."[13]

The Revolutionary Character of *Common Sense*

Common Sense would fundamentally change the nature of the debate over America's relationship with England and with England's vaunted constitution. By January of 1776 there were many in the Continental Congress—some openly and some privately—who were advocating independence. But the framework of all of the discussions in the Congress, both among those who were advocating independence and among those urging caution and further attempts at reconciliation, was shaped by a common devotion to and defense of the "true principles" of the English constitution. During the period from 1765 to late 1774, most of America's political leaders found themselves in one of two camps. On the one hand, men like John Jay and James Duane, and possibly John Dickinson, agreed that Parliament had no right to levy taxes of any kind on the colonies but were prepared to concede some parliamentary authority over other issues that affected the welfare of the entire empire; the most commonly cited example of this was the regulation of trade "for the good of the empire," by which was meant the right to levy taxes on trade for purposes other than raising a revenue. Increasingly though, Americans, including Dickinson, were beginning to see that the distinction between taxation and other forms of parliamentary legislation was a fuzzy, and perhaps an untenable, one. Beginning in the early 1770s, and especially with the publication in 1774 of both Thomas Jefferson's *Summary View of the Rights of British America* and James Wilson's *Considerations on the Nature and Extent of the Legislative Authority of the British Parliament,* most Americans had arrived at the position that Parliament had no legislative authority over the colonies whatsoever. In their view—a view endorsed by the First Continental Congress by the time it adjourned in late October of 1774—Parliament could not enact any law affecting the colonies without the consent of those colonies. In their view of the English constitution—a view that in the decades after the American Revolution would come to form the intellectual basis for the British Commonwealth—the king and the king alone was the sole entity having any authority over the constituent parts of the British empire.

By January of 1776 nearly everyone in the Congress had moved toward Jefferson's and Wilson's position. And, increasingly, many, especially those who were advocating independence, were framing their arguments not only with reference to the English constitution, but also to "the laws of nature"—those natural rights of mankind on which the true principles of that English constitution were founded. But those in the Congress advocating independence only invoked the laws of nature as a last resort—as the only alternative open to them given the failure of the king to recognize those "true principles" of the English constitution. That constitution remained not only at the core of their connection to Great Britain, but also at the core of the set of political values that defined their own polities.[14]

In January of 1776, the principle source of division in the Continental Congress was not so much an intellectual, as an emotional, one. Men like John and Sam Adams believed that the time had long passed when America's political leaders could convince the king of the merits of their constitutional position. Their only alternative then was to appeal to a higher law—the laws of nature—to justify independence from that king and his empire, on the grounds that he had irretrievably strayed from the principles of the English constitution. But even for those advocating independence, the English constitution—or at least their idealized view of it—remained the standard for what was good and true. Men like Dickinson, who were fast finding themselves in a minority, continued to hope—increasingly against all evidence—that the king would somehow come to see the light. But for both sides, the English constitution embodied the very essence of a benevolent and just government.

The opening pages of Tom Paine's *Common Sense* entirely and emphatically rejected that logic—and the reading of English history that formed the basis of that logic. "The so much boasted constitution of England," Paine wrote, may have been "noble for the dark and slavish times in which it was erected. When the world was overrun with tyranny, the least remove therefrom was a glorious rescue. But that it is imperfect, subject to convulsions, and incapable of producing what it seems to promise, is easily demonstrated."[15]

With that emphatic, even contemptuous, dismissal, Paine then embarked on a passionate attack, phrased in plain but riveting language, on the very institutions that lay at the heart of the English constitution. Although he devoted a few passages pointing to the injustice and, indeed, the ridiculousness, of a hereditary aristocracy, he reserved his greatest ire for the one institution to which most Americans, even in January of 1776, still felt their greatest affection—the monarchy:

> There is something exceedingly ridiculous in the composition of the monarchy; it first excludes a man from the means of information, yet empowers him in cases where the highest judgment is required. The state of the King shuts him from the world, yet the business of a King requires him to know it thoroughly; wherefore, the different parts, unnaturally opposing and destroying each other, move the whole character to be absurd and useless.[16]

He continued his assault on the monarchy with a discourse on equality that would have implications far beyond the question of America's relations with George III. "Mankind being originally equal in the order of creation," he wrote, "the equality could only be destroyed by subsequent circumstances." Acknowledging with some regret the distinctions that existed, and perhaps might always exist, between rich and poor, Paine went on to condemn

> another even greater distinction for which no truly natural or religious reason can be assigned, and that is the distinction of men into KINGS and SUBJECTS. Male and female are the distinctions of nature, good and bad the distinctions of heaven; but how a race of men came into the world so exalted above the rest, and distinguished like some new species, is worth enquiring into, and whether they are the means of happiness or misery to mankind.[17]

Paine's assault on the monarchy did not depend on that institution's illogic alone. He next embarked on a contemptuous survey of its history; it was an institution

> first introduced into the world by the Heathens, from whom the children of Israel copied the custom. It was the most prosperous invention the Devil ever set on foot for the promotion of idolatry. The Heathens paid divine honors to their deceased kings, and the Christian world hath improved on the plan by doing the same to their living ones. How impious is the title of *sacred majesty* applied to a worm, who in the midst of his splendor is crumbling into dust.

Paine then launched into a wrathful survey of the sins and "savage manners" that marked the behavior of kings throughout the ages, ending with his assessment of the operation of the monarchy in the country of his birth:

> England, since the conquest, hath known some few good monarchs, but groaned beneath a much larger number of bad ones, yet no man in his senses can say that their claim under William the Conqueror is a very

honorable one. A French bastard landing with an armed banditti, and establishing himself king of England against the consent of the natives, is in plain terms a very paltry rascally original. It certainly hath no divinity in it.[18]

George III, the "royal brute of England," seemed to Paine the personification of the utter ridiculousness of the notion of hereditary monarchy, and at this point, he unleashed his anger with full force. "Even brutes," he said, "do not devour their young, nor savages make war on their own families." But "this wretch . . . with the pretended title of FATHER OF HIS PEOPLE can unfeelingly hear of [the American colonists'] slaughter, and composedly sleep with their blood upon his soul."

Paine's imagery was not unfamiliar to his American readers. Americans had routinely referred to the king, the sovereign leader of their mother country, as their father. Whatever the psychological wellsprings of Paine's fury, his anger leaps off the page. By the dictates of the English constitution, Paine observed, "the King Is law, [but] in free countries, the law *ought* to be King." If George III refused to recognize this, Paine asserted, then "let the crown . . . be demolished, and scattered among the people whose right it is." There was no alternative, he concluded, but to acknowledge that "the King is dead; his power is the people. . . . Of more worth is one honest man to society, and in the sight of God, than all the Crowned ruffians that ever lived."[19]

The logic and compelling language of Paine's assault on the king, and by implication, on the corrupted constitution that allowed the king to exercise his powers so tyrannically, are the most emotionally powerful parts of *Common Sense*. But there were two other equally important components to his argument. One of these—the "common sense" aspect of his pamphlet—was aimed at demonstrating the folly of the very structure of the British empire, a structure that required America to occupy a subordinate, colonial status in relation to a mother country. The second was a form of pep talk to Americans, aimed at convincing his readers that they had the virtue, the resources and the strength to achieve independence.

Paine was mindful that while many of his readers may have still felt an emotional attachment to the king, many also cherished their identity as subjects of the British empire. He acknowledged that America may have "flourished under the former connexion with Great Britain," but he rejected the notion "that the same connexion is necessary toward her future happiness." Nothing, he averred, "can be more fallacious than this kind of argument. We may as well assert that because a child has thrived on milk, that it is never to have meat, or that the first twenty years of our lives is to become a precedent for the next twenty." And, anticipating the counterargument that the benefits of being ruled by their mother country far outweighed any of the burdens, Paine scoffed: "Small islands not capable of protecting themselves, are the proper objects for kingdoms to take under their care; but there is something very absurd in supposing a continent to be perpetually governed by an island."[20]

And there was no doubt about it—America possessed the means by which to reverse that absurd relationship. The American colonies possessed, Paine claimed (in what may have been at least one instance of overoptimism and perhaps of outright falsehood in his argument), the largest and most well-disciplined army in the world. Moreover, the American economy was strong and free of debt. And, looking to the necessity of raising a navy to combat British attempts to blockade American ports, Paine boasted that supplies of timber, iron and cordage—the staples of shipbuilding—as well as tea, were more abundant in America than anywhere in Europe.[21]

One of the most striking features of *Common Sense* is the way in which it consciously avoided any reference to the situation or interests of any of the individual American colonies. In contrast, in the journals of the Continental Congress and the correspondence of particular members of that Congress, the provincial interests of particular colonies were always on display. Paine's arguments, on the other hand, were always directed at a *united* America, even if that united America was in January of 1776 more a hope than a reality.

One of America's great strengths, Paine asserted, was the success of the colonies in manifesting a "spirit of good order and obedience to continental government." One of the most powerful arguments in favor of independence, he asserted, "is that nothing but independence, i.e., a continental form of government, can keep the peace of the continent and preserve it inviolate from civil wars." Paine's description of the strength of the "continental" bonds that held the colonies together was at the moment he wrote *Common Sense* exceedingly overoptimistic. But it was at the same time self-fulfilling, for one of the most potent effects of *Common Sense* would be to cause those across the expanse of the British mainland colonies who read it to think of themselves not as settlers of the British colony of Georgia, Maryland or New York but as Americans.[22]

As he was writing *Common Sense* in his room above Robert Bell's bookshop on Third Street in Philadelphia and in close touch with advocates of independence such as Rush, Franklin and Sam Adams, Paine was well aware of the divisions within the Continental Congress between those arguing for continuing efforts at reconciliation and those who had given up all hope for such an outcome. For that very reason, his arguments were aimed not only at mobilizing the public to embrace the idea of independence but also to energize them into pressing their congressional representatives to embrace that idea as well. Professing what was probably not a wholly sincere desire to avoid giving offense to those in and outside the Congress who had been advocating reconciliation, Paine went on to place those men in several highly unflattering categories: "interested men who are not to be trusted; weak men who *cannot* see; prejudiced men who *will not* see; and a certain set of moderate men, who think better of the European world than it deserves; and this last class by an ill-judged deliberation, will be the cause of more calamities to their continent than all the other three."[23]

Paine knew well the identity of that "last class" of men—John Dickinson foremost among them—and certainly one aim of *Common Sense*, an aim endorsed by Paine's Philadelphia patrons, was to increase the pressure on them to stop their equivocation and get on the revolutionary bandwagon.

And *revolution* was what Paine had in mind. In one of the concluding passages of an extra section that he added to the second edition of *Common Sense*, published just a few weeks after the first edition, he observed that there are three different ways by which an independency may hereafter be effected; and that *one* of the *three* will one day or other, be the fate of America, viz. By the legal voice of the people in Congress; by a military power; or by a mob. It may not always happen that our soldiers are citizens, and the multitude a body of reasonable men; virtue . . . is not hereditary, neither is it perpetual. Should an independency be brought about by the first of those means, we have every opportunity and every encouragement before us, to form the noblest, purest constitution on the face of the earth.[24]

Although Tom Paine has come to be known as the most radical of the American revolutionaries, he understood, at least at this stage in his long and controversial career as a pamphleteer and polemicist, that a military coup was not likely to produce justice. Nor could the mob on the street be counted on for virtue or good judgment. It was only by "the legal voice of the people in Congress"—an important validation of Congress's legitimacy—that a truly just and lasting independence could be achieved.

The opportunity offered by that united effort, endorsed both by the Congress and the people at large, was awe-inspiring. Americans could, he believed, create "the noblest, purest constitution on the face of the earth." In what was probably the most stirring and optimistic passage in a pamphlet largely devoted to angry denunciations of the British king and the system of government he embodied, Paine exulted:

We have it in our power to begin the world over again. A situation, similar to the present, hath not happened since the days of Noah until now. The birth-day of a new world is at hand, and a race of men perhaps as numerous as all Europe contains, are to receive their portion of freedom from the event of a few months. The Reflexion is awful—and in this point of view, How trifling, how ridiculous, do the little, paltry cavellings, of a few weak or interested men appear, when weighed against the business of a world.[25]

America, indeed, the world, had never seen anything like *Common Sense*. Within ten days copies of the pamphlet were already circulating in Virginia and Massachusetts. The first edition of 1,000 copies sold out in a few weeks. At that point, the cantankerous Paine got into a bitter argument with Robert Bell, both over his share of the profits and over additional arguments he wished to add to a second edition. He then arranged with another printer for a run of 6,000 copies of the expanded edition and contracted with the Philadelphia printers and entrepreneurs Thomas and William Bradford to sell them. As part of that agreement, Paine took the extraordinary step of forswearing any profits for himself, instead donating his share to the Continental Army for the purchase of mittens for its soldiers.[26]

Within three months of its January 10 publication, 100,000 copies of *Common Sense* had been sold throughout the colonies. By the end of the year, the number of copies sold had risen to between 150,000 and 250,000 worldwide. While pamphlets and broadsides had been a standard means of political expression in England and America for well over a century, the world had never seen anything like *Common Sense*. A Connecticut reader, writing in the *Connecticut Gazette*, gave testimony to the effect that Paine's words were having all across America. "You have," he wrote, "declared the sentiments of millions. Your production may justly be compared to a land flood that sweeps all before it. We were blind, but on reading these enlightening words, the scales have fallen from our eyes."[27]

Moreover, the impact of Paine's pamphlet went beyond its sales. In Philadelphia, it was "read to all ranks," including artisans, mechanics and merchant seamen who may not have acquired the level of literacy to read it themselves. In February, one Philadelphia writer noted that "the progress of the idea of Colonial independence in three weeks or a month" had been nothing short of astonishing: "surely thousands and tens of thousands of common farmers and tradesmen must be better reasoners than some of our untrammeled *juris consultores*, who to this hour feel a reluctance to part with the abominable chain."[28]

The publication and extraordinarily wide and rapid circulation of *Common Sense* did more than any event of the previous decade to awaken public consciousness across all of America and across all lines of occupation and social class to the idea of independence. But in spite of its impact among the general populace, those members of the Continental Congress who had been reluctant to embrace the idea of independence were slow to understand its revolutionary impact. Most members of the Congress did not even mention the pamphlet in their correspondence to friends and relatives back home. But some did, however offhandedly. Henry Wisner, who served in the Congress as a representative for New York only for a month in January and February of 1776, briefly mentioned it in a letter to a friend without commenting on it, simply asking his friend to send it to the Orange and Ulster Committees of Safety and to solicit their opinion of it. On January 13 Sam Adams wrote his trusted friend James Warren telling him that he had sent a copy of *Common Sense* to Adams's wife, Elizabeth. He recommended that Warren borrow the copy from Elizabeth, but at the same time asked his friend "not to be displeased with me if you find the Spirit of it totally repugnant of your Ideas of Government." Warren, like Adams, was an ardent advocate of independence, but he, also like Adams, was concerned first and foremost with defending the autonomy of his home colony. Adams's concerns about Warren's reaction to the pamphlet were therefore probably related to those sections of *Common Sense* that emphasized the need for a supreme "continental" government capable of ruling a new American "empire."[29]

There were a few members of the Congress who were more unambiguously positive about *Common Sense*. Josiah Bartlett, one of the first delegates to read it, quickly sent a copy to his fellow New Hampshire colleague John Langdon, noting that it was "greedily bought up and read by all ranks of people" in Philadelphia. And of course Benjamin Franklin, who, if not an active collaborator in the production of the pamphlet, was at least an approving supporter, fully embraced the logic and implications of Paine's argument, although even he, when sending it to a friend in Paris, commented that Paine's "rude way of writing" might "seem strong on your side." That "rude way of writing" was of course a hugely important part of its appeal. Many of those who engaged in political writing in eighteenth-century England and America were at least as interested in displaying their own superior education and erudition as they were in winning converts to their cause, and the tone of their writing was formal, even florid. By contrast, Paine's writing style was more direct and less formal. Although at times he allowed his anger at England and English institutions to fly off the pages, *Common Sense* was far from being rude or crude—indeed, its eloquence also leapt off those pages. As Edmund Randolph of Virginia later noted, it was indeed a style of writing "hitherto unknown on this side of the Atlantic." It made no effort to display the author's classical learning and, in its avoidance of the sorts of legalism that marked the political writings of American patriots such as Dickinson, Maryland's Daniel Dulany and John Adams, it was successful in ways that those writers were not in reaching a mass audience.[30]

As for John Adams, it would have been very odd indeed if the Braintree lawyer and activist had not expressed his own opinions about *Common Sense*. Adams had left Massachusetts to travel back to Philadelphia in late January and had apparently not seen a copy of *Common Sense* before his departure. Taking a circuitous route back to the Congress, he did not lay his hands on the pamphlet until he happened upon a copy while traveling through New York in mid-February. He immediately sent a copy to Abigail commenting that he thought the sentiments expressed in it would soon become "the common faith." By April of 1776, when it was clear to all that Paine's work had become a runaway best seller and was having a profound influence on public opinion, Adams began to mix grudging approval with sniping criticism. He acknowledged that *Common Sense* was a "meritorious Production" which was to be commended for its "elegant Symplicity," but he then went on to criticize it in nearly every aspect. "In Point of argument there is nothing new," he commented. "I believe that every [argument] that is in it had been hackneyd in every Conversation public and private, before that Pamphlet was written." By May of 1776 Adams had ramped up his ire at *Common Sense*. Focusing on Paine's advocacy of annually elected, single house legislatures in the individual states, he railed against the pamphlet as doing "great Evil." And while acknowledging the power of Paine's writing style, he pronounced him "very ignorant of the Science of Government."[31]

In the months following publication of *Common Sense*, as the pamphlet gained in popularity and as Adams became more and more annoyed by the growing popularity of Paine's ideas about the virtues of "democratical" state governments, the Braintree lawyer was moved to take more direct action to counter Paine's views. In late March of 1776, writing anonymously in the form of "A Letter from a Gentleman to his Friend," he produced his own pamphlet, *Thoughts on Government*, in which he attempted a systematic refutation of Paine's ideas, pointing to their anarchical consequences. Soon after, Paine engaged him in a discussion of their conflicting views, a exchange that Adams characterized as being marked on Paine's part by a "conceit of himself and a daring Impudence."[32]

Adams would never let go of his animus, likely motivated in the main by pure envy, toward both Paine and *Common Sense.* Later in life, as he was writing his autobiography, he indulged himself in an extended diatribe. Although he could not disassociate himself from Paine's advocacy of independence, he brushed aside Paine's arguments for separation from Great Britain as wholly unoriginal—"a tolerable summary of the Arguments which I had been repeating again and again in Congress for nine months." This assessment was preposterously wide of the mark. Adams had been a vigorous advocate of independence inside the walls of the Pennsylvania State House, but his arguments even in that closed forum were more legalistic and less unified than Paine's. Whatever the depth of his intellect or the passion of his beliefs, Adams was never able to put together a single argument in favor of independence in which the whole equaled more than the sum of the parts. *Common Sense,* by contrast, went straight to the minds and hearts of Americans.[33]

Some of Adams's venom no doubt came from the simple fact that the personalities, temperaments and intellects of the two men truly did spring from different sources. And some of it came from the very different cultural backgrounds of the Braintree Puritan and the newly arrived English immigrant. Adams could not resist noting, for example, that Paine only seemed able to write after "he had quickened his Thoughts with large draughts of Rum and Water," a habit that contributed to his "intemperate" writing style. In sum, Adams pronounced Paine to be "a bad Character and not fit to be placed" in any position of real responsibility. And from the late spring of 1776 until his death, Adams never let go of his hostility. In 1819, writing to Thomas Jefferson, he was still complaining: "What a poor, ignorant, malicious, short-sighted crapulous mass, is Tom Paine's Common Sense."[34]

Had Adams's feelings about *Common Sense* been guided less by his intellectual and personal egotism and more by a pragmatic desire to move his fellow Americans closer to the decision in favor of independence, then he certainly would—*should*—have put his reservations about that part of Paine's pamphlet with which he disagreed and embraced it enthusiastically. After all, on the most immediate issue facing both the Continental Congress and the American people, he and Tom Paine were on the same side.

And what of Adams's longtime intellectual rival? John Dickinson's *Letters from a Farmer in Pennsylvania*, had established his reputation throughout America as perhaps the most articulate defender of American rights. It was arguably the most important political pamphlet published in America up to that time and would remain so until the publication of *Common Sense*. Dickinson, who still believed in the virtues of the English constitution and still earnestly wished to find some path toward reconciliation, nevertheless refrained from any public or private response to *Common Sense*. Although he almost certainly disagreed with Paine's unrelenting hostility toward the "vaunted English constitution," he was at that moment in his career not inclined to pick any additional fights with those with whom he disagreed politically. The Philadelphia Yearly Meeting, the most visible and influential representative of Quaker opinion about the unfolding hostilities between Great Britain and America, would exercise no such restraint. On January 20, the meeting issued a "testimony" addressed not only to fellow Quakers, but also to the "people in general" of America. They professed that

> It hath ever been our judgment and principle, since we were called to profess the Light of Christ Jesus . . . that the setting up, and putting down kings and governments, is God's peculiar prerogative; for causes best known to himself; and that it is not our business, to have any hand or contrivance therein; nor to be busy bodies above our station, much less to plot and contrive the ruin, or overturn of any of them, but to pray for the king, and safety of our nation, and good of all men.

Tom Paine was sufficiently outraged by the Quakers' pusillanimity that he added yet another appendix to the third edition of *Common Sense* in April of 1776, an appendix that, after avowing his own devotion to God and religion, went on to mount a scathing attack on the very principles of Quakerism, which, he asserted, "have a direct tendency to make a man the quiet and inoffensive subject of any, and every government which is set over them."

Dickinson, though he had never been a member of the Society of Friends, or, indeed, any other organized religion, nevertheless was seen as being in sympathy with the general principles of Quakerism, if not their precise practices and doctrines. For that reason, many in Philadelphia believed that he was sympathetic to the anti-independence position articulated in the Philadelphia Yearly Meeting's "testimony." His Pennsylvania colleague Charles Thomson lamented the fact that Dickinson's Quaker mother and wife were "continually distressing him with their remonstrances." And of course Dickinson's longtime rival John Adams saw the Philadelphia Yearly Meeting testimony as one more sign that Dickinson's views toward independence were "warped by the Quaker interest."[35]

In fact, though, however much Dickinson may have dissented from the opinions expressed in *Common Sense,* he not only refrained from engaging in the debate over it, but also went on record as disavowing the sentiments expressed in the Philadelphia Yearly Meeting's testimony. Dickinson was struggling mightily to remain true to what he conceived to be "Quaker principles," but he never came close to advocating the sort of submission implicit in the Yearly Meeting's testimony. In describing his Quaker principles he talked about actions that were simultaneously "turbulent" and "pacific," at one point indicating in his notes that he favored a "peaceable War."[36]

Nor was it the statement of the Philadelphia Yearly Meeting alone that caused Philadelphians, and Americans more generally, to question Dickinson's steadfastness in support of the patriot cause. In April of 1776 a wealthy Maryland plantation owner and future loyalist, James Chalmers, published *Plain Truth,* an anonymous, and militantly hostile, response to *Common Sense,* praising the "beautiful system" created by the English constitution and attacking the "demagogues" within America advocating for independence. Not only was the pamphlet dedicated to Dickinson, but rumors circulated widely that Dickinson was in fact the pamphlet's author. Dickinson was sufficiently concerned about those rumors that he penned a response under the pseudonym "Rusticus" emphatically denying both authorship and any agreement with the views put forward in *Plain Truth*. At the same time, however, he made it clear that he was not at that moment prepared "to declaim in favor of Independency."[37]

As the events of 1776 unfolded, John Dickinson truly did stand between several rocks and several hard places. On the one hand, he was on record as rejecting the pronouncements of King George III, disagreeing with the principles espoused in the Quaker Yearly Meeting and publicly disassociating himself from one of Paine's critics. But at the same time, he found himself increasingly alienated from his fellow congressional delegate John Adams and many of Adams's colleagues and quietly dissenting from the arguments of a pamphlet from an obscure Englishman that was being rapidly embraced by tens of thousands of Americans. He was left with the only option of repeating—again and again in slightly varying forms—his fundamental items of political faith: "The first wish of my soul," he wrote, "is for the Liberty of America. The next is for constitutional reconciliation with Great Britain. If we cannot obtain the first without the second, let us seek a new establishment." That statement of political faith would, in the end, cause him to embrace, however reluctantly, American independence. But neither John Dickinson, nor many of his congressional colleagues, nor, indeed, many colonists throughout America, were prepared, even in the spring of 1776, to make that difficult choice.[38]

Whatever anguish John Dickinson may have felt over the difficult personal and political decision that he faced, and whatever animus John Adams may have felt toward both Dickinson and the English pamphleteer who had dropped the printed bombshell upon the American people and helped move them to embrace the position that Adams had long advocated, there was no denying the fact that the publication of *Common Sense* had caused the scales to fall from many Americans' eyes. *Common Sense*, because of its enormous impact on public opinion throughout America, would without question propel the movement for independence forward. But it remained to be seen whether either the members of the Continental Congress or the provincial legislatures that had elected them were inclined to keep up with the rapidly changing temper of public opinion throughout their country.

TWENTY-ONE

"THE CHILD INDEPENDENCE IS NOW STRUGGLING FOR BIRTH"

THE PUBLICATION OF *Common Sense* marked a moment when many in America would, in their zeal for independence, move well beyond their representatives to the Continental Congress. As Paine's message spread around the colonies, and the war escalated, the delegates suddenly found themselves out of touch and, at least occasionally, out of synch with the people. But it was not the members of Congress alone who found themselves in that situation. They were, after all, only the servants of the colonial legislatures that had elected them, and in many colonies—particularly those in the mid-Atlantic and in parts of the South—the politicians serving in those legislatures were lagging even further behind public opinion.

The Congress had not yet become a true agency of the "people." At least a part of the reason for the disjunction between the reaction to *Common Sense* among the delegates to the Congress and that of the people at large lay in the fact that the Congress remained a body that was conducting its meetings entirely *in secret*. Its members were sternly enjoined not to discuss their business with members of the public out of doors. Not only were the people of Philadelphia, and of America, kept in the dark about what was going on inside the Assembly Room of the Pennsylvania State House, but it sometimes seemed as if the members inside that room were

either oblivious to or simply neglectful of what was going on outside their secret conclave.[1]

In the unlikely event that there was a regular reader of all of Philadelphia's six newspapers during the months between January and May
of 1776, that reader would have found precious little information
about what the members of the Congress were actually doing. They
continued to meet every day, but little of what they were discussing or
of actions they were taking was ever shared with the public. Occasionally they would order the publication of certain events—the memorial
for General Montgomery, decisions relating to the appointment of
military commanders or an occasional announcement of the election
of new delegates from one of the colonies—but there was little that a
Philadelphia resident could learn, outside of the rumor mill, about
what was actually being debated in the Congress.

By contrast, there was no shortage of commentary in those newspapers from letter writers and essayists about the proper course that the
colonies and the Congress should take. Indeed, the period leading up
to independence in Philadelphia and in America at large witnessed
something like a communications revolution, with the number of
newspapers being published expanding rapidly, and the number of individuals from all walks of life voicing their political opinions in those
newspapers increasing accordingly. Because of the continuing political
influence both of the Quakers and other conservative members of the
Philadelphia elite, much of what was published in that city's newspapers continued to support the Pennsylvania Assembly's efforts at
slowing down any move toward independence. But elsewhere in
America, *Common Sense* prompted numerous writers to urge for bold
steps to combat British oppression. As a correspondent from Virginia,
writing in New York's *Constitutional Gazette,* observed, "[Tom Paine]
has made many converts here. Indeed every man of sense and candour,
with whom I have had an opportunity of conversing, acknowledges the
necessity of setting up for ourselves, having already tried in vain every
reasonable mode of accommodation."[2]

It would have been impossible for any member of Congress to ignore entirely the growing body of sentiment out of doors in favor of
independence. But the cautious way in which the Congress proceeded
during the months between January and May of 1776 may have given

that impression. As late as April 22, 1776, a writer in John Dunlap's *Pennsylvania Packet* asserted approvingly that "a re-union with Great Britain upon constitutional principles has been the favorite object of the Continental Congress, whose conduct has been steadily marked with defensive movements, and nowhere giving way to revenge or resentment. . . . They have made a redress of grievances, and the protection of America, their only care."[3]

The Congress was not, as some have since claimed, divided between patriots and future loyalists. Joseph Galloway was the one future loyalist who left the Congress early, refusing to attend the opening session of the Second Continental Congress in May of 1775. Only four other congressional delegates—Joachim Zubly of Georgia, Robert Alexander of Maryland, Andrew Allen of Pennsylvania and Isaac Low of New York—would ultimately side with the British. Rather, the division—which seemed by late January to be approaching a stalemate—was between those who were advocating independence and those, like John Dickinson, his fellow Pennsylvania delegate James Wilson and New Yorkers James Duane and John Jay, who were asking for more time to make further attempts at reconciliation.[4]

As we have seen, James Wilson, aided by John Dickinson and almost certainly supported by members of the New York delegation, had attempted to draft a conciliatory response to the king's combative October speech to Parliament. The Congress had only learned about the speech on January 8, two days before the publication of *Common Sense*. But Wilson's proposed address, which vowed that "an independent empire is not our wish," went nowhere. Yet most delegates, including those who were unequivocally in favor of independence, knew that the time was not yet ripe for a formal proposal advocating that momentous step.[5]

Increasingly though, others were not so cautious when it came to independence. John Adams fumed about the unnecessary delay in moving forward with a resolution for independence. Writing to Abigail in mid-February, he claimed, perhaps disingenuously, that he would support any credible plan for reconciliation but added that there was "no Prospect, no Probability, no Possibility" of such an outcome. He then launched into a rant, aimed most likely at John

Dickinson: "I cannot but despise the Understanding, which sincerely expects an honourable Peace, for its Credulity, and detest the hypocritical Heart, which pretends to expect it, when in Truth it does not." Sam Adams, though no doubt just as earnest in his desire to move a proposal for independence forward, had a much better sense of where the votes would fall if his hotheaded cousin were to push for a precipitous decision. As late as April of 1776, he was still urging the importance of having all of the colonies—even the often maddeningly recalcitrant New York and Pennsylvania—on board. Although he confessed that he was disappointed that things seemed to be moving so slowly, perhaps relying on his Puritan faith, he wrote that he was "disposd to believe that every thing is ordered for the best." He went on to observe, sagely, that "we cannot make Events [for] it requires time to bring honest Men to think & determine alike even in important Matters." But however necessary—and wise—Sam Adams's patience may have been, the months from mid-January to mid-May were nevertheless frustrating ones, as the Congress continued to oversee the often depressing military situation, attempted to deal with the demands and needs of the individual colonies, and, most important, to forge a consensus among its delegates about America's ultimate relationship with Great Britain.[6]

By the end of February, the delegates had learned of yet another action by the king and Parliament that erected further obstacles to any possible path toward reconciliation. On December 22, 1775, Parliament had passed the Prohibitory Act, essentially declaring war on American commerce and stipulating that any ships found trading with the colonies would have their cargoes confiscated and be treated "as if the same were the ships and effects of open enemies." If the colonies and the British had initiated their land war at Lexington and Concord on April 19, 1774, the passage of the Prohibitory Act, which went into effect on January 1, 1776, marked the beginning of the naval war.[7]

Not surprisingly, when news of the act reached the colonies in late February of 1776, those already in favor of independence saw this as the final proof, if such proof were needed, of the inevitability of their separation from England. Connecticut's Oliver Wolcott, who had earlier been among those delegates counseling moderation, labeled it "the inhuman pirating Act," and resolved that the time had come for "us therefore to take care of ourselves." Joseph Hewes of North Carolina, who as recently as December of 1775 had been among those urging further attempts at peacemaking, had clearly changed his mind as well. Upon hearing news of the passage of the Prohibitory Act, he admitted that he could no longer see any "prospect of a reconciliation; nothing is left now but to fight it out." And of course John Adams could only say "I told you so." As if he needed any further evidence of the impossibility of reconciliation, Adams noted that the act was being referred to by a variety of names—the "restraining Act, or prohibitory Act, or piratical Act, or plundering Act, or Act of Independency." Of all of those, he believed that the "Act of Independency" was the most apt, for, he predicted, by "throw[ing the] thirteen Colonies out of the Royal Protection," its effect would surely be to unite those colonies once and for all in a desire for independence.[8]

Although the Prohibitory Act was in essence a declaration of naval war, some in the Congress discerned a glimmer of hope in it. Lord North, in drafting the act, had included the creation of a "peace commission," which, if it found that some or all of the American colonies were willing to cease their belligerent behavior, would have the power to suspend some of the most punitive features of the Prohibitory Act. Historians on both sides of the Atlantic have differed on whether the inclusion of the idea of a peace commission represented a genuine effort at reconciliation or merely a ploy to keep the moderates within America from going over to the side of those favoring independence. It seems likely that Lord North himself was genuinely serious about exploring every possible avenue toward reconciliation, even in the face of opposition from members of Parliament, many of whom had no desire to soften their stance toward the rebellious Americans. But however sincere North may have been, "peace," if there were to be peace, would be on his terms, not on those that would have been found acceptable by virtually any member of the Continental Congress.[9]

As relations with England continued to worsen, John Dickinson found himself in an increasingly uncomfortable position. On the one hand, he went out of his way to demonstrate his determination to defend America at all costs. Although he was entitled to a waiver from military duty because of his service both in the Pennsylvania Assembly and the Continental Congress, he not only refused that waiver but requested he be made commander of the four Philadelphia battalions then being mobilized to defend that city against possible British attack. That request was granted, and on February 13 Dickinson gave a rousing speech to the troops, filled with "great vehemence and pathos," that even John Adams agreed was "much talked of and applauded."[10]

But Dickinson continued to spend a good deal of time drafting lengthy speeches, none of them ever delivered, in which he tried to find some small areas—mostly relating to the regulation of trade and the king's control over Crown lands—in which the colonies could cede authority to the king and Parliament without ceding their liberties. And in anticipation of the formation of a peace commission, he spent much of his time writing proposals, never formally presented, laying out the guidelines by which a peace negotiation might be conducted. Finally, as the most influential man serving in the Pennsylvania Assembly, he persuaded a majority of members of that body to continue to state their explicit objection to any move that would lead toward independence. As Dickinson's biographer Milton Flower has observed, all of Dickinson's patriotic actions and beliefs, including his willingness to alienate most of his Quaker friends and relatives by assuming a position of leadership in the Philadelphia militia, were becoming "invisible" to his opponents in both the Assembly and the Congress, for, increasingly, their litmus test of "patriotism" was whether one supported or opposed independence.[11]

To make matters worse for individuals like Dickinson, the promise of a peace commission was daily growing more dubious. Some had always believed that the whole idea was either a ruse by the British or simply unworkable. Oliver Wolcott referred to the proposal as an "insidious Manoeuvre." Josiah Bartlett believed it a mere "pretence" on the part of the British ministry. And William Whipple, a New Hampshire delegate who had just joined the Congress in late January of 1776, labeled the still-invisible commissioners "their Low Mightenesses" and said that though he hoped they would be treated with civility, he also believed that they should be "sent back with a flea in the ear, for I cannot possibly think they are commissioned for any good." Whipple added that, however much some in the Congress may have been pinning their hopes on the commissioners, "some people here (I mean out of doors) are for shutting them up the moment they land." And of course John Adams, who had been contemptuous of the idea from the beginning, became more and more irate as each day passed without their appearance. Writing to Abigail, he fulminated against the way in which the whole idea had "duped" the colonies into paralysis: "A more egregious Bubble was never blown up than the Story of Commissioners coming to treat with the Congress. Yet it has gained Credit like a Charm." Sam Adams had very much the same views on the subject. As late as mid-April, noting that "moderate gentlemen" in the Congress were still "flattering themselves with the prospect of reconciliation" as soon as the peace commissioners arrived, he characterized their hope as a "mere Amusement indeed. When are these Commissioners to arrive?"[12]

As time passed and there was still no sign of the commissioners, that question was on everyone's mind. Robert Morris, Philadelphia's wealthiest merchant and a recently elected delegate to the Congress, had urged patience and reconciliation, but by early April he was running out of patience. Writing to General Horatio Gates, he exclaimed in frustration: "Where the plague are these commissioners? If they are to come, what is it that detains them?" Morris too was coming to believe that "it is time we should be on a Certainty & know positively whether the Libertys of America can be established & Secured by reconciliation, or whether we must totally renounce Connection with Great Britain & fight our way to a total Independence." A few weeks earlier, Oliver Wolcott had derisively spoken of the way in which the moderates in the Congress had deluded themselves into believing in the "Phanptom of Commissioners coming over with the Proffers of Peace."[13]

The individual most incensed by the way in which the fiction of the British peace commissioners had caused Americans to deceive themselves about the prospects of peace was not the voluble John Adams, but the ever-self-controlled General Washington. On a visit to Philadelphia at the end of May to confer with members of Congress on a wide range of future military strategies and operations,

Washington heard altogether too much talk among at least some members about the possibility that the arrival of a peace commission might bring the crisis with England to an end. He was angered at such talk, considering it hopelessly unrealistic, for he was convinced that the promise of a peace commission had been intended solely to mislead Americans. Reporting his experience in Philadelphia in a letter to one of his brothers, he let loose his contempt for those members of Congress "still feeding themselves upon the dainty food of reconciliation." The only "commissioners" likely ever to appear in America, Washington, predicted, would be "Hessians and other Foreigners"—that is, mercenary troops.[14]

Meanwhile, during the late winter and early spring of 1776, America's military fortunes showed modest signs of improvement after the disastrous defeat in Quebec in January. In late February, a hastily assembled corps of North Carolina militiamen had won a minor, highly localized skirmish over an even more motley group of North Carolina loyalists at Moore's Creek. And a newly outfitted version of an "American navy" fought an inconclusive battle with British ships in Nassau, in the Bahamas, on March 3–4.[15]

At nearly the same time, George Washington's army scored its first really important victory at Dorchester Heights in Boston. Ever since his arrival in Boston, Washington had understood that the 100-foot-high bluff at Dorchester, which looked out over Boston from the south, was of even greater strategic value than Breed's Hill and Bunker Hill. The British general in Boston, William Howe, had never bothered to fortify the area because he was confident that British troops could simply sally forth and repel any American attempt to occupy the bluff. Washington had a brilliant move up his sleeve. He arranged to have a herd of oxen pull tens of thousands of pounds of captured British cannons that had recently been hauled to Boston from Fort Ticonderoga up the hill in the dead of night. And then, on the night of March 4, 1776, some 2,000 of his troops moved up the hill into the Dorchester Heights. They immediately began to install prefabricated fortifications to enable them to defend themselves should Howe and his troops attempt to retake the position. The British general, when confronted with this surprise takeover of the most strategic position in all of Boston, had two options. He could unleash his own army of some 2,400 men to retake the Heights, or he could allow Washington's men to remain there, a decision tantamount to giving Washington's army effective control over Boston. Unwilling to cede Boston so easily, Howe was planning a counterattack, but as he was ready to launch it, a huge snowstorm descended late in the day on March 5, frustrating his plans. Forced to reconsider his tactics, Howe informed Washington on March 8 that he and his troops were prepared to leave the city, and leave it undamaged, if Washington would guarantee their safe departure. Washington, although he was fully ready for battle, agreed, and on March 17, Howe and his forces left Boston. Washington was understandably gleeful at his long-awaited success in Boston, but his self-restraint and sense of dignity must have been tested constantly both by the paucity of arms, ammunitions, supplies and troops provided him by the Congress and by the extent to which members of Congress continued to attempt to micromanage his command.[16]

Alas, the news from Canada, which both Washington and the Congress were committed to occupying, was going from bad to worse. In spite of ongoing attempts to win the minds, hearts or military garrisons of the British and French in Canada, the American army's efforts there continued to prove disastrous. In mid-March Congress decided to send a mission to Canada, including two of its own members, Benjamin Franklin and Samuel Chase, to inspect the situation first hand. It took a while for the commissioners to get organized, and they did not leave until early April. The trip proved to be an unbelievably arduous one, so much so that Franklin, seventy years old and feeling "a fatigue that at my time of life may prove too much for me," sat down "to write a few Friends by way of Farewell." And what the American commissioners saw caused them nothing but gloom. By May 1 they had concluded that there was no hope of winning the Canadians over to the American side, and by the end of May they had become convinced that the American troops there were hopelessly outmatched by British forces. Indeed, they were appalled by the state of the American army. They described its officers as "unfit," the regular soldiers essentially out of control and the supplies "scanty & precarious," reduced to "a few half Starved cattle & trifling quantities of flour."[17]

Quite simply the Canadian venture had proved a disaster. By June 4, John Hancock, as president of the Congress, finally wrote to the legislatures of the American colonies that "by the best Intelligence from Canada, it appears, that our Affairs in that Quarter wear a melancholy Aspect. . . . Our Continental Troops alone are unable to stem the Torrent." To some, the Americans' travail in Canada seemed only to provide further proof of the pernicious character of British rule, and therefore to make an American declaration of independence all the more urgent. To others, however, and to John Dickinson in particular, the clear evidence of America's military weakness in that part of the continent reinforced the belief that a premature American declaration of independence might result in political and military humiliation for the colonies.[18]

The Congress's earlier agreement on a boycott on trade with Great Britain was already beginning to have negative effects on American commerce. One obvious way to offset those effects was to begin to develop trading relationships with other nations outside the British mercantilist system. But now, in the aftermath of the Prohibitory Act, the delegates also needed to agree on more aggressive policies aimed at combating the British declaration of war on American commerce. Looking ahead at least to the *possibility* of independence, the Congress began to make overtures to other European nations, France in particular, to form alliances that would not only bolster American trade but perhaps also provide the necessary aid to strengthen the American war effort. And now, at least a few in the Congress, led by Sam Adams and Benjamin Franklin, began to press the delegates to think about a formal union among the "united states" once independence was declared.

On February 14, even before they had gotten word of the passage of the Prohibitory Act, the delegates had begun to discuss the importance of foreign alliances. John Penn of North Carolina wrote to a member of his colony's provincial congress expressing his concern that the British might create military and trade alliances with other nations to bring America to its knees and suggested that the "united colonies" needed to do the same thing. At the same time, Penn recognized the consequences of doing so; he understood that in order to forge alliances with other nations, particularly countries like France that had a natural enmity with Great Britain, America might need to convince those nations that Americans were serious about effecting a "total separation" from the British Empire.[19]

Penn's analysis was right on target both with respect to the necessity of entering into foreign alliances and of the potential consequences of doing so. Two days later, on February 16, George Wythe of Virginia reported that the Virginia Convention, following the same logic articulated by John Penn, had passed a resolution proposing that all American ports should be opened to all nations except Great Britain, Ireland and the British West Indies. And the Virginians were willing to go further. To protect American ships involved in that trade, they were prepared to grant letters of mark to private citizens, authorizing them to arm their vessels and seize British ships on the high seas. Wythe thought that the Congress should go even further than the action proposed by the Virginia Convention. Believing that a vital part of opening up trade to the Americans as well as combating British attacks on American ships was to move decisively to enter into commercial treaties with other foreign powers, particularly France and Spain, he introduced a formal proposal to that effect.[20]

Wythe's proposals apparently produced a lengthy argument in the Congress, for everyone in the room realized the consequences of moving in that direction. The combination of the boycott on trade with Great Britain and an aggressive attempt to open up trade with nations outside the British Empire would amount to a decision to abandon the most important connection—mutually beneficial trade—holding the empire together. The inevitable result, almost everyone understood, might well be an "independency" from that empire. They would debate the matter off and on for several weeks until, on March 19, the Congress finally agreed to arm vessels to defend themselves against, and even aggressively attack, any British ships that threatened their commerce. In the midst of the debate on how to implement the specifics of that policy, Wythe and Richard Henry Lee proposed adding language to the preamble of the proposal stating that King George III, and not Parliament, was "Author of our Miseries." Again, everyone in the room understood the significance of those words—by speaking of the king in that way in a formal resolution, the delegates would be taking one more step, as one delegate phrased it, toward "severing the King from Us forever." The delegates rejected Wythe and Lee's language, but the escalation of America's naval battle with the British narrowed still further any hope for reconciliation.[21]

Congress continued to dither, however, over whether to open all American ports to trade with Great Britain's foreign rivals. While the concern that such a step might amount to a virtual declaration of independence weighed heavily, there was also a significant, and realistic, concern among some that the complexities of negotiating diplomatic alliances with other nations would create new problems. John Adams, who was emphatically in favor of opening American ports to all trade except that of the British, nevertheless clearly understood the obstacles. As early as October of 1775, Adams had begun to make a list of questions that needed to be answered. In a series of letters to James Warren, he began to explore the "complicated subject of Trade." In the absence of reliable trading relations with foreign nations other than Great Britain, the effect on the American colonial economy could well be devastating. It would require, Adams observed, a fundamental change in "our Habits, our Prejudices, our Palates, our Taste in Dress, furniture, Equipage, Architecture, &c." Did Americans, he asked, have sufficient virtue to give up on some of the luxuries they had enjoyed, to become "mere Husbandmen, Mechanicks & Soldiers?" He acknowledged that they might be able to bear such deprivation for a while, but how long could they hold out—a few months, a year? Embedded in Adams's question was a condescension toward the life styles of Americans less privileged than a Braintree lawyer, but the question was nevertheless on target. And the answer was not clear. He posed a similar list of questions about the likelihood of replacing the lost trade from the British with new trading relations with foreign nations. Would other nations, with no strong attachments to America, be willing to "run the risque of escaping Men of War, and the Dangers of an unknown Coast?" Again, the answers were not clear.[22]

Back in November of 1775, the Congress had established a Secret Committee to "correspond with our friends in Great Britain, Ireland, and other parts of the world," but whose most immediate task would be to quietly test the waters about the likelihood of obtaining useful foreign alliances. Initially composed of Benjamin Franklin, Thomas Johnson, John Dickinson and John Jay, the committee later added the wealthy and worldly Philadelphian Robert Morris, who perhaps knew the world of international commerce better than any other American. It has been argued with considerable persuasiveness that this Secret Committee was, in effect, the beginning what we now call the Department of State. Its primarily moderate members (excepting Franklin) immediately began to reach out to diplomats in other nations. Their early efforts were facilitated by the presence in Philadelphia of a Frenchman, Julien Achard de Bonvouloir, who though claiming to be a "traveler out of curiousity," had in fact been sent by the French government to see if France might gain some advantage from the trouble between Britain and America. In late January, two other French emissaries, Pierre Penet and Emmanuele de Pliarne, also began discussions with members of the Secret Committee.[23]

Encouraged by their discussions with the three Frenchmen, the Secret Committee decided in early March of 1776 to send immediately Silas Deane of Connecticut to France to begin exploring the possibility of an alliance. The committee hoped that Deane would be able to ingratiate himself with the wily French foreign minister, the Comte de Vergennes, in the hopes of getting him to agree to provide more substantive aid to the American colonies. Unfortunately, the ship on which Deane was supposed to sail was involved in an accident as it was leaving port, and even when he did finally make it to France, it was clear that the French were not yet ready to commit themselves to an American cause whose outcome was anything but certain.[24]

The eventual failure of Silas Deane's mission lent credibility to John Adams's earlier skepticism about whether other nations would be willing to "run the risque" of an alliance with the colonies. The members of Congress found themselves in a triple bind. First, those reluctant to declare American independence feared that entering into trade and diplomatic alliances with England's enemies would make such a declaration inevitable. Yet, it would be significantly more difficult to win the war and achieve a secure and durable peace without first obtaining some commitments from nations like France and Spain, which had both the commercial markets and the military power to help America look after its own interests in a highly competitive European environment with a shifting balance of power. But France and Spain, were unlikely to make any meaningful commitments to the Americans unless they had some strong guarantees that the colonies would not back down and accept some offer of conciliation from the British. It was simply not in their interest to commit resources to America if the only consequence of that would be to allow the Americans the leverage to be reunited with their mother country, thereby strengthening Great Britain's position within the balance of power of Europe.

On April 6, still plagued by uncertainty about the likelihood of establishing successful alliances with nations like France and Spain, the Congress nevertheless moved forward to adopt the resolution that the Virginians and the New Englanders in particular had been agitating for:

> Resolved, That any goods, wares and merchandises, except such as are of the growth, production or manufacture from any country under the dominion of the king of great Britain, and except East India tea, may be imported from any other parts of the world to the thirteen United Colonies by the inhabitants therof.

The exclusion of East India Company tea, a product from a country not formally under British dominion, was hardly a subject of controversy given the fact that it was that much-maligned tea that had set off so much of the ensuing ruckus in the first place. And there was one other noteworthy provision as well: as had been the case with the adoption of the Articles of Association, the importation of slaves from any part of the world was expressly prohibited.[25]

The important step of opening up American trade to the rest of the world, coming just a few weeks after news of the retreat of the British out of the capital of Boston, provided at least a temporary boost to many delegates who had been suffering through a frustrating first quarter of the year 1776. But as April dragged into May, with still no sign of the "phantom" peace commissioners, the patience of many of the delegates—not to mention that of the people out of doors—began to fray. "This Story of Commissioners," John Adams wrote Abigail, "is as arrant an Illusion as ever was hatched in the Brain of an Enthusiast, a Politician, or a Maniac. I have laugh'd at it—scolded at it—griev'd at it—and I don't know but I may at an unguarded Moment have rip'd at it, but it is vain to Reason against such Delusions." Sam Adams, writing to his good friend and fellow Bostonian James Warren on April 16, acknowledged that the interminable wait for the nonexistent peace commissioners "trys my Patience." Unlike his cousin, he had largely kept his annoyance with the "moderate prudent Whigs" who were still dragging their feet to himself. But by mid-April he too was running out of patience. "*Their* Moderation has brought us to this Pass," he observed, "and if they were to be regarded, they would continue the conflict a Century." He wrote, with remarkable eloquence, "The Child Independence is now struggling for Birth. I trust that in a short time it will be brought forth, and in Spite of Pharaoh all America shall hail the dignified stranger."[26]

While Tom Paine's *Common Sense* may have laid out the logic of independence in plain and bold language, in April of 1776, it was apparent that words alone would not propel Americans—or their representatives in Congress—to take that audacious leap. The path toward independence was by no means a straight one, and there remained many bumps along the way.

TWENTY-TWO

FOURTEEN PATHS
TO INDEPENDENCE

AMERICA'S DECISION FOR independence was never one that a single Congress, representing the supposedly "united colonies," could make alone. While it was gaining in authority as the body responsible for overseeing America's military defense against Great Britain, the Continental Congress remained the servant, not the master, of the thirteen legislative bodies to which the Congress's delegates reported. During May and June of 1776, it became more and more apparent that the decision-making process involved, at the very least, fourteen political agencies. While the decision of the delegates to the Continental Congress on July 2, 1776, to approve a resolution endorsing American independence would prove, in John Adams's words, "the most memorable epocha in the History of America," the legitimacy of that decision rested on the approval of the thirteen colonial legislative bodies that had elected them.

By May 1776, with most of the thirteen provincial legislatures in the American colonies operating as extra-legal conventions or congresses, the claims of those bodies to any legitimacy rested not on royal charters but on the opinions of the people in the colonies in whose name they claimed to be acting. Similarly, the three assemblies that remained legally intact—those in the proprietary colony of Pennsylvania and in the independently chartered colonies of Rhode Island and Connecticut—were by May 1776 increasingly sensitive to the fact that their authority rested not on some ancient charter but on the will of the people. Indeed, more and more, the thoughts and actions of each of America's colonial legislatures were being influenced by the actions of a wide variety of extra-governmental groups—local committees of correspondence and committees of safety that claimed to be speaking and acting on behalf of the citizenry at large. To an extent greater than ever before, the dynamic of events during the months of May and June of 1776 would involve a dialectic among all of the agencies of political action—official and extra-governmental, local, provincial and continental—all across America.

Moving the Ball Forward in Congress

In the middle of May, John Adams, writing to James Warren, gave his assessment of the state of play across the country. He claimed that "the four Colonies to the Southward"—Virginia, North Carolina, South Carolina and Georgia—had come around to agree with the four New England colonies—New Hampshire, Massachusetts, Rhode Island and Connecticut—that independence was the only course. He noted, though, that the "five in the middle"—New York, Pennsylvania, New Jersey, Delaware and Maryland—were not quite there. Though he expressed frustration at New York and Pennsylvania's continued obstinacy, he was confident that Delaware and New Jersey would soon come around to his side. He was less optimistic about Maryland: "That is so excentric a Colony—sometimes so hot, sometimes so cold—now so high, then so low—that I know not what to say about it or to expect from it." In fact, Adams may have been a bit overoptimistic. South Carolina and Georgia were not nearly as solid in their commitment to independence as he believed them to be, and it would be many weeks before New Jersey and Delaware would begin to tip in that direction.[1]

But Adams, and many other members of the Congress who were now openly advocating independence, were not willing to sit by passively and wait for the tide of opinion in many of the more reluctant colonies to change. On May 10, led by Adams, the advocates of independence made a move that would spur at least some of the legislatures into action. Meeting as a committee of the whole, the Congress unanimously adopted the following resolution:

Resolved, That it be recommended to the respective assemblies and conventions of the United Colonies, where no government sufficient to the exigencies of their affairs have been hitherto established, to adopt such government as shall, in the opinion of the representatives of the people, best conduce to the happiness and safety of their constituents in particular, and America in general.

There was nothing in the resolution that spoke of independence per se. But five days later, after a significantly more contentious debate, the Congress adopted a preamble to the resolution, and its intent was clear. The preamble was significantly longer than the resolution itself. It began with a familiar list of the many incursions on American liberties committed by the king and Parliament. Added to the list, however, was a new one—a denunciation of one of Great Britain's most recent provocations, the hiring of German mercenaries to bolster their armed forces in America—an action the preamble declared to be solely intended "for the destruction of the good people of these colonies."

The preamble's final section made clear that the purpose of the May 10 resolution was not simply to establish "governments sufficient to [the colonies'] affairs." It defended the call to establish new governments on the grounds that it was "absolutely irreconcilable to reason and good conscience, for the people of these colonies now to take the oaths and affirmations necessary for the support of any government under the crown of Great Britain." Going even further, it asserted that "every kind of authority under the said crown should be totally suppressed . . . for the preservation of internal peace, virtue and good order, as well as for the defence of their lives, liberties, and properties, against the hostile invasions and cruel depredations of their enemies."[2]

Although the preamble was drafted by a committee consisting of John Adams, Edward Rutledge and Richard Henry Lee, Adams, predictably, claimed full credit for its content, and, indeed, later in life, criticized George Washington among others for not giving him such credit. One of the reasons for his insistence on authorship is that he considered its language and its passage by the Congress a virtual declaration of independence, something he had been fighting for, if not explicitly admitting that he was doing so, for more than a year. Looking back on that moment a quarter of a century later, in his autobiography, he had lost none of his passion, or his sense of aggrievement:

> It was a measure which I had invariably pursued for a whole Year, and contended for, through a Scaene and Series of Anxiety, labour, Study, Argument, and Obloquy, which was then little known and is now forgotten. . . . Millions of Curses were poured out upon me, for these Exertions and for these Tryumphs over them, . . . for there were such at that time and have continued to this day in every State in the Union; who whatever their pretences may have been have never forgotten nor cordially forgiven me. [3]

A Revolution in Pennsylvania

Of all of the colonies north of the Mason-Dixon line, Pennsylvania was the one with the greatest population, wealth and political prestige. It, along with New York, was also a colony where the political ruling class that dominated the provincial legislature was most resistant to any move that might lead to independence. During the months of May and June, the conflict among Pennsylvania's delegates to the Continental Congress, the members of its provincial assembly and the people at large would escalate to a level far higher than in any other colony in America. By the beginning of July of 1776, those conflicts would culminate in a genuine internal revolution in the politics and governance of the colony.

One of the sparks that ignited many underlying differences of political opinion within Pennsylvania into open conflict was the Congress's May 10 resolution. During the debate over it, James Wilson acknowledged the appropriateness of earlier actions by the Congress giving the colonies of Massachusetts, New Hampshire, South Carolina and Virginia permission to organize their own governments. But he was deeply disturbed by the implications of the preamble for his own province of Pennsylvania. "In this Province," he predicted, "if that Preamble passes there will be an immediate Dissolution of every Kind of Authority. The People will be instantly in a State of Nature. Why then precipitate this Measure? Before We are prepared to build the new House, why should We pull down the old one, and expose ourselves to all the Inclemencies of the Season?"[4]

In the context of the highly conflicted politics of Pennsylvania, James Wilson had ample cause for concern. In most colonies, the substance of the resolution authorizing the creation of new governments was relatively uncontroversial. Ardent advocates of independence like John Adams hoped it would be a spur to colonies sitting on the fence to get off that fence by the act of creating their own, independent governments. And most moderates in the Congress could support it on the grounds that it merely gave their colonies permission to reorganize their governments, without requiring that they do so. And, indeed, in most colonies governed by a royal charter, the steady dissolution of any semblance of royal authority heightened the urgency of taking some step to reconstitute their governments.

Pennsylvania, as a proprietary colony without a royal charter, with a governor who did not have to answer directly to the king and with a provincial assembly that was still dominated by opponents of a too-hasty move toward independence, presented an altogether different situation. Pennsylvania's proprietary governor, John Penn, the grandson of the colony's founder, William Penn, had maintained generally cordial relations with the colony's ruling elite, thus mitigating some of the personal and political animosity that caused relations between Crown officials and provincial leaders in most of the colonies governed by a royal charter. Further, moderates John Dickinson, Robert Morris and James Wilson had retained their positions as the province's political leaders and viewed the language of the preamble with grave concern, believing it amounted to an open call for an internal revolution in Pennsylvania.

And the fears of Dickinson, Morris and Wilson seemed to be well grounded. Virginia's Carter Braxton, in a letter to his neighbor Landon Carter, noted that "those out of doors" in Pennsylvania were interpreting the May 10 resolution and the May 15 preamble as not only a call for independence but also as a mandate to dissolve the existing Pennsylvania government. Indeed, as news of James Wilson's opposition to the preamble became public, the residents of his legislative district in Carlisle turned out for a public protest of his behavior, and the attacks on him in Philadelphia were so great that twenty-two delegates to the Congress, including, interestingly, John Adams and Thomas Jefferson, felt compelled to sign a formal "Defense" of his integrity.[5]

On a rainy Monday, May 20, some 4,000 citizens gathered in the State House Yard, to rally not just for repeal of the Pennsylvania Assembly's instructions to its delegates to vote against any resolution for independence but also in support of a change in the Pennsylvania government. Thomas McKean, who owned property both in Pennsylvania, where he was a colonel in the militia, and in Delaware, where he served as a delegate from that colony to the Congress, delivered a passionate speech denouncing the sluggishness of the Pennsylvania Assembly in rallying behind the common cause. He then proposed both the creation of a new government through the means of a constitutional convention and a resolution demanding that the Pennsylvania Assembly, still bound by its instructions proclaiming their allegiance to the king, be replaced by a government instituted by the people. The crowd enthusiastically endorsed the proposals. William Bradford, Jr., a young militia captain who attended the meeting, recorded in his diary that the meeting's outcome marked "a *coup de grace* to the King's authority."[6]

John Dickinson traditionally left the city in the late spring to spend time at Fair Hill, on the city's outskirts, and he was not inclined to allow any turmoil in Philadelphia to interrupt his usual schedule. Accordingly, he departed for Fair Hill sometime in the early May. Thus, he did not participate in the debate in Congress over the resolution calling for the establishment of new colonial governments, and he was absent from the Pennsylvania Assembly during that same period. Nor was Dickinson seen on the streets of Philadelphia during the boisterous town meeting of May 20. But he could not stay clear of the fray for long. In yet another sign that the mood of the people out-of-doors was much more militant than that of the cautious majority in the Pennsylvania Assembly, the residents of the western Pennsylvania county of Cumberland (which included James Wilson's legislative district of Carlisle) petitioned the assembly on May 28 demanding that it repeal the instructions opposing independence it had given to the Pennsylvania delegation to the Continental Congress. That petition, along with news that Virginia was about to establish a new govern-

ment *and* to instruct its delegates to *support* independence, would energize those calling for change in Pennsylvania.[7]

On June 5 the Pennsylvania Assembly, meeting upstairs in the
Long Room of the Pennsylvania State House at the same time that
the Congress was meeting downstairs, voted to appoint a committee
to deliberate on a new set of instructions for its congressional delegates. John Adams was among those keeping a close watch on the deliberations occurring on the floor above him. For more than a year he
had been castigating the Quaker "broad brims" in the assembly for
"clogg[ing]" any and all efforts toward independence, but when he
heard that the assembly was in the midst of drafting new instructions
to its congressional delegates, he exulted: "these cloggs are falling off,
as you will Soon see." But Adams may have been a bit premature in
his exultations. When the Assembly moved on June 5 to appoint a
committee to draft the new set of instructions, its members named
none other than John Dickinson as the committee's chairman. Whatever popular pressure they were feeling from outside their walls, a
majority of members in the Assembly still retained their faith in
Dickinson not only as the most able, but also the most reasonable,
member of their body.[8]

There was never any doubt that Dickinson, as the committee's
chair, would be the person to draft the new set of instructions. He
completed the draft the next day, June 6, and submitted it to the Assembly. He knew that the change going on around him, from the ag-
itation in his own colony, to Virginia's impending endorsement of
independence, required something more than a simple reiteration of
the Assembly's previous position to be acceptable, both within the
Assembly and out of doors. But still, he was not ready to embrace
independence.

Dickinson began his draft by acknowledging that "the situation
of public affairs is greatly altered." The contemptuous rejection of
the Olive Branch Petition, the passage of the Prohibitory Act, the
hiring of foreign mercenaries—these indicated that "all hopes of a
reconciliation, on reasonable terms, are extinguished." But then the
next sentence seemed to contradict what had preceded it: "Nevertheless," Dickinson wrote, "it is our ardent desire that a civil war, with
all its attending miseries, could be ended by a secure and honorable

peace." The operative section of the new set of instructions then authorized Pennsylvania's delegates to "concur with the other Delegates in Congress in forming such further compacts between the
United Colonies, concluding . . . treaties with foreign kingdom and
states, and in adopting such other measures as shall be judged necessary for promoting the liberty, safety, and interests of America."
There was little point in giving the Pennsylvania delegates to the
Congress permission to enter into treaties with foreign nations, for it
had already agreed to do that without Pennsylvania's permission. But
the Congress had not yet moved to form "compacts between the
United Colonies." Since Dickinson had been among those members
of Congress most strenuously opposing Benjamin Franklin's and
Sam Adams's proposal in mid-January for an intercolonial union, the
new instructions signified that the events of the past month had
moved him a little closer to accepting the possibility that independence might be America's only option.

The draft of the instructions concluded with what could be considered, at best, a highly equivocal endorsement of independence as
an extreme last resort. Echoing sentiments expressed by Dickinson in
the past, it asserted that the "happiness" of the colonies had always
been the Assembly's first wish, and "reconciliation with Great-Britain
our next." As much as Dickinson and his colleagues "prayed for the
accomplishment of both . . . , if we must renounce the one or the
other, we humbly trust in the mercies of the Supreme Governor of
the Universe, that we shall not stand condemned before his throne, if
our choice is determined by that over-ruling law of self-preservation,
which his divine wisdom has thought fit to implant in the hearts of
his creatures." It came close perhaps, but it stepped back from the
precipice; nowhere in those instructions could one find the word
"independence."[9]

The Pennsylvania Assembly apparently put all other business aside
and devoted three days to discussing Dickinson's draft, after which,
with dissenters on both sides, it endorsed the instructions. But Dickinson's attempt to straddle the line between continuing delay and an
outright endorsement of independence, in addition to raising the
hackles of both radicals and conservatives within the Pennsylvania
Assembly, was clearly insufficient to change the tide of opinion in the

other body in which he had laid a claim to leadership—the Continental Congress. As Dickinson would discover, on June 7, the day after he presented his draft of the instructions to the Pennsylvania Assembly, Richard Henry Lee, acting on the instructions of Virginia's extra-legal provincial legislature, the Virginia Convention, introduced a resolution to the Congress that would provide a more urgent focus on the debate relating to Americans' relationship with their mother country.[10]

Virginia Forces the Issue

On May 6, 1776, the opening day of the meeting of the Virginia Convention, Patrick Henry showed up with a set of resolutions formally proposing the independence of the "United Colonies" from Great Britain. More conservative members of the Convention such as Edmund Pendleton delayed discussion of Henry's resolutions until May 14, but, after undergoing extensive revisions, and after considerable debate, they were put to a vote the following day. The final version proclaimed:

> These United Colonies are, and of right ought to be free and independent States, that they are absolved from all allegiance to the British Crown, and that all political connection between them and the State of Great Britain is, and ought to be, totally dissolved.

The nine days of behind-the-scenes discussion of Henry's original resolutions, though perhaps annoying to the radical Virginia patriot, would prove important to the unity of the revolutionary movement in that colony and beyond. When the Virginia Convention finally voted on the resolutions on May 15, it unanimously endorsed them. The importance of the strong consensus behind Virginia's recommendation favoring independence could not have been lost on the delegates to the Continental Congress.[11]

The Delegates Debate Independence—Briefly

On June 7, 1776, Richard Henry Lee formally introduced the Virginia resolutions for independence into the Continental Congress.

In addition to their call for the end to all political connection between the colonies and Great Britain, they also urged the Congress
to move forward as quickly as possible to form foreign alliances and
for it to begin to prepare a "plan of confederation" for submission to
the colonies. In fact, it would be another two years before the "united
States" would be successful in negotiating a treaty with a foreign
power, and another five years after that before all thirteen states
could come to an agreement on their "plan of confederation."[12]

The Virginians had managed to reach consensus on their resolutions in nine days; it would take the members of Congress—and the
colonial legislatures of the colonies they represented—nearly a month
to reach a similar decision. Discussion was postponed until the following day, Saturday. Once that discussion began, it lasted until seven
in the evening, an unusual event in a body that normally adjourned
by three or four in the afternoon. According to the notes on the debate made by Thomas Jefferson, who had only recently returned from
an extended stay in Virginia, James Wilson, John Dickinson, Robert
Livingston of New York and, in what must have been particularly
annoying to John Adams, his frequent rival Edward Rutledge of
South Carolina, led the opposition to Lee's motion. Indeed, Rutledge
was particularly upset about the precipitous nature of Lee's resolution. Sitting down at ten that evening, he wrote John Jay, whom he
knew would be a sympathetic listener, that the only reasoning behind
the measure was that "of every Madman, a Shew of our Spirit." According to Rutledge, he, and a majority of the other delegates in the
Congress,

> saw no Wisdom in a *Declaration* of Independence, nor any other Pur-
> pose to be answer'd by it, but placing ourselves in the Power of those
> with whom we mean to treat, giving our Enemy Notice of our Inten-
> tions before we had taken any Steps to execute them there by enabling
> them to counteract us in our Intentions & rendering ourselves ridicu-
> lous in the Eyes of foreign Powers by attempting to bring them into an
> Union with us before we had united with each other.[13]

Rutledge's contemptuous dismissal of those favoring independence
was perhaps even more off-target than the intolerance that delegates

like John Adams displayed toward those who did not share their opinion on the subject. John Dickinson, the one person in the Congress whose cautious views toward independence still commanded some respect from the delegates, now spoke on that Saturday. He embarked on an extended analysis of why a premature declaration of independence, phrased in the unequivocal terms of Lee's resolution, would not only compromise America's leverage in dealing with foreign powers but also make it nearly impossible for America to achieve a "Reconciliation with Great Britain," which Dickinson thought both likely and desirable "in a Year or two." He pleaded, "Do not let Us turn our Backs on Reconciliation till We find it a Monster too dreadful to approach." And, ignoring the impact of Tom Paine's demolition of the very idea of an English constitution, Dickinson insisted that all of America's actions up to that point had been based on the precepts of that constitution. To declare independence, he insisted, would amount to the dissolution of that noble instrument. While acknowledging that the time might come when that would prove necessary, he was adamant in his belief that that time *had not yet come*. And, indeed, if it should come, then the authority for discarding the English constitution and forming a new one was vested "in our Constituents, not in Us, [and] they have not given it to Us."[14]

The arguments put forth that day by Dickinson and others opposing Lee's resolution were filled with "what if's." If independence were declared without the formal authorization of the provincial legislatures that were up to that point resisting an outright authorization of that sort, then the delegates from those colonies would have to leave the Congress, and indeed, their colonies might well have to "secede from the Union." And if that happened, would any foreign power agree to enter into an alliance with a group of divided colonies? And how could Americans trust the corrupt foreign nations of Europe in the first place? Was it not likely, for instance, that France and Spain, rather than give the colonies control over the North American continent, would either combine to strip Americans of "all of their . . . possessions" or, alternatively, ally themselves with Great Britain in partitioning America? None of these "what if's" was implausible, and for that reason, they were, given the uncertainty in many delegates' minds, unanswerable.[15]

The Virginia resolution produced the longest day of speeches yet, but, in the end, few minds were changed. It was clear that the push for independence had not yet received anywhere near the unanimity—or even strong consensus—of sentiment that was necessary if such a bold move were to succeed. Some—the delegates from Pennsylvania and Maryland—had been explicitly instructed not to support a resolution of the sort offered by Lee. Others—those from New York, New Jersey and Delaware—while not prohibited from supporting independence, believed they had to wait for some positive authorization from their legislatures. Still others were, in Jefferson's words, "not ripe for bidding adieu to British connection." When the Congress reconvened on Monday morning June 10, those opposing the resolution had their way for the moment. The Congress agreed, apparently without dissent, to postpone consideration of the first part of Lee's resolution—that proposing independence—until July 1. But at the same time, in order "that no time be lost," a committee would be appointed to prepare a declaration "to the effect of the said first resolution." The following day the Congress, continuing to act as a committee of the whole, elected Thomas Jefferson, John Adams, Benjamin Franklin, Roger Sherman and Robert Livingston to prepare that declaration. And it proposed the creation of two other committees, one to "prepare and digest the form of a confederation to be entered into between these colonies" and another "to prepare a plan of treaties to be proposed to foreign powers." Those committees were constituted on June 12, with one representative from each colony to serve on the committee to draw up a plan for a confederation, and a committee consisting of John Dickinson, Benjamin Franklin, John Adams, Benjamin Harrison and Robert Morris to draw up drafts of potential treaties.[16]

All of the members of the committee to draft a declaration of independence, with the exception of Robert Livingston, were firm advocates of independence. It would have been not only inappropriate but also disruptive to put someone as vocally opposed to independence as John Dickinson on the committee. But Dickinson, in addition to serving on the committee charged with making drafts of treaties with foreign powers, was also elected to serve as Pennsylvania's representative on the committee drawing up a proposed plan of confederation. Indeed, as the delegate receiving the most votes in the balloting for that committee, he was selected to serve as the committee's chair and the lead draftsman of the proposal that would emerge from it. John Dickinson may have been playing defense on the question of independence, but he was in no way out of the game.[17]

The State of Play in the American Colonies

Even though Richard Henry Lee's June 7 resolution put the question of independence squarely before the Congress, the members of that body remained entirely dependent on the authorizations of their respective legislatures as to how, or whether, they should respond to that resolution. From June 7 to July 2, the most important events were occurring not in the Assembly Room of the Pennsylvania State House, but in the colonial capitals of government, and in some cases, in the streets, of the thirteen North American colonies.

If Virginia had taken the lead in putting the question of independence on the table inside the Assembly Room of the State House, the actions of other colonies, counties and local committees would soon prove every bit as important as the eventual declaration by Congress itself. While the Continental Congress was gaining in authority as the body responsible for overseeing America's military defense against Great Britain, it remained the servant, not the master, of the various colonial legislatures when it came to political decision making. And increasingly, the colonial legislatures themselves were learning that they were the servants, not the masters, of the people at large.

The legislature of North Carolina had been the first representative body in America to state unequivocally its commitment to independence. On April 12, nearly two months before Richard Henry Lee introduced Virginia's resolution into the Continental Congress, the members of the North Carolina Provincial Congress, buoyed by the recent victory of their patriot militia over a loyalist army at Moore's Creek Bridge, and supported by the fervor for independence among virtually all of their constituents, unanimously endorsed the idea of independence. Concluding that "no hopes remain of obtaining a redress" of grievances from Great Britain, they "Resolved, That the delegates for this colony in the Continental Congress be empowered to concur with the delegates of the other Colonies in declaring Independency, and forming foreign alliances, reserving to this Colony the sole and exclusive right of forming a Constitution and laws for this Colony." This resolution did not explicitly require North Carolina's delegates to the Congress to vote for independence, but they were already sufficiently inclined in that direction to make it clear that they could be counted on to support independence.[18]

In early April 1776, the South Carolina Provincial Congress finally got around to adopting a new constitution—a step recommended to it by the Continental Congress back in November 1775. In so doing, it expressed its hope for "an accommodation with Great Britain," adding in parentheses, "an event which, though traduced and treated as Rebels, we still earnestly desire." At about that same time, the Congress "authorized and empowered" its delegates to the Continental Congress "to concert, agree to, and execute, every measure which they . . . , together with a majority of the Continental Congress, shall judge necessary for the defence, security, interest, or welfare of this colony in particular and of America in general." That authorization was nowhere near as explicit as North Carolina's endorsement of independence, and the state of mind of South Carolina's delegates to the Continental Congress with respect to independence was far more divided than that of their neighbors to the north. But the South Carolina resolution, without mentioning the crucial word, had taken at least a step forward in authorizing its delegates to fall in line with the majority sentiment in the Continental Congress.[19]

On April 5, the Georgia legislature issued a set of instructions to its delegates essentially allowing them to use their own judgment with respect to the question of independence. Georgia had held elections for new delegates to the Congress on February 2, 1776, but it took until May 20, for the first two of those delegates, Button Gwinnett and Lyman Hall, to make it to Philadelphia, with a third, George Walton, arriving a few days before the final vote on independence. But with the arrival of Gwinnett and Hall, it seemed likely that the Georgia delegation, such as it was, could be counted on to support independence.[20]

On May 4, to the surprise of no one, the Rhode Island legislature passed a set of resolutions formally terminating British authority over the colony and proclaiming that in the future the issuing of legal documents from the colony would be done in the name of "the Governor and Company of the English Colony in Rhode Island and Providence Plantations," and not in the name of the king. At the same time it issued instructions to its representatives to the Continental Congress authorizing them to support independence, although, pointedly, the legislature did not use that word in its authorization. As they were debating their rejection of all royal authority, the Rhode Island legislators also discussed whether to poll their citizens on the subject but decided against doing so, in part for logistical reasons, but in part too, according to Rhode Island Governor Nicholas Cole, because "although a very great majority of the Colony were perfectly ripe for such a question, yet, upon its being canvassed, several towns would vote against it," creating an "appearance of disunion [that] would be injurious to the common cause." And the very word "independence," the governor feared, might frighten "many honest and ignorant people" into believing they were committing themselves to "eternal warfare." So, even in supposedly "radical" Rhode Island, the decision to support independence was neither an easy nor an uncontested one.[21]

Even in Virginia—within both the Virginia Provincial Convention and the colony's congressional delegation—there were murmurings of dissent. On April 20, Richard Henry Lee had written to Patrick Henry urging him to get Virginia to take the lead in rousing America "from the fatal lethargy into which the feebleness, folly, and interested views of the Proprietary governments [Maryland and Pennsylvania], with the aid of Tory machinations, have thrown her most unhappily." Henry, who was proving to be a much more effective political force in the Virginia Provincial Convention than he had been in the Continental Congress, swung into action, working overtime to get the near unanimous vote favoring the May 15 resolution for independence (only Robert Carter Nicholas had abstained, but he also promised to "rise and fall" with the patriot cause). But within Virginia's delegation to the Continental Congress, at least one individual, Carter Braxton, continued to work with moderates from other colonies to forestall independence.[22]

Interestingly, the people of Massachusetts were slow to take the formal step of instructing their delegates to support independence. Although Massachusetts was widely seen as the driving force behind independence, in reality, by the end of 1775, the colony's delegation to the Congress found itself bitterly divided on ideological and personal issues. Much to the chagrin of John and Sam Adams, both Thomas Cushing and Robert Treat Paine dragged their feet on independence, in part because they were not as convinced as the Adamses that the towns of Massachusetts were uniformly in favor of such a step. And the Adamses were distinctly suspicious of John Hancock. They had never forgiven him for not having relinquished the presidency of the Congress on the return of Peyton Randolph, while Hancock's animosity toward the Adamses had increased after they had supported Washington over him as commander of the Continental Army. And so they may have sought to replace all three. When members of the Massachusetts General Court, the colony's provincial legislature, voted for new delegates to the Continental Congress on December 15, 1775, the Adamses' supporters succeeded in replacing Cushing with Elbridge Gerry, but they failed to replace Paine and Hancock, who still had enough support in their legislature to retain their positions. Cushing, who was bitterly disappointed by his rejection, wasted no time in telling Hancock that "you as well as myself had been placed in a disagreeable light and measures taken to hurt our Influence." He went on to say to Hancock that he was "well acquainted" with the "names & characters" of those who were, "by their little, low, Dirty & sly Insinuating Actes & Machinations," responsible for the move to oust them.[23]

With the addition of Elbridge Gerry, a majority of the Massachusetts delegates to the Congress now favored independence, but they were unable to persuade the General Court to aid them in their cause. In late March, Gerry wrote to James Warren, who had served in the Massachusetts legislature since the time of the Stamp Act crisis, urging him to "originate instructions . . . in favor of independence" in the legislature. But the legislature continued to procrastinate, at least in part because support for independence in some of the colony's towns was not as great as the Adamses believed it to be and as Cushing and Paine well knew. James Warren, perhaps feeling a little defensive after receiving numerous letters from both Sam and John Adams complaining about the legislature's inaction, was left merely to shrug it all off, telling his correspondents that their fellow Massachusetts politicians had gotten too bogged down in petty issues to concern themselves with "the grand question." In fact, the Massachusetts General Court never got around to formally endorsing independence until after independence had been formally declared.[24]

On June 14, the Connecticut legislature, apparently unaware that the Virginia Convention had already instructed its delegates to introduce a resolution for independence into the Congress, instructed its delegates to propose that the Congress "declare the United American Colonies free and independent states." New Hampshire's two delegates to the Continental Congress, Josiah Bartlett and William Whipple, when they learned on May 28 that the Virginia Convention had asked its delegates to introduce a resolution for independence into the Congress, immediately wrote to their colleagues back home asking them to endorse that move. On June 15, the New Hampshire House of Representatives instructed its delegates to Congress "to join with the other Colonies in Declaring *The Thirteen United Colonies, A Free & Independent State.*"[25]

Whatever the procrastination and infighting in Massachusetts, it was clear to all that the New England colonies were on board with the move for independence. And although the state of mind of at least some of the South Carolina delegates remained uncertain, the other colonies from Virginia southward were of a similar mind. Which left the two proprietary colonies—Pennsylvania and Maryland—and New Jersey, Delaware and, perhaps most problematic, New York, in the undecided column.

John Dickinson was fighting a battle for control on two fronts, in the Congress and in his own legislature one floor above in the State House. As we have seen, on June 6 Dickinson drafted a revision of the Pennsylvania Assembly's earlier instructions prohibiting its delegates to the Continental Congress from supporting independence. Dickinson's draft, while stopping well short of authorizing independence, did give the delegates the power to take any necessary steps "for promoting the Liberty, Safety, and Interests of America." Perhaps Dickinson believed that this would buy him and his moderate colleagues in the legislature some time to continue their efforts at reconciliation. But time was running out, for events in the legislature and out of doors were unfolding rapidly. Although Dickinson was successful in persuading the

Pennsylvania legislature to adopt his revised set of instructions on June 8, the radicals in the legislature, still in a minority but buoyed by their support from ordinary Philadelphians, were doing everything possible to delegitimize the legislature itself.

Responding to the demand in the May 20 town meeting, moderates in the legislature, still in a bare majority in that body, attempted to arrange for a constitutional convention to be called under the Assembly's authority. It was a move, they hoped, that would place them in control of the framing of a new constitution. But radicals in the Assembly blocked the move by absenting themselves from the chamber, thus preventing the proposal from being passed because of the lack of a necessary quorum.

Faced with the continuing non-attendance of the radical minority, the Assembly, unable to function, adjourned on June 14. The *Pennsylvania Packet*, still loyal to Dickinson and the moderates in the Assembly, castigated the radicals for "desertion and cowardice." In fact, though, the adjournment led to a power vacuum that would be filled four days later when an extra-legal Provincial Conference, convened in the original meeting place of the Continental Congress, Carpenters' Hall. Among the delegates to the Provincial Conference were a few known advocates of independence from the Continental Congress, such as Benjamin Franklin and Benjamin Rush, but perhaps more important, delegates who had not been part of the provincial ruling elite in the former Provincial Assembly, including new ones from the previously underrepresented western counties. Not only did the residents of those counties tend to be more favorably inclined toward independence, but their radical frame of mind was further buttressed by the decades of resentment toward the eastern elite that had dominated the Assembly and deprived them of an equitable voice in the affairs of the colony.

On June 24, the Provincial Conference approved a resolution stating: "We the deputies of the people of Pennsylvania . . . do in this public manner in behalf of ourselves, and with the approbation, consent, and authority of our constituents, unanimously declare our willingness to concur in a vote of the congress, declaring the united colonies free and independent states." While the delegates to the Conference had not declared independence, or even instructed Pennsylvania's delegates to the Continental Congress to vote in favor of independence, they had made clear their support of such a move and, perhaps more important, had asserted emphatically that they, not the now-dormant Provincial Assembly, were the true representatives of the people of their colony. For all practical purposes, people like John Dickinson, whatever their status within the Continental Congress, were finding their power and influence within provincial Pennsylvania politics rapidly eroding.[26]

As the critical July 1 debate on independence neared, Pennsylvania was in the unusual position of having an extra-legal Provincial Conference whose members emphatically favored independence and a delegation to the Continental Congress, most of whose members opposed it. The dynamic of events in Pennsylvania is perhaps the best example of an "internal revolution" accompanying America's move toward independence. And, indeed, in the aftermath of independence, that internal revolution, motivated by the people out-of-doors, would result not only in a radical change in the political leadership within Pennsylvania politics, but also in the most democratic state constitution in all of America—extending the franchise to all taxpaying adult male citizens and establishing a unicameral legislature with annual elections to it and without a chief executive.

The political and economic fortunes of the colony of Delaware had always been closely tied to those of Pennsylvania. They were so close that most people still referred to the Delaware colony as the "three lower counties," viewing its three counties as essentially appendages of Pennsylvania. Indeed, John Dickinson, who spent much of his leisure time at his country estate, Poplar Hill, near Dover, Delaware, was often considered as much a Delawarean as a Pennsylvanian. When the Continental Congress passed the resolution urging each of the colonies to set up its own government, both radical and moderate patriot leaders in Delaware were eager to take advantage of the offer, for they were in the midst of a confrontation, both verbal and military, with a substantial group of British sympathizers in Sussex and Kent Counties. Moreover, the presence of British naval vessels in the Chesapeake Bay offered a threat that Delaware was wholly unequipped to repel.

Caesar Rodney, one of Delaware's delegates to the Continental Congress, was quick to support the idea of forming a new government.

He, like Dickinson, believed that a "well-regulated government," with a "Good Executive," would not only be important in withstanding the British threat, but in so doing, might provide further leverage for some sort of reconciliation with the British. On June 14, Thomas McKean, the same man who chaired the town meeting in Philadelphia on May 20 demanding the organization of a new government in that colony, introduced a resolution into the Delaware Assembly proposing that a constitutional convention be held to draw up a new frame of government. The resolution also authorized its delegates to the Continental Congress to cooperate in entering into treaties with foreign nations and to pursue other measures for "promoting the liberty, safety, and interests of America." But the word "independence" was conspicuously absent from the Delaware resolution. Delaware would delay until the middle of August before creating a new government, and as the month of June came to an end, neither the legislature nor the colony's delegates to the Continental Congress had made a commitment to independence. Like its dominant neighbor to the north, Delaware would remain in the "undecided" column nearly to the end.[27]

Events in New Jersey moved somewhat more swiftly than those in Delaware. In January 1776, New Jersey dissolved its old legislature and created a new Provincial Congress. There were clear signs that its royal governor, Benjamin Franklin's son William Franklin (from whom Franklin by this time was wholly estranged), was fast losing favor. The new Provincial Congress, however, did not take any steps to repudiate the instructions issued by the old Assembly in November of 1775 stipulating that the colony's delegates should not vote in favor of independence. But by June 1776, public opinion in the colony had changed, and when a newly elected Provincial Congress met on June 10, most of its members seemed ready to act. By a vote of 48 to 10 they condemned Governor William Franklin as "an enemy to the liberties of this country," and voted at the same time to form a new government under a new constitution. Although it would take another two weeks for a formal draft of a new government to be approved, the delegates to the New Jersey Provincial Congress agreed at the outset that the actions of the British had left the colony "in a state of nature." Once they had admitted to being in that state, it would be virtually impossible for

New Jersey's political leaders to move out of it and back under the authority of an unwritten English constitution.[28]

Maryland posed a far more difficult problem. Like Pennsylvania, it was a proprietary colony, and for that reason did not have a single representative of the crown such as Virginia's Lord Dunmore, Massachusetts' General Gage or New Jersey's William Franklin to serve as a lightning rod for colonists' hostility. And whereas Dunmore's proclamation promising freedom to the slaves of Virginia if they fought on the side of the British served to rally Virginians *against* the royal government, the proclamation seemed to have the opposite effect in Maryland, causing some of that colony's leading planters to try even harder to seek reconciliation with the British. On May 15, 1776, the day the Continental Congress adopted the preamble to the resolution asking the colonies to form new governments, Maryland's delegates to the Congress walked out, claiming they could not legally carry out the Congress's mandate until the Maryland Provincial Convention issued new instructions telling them how to proceed "upon this alarming occasion." The Maryland Convention received Congress's preamble five days later, on May 20, and on May 21 unanimously agreed that there was no need to organize a new government, reaffirming the legitimacy of its own authority and refusing to repudiate that of the king. It then re-elected its delegation to the Continental Congress, reiterated its commitment to reconciliation with Great Britain "on constitutional principles" and, finally, instructed its congressional delegates to continue to adhere to their previous instructions to vote against independence.

When the Continental Congress began debate on Richard Henry Lee's resolution for independence, the Maryland delegates found themselves in a vexing situation. Although some of them clearly favored independence, they felt powerless to act until the Maryland Convention, which had adjourned on May 25, altered their instructions. John Adams persistently badgered Samuel Chase, Maryland's most influential delegate and a strong supporter of independence, to do something about his colony's recalcitrance, warning him that if Maryland delayed much longer they would "be left alone." Responding in part to Adams's prodding, Chase left for Maryland on June 14 to try to persuade his colony's political leaders to call their convention back into session and to endorse independence. He evidently succeeded in getting a number of county committees of safety to endorse independence, but on June 21, when the provincial convention met again, its members dug in their heels, ordering the Maryland delegates in Philadelphia to come home to attend the convention, but not to leave Congress before receiving guarantees that the Congress would not vote on the question of independence in their absence. Since Congress had already agreed to take up Richard Henry Lee's resolution for independence on July 1, the Maryland delegates found themselves in an even more difficult position.[29]

On June 24 John Adams once again wrote Chase, who was still in Maryland trying to drum up support for independence. Beginning with the plea "Don't be angry with me," Adams nevertheless went on to tell Chase that it was out of the question for the Congress to delay its July 1 discussion of independence until Maryland got its act together. Such a delay, Adams insisted, "would hazard Convulsions and dangerous Conspiracies." Adams was plainly annoyed with the Maryland legislature's procrastination, but as annoyed as he may have been, Maryland's delegates to the Continental Congress were even more so. Most of them were committed to voting in favor of independence, but they faced the prospect of going into the crucial debate on July 1 having to sit on their hands, with their colony still very much in the "undecided column."[30]

And then there was New York, which from the moment the First Continental Congress convened in September 1774, had tried to put the brakes on any actions that might lead to a break with the mother country. New York's established ruling elite, like that in Pennsylvania, had supported the idea of a Continental Congress as a means of quieting some of the more radical, popular voices in the wake of the passage of the Coercive Acts. Even more than in Pennsylvania, the politics of New York—both in and out of doors—had been driven by division between radical political organizers of the same bent of mind as Boston's Sam Adams, such as Isaac Sears and Alexander McDougall, and by more conservative members of the traditional ruling elite—men like John Jay, James Duane and members of the Livingston family. Whereas in Pennsylvania the Assembly continued to be the colony's official legislative body right up until its adjournment on June 14, 1776, the New York Assembly gave way to an extra-legal Provincial Congress in April of 1775 at nearly precisely the moment of the outbreak of war at Lexington and Concord. Conservative politicians in New York, although nervous, had supported that move, and as a consequence, they maintained their control over the Provincial Congress, and, therefore, their control over the selection of delegates to the Continental Congress. But even more than in Pennsylvania, radical insurgents led by men like Sears and McDougall constantly posed a threat to the political dominance of New York's traditional ruling elite. The existence of a wealthy, powerful minority of landowners sympathetic to the British in New York's Hudson River valley, further confused the political situation in the colony.[31]

Most alarming, the British, after being driven from Boston, had decided to make their stand in New York City. General Washington, realizing this, had arrived in New York with a substantial contingent of troops in mid-April, but even Washington was not prepared for what he witnessed on the morning of June 29. As New Yorkers awoke that day they saw forty-five British ships in the harbor, a fleet so massive that one Pennsylvania rifleman who observed the scene declared "that I thought all London was afloat." And as those ships began to unload thousands of British and Hessian troops on Staten Island, it became clear that the military threat to New York made that of earlier British efforts to subdue Massachusetts pale in comparison.[32]

Unlike Pennsylvanians like Dickinson, Wilson and Robert Morris, who had greeted, with a mixture of ambivalence and nervousness, the congressional resolution of May 15 calling for the colonies to organize their own governments, New York's conservative elite quite accurately saw it as an opportunity to strengthen their political control over their colony. (The fact that the radical activists Isaac Sears and Alexander McDougall were temporarily absent from the political scene because they had joined the military effort by serving in the New York militia no doubt gave the elite added incentive to make their move at this time.) Robert Livingston, writing from Philadelphia, commented on the different situations in New York and Pennsylvania in a letter to his son-in-law, John Jay, on May 17. He noted that the May 15 resolution had occasioned "great alarm" among many of the Pennsylvanians, who "are very fearful of its being attended with many ill consequences next week when the Assembly are to meet"— a fear that, as things turned out, was wholly justifiable. Livingston was sufficiently apprehensive about the consequences of a change in government in New York that he asked Jay (who had absented himself from the Continental Congress and was serving in the Provincial Congress in order to keep in control of things there) to keep constantly in touch with him should he need to come back to New York to help influence the course of events. But he seemed confident that "our people," by which he meant the established ruling elite of his colony, were "satisfied of the necessity of assuming a new form of Government." Jay, like Livingston, still hoping for reconciliation rather than independence, emphatically agreed with Livingston on the need for a new government in New York: the present one, he believed, was badly flawed, and "will no longer work anything but mischief."33

But as was the case in Pennsylvania, New York's ruling elite, whatever its dominance within its Provincial Congress and within its delegation to the Continental Congress, would find it more and more difficult to resist popular pressure for an endorsement of independence. On June 8, the first day of debate over Richard Henry Lee's resolution for independence, four of New York's delegates sent an urgent letter to the New York Provincial Congress informing them that "the question of independence will very shortly be agitated." Since at least some of the New York delegates considered themselves "as bound by our instructions not to vote on that question," and since "the matter will admit of no delay," they pleaded with their colleagues back home to send them new instructions. Their letter reached New York two days later, but members of the Provincial Congress simply procrastinated. On June 11, John Jay introduced a set of resolutions into that body attempting to slow things down even further. The resolutions were extraordinarily convoluted, perhaps purposely so. The first reminded the New York delegates to the Continental Congress that they were not authorized to add New York's endorsement to the resolution for independence. The second resolution informed the delegates that since the "good people" of New York had not yet made their sentiments on that great subject known, it would not be possible for the Provincial Congress to change its instructions to the delegates on that subject. In what must have been an infuriating bit of obfuscation to at least some of New York's delegates to the Continental Congress, the resolutions then informed the delegates that "it would be imprudent to inquire into the sentiments of the people relative to the question of independence, lest it should create division." In other words, the Provincial Congress was unwilling to authorize the delegates to vote for independence until they had been given authorization to do so by the good people of the colony, but the Congress was at this point not willing to take steps to discern what popular opinion on that all-important question might be. The resolutions ended with what could hardly have seemed much of a consolation: namely that the Provincial Congress would try to discern the "sentiments of the people of this colony" at "the earliest opportunity."[34]

Truly, Jay and his conservative New York colleagues had created a Catch-22 situation for the advocates of independence. They insisted that the only true authority for authorizing independence should come from the people themselves, but at the same time said that it would be "inconvenient" for the people's voice to be consulted. And there things would stand until the reopening of debate on Lee's resolution on July 1. The New York delegation to the Congress was left to sit on its hands all through the remainder of the month of June.

On June 29, South Carolina's Edward Rutledge, still emphatically opposing independence, wrote an urgent letter to John Jay, pleading with him to return to Philadelphia to be present for the debate on independence that would take place two days later. Acknowledging that Jay was doing important business in New York in keeping the advocates of independence at bay, he nevertheless was convinced that Jay's attendance in Philadelphia would be absolutely necessary if the rising tide toward independence was to be turned back. "Whether we shall be able effectually to oppose [independence]," Rutledge wrote, "will depend in a great Measure upon the Exertions of the Honest and sensible part of the Members." Most of the New York delegates present at the Congress at that moment, Rutledge observed, "never quit their Chairs," and were not up to the task of effectively arguing against independence. "You must know the Importance of these Questions too well not to wish to be present," Rutledge pleaded. For Rutledge, the voices of prominent, respectable members of the traditional ruling elite such as John Dickinson and John Jay were the only hope for those who wanted to turn back that tide of opinion favoring independence. Clearly, that tide was rising, but Rutledge still believed that the voices of a few influential delegates might be sufficient to turn it back.[35]

TWENTY-THREE

"THE GREATEST
DEBATE OF ALL"

T HE FIRST FOUR days of July 1776 would prove not only to be among the most significant in all of American history, but in the history of the Western world. The Americans' decision for independence, and their subsequent defense of that action in the Declaration of Independence, would set in motion a string of ideas—that of political self-determination, of the people as the ultimate source of government power and, perhaps most important, of the fundamental equality of all of mankind—that continues to play out even today.

July 1: The Debate Begins

The operations of the Continental Congress on the morning of July 1 seemed little different from that on many others, with John Hancock spending the first part of the day going over routine business, reading letters from General Washington and several other army officers reporting on the state of military affairs, reading a report from the army's paymaster in the southern colonies and agreeing to draw $6,000 from the treasury to pay for defense costs in Virginia.[1]

But July 1, 1776, would not be just any other day. Earlier that morning, an express rider had appeared suddenly to report that the Maryland Provincial Congress had unanimously instructed its delegates to the Congress to support independence. With the news of Maryland's change of heart before them, the Congress was ready to begin what John Adams termed "the greatest Debate of all"—the discussion of the resolution for independence first introduced by Richard Henry Lee on June 7.[2]

The first step in organizing that discussion was to agree to operate as a committee of the whole. The Congress then selected Virginia's Benjamin Harrison to moderate the discussion, so he took John Hancock's place behind the table on the raised dais in the front of the room. As the debate began, the delegates knew that their congressional colleagues from New Hampshire, Massachusetts, Rhode Island, Connecticut, Virginia, North Carolina, Georgia and now Maryland were solidly in the pro-independence camp. The state of play in New Jersey and Delaware was still unknown. The South Carolina delegates, though they had been given permission to vote in favor of independence, were, at best, divided on the question. The balance of opinion among the Pennsylvania delegation was still an open question, and New York's delegates, still under a restriction from their legislature, were known to be required to abstain from any vote on the question. Under the rules of the Congress, approval of nine of the thirteen colonies was necessary for the resolution to pass. That left the advocates of independence one colony short. More important, most delegates understood that the nine-vote minimum was a formality. If colonies such as South Carolina, Pennsylvania and New York continued to dissent, or even to abstain, the legitimacy of any vote on independence would be problematic.

Of all the men in the Assembly Room of the Pennsylvania State House that day, John Dickinson perhaps faced the most pressure. He likely knew that the position he was about to take against independence would not only not prevail, but might also cast him indelibly as a weak and cowardly servant to his British masters. But Dickinson would not back down. A better writer than an orator, he had spent the weekend carefully laying out the argument that he intended to present on Monday.

Sometime in the early afternoon, Dickinson would be the first to rise behind the closed doors and windows of the Assembly Room of the State House, on one of the hottest days of the year thus far, with the temperature above ninety degrees. "The Consequences involved in the Motion now lying before You are of such Magnitude," he began, "that I tremble under the oppressive Honor of sharing in its Determination. I feel Myself unequal to the Burthen assigned Me. I believe, I had almost said, I rejoice, that the Time is approaching, when I shall be relieved from its Weight." Noting that his position was unlikely to improve his popularity, he insisted that he would rather sacrifice the latter than put in danger "the Blood and Happiness of my Countryman. . . . I must speak, tho I should lose my Life, tho I should lose the Affections of my Countrymen."

Dickinson, ever pious even though, all his life, he rejected any formal religious affiliation, ended his prefatory remarks with a prayer, imploring "Almighty God" not only to "enlighten the Members of the House," but also to "enable Me to speak the Precepts of sound Policy on the important Question that now engages our Attention." Then he launched into the main body of his speech, a carefully argued reiteration of all of his fears about a precipitous leap into independence that he had been voicing for the better part of a year. The continuing theme, the continuing plea, in his speech was the need for "prudence." At this point, having given up any hope that the British would come around to accept the righteousness of America's constitutional position, prudence, for Dickinson meant delaying a decision on independence until America had received firm assurance from the French of their aid to the cause. To do otherwise, he argued, was to treat them with "Contempt," thus endangering the possibility of French aid. Prudence also meant putting aside unrealistic expectations about the good will of either France or Spain. In the case of France, that nation might well be more interested in using its leverage in the conflict to retake Canada from the British. And the Spanish were more likely to view a united and independent American nation at their door as a threat rather than a benefit. Prudence required therefore, that rather than "proclaiming American independence to the world," America should engage in careful, behind-the-scenes negotiations with those powers.

Dickinson then proceeded to catalogue the catastrophic cost to America that would surely result from an unlimited war with Great Britain—a staggering financial debt, "Burning Towns, [and] Letting Loose Indians on our Frontiers." Reminding his listeners of the travail already suffered by the Continental Army—the debacle in Canada firmly in mind—he warned that a rash war for independence might well leave the Americans in a position where they were forced "to brave the Storm in a Skiff made of Paper."

Perhaps even more serious than the cost in money or in human life was the danger to the internal unity of the colonies. Dickinson was convinced that a premature declaration of independence would result in "partition" rather than union. In his position as chair of the other committee created in response to Richard Henry Lee's resolution for independence—that charged with drafting a plan for a "confederation" among the independent states—he was already beginning to see the way in which the jealousies and self-interests of individual colonies might thwart an effort toward a workable union. Dickinson was convinced that the "Calamities" of war would only increase those jealousies, leaving the so-called common cause of America's revolution a cruel joke, an idea undermined by jealousy and animosity.[3]

It was an unusually long speech, lasting perhaps until two in the afternoon, and the day was growing hotter. And Dickinson's rhetoric, normally so cool and controlled, even legalistic in its tone, grew more overheated as he reached his conclusion. "I should be glad," he concluded, "to read a little more in the Doomsday Book of America—Not all—that like the Book of Fate might be too dreadful." In his reference to the Domesday Book—the ancient survey of the lands of England—Dickinson no doubt intended to call attention once again to the fragility of any attempt at union among the colonies across the vast American landscape; and his reference to Voltaire's *Zadig: Or the Book of Fate* was yet another warning about attempting to tamper with matters beyond human control—both illusions highly revelatory of his essential conservatism. Dickinson concluded with a different vision for America—a different reading of *America's* Domesday book. If Americans could achieve reconciliation with Great Britain, if they could avoid the calamities that would surely result from a rash rush into independence, then, Dickinson told his fellow delegates, perhaps they would see "in 20 or 30 Years this Commonwealth of Colonies"—a commonwealth happily existing within the British Empire, in a content and prosperous state.[4]

John Adams, in the heat of the moment, told Samuel Chase that he considered the whole debate over independence that day to be "an

idle Mispence of Time, for nothing was Said but what had been repeated and hackneyed in that Room before an hundred Times, for
Six Months past." But looking back on the event a quarter of a century later, he had a slightly more benign view of the nature of the debate that day and a decidedly more laudatory view of his own role in
that debate. Writing in his *Autobiography*, Adams acknowledged that
his nemesis, although relying on nothing but "familiar" arguments,
had nevertheless spoken "not only with great Ingenuity and Eloquence, but with equal Politeness and Candour." But perhaps this
uncharacteristic generosity toward his rival was only a means of putting the spotlight on his own role following Dickinson's speech. According to Adams, "No member rose to answer" Dickinson, and
"after waiting some time, in hopes that someone less obnoxious than
myself, who had been all along for a Year before, and still was represented and believed to be the Author of all the Mischief, I determined to speak." Unlike Dickinson, who had carefully prepared his
speech, Adams used no notes. In fact, he could later remember little
of what he had said, other than an opening statement to the effect
"that this was the first time of my Life that I had ever wished for the
Talents and Eloquence of the ancient Orators of Greece and Rome,
for I was very sure that none of them ever had before him a question
of more Importance to his Country."[5]

John Adams was no Demosthenes or Cicero, but he had, through
hard work, become a darned good courtroom lawyer. Over the past
year and more, he had been making the case for the necessity of independence, and so doubtless he provided a convincing rebuttal to Dickinson's argument—convincing at least to those who already agreed
with him. According to Adams's later recollection, as he was finishing
his rebuttal, three newly elected delegates from New Jersey—Richard
Stockton, John Witherspoon and Francis Hopkinson—entered the
chamber and Stockton asked if Adams could summarize his remarks
for them. Adams then recalled:

> All was silence. No one would speak: all eyes were Turned upon me.
> Mr. Edward Rutledge came to me and said laughing: Nobody will speak
> but you, upon this Subject. You have all the Topicks so ready, that you
> must satisfy the Gentlemen from New Jersey. I answered him laughing,

that it had so much the Air of exhibiting like an Actor or Gladiator, for the Entertainment of the Audience, that I was ashamed to repeat what I had said twenty times before, and that nothing new could be advanced by me. The New Jersey Gentlemen however, still insisting, on hearing at least a Recapitulation of the arguments and no other Gentleman being willing to speak, I summed up the Reasons, Objections, and Answers, in as concise a manner as I could, till at length the Jersey Gentlemen said they were fully satisfied and ready for the Question, which was then put and determined in the Affirmative.[6]

Adams's recollection is misleading on a number of counts. Although it is indeed likely that he made one of the most impassioned and persuasive speeches that day, it is unlikely that he was the only one who spoke in favor of independence. And while it appears to be the case that at least two members of the New Jersey delegation arrived that day and, by the casting of their votes, added a ninth colony to the ranks of those favoring independence, there is little evidence beyond Adams's twenty-five-year-old recollection that his summary of his earlier speech was the deciding factor in their decision. The New Jersey legislature had, after all, already ordered the arrest of their royal governor, William Franklin, and by their vote on June 22 authorizing their congressional delegates to vote in favor of independence if they considered it "necessary and expedient" for the purpose of defending American liberty, had taken all but the final step in committing itself to independence.[7]

By the time Adams ended his speech, it was probably well after the Congress's usual four p.m. adjournment time. The temperature inside the Assembly Room had cooled considerably, for a powerful thunderstorm had passed over the city during Adams's speech, heavy rainfall driving down the temperature. The delegates, still operating as an informal committee of the whole, apparently took the equivalent of a straw vote to see where they stood on the question they had been debating all afternoon. Pennsylvania and South Carolina voted against Lee's resolution for independence; Delaware, which at that moment had only two delegates present, was divided; and New York's delegation had been prohibited by its legislature from casting a vote on the question.[8]

Nine in favor, two opposed, one colony divided and another abstaining. Could that be considered a sufficient endorsement of a decision of this magnitude? Few believed that it could. But what to make of it, and what to do next?

In spite of South Carolina's "no" vote that day, it was likely that a majority of the delegation favored independence, and that the vote in the negative was a temporary gesture of respect to Edward Rutledge, who was the South Carolinian most opposed to independence. There was, therefore, some hope that South Carolina would come around. Pennsylvania's delegation found itself in an awkward situation, as many of its delegates were at odds with the newly elected Provincial Congress, which emphatically favored independence. That body had scheduled a vote to replace its delegates for July 20, and until then Dickinson and his colleagues were lame ducks. John Morton, Benjamin Franklin and James Wilson voted in favor of Richard Henry Lee's resolution for independence; Dickinson, Robert Morris, Thomas Willing and Charles Humphreys against. The Delaware vote on that day had Thomas McKean voting in the affirmative, George Read in the negative. The third delegate, Caesar Rodney, back home in Delaware dealing with a potential Loyalist uprising, was absent. And of course New York's delegates were left with no choice but to remain silent.

Faced with a less than unanimous endorsement of the resolution for independence, the Congress, still sitting as a committee of the whole, embraced a motion by Edward Rutledge that "the determination thereof [be] postponed till tomorrow."[9]

July 2: Day of Decision

We know frustratingly little about what happened between the time that the Congress adjourned on July 1, possibly as late as seven p.m., and the morning of July 2. John Adams was hopeful that the resolution would pass by a larger majority the second time around, "perhaps with almost Unanimity." But he remained concerned, and annoyed, about the situation with the Pennsylvania delegation, for he feared that Dickinson and his moderate Pennsylvania colleagues would continue to "vote point blank against the known and declared sense of their constituents." And although few may have been aware of it at the time, Delaware's Thomas McKean had sent a message to Caesar Rodney, a known supporter of independence since the spring of 1776, that he had better get on his horse and get to Philadelphia *post haste.*[10]

The weather on July 2 had improved a bit. The heat of the previous day had been reduced by the heavy rain the previous evening. Once again John Hancock began the day's proceedings by introducing some routine business—a letter from George Washington accompanied by reports on several military matters, a communication from the Council of Massachusetts Bay dated June 26 and other letters related to the details of financing the war. At that point, Charles Thomson's pitifully scant journal of the proceedings reads:

> The Congress resumed the consideration of the resolution reported from the committee of the whole; which was agreed to as follows: "Resolved, That these United Colonies are, and, of right, ought to be, Free and Independent States; that they are absolved from all allegiance to the British crown, and that all political connexion between them, and the state of Great Britain, is, and ought to be, totally dissolved."[11]

What is absent from that monumentally unhelpful journal entry is any hint on how much time was spent on the question, any hint of the nature of the debate on the matter and any details on the actual vote on the question. In fact, there is ample testimony from delegates who were present on that day that the vote was unanimous among the twelve colonies that voted, with the New York delegates continuing to abstain. But we are left only to make educated guesses about what happened between the early evening of July 1 and the morning of July 2 to cause the South Carolina, Delaware and Pennsylvania delegations to decide to support the resolution for independence.

South Carolina's Edward Rutledge gave some hint of the likely switch in his delegation's vote as the debate came to a close on July 1. According to Thomas Jefferson's account of the proceedings, Rutledge, when he had asked the Congress to put off their decision for another day, indicated that "he believed his colleagues, tho' they disapproved of the resolution, would then join in it for the sake of una-nimity." Since Rutledge himself was the South Carolinian most adamantly opposed to independence, the "colleagues" he was speaking of were actually probably only one: himself! At the time, the South Carolina delegation consisted of four delegates—Rutledge, Thomas Heyward, Arthur Middleton and Thomas Lynch, Jr. Whatever the reasons for the switch in the South Carolina vote—a willingness to sacrifice their own views for the sake of American unity, the massag-ing of Rutledge's own sense of pride and prestige, an understanding that their constituents back home favored independence—all four ended up voting for independence and signing the Declaration of In-dependence. And, by so doing, they would have one more opportunity, on July 3, to influence the final outcome of the American decision for independence.[12]

We are able to identify the reasons for Delaware's change from a "divided" vote on July 1 to an affirmative one on July 2 with more cer-tainty. Caesar Rodney's role in the adoption of the resolution for in-dependence has long been part of the lore of American history—a mythology etched even deeper in Americans' minds by the Broadway musical, later made into a highly popular motion picture, *1776*. In that utterly charming, and occasionally accurate, bit of historical artistry, the very decision for independence hangs on the heroic actions of the forty-eight-year-old Delaware lawyer. John Adams described him as "the oddest looking Man in the World," an observation provoked in part by the fact that Rodney was suffering from the effects of ad-vanced skin cancer, which had badly disfigured his nose and one side of his face, a condition which was sufficiently visible that he often hid that part of his face with a silk scarf.[13]

According to the recollection of Rodney's Delaware colleague Thomas McKean, after the vote on July 1, he immediately sent a message to Rodney, who was about seventy miles away in Dover, Delaware, to hightail it back to Philadelphia by early the next morn-ing. McKean's recollection may have been blurred by the passage of time, for it would have taken a miracle for McKean's message, which could not have been sent any sooner than the early evening of July 1, to have reached Rodney, and then for Rodney to have mounted his horse and made the ride to Philadelphia in time to show up at the State House on the morning of July 2. It is more likely that the messenger sent to get Rodney moving left sometime earlier in the day on July 1, while the debate in the Congress was still going on. But whatever the precise timing of the journey from Philadelphia to Dover, there is no doubt that Rodney undertook a hurried, perhaps even perilous ride, to make it to the State House on time. By his testimony and that of several others, he rode all night through thunder and rain, to arrive at the State House still wearing his boots and spurs. Again according to McKean, after taking his seat in the Congress, Rodney announced: "As I believe the voice of my constituents and of all sensible and honest men is in favor of Independence and my own judgment concurs with them, I vote for Independence." Although this version of Rodney's midnight ride may not be quite as dramatic as that portrayed in the Broadway musical, his appearance that morning at the State House, expected by few other than his colleague Thomas McKean, was nevertheless both a surprise and a pleasure to the assembled delegates.[14]

The change in Pennsylvania's vote on July 2 was the most surprising to the members of Congress at the time and remains a source of some puzzlement to the present day. As the vote on independence neared that day, John Dickinson and Robert Morris left the table around which the Pennsylvania delegates were seated, pulling themselves "behind the bar," that rail which to this day keeps visitors to the Assembly Room of Independence Hall from actually walking into the space where the delegates to both the Continental Congress and the Constitutional Convention of 1787 carried out their deliberations. This removal left the decision up to the remaining five Pennsylvania delegates—John Morton, Benjamin Franklin, Thomas Willing, Charles Humphries and James Wilson. Morton and Franklin were clearly in favor of independence, Willing and Humphreys clearly opposed. James Wilson, although John Dickinson's protégé and a strong supporter of Dickinson's arguments in favor of reconciliation over the course of the past two years, had already made a reluctant break with his mentor on the July 1 vote, and once again on July 2 became the decisive vote within the Pennsylvania delegation in favor of independence, thus assuring a unanimous endorsement (with New York still abstaining) of that epochal decision in American history.[15]

James Wilson explained his decision to vote for independence as an act of respect to the power of the people of his colony, who had made their will apparent in the dramatic changes in the Pennsylvania government over the course of the previous weeks. Just a few years later, the "people" would be less than respectful to him when they launched a full-scale attack on his Philadelphia residence in protest against what they believed to be his excessive sympathy toward Loyalists, but Wilson, whatever the ups and downs of his personal relations with his fellow Philadelphians, was a sincere believer in the ultimate power of the people.[16]

Robert Morris, writing to a fellow Pennsylvanian three weeks after the Congress had voted in favor of independence, repeated his belief that that vote had been premature. He continued to hold out hopes that a peace commission would arrive from England and present General Washington with acceptable terms for a reconciliation between the two sides in the conflict. But, he added, if that did not come to pass, it would then be clear that "our *United Efforts*" to combat British tyranny and to "support the Independency" would be necessary. Although he was not persuaded that that moment had not yet come to pass, on that critical day, July 2, he apparently felt strongly enough about the importance of presenting to the world the *appearance* of American unity, that he absented himself from the vote. In the end, when the Declaration of Independence was finally put on parchment and presented to the delegates sometime in August, Morris would affix his signature to the document.[17]

John Dickinson never explained his decision not to vote that day. But one thing is certain: his decisions not to support independence *and* to absent himself from the vote that day were based entirely on his own moral sense of what was right. In spite of the decision of the Pennsylvania Provincial Congress supporting independence, Dickinson could be reasonably confident that his constituents would respect any decision that he might make on that question. His speech of July 1 was a necessary display of his conscience and integrity, and having made that speech, he simply could not, either emotionally or morally, reverse himself and vote in favor of independence the following day. But, like Morris, he recognized the need for the Congress to speak with a single, united voice, and for that reason, withdrew himself.[18]

He would pay a price. Ezra Stiles, a contemporary Connecticut minister who would soon become the president of Yale College, as it then was known, commented that Dickinson "now goes into oblivion or a dishonorable reminiscence with posterity," and John Adams, ever spiteful toward his rival, was still ranting about the "timid and trimming Politicks of some men of large Property here." But neither of those assessments was a fair measure of either Dickinson's motives or his actions during that critical time. It is noteworthy that immediately after America declared her independence, Dickinson led his Philadelphia battalion to Elizabethtown, New Jersey, to do battle with the British, while Adams, expressing his desire to "leave the War to be conducted by others" and complaining about being "weary, thoroughly weary" and in need of "a little Rest," planned to return home to Massachusetts as soon as possible.[19]

Dickinson never explained his failure to vote that day and never attempted a public defense of it. But he did, in a letter to an unknown correspondent written in August of 1776, defend the principled nature of his conduct during those trying weeks leading up to independence. "What can be more evident than that I have acted on Principle?" he asked. "Was there a Man in Pennsylvania that possessed a larger share of the public Confidence . . . than I did? Or that had a more certain Prospect of personal advantages from Independency, or of a small chance of advantages from Reconciliation?" He went on to recall his prediction in his July 1 speech that he would surely "lose a great deal of my popularity" by opposing independence, and asked, rhetorically, "What would be my object & whom was I trying to please?" He then ran through the list of possibilities. The supporters of the proprietary governor of the colony? Hardly, for they had been "uniformly my deadly foes throughout my Life." The Quakers? John Adams, who always linked Dickinson with the "broad brims," would have answered "surely," but Dickinson, although sympathetic to Quaker principles and closely connected to the religion through family ties, had never been afraid to stand up to the religious sect of which he was not a member. And besides, Dickinson noted, "All things were converging to a Revolution in which they would have little Power." Dickinson's prediction about the future decline in the popularity and political power of the Quakers in post-revolutionary Pennsylvania was right on target, but, unfortunately for him, though not a Quaker and not a spokesman for that religious sect, Dickinson's reputation and popularity would suffer in much the same way. As Dickinson himself put it, perhaps a bit self-righteously and hyperbolically, "I have so much of the spirit of Martyrdom in me, that I have been conscientiously compelled to endure in my political Capacity the Fires & Faggots of persecution."[20]

On the day after the July 2 vote on independence, John Adams wrote two letters to Abigail. The first was primarily concerned with local matters in and around Boston, but he concluded with some reflections about the extraordinary events that occurred during the past fifteen years of his professional and public life. Looking back to the year 1761, when he was involved in a legal argument over the British issuance of Writs of Assistance and which he regarded as "the Commencement of the Controversy" between the two countries, he marveled at "the Suddenness, as well as Greatness of this Revolution," a revolution which, he believed, was divinely ordained, for, he said, "it is the Will of Heaven that the two Countries should be sundered forever."

Adams's second letter to his wife was devoted entirely to the events leading to independence, but far from marveling at the "Suddenness" of the decision for independence, he complained that "Had a Declaration of Independency been made seven months ago, it would have been attended with many great and glorious effects"—alliances with foreign states, the successful conquest of Quebec and, indeed, the possession of all of Canada. Once again he railed against the "jarring Views, Wishes, and Designs" of others, which slowed the progress of "many salutary Measures" that would have given American greater advantage in the military engagements still to be fought. But the ever-mercurial Mr. Adams concluded on a note of optimism and with one of the most famous mis-predictions in all of American history. "But the Day is past," he wrote.

The Second Day of July 1776 will be the most memorable Epocha, in the history of America. I am apt to believe that it will be celebrated, by succeeding Generations, as the great anniversary Festival. It ought to be commemorated, as the Day of Deliverance by solemn Acts of Devotion to God Almighty. It ought to be solemnized with Pomp and Parade, with Shews, Games, Sports, Guns, Bells, Bonfires, and Illuminations from one End of this Continent to the other from this Time forward forever more.

He was close, but slightly off the mark. John Adams had been on center stage in the Pennsylvania State House for much of the past twenty-two months, but he would now have to share, perhaps even yield, the stage to a young Virginian from Albemarle County.[21]

TWENTY-FOUR

THOMAS JEFFERSON'S DECLARATION OF INDEPENDENCE

IT IS, ALONG WITH the United States Constitution, America's most cherished document. It succeeds masterfully in laying out the reasons for America's audacious decision to break all ties of constitutional and emotional connection with the king and the empire over which he ruled. But the Declaration of Independence does more than that—in its eloquent preamble it lays out an idealistic, if idealized, vision of America's future, as a country committed to the principle of equality and to the protection of mankind's "unalienable rights." Its author, Thomas Jefferson, went on to accomplish many extraordinary things in his long and productive life, but among all of those accomplishments, his writing of the Declaration of Independence would come to be the most remembered, most revered, by successive generations of Americans.

But during the last few weeks in June and the first days of July in 1776, few in the Continental Congress were aware either of the importance of the task assigned to Jefferson, or of its lasting impact on the American consciousness. And, as these two concluding chapters will demonstrate, the remarkable achievement of the Declaration of Independence was not Thomas Jefferson's alone. *America's* Declaration of Independence was the collective accomplishment of the members of the Continental Congress, a congress that had been struggling to define America's future for the past twenty-two months.

Thomas Jefferson left Philadelphia in late December of 1775, eager to return home to his wife and family, as well as to his newest passion in life—his plantation-in-progress, Monticello. Although he did not set any specific timetable for his return to Congress, his mother's unexpected death on March 31, 1776, followed by an acute onset of what we would today call a migraine headache, caused him to delay his return to Philadelphia for nearly six weeks.

Whatever the sadness provoked by the death of his mother or the intensity of his headaches, at least some of his delay in returning was the result of his deep infatuation with his pastoral life at Monticello. At his hilltop estate in the western Virginia county of Albemarle, he was safely removed from the military conflict that had erupted in Norfolk in early January, where the combination of Lord Dunmore's naval forces and riotous Norfolk residents had essentially burned the town to the ground. Jefferson's correspondence later in life was voluminous—indeed, so much so that it is a wonder he had any time left over to accomplish all of the things that he was able to during his long career. But the written record during his five-month retreat at Monticello in the first half of 1776 is remarkably sparse. We know that he received occasional reports of the disastrous military campaigns in Canada, and that a few of his friends wrote him about issues relating to Virginia's military preparations, but he apparently was not moved to comment on those reports, at least in writing. Indeed, three days after he arrived in Philadelphia, he wrote his friend John Page that "I have been so long out of the political world that I am almost a new man in it."[1]

Jefferson did undertake one extended piece of political writing during his retreat at Monticello, a "Refutation of the Argument that the Colonies Were Established at the Expense of the British Nation," apparently written after he had received news of the content of the king's speech to Parliament denouncing the colonies on October 26, 1775. Jefferson wrote the piece at nearly the exact time of the publication of Tom Paine's *Common Sense*, although he did not receive a copy of Paine's pamphlet until three or four weeks later. Although Jefferson, unlike John Adams, came to hold a high opinion of Paine's contributions to the cause of independence, there is no evidence that Paine's pamphlet had much of an influence on Jefferson's thinking at the time. Indeed, whatever mutual admiration may have existed between Paine and Jefferson, their temperaments, and their writing styles, were entirely different. Jefferson's refutation of the king's speech, which was never published, was a scholarly, historical treatise, aimed not at rallying the American people to action, but, rather, at clarifying in his own mind some of the historical details relating to the founding of the American colonies. Although some of the logic of his privately composed treatise would ultimately find its way into the Declaration of Independence, Jefferson was content, at least at that time, to keep his thinking to himself.[2]

Returning to Philadelphia

Jefferson left Monticello, accompanied by his slave Bob, the brother of his servant and future companion, Sally Hemings, for Philadelphia on May 6. On his trip to Philadelphia in 1775 he had traveled with a veritable entourage—three slaves, a carriage and four horses—but having discovered that the cost of boarding his horses in Philadelphia was nearly twice that of his own lodgings in the city, this time he and Bob were on horseback, riding for eight days through the Shenandoah Valley and upland to reach Philadelphia from the west. Upon his arrival he would take up lodgings, at least temporarily, once again at the boardinghouse of Benjamin Randolph, but after eight days he moved to a three-story brick house on Seventh and Market Streets, completed just the year before by Jacob Graff, a recently married bricklayer. Jefferson lived in two rooms—a bedroom and a parlor, on the second floor. Visitors to the Graff House today see a compact house, snugly positioned on the corner of a bustling thoroughfare, but in May 1776, its location was quite literally on the outskirts of the city, with fields and a stable located just across the street.[3]

Although Jefferson may not have realized it at the time, the timing of his arrival was propitious. On May 15, the day after he arrived but perhaps before he had taken his seat inside the Assembly Room of the Pennsylvania State House, the Congress agreed to the preamble to the May 10 resolution requesting the colonies to begin to organize their own governments. The preamble stated that it was "irreconcilable to reason and good conscience" for any colony to give support to any government under the authority of "the crown of Great Britain." This was the same day that some 290 miles to the south, in Williamsburg, the Virginia Convention had instructed its delegates to the Continental Congress to introduce a resolution into that body proposing independence. Although Jefferson no doubt had some sense of the direction in which the political winds in his home colony were blowing, he was probably not aware of the specific nature of the Virginia Convention's action when he arrived in Philadelphia. But he soon would be.

Although upon his arrival in Philadelphia he had claimed to have felt removed from the political world, he immediately threw himself into the maelstrom of political activity in Philadelphia. Although only distantly aware of the events in Canada while at Monticello, he immediately became actively involved in committee work aimed at mitigating the debacle there, drafting reports and recommendations, as well working with George Wythe in the drafting of a letter to German mercenaries, who were being sent by the British to bolster their army in America. This last missive was hardly a friendly one. The two Virginians announced, "with no small pleasure . . . that we can affirm you to be unprovoked enemies," and then went into a tirade at their willingness to "undertake the bloody work of butchering" the innocent inhabitants of America.[4]

As much as he was preoccupied with continental affairs, Jefferson soon became aware that the Virginia Convention, on the same day that it had passed the resolution advocating independence, had agreed to begin drafting a new constitution for the aspiring-to-be-independent colony. Jefferson was at this stage in his career every bit as much a Virginian as he was an American political leader and felt torn between his desire to be part of that effort and his duties in the Continental Congress. On May 16 he actually suggested to his friend Thomas Nelson that the entire Virginia delegation to the Continental Congress return home for the purpose of assisting in the writing of a new constitution—"a work of the most interesting nature"—for the colony. Given the important business facing the Congress, this was a wholly unrealistic suggestion, but Jefferson nevertheless spent much of his time in early June writing multiple drafts of a constitution for his homeland, the final version of which he sent to the Virginia Convention, probably on June 13.[5]

There has been considerable speculation—and disagreement—about the extent to which Jefferson's drafts influenced the final version of Virginia's frame of government, which has generally been attributed to George Mason. It seems likely that Jefferson's drafts arrived in Williamsburg too late to receive a thorough appraisal, and the preponderance of evidence suggests that Mason's drafts of the Virginia Constitution and the declaration of rights that preceded it were much more influential in shaping the final product than Jefferson's. But one thing is clear: Jefferson's own work on his drafts of the Virginia Constitution, occurring immediately before and during his work on another assignment given to him by the Continental Congress, would have a profound effect not only on some of the language of the Virginia Constitution but also on the other document that would become America's official justification for its separation from Great Britain.[6]

As we have seen, when Richard Henry Lee introduced Virginia's proposed resolution for independence into the Continental Congress on June 7, the Congress ended up deferring further discussion of the resolution until July 1. But it set up a committee to draft a justification for such an action in order that no time would be lost should Congress eventually endorse the resolution. The delegates elected Thomas Jefferson, John Adams, Benjamin Franklin, Roger Sherman and Robert Livingston to serve on that committee. Among that group of five, only Livingston still harbored any reservations about the wisdom of independence. There is no formal statement from the Congress affirming that Jefferson was selected as chair of the committee, although John Adams, writing forty-six years later about the events of that day, recalled that "I think [Jefferson] had one more vote than any other, and that placed him at the head of the committee." Whatever the precise tabulation of the vote, since the normal procedure of the Congress was to appoint the individual receiving the largest number of votes in the election of a committee as its chair, Jefferson probably did receive the highest number of votes.[7]

Adams's other, more famous recollection of the circumstances surrounding the decision to allow Jefferson to write the first draft occurred around 1805, when he was composing his *Autobiography*. His recollections at that time were self-deprecating with respect to his own talents, but rather mean-spirited as they related to Jefferson's prior contributions to the Congress. Jefferson, he recalled, "had been now about a Year a member of Congress, but had attended his Duty in the House but a very small part of the time and when there had never spoken in public." Indeed, Adams claimed, "during the whole Time I satt with him in Congress, I never heard him utter three Sentences together." The only speech of consequence that Adams could remember was one in which Jefferson uttered "a gross insult on religion . . . for which I gave him immediately the Reprehension, which he richly merited."[8]

So how was it that Jefferson was included on the committee, particularly when men like Richard Henry Lee, who had introduced the resolution for independence, had served in the Congress longer and whose reputation at that time was probably more distinguished than Jefferson's? Again according to Adams, because of Virginia's role in shaping events up to that point, it was important that someone from that colony be on the committee. And besides, Adams admitted, "Mr. Jefferson had the Reputation of a masterly Pen." Equally important, Adams claimed, was that Lee "was not beloved by most of his Colleagues from Virginia, and Mr. Jefferson was sett up to rival and supplant him." There is little evidence to support that assertion. In fact, it is likely that Lee purposely deferred to Jefferson because, after introducing the resolution for independence, he was anxious to return home to work on Virginia's new constitution. Indeed, Lee did leave Philadelphia to go to Virginia on June 13 and did not return until after the Declaration of Independence had been adopted, although he later signed the document. The strong support for Jefferson almost certainly owed less either to animosity toward Lee or lack of desire to serve on Lee's part than it did on Jefferson's well-deserved reputation as a masterful writer.[9]

Unfortunately, we have no other account about the rationale for the selection of committee members other than Adams's belated recollections. The Congress's secretary, Charles Thomson, true to his casual note-taking practices, provided no details of the selection process, and none of the other delegates left behind any written comments on the matter. It seems likely, however, that among the factors that led to the selection of the other four delegates—Adams, Franklin, Roger Sherman and Robert Livingston—was a desire for some approximation of geographic balance, with Adams and Sherman the two New Englanders, Franklin and Livingston representing two important and populous mid-Atlantic colonies and Jefferson the southerner.

The selections of Adams and Franklin were probably foregone conclusions. Adams, however annoying his obsessive and self-aggrandizing manner may have been to some, had demonstrated a combination of intellect and persistence that earned him a place on the committee. And Franklin's selection owed to the fact that, well, he was *Franklin*—along with General Washington the most distinguished and respected man in America. The fact that he was also widely known and, in at least some circles, respected in Britain provided even more of a rationale for his selection.

The fourth member of the committee, Roger Sherman of Connecticut, is relatively unknown to most Americans today, but on the eve of independence he had a reputation as a man of admirable diligence and uncommon good sense. Fifty-five years old in 1776, Sherman was one of just a few of America's revolutionary political leaders—Benjamin Franklin notably being among that small group—who began life in genuinely modest circumstances. Sherman's father, a shoemaker who died when Roger was nineteen, left his family little more than a modest farm and his cobbler's tools. Sherman may also have been the only one of America's Founding Fathers to rise to prominence by serving in public, salary-paying offices. During the forty-eight-year period between 1745 and his death in 1793, Sherman served as a jury man, tax collector, inspector of pennies, town clerk, deacon of his Congregational church, town agent to the Connecticut Assembly, justice of the peace, justice of the county court, representative in the lower house of the Connecticut Assembly, member of the upper house of the Assembly, commissary for the Connecticut militia and, finally, judge of the Connecticut superior court. His service to the continental government was just beginning. He was a delegate from Connecticut in both the First and Second Continental Congresses. In addition to being on the drafting committee for the Declaration of Independence, he would also be on the committee charged with drafting the Articles of Confederation, and, most notably, would go on to become the foremost proponent of the compromise between large states and small states on the subject of representation in the Constitutional Convention of 1787.[10]

John Adams considered Sherman to be "one of the soundest and strongest pillars of the Revolution," and counted him "one of the most cordial friends which I ever had in my life." Like most others who first encountered Sherman, however, Adams was struck by his awkward and ungainly public persona. He described Sherman's appearance as "the reverse of grace." Some years later a Georgia delegate to the Constitutional Convention would comment similarly, calling Sherman "the oddest shaped character I have ever met with" and assessing his manner of private and public speaking as "grotesque and laughable." But whatever his physical awkwardness, Sherman was not a man to be messed with. One political rival in Connecticut wrote a friend warning him that Sherman was as "cunning as the devil, . . . and if you are trying to take him in, you may as well catch an eel by the tail." But neither Adams nor Jefferson had any reason to worry about Sherman being a disruptive force on their committee, for he had been a forceful advocate for independence since at least Lexington and Concord.[11]

The one member of the committee who must have caused the others some concern was Robert Livingston. At the time the committee was chosen he was under orders from New York's legislature not to vote in favor of independence. And Livingston didn't need any such admonishment, for he had gone on record opposing a precipitous move toward independence. But in spite of his personal opposition to independence, he had also made it clear that he was willing to support that move should a majority of the Congress endorse it. Moreover, Livingston had proven himself a competent, conscientious member of the Congress who had been elected by his colleagues to serve on a wide range of important committees. His presence would not change the balance of power on the committee, and, just perhaps, his involvement might cause him to re-evaluate his position advocating further efforts at reconciliation.[12]

We know that on June 11 the committee chose Jefferson to compose the first draft of the Declaration, a seemingly logical choice
since Jefferson had been selected as chair of the committee. But the
recollections of John Adams have made the decision a matter of some
speculation. Adams provided the only extended description of that
process, first in his autobiography in 1805 and later in a long letter to
Timothy Pickering in 1822. According to Adams, when the committee first met, "Mr Jefferson desired me to take [the minutes of the
Congress] to my Lodgings and make the Draught." But, according to
Adams, he declined to write the first draft, insisting instead that Jefferson take on the task. In writing his 1805 autobiography, he listed
the reasons as follows:

> 1. That he was a Virginian and I a Massachusettsensian. 2. That he was
> a southern Man and I a northern one. 3. That I had been so obnoxious
> from my early and constant Zeal in promoting the Measure, that any
> draught of mine, would undergo a more severe Scrutiny and Criticism
> in Congress, than one of his composition. 4thly and lastly and that
> would be reason enough if there were no other, I had a great Opinion of
> the Elegance of his pen and none at all of my own.

Adams gave a similar version of events in his letter to Pickering in
1822, although in it Adams described Jefferson as modestly acqui-
escing, saying "Well, if you are decided I will do as well as I can."[13]

The first three of the four reasons that Adams cited have a ring of
truth to them. It was certainly preferable, from a purely political point
of view, to have someone from Virginia—America's oldest and most
populous colony—rather than one of the "radical New England fanatics" as they were sometimes viewed, do the drafting. The New England colonies were all within the independence camp. At the time
the committee was selected, however, Delaware's, Maryland's and
South Carolina's support of independence was in doubt. And so the
selection of Jefferson, a southerner, it was perhaps felt, might help
sway these more southerly delegates. And Adams was certainly correct in recognizing that his zealousness in promoting the cause of independence might well have rendered him "obnoxious" to at least
some of the delegates in the Congress. If it's unlikely that Adams had

admitted to Jefferson that the "elegance" of the Virginian's pen was greater than his own (in his letter to Pickering he went even further, recalling that he had told Jefferson that "You can write ten times better than I can"), it is at least true that Adams, and the other members of the committee, held Jefferson's writing ability in high regard.

The other three delegates on the committee—Franklin, Sherman and Livingston—never recounted the discussion held among themselves that day. And it took Jefferson until 1823, after seeing a published version of a Fourth of July oration by Timothy Pickering based on Adams's letter to him, before he gave his own version of events. Writing to James Madison, Jefferson insisted that "Mr Adams memory has led him into unquestionable error. . . . At the age of eighty-eight and forty-seven years after the transactions of Independence, [his memory] is not wonderful." Jefferson was eighty at the time he wrote to Madison, so he was no spring chicken himself. He was well aware of this, telling Madison, "Nor should I . . . venture to oppose my memory to his, were it not supported by written notes, taken by myself at the moment and on the spot." According to Jefferson, there was no exchange between him and Adams about who might be better qualified to produce a first draft. Quite simply, Jefferson recalled, the members of the committee "unanimously pressed upon myself alone to undertake the draught. I consented, I drew it."[14]

John Adams, in his autobiography, said that the drafting committee had several meetings before the actual drafting of the Declaration got under way, and during those meetings it is likely that all of the members of the committee voiced their opinions about the shape of the document. But at some point, probably on either Wednesday or Thursday, June 12 or 13, Jefferson repaired to the second-floor parlor of his lodgings at the home of Jacob Graff, and seating himself in a swiveling Windsor chair and with a wooden writing box specially made for him by his former Philadelphia landlord, the master cabinet maker, Benjamin Randolph, he began to put pen to paper. John Adams later claimed that Jefferson wrote that first draft in just "a day or two," after which he "produced to me his draught." Jefferson was in fact an exceptionally efficient writer, so Adams may not have been too far off the mark. Indeed, Jefferson had other responsibilities at the time he was writing the Declaration. During the weeks before the final debate on independence he served on three other committees: one to "digest and arrange" all of the resolutions regarding the disastrous Canadian campaign, another to "enquire into the causes of the miscarriages in Canada" and a third to draw up rules and regulations for congressional debates. Although subsequent generations of Americans came to see the writing of the Declaration of Independence as the single most important literary task ever undertaken in all of America's history, Jefferson and Adams probably did not consider it as such at the time. As we have seen, Jefferson was so emotionally and intellectually involved with the task of constitution making in Virginia that he wanted to leave the Congress before being appointed to the committee to draft the Declaration. Meanwhile, many in the Congress believed that the work of the committee to draft a "plan of confederation" for the "united colonies"—a committee chaired by none other than the reluctant revolutionist John Dickinson—was more important than that of the committee to draft the declaration.[15]

While over the course of more than two centuries Jefferson has come to be known as the principal author of the Declaration, the details of the editing of various drafts of the document are less clear. According to Jefferson, before giving his initial draft to the entire committee of five, he "communicated it separately to Dr. Franklin and Mr. Adams requesting their corrections." Those corrections, Jefferson claimed, "were two or three only, and merely verbal. I then wrote a fair copy, reported it to the committee, and from them, unaltered to the Congress."[16]

In all likelihood, the process of drafting and editing the Declaration was far more complicated than that. Jefferson probably composed several "fragments" of the Declaration and then combined them into what he later called "the original rough draft," which he shared with Adams and Franklin. Moreover, after Adams and Franklin offered their comments on that rough draft, Jefferson asked Franklin to look at his revised draft one more time. On a "Friday morn" in June, possibly June 21, he attached a note to that revised draft telling Franklin that "the inclosed paper has been read and with some small alterations approved of by the committee. Will Doctr. Franklyn be so good as to peruse it and suggest such alterations as his more enlarged view of the subject will dictate?"[17]

When one compares the draft of the Declaration that was delivered to Congress on June 28 with Jefferson's "original rough draft," one can discern a total of twenty-six alterations—two in Adams's handwriting, five in Franklin's and sixteen in Jefferson's. The draft submitted to Congress also contained three additional paragraphs in Jefferson's hand. In analyzing Jefferson's original rough draft, it is sometimes difficult to tell whether the changes were made by Jefferson or by others and merely recorded in Jefferson's handwriting. But though Jefferson would later complain of the "mutilations" to which his original draft was subjected, most of the changes suggested by his colleagues made the finished document more elegant and forceful.

The Preamble

Of all the parts of the Declaration of Independence, the Preamble has become most firmly embedded in American culture. It is, moreover, the quintessential expression of American values and ideals. The words and ideas in Jefferson's preamble, whether in their initial or revised form, did not, however, spring unaided from Jefferson's brain. Jefferson later claimed that he "turned toward neither book nor pamphlet" while writing the Declaration. But he carried in his head a rich intellectual heritage, including the writings of John Locke, and especially *The Second Treatise of Civil Government*, which explored in detail the idea of mankind's "natural rights," and also the works of a group of eighteenth-century Scottish philosophers including Francis Hutcheson, David Hume and Adam Smith.[18]

The first paragraph of that preamble was essentially a restatement of the May 15 resolution of the Virginia Convention, which began, "Forasmuch as all of the endeavours of the United Colonies by the most decent representations to the King and parliament of Great Britain, to restore peace and security to America . . . have produced, from an imperious and vindictive administration, increased insult, oppression, and a vigorous attempt to affect our total destruction." The version of the preamble that Jefferson and his fellow committee members submitted to Congress avoided legalistic words such as "forasmuch" and "whereas," and began far more elegantly:

When in the course of human events it becomes necessary for one people to dissolve the political bands which have connected them with another, and to assume among the powers of the earth the separate and equal station to which the laws of nature & of nature's god entitle them, a decent respect to the opinions of mankind requires that they should declare the causes which impel them to the separation.[19]

This single sentence announced the Americans' intention of declaring their independence, of breaking the ties that had bound them to England. The justification for this unprecedented act was to be found in "the laws of nature and of nature's god." Jefferson, a deist who did not believe that God played an active role in the daily affairs of mankind, nevertheless did believe, with John Locke, that certain natural rights were God-given. This first sentence also conveyed Jefferson's awareness that a compelling public statement of the reasons for the decision to seek independence from England was necessary if America's political leaders were to earn the support not only of their constituents in the colonies but, equally important, of foreign nations like France. Much of the opposition to independence from men like John Dickinson was based on the uncertainty of gaining either commercial or military aid from France, and a firmly stated commitment to independence from Great Britain, France's bitter enemy, might be a way of winning that nation over to the American cause.

It is of course the second paragraph of the preamble, and, in particular the first sentence of that paragraph, that, in their final form, have become a vital part of American memory and American ideals:

We hold these truths to be self-evident, that all men are created equal, that they are endowed by their Creator with certain unalienable Rights, that among these are Life, Liberty and the Pursuit of Happiness.—That to secure these rights, Governments are instituted among Men, deriving their just powers from the consent of the governed.—That whenever any Form of Government becomes destructive of those ends, it is the Right of the People to alter or abolish it, and to institute new Government, laying its foundation on such principles and organizing its powers in such form, as to them shall seem most likely to effect their Safety and Happiness.

Although the opening words of that second paragraph of the preamble are significantly indebted to the writings of John Locke, the more immediate influence on Jefferson's composition of that passage, occurring virtually simultaneously with his duties as chair of the Continental Congress's Committee of Five, was his intense intellectual and emotional involvement in the crafting of the Virginia Constitution and Declaration of Rights. However frustrated he may have been that he was not in Williamsburg to take the lead in that effort, his involvement from afar had a direct impact on his drafting of the preamble of America's Declaration of Independence.

On June 12, the *Pennsylvania Gazette* printed the Virginia Convention committee's first draft of the Declaration of Rights, a draft most likely crafted by Jefferson's senior Virginia colleague, George Mason. It is likely that Jefferson read the draft just as he was beginning his composition of the Declaration of Independence. The draft of the Virginia Declaration printed in the *Pennsylvania Gazette* began: "That all men are born equally free and independent, and have certain inherent natural rights, of which they cannot by any compact deprive or divest their posterity; among which are the enjoyment of life and liberty, with the means of acquiring and possessing property, and pursuing and obtaining happiness and safety." Although Jefferson could not have known it at the time, the Virginia Convention, when it eventually adopted the draft of the Declaration of Rights, made one small, but highly significant change, adding, between the phrases "of which" and "they cannot" another phrase—another qualifying phrase: "when they enter into a state of society." Thus with italics added: "That all men are by their nature free and independent, and have certain inherent rights, of which, *when they enter into a state of society,* they cannot by any compact deprive or divest their posterity; namely the enjoyment of life and liberty, with the means of acquiring and possessing property, and pursuing and obtaining happiness and safety." That seemingly innocuous (and perhaps purposely ambiguous) phrase was in fact of momentous importance, for when members of the Virginia Convention read the original phraseology, many of them protested that such an open-ended assertion of mankind's inherent rights of life and liberty might be "misinterpreted" to apply to the colony's slave population, and thus the Convention added the phrase "when they enter into a state of society" to avoid any such misconception.[20]

Jefferson's initial articulation of the fundamental natural rights of man did not include that qualification and was somewhat more elegant than the version in the Virginia Declaration of Rights, but it was nevertheless inferior to the language of the final draft. In his initial composition, he wrote:

> We hold these truths to be self-evident, that all men are created equal & independent; that from that equal creation they derive rights inherent & inalienable, among which are the preservation of life, & liberty, & the pursuit of happiness.

The final draft was not only more concise, but more elegant than either the Virginia Convention's version or that in Jefferson's initial draft. And it did not include the qualification of "when they enter into a state of society," which excluded forty percent of Virginia's population from the guarantee of the blessings of liberty. There is little doubt that Jefferson's own conception of the promises of equality, life, liberty and the pursuit of happiness was, at least implicitly, far more limited than ours today, but the fact that the language of the preamble did *not* include that qualification has proven enormously important over the course of America's history.

The famous opening lines of the preamble's second paragraph were in fact intended as just a preface to the paragraph's real punch line—the assertion of Americans' right to rebel against the government of England. Jefferson, like Tom Paine, reminded his readers that the very purpose of government is to protect the natural rights of mankind. Since governments, at the time of their creation, base their authority on the consent of the people over whom they are to govern, then it is also the right of the people to "alter or abolish" their government if its actions threaten the very liberties that the government was created to protect. And, though Jefferson may have been seen as a "radical" by some within the elite body of the Continental Congress, he was certainly no anarchist. Like Paine, he recognized the dangers of living in a society *without government* and was quick to assert that once the people had severed their ties to an old, corrupt government, they must move on to form new governments committed to promoting the people's "Safety and Happiness."

The preamble, in its final form as approved by Congress, ended with an emotional, if somewhat self-righteous, invocation of the patience with which Americans had endured the "sufferances" imposed upon them by Great Britain:

> Prudence, indeed, will dictate that Governments long established should not be changed for light and transient causes; and accordingly all experience hath shewn, that mankind are more disposed to suffer, while evils are sufferable, than to right themselves by abolishing the forms to which they are accustomed. But when a long train of abuses and usurpations, pursuing invariably the same Object evinces a design to reduce them under absolute Despotism, it is their right, it is their duty, to throw off such Government, and to provide new Guards for their future security.— Such has been the patient sufferance of these Colonies; and such is now the necessity which constrains them to alter their former Systems of Government. The history of the present King of Great Britain is a history of repeated injuries and usurpations, all having in direct object the establishment of an absolute Tyranny over these States. To prove this, let Facts be submitted to a candid world.[21]

The Declaration of Independence as a whole was intended for multiple audiences, both at home and abroad, but this particular passage was perhaps aimed most directly at those in and out of Congress who were still hoping that some solution short of independence might be found. As we have seen, the decision for independence was reached slowly and, indeed for many, painfully. So it was important to signal to the world that the decision had not been arrived at rashly—that the delegates to the Congress had done everything within their power to find some alternative and that only a "long train of abuses" had driven them to this final, decisive action.

The phrasing of that section of the preamble was again shaped by multiple sources. In his *Second Treatise of Civil Government,* John Locke had written that the people could "rouze themselves" and deny the legitimacy of their government only after "a long train of Abuses, Prevarications, an Artifices, all tending the same way," had justified such a drastic step. And Jefferson himself, in his 1774 *Summary View of the Rights of British America*, referred to the "rapid and bold succession of injuries" to which the colonies had been subjected, concluding that "single acts of tyranny may be ascribed to the accidental opinion of a day; but a series of oppressions, begun at a distinguished period, and pursued unalterably thro' every change of ministers, too plainly prove a deliberate, systematical plan of reducing us to slavery."[22]

Many people at the time regarded the words of the preamble as having little substantive importance. John Lind, a Loyalist critic of the Declaration of Independence, claimed that "Of the preamble I have taken little or no notice," and the embittered former Massachusetts royal governor, Thomas Hutchinson, gave it only cursory attention in his critical dissection of the Declaration. But it was not Loyalists alone who ignored the preamble. For most American patriots, the heart and soul of the Declaration was the list of specific grievances, which, making up more than two-thirds of the document, were aimed at proving to the world that the king was indeed guilty of "repeated injuries and usurpations" that justified independence.[23]

It is in the list of grievances that we see Jefferson the lawyer, rather than Jefferson the philosopher, display his argumentative skills. The list is in no way a fair-minded or evenhanded assessment of the conflict, but, rather, a one-sided bill of indictment aimed not only at persuading those Americans who remained undecided on the question of independence, but, equally important, at signaling to potential European allies that Americans were utterly serious about their intent to break with England.

The fact that Jefferson was nearly simultaneously engaged in drafting a version of the Virginia Constitution made this part of his job in drafting the Declaration significantly easier. He prefaced his draft of the Virginia document with twenty itemized grievances against the king that differed only slightly from the list of twenty-eight complaints that he included in his draft of the Declaration.[24]

There is a monotony to the recitation of the injustices, but, as the grievances accumulate, Jefferson's tone, much like that of a prosecuting attorney delivering his summation to a jury, grows steadily more belligerent, more fiery in its sense of outrage. Nor was it merely the British actions that elicited Jefferson's contempt. Even worse was the British *intent.* Jefferson portrayed King George III as not merely guilty of bad policies, but of proceeding with malevolent motives. The grievances laid out in Jefferson's list are not merely *constitutional* in nature, but intensely *personal.*

Buried in the list of grievances—number sixteen in the "fair copy" that he and the Committee of Five sent to Congress—was the complaint that had started it all, the denunciation of the king and Parliament for "imposing taxes on us without our Consent." Several other grievances were direct consequences of the decision to tax the colonies—one accusing the king of "sending swarms of Officers to harass our people," an accusation that referred to the customs officials sent to America to collect the taxes; and another condemning the king for sending "Standing Armies" to America in "times of peace," a direct outgrowth of the inability of the customs officers alone to carry out their duties. Adding insult to injury, the decision to send troops to America was accompanied by another parliamentary act requiring the colonists to provide lodging for those troops—the subject of another of his specific grievances. The thirteenth grievance on Jefferson's original list was one of the most convoluted, charging the king with combining "with others to subject us to a jurisdiction foreign to our constitution"; the "others" referred to in that grievance were the Parliament, which in the Declaratory Act had declared its right to legislate for the colonies in "all cases whatsoever," and the Board of Trade, which was charged with enforcing the new taxes imposed on the Americans.

A significant number of the grievances in the draft that Jefferson and the committee sent to Congress—nine in all—dealt with encroachments on the prerogatives of the colonial legislatures. Jefferson blamed the king for refusing to approve laws passed by those legislatures; for instructing his governors to prevent laws already passed from going into effect; for not allowing laws to go into effect unless the people gave up their right to representation in the legislature; for calling the legislatures into session in places and times "unusual, uncomfortable, and distant," all with an aim of "fatiguing" the people into "compliance with his measures; for dissolving the legislatures whenever they displayed "manly firmness" in opposing his measures; for refusing to call for new elections of representatives, thus making it impossible for the legislatures to meet; for refusing to agree to laws passed by the legislatures establishing provincial courts; for revoking colonial charters—a grievance aimed particularly at his actions toward the Massachusetts government; and, finally, for suspending many of the legislatures, thus depriving the colonies of their right to govern themselves.

It is not surprising that Jefferson devoted so much space in his list of specific grievances concerning violations of the rights of provincial legislatures. Nearly all of the members of the Congress who would be asked to endorse his draft of the Declaration of Independence had been members of those legislatures. They felt great pride not only in the independence and autonomy of their representative assemblies but also in the prestige they had earned and the power they exercised while members of those legislatures. The encroachments upon the rights and prerogatives of their legislatures were therefore not only *constitutional* violations, but also intensely *personal* assaults on their prestige and dignity.

Several of the grievances in Jefferson's draft dealt with imperial threats to American judicial processes: making colonial judges dependent on the British government for their continuation in office and for their salaries; depriving the colonists of their right to trial by jury; attempting to transport colonists accused of crimes back to Great Britain to be tried there rather than by a jury of their peers at home; and protecting British troops, "by a mock-trial, from punishment for any murders which they should commit on the inhabitants of these states," a likely reference to the 1774 Administration of Justice Act.

If the American grievances began with acts of taxation and then spread to more general threats to American legislative and judicial processes, still other grievances came to the fore in the years immediately preceding independence. The twelfth and twentieth points of argument in Jefferson's draft, which accused the king of rendering the military superior to civilian power and of "altering fundamentally the forms of our governments," were clearly aimed at those parts of the Coercive Acts suspending Massachusetts government and installing General Gage as a military governor of the colony. The fifteenth item on his list, which complained of British edicts that cut off

American trade "with all parts of the world," was aimed at both the Boston Port Act and the Prohibitory Act of December 1775. The nineteenth, condemning the king for "abolishing the free system of English laws in a neighboring province," amounted to a broad-brushed, and unfair, attack on the Quebec Act, which, as we have seen, was aimed at protecting the liberties of the French Catholic residents of that province, not at destroying American liberties.

The final grievances in Jefferson's draft list built to a crescendo of outrage over British actions occurring after military hostilities broke out at Lexington and Concord. The twenty-third, with the charge that the king had "plundered our seas, ravaged our coasts, burnt our towns, and destroyed the lives of our people," while technically true, was certainly a one-sided depiction of the tragic outcomes of any state of war. The twenty-fourth grievance condemned the king for sending foreign mercenaries to "compleat the works of death, desolation, and tyranny, already begun with circumstances of cruelty & perfidy unworthy the head of a civilized nation." Another grievance, the twenty-seventh on Jefferson's original list and the twenty-sixth on the list eventually approved by Congress, blamed the king for forcing "our fellow citizens taken captive on the high Seas to bear arms against their Country." This grievance was aimed at the effects of the Prohibitory Act, which not only declared war on American commerce but also called for the impressment of American sailors into the British navy.

When Thomas Jefferson was working on his drafts for the Virginia Constitution, he included, midway through his list of grievances, two items in the preamble that leap out at the reader in their intensity and passion. One denounced the king for "prompting our negroes to rise in arms among us," a reference to Lord Dunmore's proclamation offering freedom to Virginia slaves who fled their masters and fought on the side of the British. The irony of that particular juxtaposition of slavery and liberty has already been noted, but it was not the arming of slaves alone that incited Jefferson's fury. Jefferson also included in the Virginia Constitution drafts another grievance blaming the king for bringing "on the inhabitants of our frontiers, the merciless Indian savages, whose known rule of warfare is an undistinguished destruction of all ages, sexes, & conditions of existence."[25]

In the draft of the Declaration presented to Congress, Jefferson changed both the order and content of grievances appearing at the end of his list. He eliminated, as a separate grievance, the charge that the king had incited "our negroes to rise in arms against us." He substituted another grievance, which had also appeared in the Virginia drafts, a condemnation of the king for inciting "treasonable insurrections of our fellow citizens, with the allurements of forfeiture & confiscation of our property." The charge referred not to Lord Dunmore's proclamation but rather to attempts to rally white American loyalists to the British side. He retained, however, in number twenty-five in the draft submitted to Congress, the wording of the grievance blaming the king for inciting warfare among the "merciless Indian savages." The placing of blame on the king and Parliament for inciting Indian violence on the American frontier was simply unfair, for it was the American colonists themselves, by their relentless move westward onto Indian lands, who did most of the inciting. But Jefferson's description of the "known rule of warfare" of the "merciless Indian savages" went beyond unfairness; it is the most shockingly ethnocentric piece of writing in a document dedicated to the principles of liberty and equality. When he penned those words, Jefferson was no doubt correct in thinking that they would be useful in strengthening his fellow colonists' commitment to band together to fight their English foe. Most eighteenth-century Euro-Americans no doubt shared that highly negative view of their Native American neighbors. But that phrase, "merciless Indian savages," has proven to be the Declaration's one piece of language that, over time, has brought no credit upon the author.

Jefferson penned one more grievance in the rough draft presented to Congress, a grievance appearing at the very end of his list. Extraordinary both in length and content, it read:

he has waged cruel war against human nature itself, violating it's most sacred rights of life & liberty in the persons of a distant people who never offended him, captivating & carrying them into slavery in another hemisphere, or to incur miserable death in their transportation thither. this piratical warfare, the opprobrium of *infidel* powers, is the warfare of the CHRISTIAN king of Great Britain. determined to keep open a market where MEN should be bought & sold, he has prostituted his negative for suppressing every legislative attempt to prohibit or to restrain this exe-crable commerce: and that this assemblage of horrors might want no fact of distinguished die, he is now exciting those very people to rise in arms among us, and to purchase that liberty of which *he* has deprived them, by murdering the people upon whom *he* also obtruded them; thus paying off former crimes committed against the *liberties* of one people, with crimes which he urges them to commit against the *lives* of another.

In that final grievance Jefferson not only included a more extensive denunciation of the attempt to incite the slave population to rise in re-bellion against their masters, but also an extended and convoluted statement blaming the king for the institution of the slave trade. His-torians have long pondered what was going on inside Jefferson's head and heart when he decided to add this lengthy excoriation of the king to the list. One can say that it is the one passage in the Declara-tion that, in its forced and labored prose, seems to lack anything ap-proaching literary grace. Moreover, while Jefferson's description of the slave trade as "piratical warfare," "execrable" and "an assemblage of horrors" may have appealed to the moral senses of many, but not all, Americans, the logic of his argument—that King George III was somehow personally responsible for instituting and perpetuating a trade in human beings that was eagerly embraced by many of the res-idents of America's southern colonies—simply strayed too far from the facts of that terrible trade. Some have read this draft of the griev-ance as a statement of Jefferson's revulsion not only at the slave trade but also at the very institution of slavery. But the final lines of the grievance are concerned with the liberties and lives of the white resi-dents of Virginia rather than of the slaves.[26]

After completing his bill of indictment against George III, Jeffer-son the lawyer moved on to his closing argument, reminding his read-ers that "in every stage of these oppressions," the American colonists had patiently petitioned for a redress of their grievances, only to be an-swered by "repeated injury." Indeed, Americans had petitioned not only the king, but also their "British brethren," seeking to enlist their support in protecting their liberties. But, he concluded, "they too have been deaf to the voice of justice and consanguinity." His original draft went on at great length—perhaps too great a length—expressing dis-

appointment with the failure of the English people to support American grievances, a situation that left Americans with no choice but to
"renounce forever these unfeeling brethren." Jefferson's anger leaps off
the pages of this part of his closing argument—an anger directed not
merely at the king, but at the British people who, Jefferson believed,
had not only not come to America's aid in a time of need, but, indeed,
had never contributed anything to America's well-being.[27]

The final paragraph of Jefferson's draft of the Declaration combined some of the Virginian's eloquence with a tendency toward dis-
cursiveness that is perhaps not untypical of a first draft produced
even by the finest of writers:

> We therefore the Representatives of the United states of America in Gen-
> eral Congress assembled do, in the name & by authority of the good people
> of these states, reject and renounce all allegiance and subjection to the kings
> of Great Britain & all others who may hereafter claim by, through, or under
> them; we utterly dissolve & break off all political connection which may
> have heretofore have subsisted between us & the people or parliament of
> Great Britain; and finally we do assert and declare these colonies to be free
> and independent states, and that as free & independent states they shall
> hereafter have power to levy war, conclude peace, contract alliances, estab-
> lish commerce, & to do all other acts and things which independent states
> may of right do. And for the support of this declaration we mutually pledge
> to each other our lives, our fortunes, & our sacred honor.

That final paragraph asserted, for the first time, that it was the representatives of the "United states," not the united colonies, who were
taking the unprecedented step of dissolving the political connections
between both the government and the people of Great Britain. And
those "United states" were not only declaring their independence but
also stating their intention to carry out a war against one of the world's
most formidable military powers, to negotiate a successful peace, to
make alliances with other nations, to promote commerce and to "do all
other acts and things which independent states may of right do." Finally, Jefferson concluded his draft with words of genuine elegance:
"And for the support of this declaration we mutually pledge to each
other our lives, our fortunes, and our sacred honor."

At some point after Jefferson wrote those final words, and no doubt after his already-revised draft of the Declaration had been read once again by his fellow members of the Committee of Five, he created a fair copy—that is, a clean copy—of his work and submitted it to the Continental Congress for their inspection and approval. As we will see, the work of writing the Declaration of Independence—*America's* Declaration of Independence, not merely *Jefferson's*—was far from complete.

TWENTY-FIVE

AMERICA'S DECLARATION OF INDEPENDENCE

The Declaration Goes to Congress

On Friday, June 28, the Committee of Five delivered its revised draft of Jefferson's draft of the Declaration of Independence to Congress. There it was read—probably by secretary Charles Thomson and not by Jefferson himself—and then "ordered to lie on the table." This was an obvious, and necessary, step, for before agreeing on a "Declaration" of independence, the delegates needed to debate and then decide on Richard Henry Lee's resolution proposing independence.[1]

Charles Thomson left only the scantest record of what transpired for the remainder of that day, but it is likely that the Congress did not discuss that draft of the Declaration at any length on the 28th. It then adjourned for the weekend, resuming discussion of Lee's resolution for independence on Monday, July 1. After the Congress adopted the resolution for independence on July 2, it moved itself into a committee of the whole to begin an open-ended discussion of the draft of the Declaration. Once again, we know little about what actually transpired, but it appears that the discussion was only a brief one, after which the delegates adjourned for the day. The real discussion of the draft would begin in earnest on July 3.[2]

Given the importance of the debate over the Declaration of Independence (or at least the importance that subsequent generations of American have attached to the process by which that document was created), it is surprising that virtually none of the delegates, other than Jefferson himself, recorded any impressions of that debate. And of course the secretary, Charles Thomson, was his usual unhelpful self. We do know from the final result that the members of Congress debated and made significant changes to the document over those days, rewriting a number of key passages and reducing Jefferson's draft by a quarter of its original size. What is likely, given what we know about how the Committee of Five operated, is that it apparently made what they called a fair copy of the Declaration, incorporating the changes to Jefferson's original draft suggested by his fellow committee members, as well as some of Jefferson's own changes, and then turned it over to the Congress. Unfortunately, that fair copy, if it existed at all, has not survived. Even if we assume that it did exist, it seems unlikely that the members of the Congress could have carried out their debate looking over one another's shoulders at a single copy. And so while it is probable that the Congress had the committee draft printed and distributed to each of the delegates, if that was the case, none of those copies has survived. Perhaps Congress had ordered them destroyed once they had agreed on the final draft, but Charles Thomson has left us no record of that action. Our basis then, for comparing the "fair copy" of the Declaration and the draft finally adopted is Jefferson's own rough draft, with his handwritten and marginal notations included. And, though we know that the changes made by the members of Congress were substantial, we have no record of who made them.[3]

For the most part, the members of Congress left Jefferson's preamble intact, aside from some minor bits of polishing (Jefferson's "inherent and inalienable rights" became "certain inalienable rights," which somehow, when the document was printed a day later, became "unalienable rights"). They made a few more changes in the paragraph leading up to the list of specific grievances, primarily eliminating some unnecessary wordiness. For example, Jefferson's original draft noted the king's "unremitting injuries and usurpations, among which appears no solitary fact to contradict the uniform tenor of the rest, but all have in direct object the establishment of an absolute tyranny of these states. To prove this, let facts be submitted to a candid world, for the truth of which we pledge a faith yet unsullied by falsehood." The final draft simply stated: "the history of the present king of Great Britain is a history of repeated injuries and usurpations, all having in direct object the establishment of an absolute tyranny over these states. To prove this let facts be submitted to a candid world."[4]

Some of the changes in wording of the specific grievances were probably intended to eliminate not merely a tendency toward wordiness but also to substitute a more accurate indictment for Jefferson's occasionally hyperbolic language. Jefferson held that the king had "suffered the administration of justice totally to cease in some of these states by refusing his assent to laws for establishing judiciary powers," when in fact, only North Carolina had lodged that grievance, and, indeed, the details of that colony's dispute with its royal governor over the operation of its courts were sufficiently complex that the claim that the king had caused the administration of justice there to "totally" cease amounted to a pretty gross overstatement. The final draft, which condemned the king for having "obstructed the administration of justice," was considerably more vague, but also less hyperbolic.[5]

And then there was the elimination of Jefferson's extended condemnation of the king for continuing the slave trade. As noted in the previous chapter, the lengthy passage in the rough draft denouncing the king for his role was jarring both in the passionate excess of its composition and in the one-sidedness of its accusation, so in that sense it is not surprising that some members of Congress would have inserted an editorial hand. Jefferson's own record of the debate during those days was sketchy, but in referring to the virtual elimination of that clause from his draft, he noted that

> the clause . . . reprobating the enslaving the inhabitants of Africa was struck out in complaisance to South Carolina & Georgia, who had never attempted to restrain the importation of slaves, and who on the contrary still wished to continue it. Our Northern brethren also I believe felt a little tender . . . under those censures; for tho' their people have very few slaves themselves yet they had been pretty considerable carriers of them to others.[6]

There has been no shortage of historical commentary both on Jefferson's motives for including the passage on the slave trade in his draft of the Declaration and on the Congress's decision to remove it. For Jefferson critics like Paul Finkelman, the very attempt to include the passage is just one more example of Jefferson's pernicious hypocrisy on the whole subject of slavery, while more sympathetic Jefferson biographers such as Jon Meacham are inclined to give the Monticello slaveowner the benefit of the doubt. As for Congress's role in deleting the passage, some have argued, as Jefferson's account implied, that the elimination of that grievance was a necessary condition for South Carolina's and Georgia's support of independence on July 2. While it is the case that South Carolina in particular was still thought by some to be on the fence that day, and that the elimination of that grievance may well have helped bring them along, there is no evidence that any delegate from either of those colonies insisted on its elimination as a condition for his affirmative vote. As for those "Northern brethren" who were involved in the slave trade, the Rhode Island delegates, representing a colony in which many merchants were still actively involved in the trade, may have felt a little sensitive about the issue. But it seems more likely that that final grievance in Jefferson's original draft was eliminated not only because of political pressure from slave-owning or slave-trading colonies but also because it was inaccurate and unfair.[7]

Whatever the case, the Congress made ample use of its editorial pen, eliminating entirely Jefferson's lengthy denunciation of the slave trade as well as that relating to "treasonable insurrections of our fellow citizens," a reference to the attempt to recruit Loyalists to fight on the side of the Crown. Reflecting the intense fear of the example set by Lord Dunmore's 1775 proclamation promising freedom to Virginia slaves who deserted their masters to fight on the side of the British, they did, however, insert into the grievance relating to warfare by the "merciless Indian savages," a condemnation of the king for exciting "domestic insurrections amongst us." Thus, the final grievance in the finished draft of the Declaration read: "He has excited domestic insurrections amongst us and has endeavored to bring on the inhabitants of our frontiers the merciless Indian savages, whose known rule of warfare is an undistinguished destruction of all ages, sexes, and conditions." It was an emotionally powerful conclusion to the long list of specific grievances—but also a grievance that was both viciously racist and outrageously unfair. Although it was undeniably true that Native American inhabitants had often engaged in brutal warfare with European settlers in a contest for control of valuable land on the North American continent, the instigators of that conflict were, more often than not, the Europeans, not the Indian combatants. And the military tactics of those European settlers who engaged in those wars were hardly just or humane. This final passage of the list in the Declaration of Independence, combining as it did a casual reference to the king's culpability for inciting "domestic insurrections" with its venomous description of the continent's Native American inhabitants, has hardly proven something in which Americans in subsequent generations could take any pride. Perhaps its only utility, in the context of the twenty-first century, is that it serves as a shocking reminder of the paradox that lay at the new American nation's core.

The Congress was also free with its editorial pen in the closing paragraphs of Jefferson's draft of the Declaration. It may well have been that Jefferson had written those final paragraphs under the pressure of time. The penultimate paragraph—that denouncing not only the king but also the British people themselves—perhaps struck many members of Congress as not only verbose but unnecessarily inflammatory. Jefferson's claim that the settlement of the colonies was done solely "at the expense of our own blood and treasure, unassisted by the wealth or the strength of Great Britain," seemed a dubious historical account of the realities of the settlement process, and his denunciation of the British people as complicit in the sending of "foreign mercenaries to invade and destroy us" was excessively combative. The concluding sentences in the draft sent to Congress, in which Jefferson announced the American intention of endeavoring "to forget our former love for [the British people], and to hold them, as we hold the rest of mankind, enemies in war, in peace friends," was, in essence, both accurate and eloquent. But in the long, rambling paragraph that preceded those sentences, Jefferson bemoaned the fact that the British people had not chosen the latter option: "We might have been a free & a great people together," he lamented, "but a communication of grandeur and of freedom, it seems, is below their dignity." Jefferson's congressional editors retained the essential idea of those concluding sentences—that of "enemies in war, in peace friends"—but cut out much of the rest. However disappointed the congressional delegates may have been about the failure of the king's subjects in Great Britain to respond favorably to their appeals to them for their support, their personal identities were still bound up with their affection for many aspects of British civilization and culture, and for the British people themselves. Their deletion of nearly half of Jefferson's wordy and inflammatory paragraph resulted in a finished product that was not only more concise, but more elegant and balanced, than Jefferson's original.[8]

When the members of Congress went to work on the final paragraph of the Declaration, probably late in the afternoon of July 3 or on the morning of July 4, they cut back again on some of Jefferson's wordiness, and at the same time added, perhaps to Jefferson's dismay, references to "the Supreme judge of the world" and to "divine Providence." That concluding paragraph, in its final form, reads:

> We, therefore, the Representatives of the united States of America, in General Congress, Assembled, appealing to the Supreme Judge of the world for the rectitude of our intentions, do, in the Name, and by the Authority of the good People of these Colonies, solemnly publish and declare, That these United Colonies are, and of Right ought to be Free and Independent States; that they are Absolved from all Allegiance to the British Crown, and that all political connections between them and the State of Great Britain, is and ought to be totally dissolved; and that as Free and Independent States, they have full Power to levy War, conclude Peace, contract Alliances, establish Commerce, and to do all other Acts and Things which Independent States may of right do. And for the support of this Declaration, with a firm reliance on the protection of divine Providence, we mutually pledge to each other our Lives, our Fortunes and our sacred Honor.

The final draft of that paragraph substituted some of the language of Richard Henry Lee's original resolution proposing independence, but at the same time retained some of the elegance of Jefferson's prose. Most important, with the exception of the addition of the words "with the firm reliance on the protection of divine Providence," Jefferson's concluding sentence remained unaltered. Americans had frequently referred to their "Lives" and their "Fortunes" in describing their commitment to resisting British tyranny, but Jefferson's addition of "our sacred Honor," creating a triad of commitment, gave to the final sentence of the Declaration, as Pauline Maier has observed, "a dignity and a mellifluousness as pleasing to the mind as it is to the ear."[9]

How did Jefferson respond to his colleagues' changes? Somewhat surprisingly, given his generally cool public demeanor, Jefferson proved a remarkably thin-skinned author. He complained to all who would listen about the "mutilations" from which his original draft suffered. And he was sufficiently upset that he wrote out in hand multiple copies of his original draft and sent them to friends in Virginia asking them "whether it is better or worse for the Critics." Richard Henry Lee, a recipient of one of Jefferson's copies, responded to his friend saying that he wished "that the Manuscript had not been mangled as it is." But Lee's response may have been prompted simply by a desire to be polite to his Virginia colleague. The final product—Congress's Declaration of Independence, not Jefferson's—was in fact superior—more concise, more constrained, and, perhaps, even more elegant than the original.[10]

The Congress Declares Independence

On the morning of July 4, arising at around six o'clock, Thomas Jefferson noted that the temperature outside of his residence at Seventh and Market Streets was 68 degrees. It would be a comfortable day, with the temperature not rising above 76 degrees. In spite of the important business awaiting him, Jefferson spent at least some of that morning shopping, buying a new thermometer and seven pairs of women's gloves, which he would later send to Monticello for his wife and, perhaps, his daughters.[11]

The Congress began its business at nine a.m., and according to Jefferson's own notes of the session that day, the members continued meeting until sometime that evening, at which time the Declaration was "agreed to by the house, and signed by every member present except Mr. Dickinson." How tempting it is to accept the word of the principal author of the Declaration on this matter. It conjures up in our minds the image of one of the most famous paintings in all of American history, by the American painter John Trumbull depicting the dramatic signing of the Declaration on that fateful day. To the extent that Americans have a mental picture of the founding of their nation, it most likely has been formed by Trumbull, who in 1818, forty-two years after the event, completed a composite portrait depicting the signing of the Declaration of Independence. Trumbull had served alongside General Washington during the Revolution, and he subsequently made it his life's work to "preserve and diffuse the memory of the noblest series of actions which have ever presented themselves in the history of man." He began the painting in 1785 in Paris, where Thomas Jefferson helped him recollect the arrangement in the Assembly Room. The finished product depicts a much grander and more lavishly appointed space than the one in which the delegates actually deliberated. Most of the images of the delegates themselves were drawn from other portraits and sketches made long after the event, with the result that many of the delegates look much older than they were at the time. And, ironically, one of the men featured in Trumbull's depiction of the signing was none other than John Dickinson, whom Jefferson himself singled out as the lone dissenter on that day.[12]

Alas, Jefferson's account, which, like Trumbull's rendering, was composed some years after the event he described took place, is no more accurate than the painting. The amount of scholarly effort devoted to determining the exact time and sequence of events surrounding the adoption of the Declaration has been both exhaustive and exhausting. The results of that research yield a picture that is far less dramatic than the scene depicted by Trumbull. Indeed, the events immediately following the adoption of the Declaration seem a bit anticlimactic.[13]

Contrary to Jefferson's recollection, most of the evidence available to us suggests that the delegates had nearly completed their discussion of the Declaration by the end of the day on July 3, and that, at most, only a few hours were needed on July 4 to complete the business. And once the delegates had approved the Declaration, rather than bursting out of the Pennsylvania State House and trumpeting the results of their labors, they instead spent the remainder of the day dealing with a wide range of mostly mundane issues, including a decision to transport quantities of flint from Rhode Island to New York, the appointment of commissioners for Indian affairs for the mid-Atlantic colonies, the appointment of an additional private secretary for John Hancock and a decision to pay "3 dollars and 54–90ths" to the express rider who had brought dispatches from Trenton, New Jersey, to the Congress. Given the volume of business before the Congress that day, the best guess is that the Declaration was approved around eleven that morning.[14]

Although Jefferson singled out John Dickinson as the only dissenter regarding the Declaration's adoption, he most likely confused Dickinson's eloquent, if unsuccessful, opposition to Richard Henry Lee's resolution for independence on July 2 with the delegates' vote on the Declaration. Indeed, although the congressional journal does make it clear that the committee of the whole approved the document, we have no record of a formal vote or even a debate on the Declaration. Nor does examining the list of signers (and nonsigners) give us much of a clue about whether there was any substantial opposition to the Declaration expressed on that day. It appears likely that John Hancock was the only member of the Congress who signed the document on July 4, with Secretary Charles Thomson adding his signature attesting to the validity of Hancock's signature. One of the reasons for the agonizing delay in voting on independence during the months of May and June was the nearly universal agreement among the delegates (except, perhaps for the always impatient John Adams) that all of the colonies— or at least as many as possible—be brought around to support that epochal decision. And on July 4 the New York delegates were still obliged by the instructions of their legislature to sit on their hands.[15]

The now-familiar Declaration of Independence begins with the words: "The Unanimous Declaration of the Thirteen United States of America." But on July 4, the delegates to the Continental Congress were not in a position to inscribe those words on a final, parchment copy. Like the New York delegates themselves, they would have to sit on their hands and wait for the approval of the New York Provincial Congress. Finally, on July 9, the New York legislature added its assent, freeing New York's delegates to the Congress to join their colleagues in endorsing the resolution for independence. Congress received official word of New York's decision on July 15, and on July 19, the delegates ordered "that the Declaration passed on the 4th be fairly engrossed." In the margins of the journal recording that action, Thomson added:

"Engrossed on parchment with the title and stile of 'The Unanimous Declaration of the 13 United States of America,' and that the same when engrossed be signed by every member of Congress."[16]

On August 2, most, but not all of the members of Congress signed the document, with those who happened to be absent on that day trickling in over the course of the next few weeks to add their signatures. The delay, although it may have lessened the drama of the moment, had some salutary effects. Pennsylvania's Robert Morris, perhaps America's wealthiest merchant, had deliberately absented himself in order to avoid casting a negative vote on independence on July 2. By August 2 he had come around and affixed his signature to the document, an enormously important act, for he would be primarily responsible for overseeing the financing of America's revolutionary war effort. Similarly, George Read, the Delaware delegate voting against the resolution for independence on July 2 (thereby necessitating Caesar Rodney's overnight ride to break the tie in the delegation and move it on the side of independence), had by August 2 also come around and signed the parchment document. The fact that men like Morris and Read had initially opposed independence, but eventually signed the Declaration, speaks volumes about the anguish that many delegates to the Congress, and many throughout America, felt about the decision for independence. "Reluctant revolutionists" they may have been, but, like John Dickinson, who refused to sign, they were not reluctant patriots. Although they had continued to advocate reconciliation rather than revolution on July 4, once the country had decided on revolution (and, in Morris's case, after he had time to think about the consequences of *not* endorsing the decision), they worked tirelessly to make sure that that decision would prove to be the correct one.[17]

Several other delegates, absent from the Congress on July 2 or July 4, added their names to the document once they arrived later that summer. The tardiest of the group, Matthew Thornton of New Hampshire, was not elected to the Congress until the fall of 1776 and did not show up in Philadelphia until November. He was the last signer of the Declaration, on November 4, 1776.[18]

If the business of the signing of the Declaration proceeded somewhat sluggishly, the Congress was much more aggressive about announcing their actions on July 4 to the world. Immediately after the delegates approved the Declaration on the morning of July 4, they sent a copy of it to John Dunlap, publisher of the *Pennsylvania Packet*, asking him to print two hundred copies as a single-page broadside to be sent to the various legislatures, conventions and revolutionary committees in order that "it be proclaimed in each of the United States." As the document was being printed, John Hancock wrote to each of the states asking them to take the steps necessary to have the document "proclaimed in your Colony in such Way & Manner as you shall judge best." He added that "the important Consequences resulting to the American States from this Declaration of independence . . . will naturally suggest the Propriety of proclaiming it in such a Mode as that the People may be universally informed of it."[19]

Although historians have had differing opinions on whether Jefferson had consciously written the Declaration in a style that would facilitate its being read aloud to large public gatherings, its elegance and relative brevity—at only 1,337 words it could just fit on a single printed page—made its distribution and public reading much easier. There is some evidence that an unofficial copy of the document was read near the Pennsylvania State House on the evening of July 4, but the official readings of the Declaration began on July 8, not only in Philadelphia, but also in Easton, Pennsylvania, and in Trenton, New Jersey. The July 8 Philadelphia reading was a dramatic affair indeed. It began with the Committees of Safety and of Inspection—both of them committees that had been in the radical vanguard of Pennsylvania's internal revolution—marching to the State House Yard. There, John Nixon, a lieutenant colonel commanding a Philadelphia battalion and a member of the radical Philadelphia Committee of Safety, had the honor of being the first person to read aloud the Declaration on an official occasion. His reading was greeted with "general applause and heart-felt satisfaction" by the "very large number of the inhabitants of the City and County" assembled there. John Adams, describing the event to Maryland's Samuel Chase, reported, "The Battallions paraded on the common, and gave Us the Feu de Joy, notwithstanding the Scarcity of Powder. The Bells rung all Day, and almost all night."[20]

The *Pennsylvania Evening Post* was apparently the first newspaper to publish the Declaration, on Saturday, July 6. But from that time forward, the news spread quickly, both in print and by word of mouth. Perhaps the most dramatic unveiling of America's call for independence came in New York City, on July 9, when General George Washington ordered officers of his Continental Army to engage in public readings of the Declaration to their troops, with the British "constantly in view." Washington believed that such readings would "serve as a free incentive to every officer, and soldier, to act with Fidelity and Courage, . . . knowing that now the peace and safety of his Country depends (under God) solely on the success of our arms. And that he is now in the service of a State, possessed of sufficient power to reward his merit, and advance him to the highest Honors of a free Country." The ceremonies in New York were not confined to dignified public readings. That same evening a mob in the city toppled an equestrian statue of George III, cutting off the head. According to one observer, "the lead from which this monument was made is to be run into bullets, to assimilate with the brain of our infatuated adversaries." And, in fact, the patriot army did make good use of the 4,000 pounds of lead in the statue, melting it down to make 42,000 musket bullets.[21]

However joyous the New York celebration of the symbolic demise of George III may have been, General Washington, looking out onto New York harbor at the ever-increasing number of British warships anchored there, realized that the battle had only begun. By mid-August Washington's army of only a little over 10,000 militiamen and a virtually nonexistent patriot navy found themselves facing a fleet of seventy British warships and over 32,000 troops. By mid-September the British had occupied all of New York City, with Washington's army fleeing north of the city. A year later, the British army marched unopposed into Philadelphia, occupying the city and causing members of the Continental Congress to scurry westward, first to a temporary capital in Lancaster and a few weeks later to York, Pennsylvania. America's citizens, their political leaders and, especially, a beleaguered continental army were realizing just how daunting their commitment of their lives, their fortunes and their sacred honor was.

ACKNOWLEDGMENTS

I HAVE SPENT the past forty-five years teaching courses on the coming of the American Revolution, and the past four years writing this book. During this time, my understanding of the dynamic driving America's audacious leap toward independence has been shaped by the works of hundreds of scholars who have written on aspects of this subject over the course of the past two centuries. I have made a conscientious effort to acknowledge my debt to those scholars in the extensive Notes section of this book.

My longtime Penn History Department colleague Bruce Kuklick is not only a dear friend, but my most perceptive and demanding critic. In his reading of this book, as in his reading of my earlier works, he has offered me exceptionally helpful advice; I may never be able to meet fully his high, critical standards, but I promise to keep trying! Professor Pauline Maier has also once again proven an insightful and generous colleague. I have assigned her book, *From Resistance to Revolution,* in my course on the American Revolution every year during my career as a teacher at the University of Pennsylvania, and in writing this book, I have relied heavily on her outstanding work on the Declaration of Independence; I am grateful to her for her critical reading of the chapters in this book on that subject. Whenever I have a question about life in eighteenth-century Philadelphia, I immediately shoot off an e-mail to Professor Billy G. Smith of Montana State University. Professor Smith always responds promptly and, after discarding the scatological information included in his response, I am always much wiser as a consequence of the exchange.

This is the second book in which I have benefitted from the superb editorial skills of Tim Bartlett. Although both Tim and I had to suffer through a summer in 2012 in which our Philadelphia Phillies put on a dismal performance, Tim's performance as editor—his impressive intellect and his sensitive handling of a sometimes cranky author—was first rate as always. Tim Bartlett's assistant, Kaitlyn Zafonte, facilitated this project in countless ways, particularly in helping me with the task of choosing the most appropriate illustrations for the book. Although I have never laid eyes on Norman Mac-Afee, in the final stages of the editorial process it seemed like we were living together, each of us working at least twelve hours a day over the course of nearly two months. The phrase "copy editor" does not begin to describe the important role that Norman—an accomplished writer and artist himself—played in shaping the style and substance of this book. I am deeply grateful to him for the combination of historical insight, literary grace and craftsmanship that he brought to this project. I am also indebted to Melissa Veronesi of Basic Books not only for her highly competent support during the final stages of production of the book, but also for her forbearance as I continued to make changes in the text and notes right up to the last minute!

I have taught thousands of undergraduates during my career at Penn, but I have never taught an undergraduate whose passion for the founding period of American history was as great as that of Alicia DeMaio. It has been my great pleasure to teach her in several courses at Penn, as well as directing her undergraduate honors thesis. But now, at the end of her undergraduate career, I have also been able to exploit both her expertise and her love of history by asking her to serve as my fact-checker and "footnote fixer." Her efficiency in those tasks easily equals her superb skills as a student of history.

My full-time literary agent, good friend and part-time psychotherapist, John Wright, continues to support all of my efforts at all times. Through his high intelligence, erudition and "old school" knowledge of the publishing business, John has helped me at every stage in this project, both as an insightful critic and an effective advocate. I look forward to working with John in many more projects still to come.

The dedication of this book to my wife, Mary Cahill, is much more than a formality. Mary has continued to serve in the difficult role of intelligent general reader; equally important, in the final, all-consuming stages of this work, while I was neglecting nearly every other aspect of our lives, she held our family and home together. I know that Mary would join me in offering a special expression of love and gratitude to our golden retriever, Abigail Adams. During the writing of this book Abigail continued to develop her skills as a true canine Frisbee champion, giving me an excuse to get up from behind my computer and go outside to clear my foggy brain. Through her joyful play, Abigail has reminded me that living in the moment is the best path to a happy life. Unfortunately, she continues to refuse to take responsibility for any errors of fact or interpretation in this book, so I'm afraid that I will have to assume that burden.

APPENDIX A:
"JEFFERSON'S DECLARATION OF INDEPENDENCE"

*The Draft from Thomas Jefferson
and the Committee of Five, with Editorial
Changes from the Continental Congress*

This rendition of the Declaration of Independence is reprinted from Carl Becker, *The Declaration of Independence* (New York, 1942), pp. 174–184. It is based on a draft copy of the Declaration sent by Thomas Jefferson to his Virginia colleague Richard Henry Lee on July 8, 1776. Although the "Fair Copy" of the Declaration that Jefferson and the Committee of Five submitted to the Continental Congress on June 28, 1776, has not survived, the draft that Jefferson sent to Lee is believed to be a close replication of that draft. Becker then took the draft that Jefferson sent to Lee and crossed out the passages deleted by Congress and added, in italics, the changes that the Congress added to the draft. The resulting document gives us a reasonably accurate sense of the difference between "Thomas Jefferson's Declaration of Independence" and the finished draft of the Declaration ultimately adopted by the Continental Congress on July 4, 1776.

A Declaration by the Representatives of the United States of America in General Congress assembled.

When in the course of human events it becomes necessary for one people to dissolve the political bands which have connected them with another, and to assume among the powers of the earth the separate and equal station to which the laws of nature and of nature's god entitle them, a decent

421

respect to the opinions of mankind requires that they should declare the causes which impel them to the separation.

We hold these truths to be self-evident; that all men are created equal; that they are endowed by their Creator with ~~inherent and~~ ∧ ^{certain un}inalienable* rights; that among these are life, liberty, and the pursuit of happiness; that to secure these rights, governments are instituted among men, deriving their just powers from the consent of the governed; that whenever any form of government becomes destructive of these ends, it is the right of the people to alter or to abolish it, and to institute new government, laying it's foundation on such principles, and organizing it's powers in such form as to them shall seem most likely to effect their safety and happiness. prudence indeed will dictate that governments long established should not be changed for light & transient causes. and accordingly all experience hath shewn that mankind are more disposed to suffer, while evils are sufferable, than to right themselves by abolishing the forms to which they are accustomed. but when a long train of abuses and usurpations, ~~begun at a distinguished period &~~ pursuing invariably the same object, evinces a design to reduce them under absolute despotism, it is their right, it is their duty, to throw off such government, & to provide new guards for their future security. such is now the necessity which constrains them to ~~expunge~~ ∧ ^{alter} their former systems of government. the history of the present king of Great Britain is a history of ~~unremitting~~ ∧ ^{repeated} injuries and usurpations, ~~among which appears no solitary fact to contradict the uniform tenor of the rest, but~~ all ~~have~~ ∧ ^{having} in direct object the establishment of an absolute tyranny over these

---

*The Rough Draft reads "[inherent &] ^{certain}inalienable." There is no indication that congress changed "inalienable" to "unalienable"; but the latter form appears in the text in the rough Journal, in the corrected Journal, and in the parchment copy. "Unalienable" may have been the more customary form in the eighteenth century.

states. to prove this let facts be submitted to a candid world, ~~for the truth of~~
~~which we pledge a faith yet unsullied by falsehood.~~

[1]* He has refused his assent to laws the most wholesome and necessary for the public good.

[2] he has forbidden his governors to pass laws of immediate & pressing importance, unless suspended in their operations till his assent
should be obtained; and when so suspended, he has ∧ neglected ~~ut-~~ *utterly*
~~terly~~ to attend to them.

[3] he has refused to pass other laws for the accommodation of large
districts of people, unless those people would relinquish the right
of representation in the legislature; a right inestimable to them, &
formidable to tyrants only.

[4] he has called together legislative bodies at places unusual, uncomfortable, & distant from the depository of their public records, for the
sole purpose of fatiguing them into compliance with his measures.

[5] he has dissolved Representative houses repeatedly ~~& continually,~~
for opposing with manly firmness his invasions on the rights of the
people.

[6] he has refused for a long time after such dissolutions to cause others to be elected whereby the legislative powers, incapable of an-
nihilation, have returned to the people at large for their exercise,
the state remaining in the meantime exposed to all the dangers of
invasion from without, & convulsions within.

[7] he has endeavored to prevent the population of these states; for
that purpose obstructing the laws for naturalization of foreigners;

---

*I have added the numbering of the specific grievances to the text. The numbers re-
fer to the grievances in the "Fair Copy." The final version of the Declaration listed
twenty-seven grievances.

refusing to pass others to encourage their migrations hither; & raising the conditions of new appropriations of lands.

[8] he has ~~suffered~~ ^obstructed^ the administration of justice ~~totally to cease in some of these states,~~ ^by^ refusing his assent to laws for establishing judiciary powers.

[9] he has made ~~our~~ judges dependent on his will alone, for the tenure of their offices, and the amount & paiment of their salaries.

[10] he has erected a multitude of new offices ~~by a self assumed power,~~ & sent hither swarms of officers to harass our people, and eat out their substance.

[11] he has kept among us, in times of peace, standing armies ~~and ships of war,~~ without the consent of our legislatures.

[12] he has affected to render the military independent of, & superior to, the civil power.

[13] he has combined with others to subject us to a jurisdiction foreign to our ~~constitutions~~ and unacknoleged by our laws; giving his assent to their acts of pretended legislation for quartering large bodies of armed troops among us;

[14] for protecting them by a mock-trial from punishment for any murders which they should commit on the inhabitants of these states;

[15] for cutting off our trade with all parts of the world;

[16] for imposing taxes on us without our consent;

[17] for depriving us ^in many cases^ of the benefits of trial by jury;

[18] for transporting us beyond seas to be tried for pretended offenses;

[19] for abolishing the free system of English laws in a neighboring province, establishing therein an arbitrary government, and enlarging it's boundaries so as to render it at once an example & fit instrument for introducing the same absolute rule into these states;

[20] for taking away our charters, abolishing our most valuable laws, and altering fundamentally the forms of our governments;

[21] for suspending our own legislatures, & declaring themselves invested with power to legislate for us in all cases whatsoever.

[22] he has abdicated government here, ~~withdrawing his governors, &~~
by *and waging war against us*
∧ declaring us out of ~~his allegiance and~~ protection∧.

[23] he has plundered our seas, ravaged our coasts, burnt our towns, & destroyed the lives of our people.

[24] he is at this time transporting large armies of foreign mercenaries to compeat the works of death, desolation & tyranny, already begun
scarcely paralleled in the most barbarous ages and totally
with circumstances of cruelty & perfidy ∧ unworthy the head of a civilized nation.

[25] *excited domestic insurrection amongst us and has*
he has ∧ endeavored to bring on the inhabitants of our frontiers the merciless Indian savages, whose known rule of warfare is an undistinguished destruction of all ages, sexes, & conditions ~~of existence.~~

[26] ~~he has incited treasonable insurrections of our fellow citizens, with the allurements of forfeiture & confiscations of property.~~

[27] *our fellow citizens*
he has constrained ∧ ~~others,~~ taken captives on the high seas to bear arms against their country, to become the executioners of their friends & brethren, or to fall themselves by their hands.

[28] ~~he has waged cruel war against human nature itself, violating it's most sacred rights of life & liberty in the persons of a distant people, who never offended him, captivating and carrying them into slavery in another hemisphere, or to incur miserable death in their transportation thither. this piratical warfare, the opprobrium of *infidel* powers, is the warfare of the *Christian* king of Great Britain. determined to keep open a market where MEN should be bought & sold, he has prostituted his negative for suppressing every~~

~~legislative attempt to prohibit or to restrain this execrable commerce: and that this assemblage of horrors might want no fact of distinguished die, he is now exciting those very people to rise in arms among us, and to purchase that liberty of which *he* has deprived them, by murdering the people upon whom *he* also obtruded them: thus paying off former crimes committed against the *liberties* of one people, with crimes which he urges them to commit against the *lives* of another.~~

In every stage of these oppressions, we have petitioned for redress in the most humble terms; our repeated petitions have been answered only by repeated injury. a prince whose character is thus marked by every act which may define a tyrant, is unfit to be the ruler of a _{free} people ~~who mean to be free. future ages will scarce believe that the hardiness of one man adventured within the short compass of twelve years only to build a foundation, so broad and undisguised, for tyranny over a people fostered and fixed in principles of freedom.~~

Nor have we been wanting in attentions to our British brethren. we have warned them from time to time of attempts by their legislature to extend ~~a~~ _{an unwarrantable} jurisdiction over _{us.} ~~these our states.~~ we have reminded them of the circumstances of our emigration and settlement here, ~~no one of which could warrant so strange a pretension: that these were effected at the expence of our own blood and treasure, unassisted by the wealth or the strength of Great Britain; that in constituting indeed our several forms of government, we had adopted one common king, thereby laying a foundation for perpetual league and amity with them: but that submission to their parliament was no part of our constitution, nor ever in idea, if history may be credited: and~~ we _{have} appealed to their native justice & magnanimity, ~~as well as to~~ [*and we have conjured them by*] ∧ the tyes of our common kindred, to disavow these usurpations, which ~~were likely to~~ [*would inevitably*] ∧ interrupt our connection∧[*s*] & correspondence. they too have been deaf to the voice of justice and of consanguinity*; ~~and when occasions have given them, by the regular course of their laws, of removing from their councils the disturbers of our harmony, they have by their free election re-established them in power. at this very time too, they are permitting their chief magistrate to send over not only soldiers of our common blood, but Scotch and foreign mercenaries to invade and destroy us. these facts have given the last stab to agonizing affection; and manly spirit bids us to renounce forever these unfeeling brethren.~~ we must ∧[*therefore*] ~~endeavor to forget our former love for them, and to hold them as we hold the rest of mankind, enemies in war, in peace friends. we might have been a free & a great people together; but a communication of grandeur and of freedom, it seems, is below their dignity. be it so, since they will have it. the road to happiness and to glory is open to us too; we will climb it apart from them, and~~ acquiesce in the necessity which denounces our ~~eternal~~ separation ∧ [*!*] [*and hold them, as we hold the rest of mankind, enemies in war, in peace friends.*]

We therefore the Representatives of the United states of America in General Congress assembled, ∧ [*appealing to the supreme judge of the world for the rectitude of our intentions*] do, in the name & by authority of the good people of these ∧ [*colonies, solemnly publish and declare, that these united colonies are and of right ought to be free and independent states; that they are absolved from all allegiance to the British Crown,*] ~~states, reject and renounce all allegiance and subjection to the kings of Great Britain, & all others who may hereafter claim by, through, or under them; we utterly dissolve~~ [*and that*] all political connection ~~which may heretofore have subsisted~~ between ~~us~~ ∧ [*them*] and the ∧ [*state*] ~~people or parliament of~~ Great Britain ∧ [*is & ought to be totally dissolved;*] ~~; and finally we do assert and declare these colonies to be free and independent states,~~ & that as free &

---

*The text in the corrected Journal reads "and consanguinity."

independent states, they have full power to levy war, conclude peace, contract alliances, establish commerce, & to do all other acts and things which independent states may of right do. And for the support of this declaration, ∧ we mutually pledge to each other our lives, our fortunes, and our sacred honor.

<small>with a firm reliance on the protection of divine providence,</small>

APPENDIX B:
AMERICA'S DECLARATION OF
INDEPENDENCE: THE FINAL VERSION

IN CONGRESS, July 4, 1776

The unanimous Declaration of the thirteen united States of America,

When in the Course of human events, it becomes necessary for one people to dissolve the political bands which have connected them with another, and to assume among the powers of the earth, the separate and equal station to which the Laws of Nature and of Nature's God entitle them, a decent respect to the opinions of mankind requires that they should declare the causes which impel them to the separation.

We hold these truths to be self-evident, that all men are created equal, that they are endowed by their Creator with certain unalienable Rights, that among these are Life, Liberty and the pursuit of Happiness.—That to secure these rights, Governments are instituted among Men, deriving their just powers from the consent of the governed,—That whenever any Form of Government becomes destructive of these ends, it is the Right of the People to alter or to abolish it, and to institute new Government, laying its foundation on such principles and organizing its powers in such form, as to them shall seem most likely to effect their Safety and Happiness. Prudence, indeed, will dictate that Governments long established should not be changed for light and transient causes; and accordingly all experience hath shewn, that mankind are more disposed to suffer, while evils are sufferable, than to right themselves by abolishing the forms to which they are accustomed. But when a long train of abuses and usurpations, pursuing invariably the same Object evinces a design to reduce them under absolute Despotism, it is their right, it is their duty, to throw off such Government, and to provide new

Guards for their future security.—Such has been the patient sufferance of these Colonies; and such is now the necessity which constrains them to alter their former Systems of Government. The history of the present King of Great Britain is a history of repeated injuries and usurpations, all having in direct object the establishment of an absolute Tyranny over these States. To prove this, let Facts be submitted to a candid world.

He has refused his Assent to Laws, the most wholesome and necessary for the public good.

He has forbidden his Governors to pass Laws of immediate and pressing importance, unless suspended in their operation till his Assent should be obtained; and when so suspended, he has utterly neglected to attend to them.

He has refused to pass other Laws for the accommodation of large districts of people, unless those people would relinquish the right of Representation in the Legislature, a right inestimable to them and for-midable to tyrants only.

He has called together legislative bodies at places unusual, uncom-fortable, and distant from the depository of their public Records, for the sole purpose of fatiguing them into compliance with his measures.

He has dissolved Representative Houses repeatedly, for opposing with manly firmness his invasions on the rights of the people.

He has refused for a long time, after such dissolutions, to cause others to be elected; whereby the Legislative powers, incapable of Anni-hilation, have returned to the People at large for their exercise; the State remaining in the mean time exposed to all the dangers of invasion from without, and convulsions within.

He has endeavoured to prevent the population of these States; for that purpose obstructing the Laws for Naturalization of Foreigners; re-fusing to pass others to encourage their migrations hither, and raising the conditions of new Appropriations of Lands.

He has obstructed the Administration of Justice, by refusing his As-sent to Laws for establishing Judiciary powers.

He has made Judges dependent on his Will alone, for the tenure of their offices, and the amount and payment of their salaries.

He has erected a multitude of New Offices, and sent hither swarms of Officers to harrass our people, and eat out their substance.

He has kept among us, in times of peace, Standing Armies without the Consent of our legislatures.

He has affected to render the Military independent of and superior to the Civil power.

He has combined with others to subject us to a jurisdiction foreign to our constitution, and unacknowledged by our laws; giving his Assent to their Acts of pretended Legislation:

For Quartering large bodies of armed troops among us:

For protecting them, by a mock Trial, from punishment for any Murders which they should commit on the Inhabitants of these States:

For cutting off our Trade with all parts of the world:

For imposing Taxes on us without our Consent:

For depriving us in many cases, of the benefits of Trial by Jury:

For transporting us beyond Seas to be tried for pretended offences:

For abolishing the free System of English Laws in a neighbouring Province, establishing therein an Arbitrary government, and enlarging its Boundaries so as to render it at once an example and fit instrument for introducing the same absolute rule into these Colonies:

For taking away our Charters, abolishing our most valuable Laws, and altering fundamentally the Forms of our Governments:

For suspending our own Legislatures, and declaring themselves invested with power to legislate for us in all cases whatsoever.

He has abdicated Government here, by declaring us out of his Protection and waging War against us.

He has plundered our seas, ravaged our Coasts, burnt our towns, and destroyed the lives of our people.

He is at this time transporting large Armies of foreign Mercenaries to compleat the works of death, desolation and tyranny, already begun with circumstances of Cruelty & perfidy scarcely paralleled in the most barbarous ages, and totally unworthy the Head of a civilized nation.

He has constrained our fellow Citizens taken Captive on the high Seas to bear Arms against their Country, to become the executioners of their friends and Brethren, or to fall themselves by their Hands.

He has excited domestic insurrections amongst us, and has endeavoured to bring on the inhabitants of our frontiers, the merciless Indian Savages, whose known rule of warfare, is an undistinguished destruction of all ages, sexes and conditions.

In every stage of these Oppressions We have Petitioned for Redress in the most humble terms: Our repeated Petitions have been answered only by repeated injury. A Prince whose character is thus marked by every act which may define a Tyrant, is unfit to be the ruler of a free people.

Nor have We been wanting in attentions to our Brittish brethren. We have warned them from time to time of attempts by their legislature to extend an unwarrantable jurisdiction over us. We have reminded them of the circumstances of our emigration and settlement here. We have appealed to their native justice and magnanimity, and we have conjured them by the ties of our common kindred to disavow these usurpations, which, would inevitably interrupt our connections and correspondence. They too have been deaf to the voice of justice and of consanguinity. We must, therefore, acquiesce in the necessity, which denounces our Separation, and hold them, as we hold the rest of mankind, Enemies in War, in Peace Friends.

We, therefore, the Representatives of the united States of America, in General Congress, Assembled, appealing to the Supreme Judge of the world for the rectitude of our intentions, do, in the Name, and by Authority of the good People of these Colonies, solemnly publish and declare, That these United Colonies are, and of Right ought to be Free and Independent States; that they are Absolved from all Allegiance to the British Crown, and that all political connection between them and the State of Great Britain, is and ought to be totally dissolved; and that as Free and Independent States, they have full Power to levy War, conclude Peace, contract Alliances, establish Commerce, and to do all other Acts and Things which Independent States may of right do. And for the support of this Declaration, with a firm reliance on the protection of divine Providence, we mutually pledge to each other our Lives, our Fortunes and our sacred Honor.

[The 56 signatures on the parchment copy of the Declaration appear in the positions indicated.]

Column 1
Georgia:
Button Gwinnett
Lyman Hall
George Walton

Column 2
North Carolina:
William Hooper
Joseph Hewes
John Penn
South Carolina:
Edward Rutledge
Thomas Heyward, Jr.
Thomas Lynch, Jr.
Arthur Middleton

Column 3
Massachusetts:
John Hancock
Maryland:
Samuel Chase
William Paca
Thomas Stone
Charles Carroll of Carrollton
Virginia:
George Wythe
Richard Henry Lee
Thomas Jefferson
Benjamin Harrison
Thomas Nelson, Jr.
Francis Lightfoot Lee
Carter Braxton

Column 4

Pennsylvania:
Robert Morris
Benjamin Rush
Benjamin Franklin
John Morton
George Clymer
James Smith
George Taylor
James Wilson
George Ross

Delaware:
Caesar Rodney
George Read
Thomas McKean

Column 5

New York:
William Floyd
Philip Livingston
Francis Lewis
Lewis Morris

New Jersey:
Richard Stockton
John Witherspoon
Francis Hopkinson
John Hart
Abraham Clark

Column 6

New Hampshire:
Josiah Bartlett
William Whipple

Massachusetts:
Samuel Adams
John Adams
Robert Treat Paine
Elbridge Gerry

Rhode Island:
Stephen Hopkins
William Ellery

Connecticut:
Roger Sherman
Samuel Huntington
William Williams
Oliver Wolcott

New Hampshire:
Matthew Thornton

ABBREVIATIONS OF
FREQUENTLY CITED WORKS

Adams, *Diary* and *Autobiography:* L.H. Butterfield et al., eds., *The Diary and Autobiography of John Adams,* 4 vols. Cambridge, MA, 1961– .

Adams Family Correspondence: L.H. Butterfield et al., eds., *Adams Family Correspondence.* 10 vols. to date. Cambridge, MA, 1963– .

Adams Papers: Robert J. Taylor et al., eds, *Papers of John Adams.* 16 vols. to date. Cambridge, MA, 1977– .

American Archives, 4th ser.: Peter Force, ed., *American Archives,* 4th series, 6 vols., Washington, DC, 1837–1846.

Boyd, *Jefferson Papers:* Julian P. Boyd et al., eds., *The Papers of Thomas Jefferson.* 38 vols. to date. Princeton, 1950– .

DAR: K.G. Davies, *Documents of the American Revolution,* 12 vols. Shannon, Ireland, 1972–1981.

GW Papers, R.S.: Philander Chase et al., eds., *The Papers of George Washington, Revolutionary Series.* 20 vols. to date. Charlottesville, VA, 1985– .

GW Papers, C.S.: W.W. Abbot et al., eds., *The Papers of George Washington, Colonial Series.* 10 vols. Charlottesville, VA, 1983–1995.

JCC: Worthington C. Ford et al., eds., *The Journals of the Continental Congress, 1774–1789.* 34 vols. Washington, DC, 1904–1937.

Smith, *Letters:* Paul H. Smith et al., eds., *Letters of Delegates to Congress, 1774–1789.* 29 vols. Washington, DC, 1976–2000.

Tyler, *"The Common Cause of America":* Richard Tyler, *"The Common Cause of America": A Study of the First Continental Congress.* Historic Research Study, National Park Service: Denver, 1974.

NOTES

INTRODUCTION

1. John Adams to Abigail Adams, July 3, 1776, L.H. Butterfield et al., eds., *Adams Family Correspondence* (Cambridge, MA, 1963–), 2: 27–28. Although the letter is dated July 3, it is possible that he wrote it late in the evening on July 2. For further details on this letter, see ibid., 2: 31n.

2. John Adams to Abigail Adams, July 3, 1776, ibid., 2: 29–31.

3. Abraham Clark to Elias Dayton, July 4, 1774, in Paul H. Smith, ed., *Letters of Delegates to Congress, 1774–1789*, 29 vols. (Washington, DC, 1976–2000), 4: 378–379; Robert Morris to Joseph Reed, July 21, 1776, in ibid., 4: 510. In spite of voting against independence, Morris would ultimately come around and sign the document sometime in August, and would later play a crucial role in the revolutionary war effort as the Director of Finance for the Confederation government.

4. John Drayton, *A View of South Carolina* (Charleston, SC, 1802), p. 217.

5. Brendan McConville, *The King's Three Faces: The Rise & Fall of Royal America, 1688–1776* (Chapel Hill, NC, 2006), pp. 130–133; John F. Watson, *Annals of Philadelphia and Pennsylvania in the Olden Time*, 2 vols. (Philadelphia, 1909), 1: 206.

6. Benjamin Rush to Ebenezer Hazard, October 22, 1768, in L.H. Butterfield, *The Letters of Benjamin Rush*, 2 vols. (Princeton, NJ, 1951), 1: 68. I first discovered a fragment of Rush's description of his experience gazing at the king's throne in Gordon Wood's magnificent study, *The Radicalism of the American Revolution* (New York, 1991), pp. 15–16. Wood's study of the Revolution, along with all of his other work on the history of this period, has, more than the work of any other historian, done the most to enhance my understanding of the period of America's founding.

7. The literature on the coming of the American Revolution is vast, but among the works covering the crucial period between 1774–1776, and in particular, the activities of the Continental Congress during that period, those that I have found most useful are John Ferling, *Independence: The Struggle to Set America Free* (New York, 2011); Jerrilyn Greene Marston, *King and Congress: The Transfer of Political Legitimacy, 1774–1776* (Princeton, NJ, 1987); Richard Tyler, *"The Common Cause of America": A Study of the First Continental Congress* (Denver, CO, 1974); David Ammerman, *In the Common Cause: American Response to the Coercive Acts of 1774* (Charlottesville, VA, 1974). Among works on the Continental Congress more generally, the most helpful have been Edmund Burnett, *The Continental Congress* (New York, 1941) and Jack Rakove, *The Beginnings of National Politics: An Interpretive History of the Continental Congress* (New York, 1979).

CHAPTER 1—THE GENESIS OF REVOLUTION, 1763-1774

1. The most comprehensive accounts of the Boston Tea Party are Benjamin L. Carp, *Defiance of the Patriots: The Boston Tea Party and the Making of America* (New Haven, CT, 2010); and Benjamin Woods Labaree, *The Boston Tea Party* (New York, 1964). My account of the Tea Party relies heavily on their research. Wyeth's account is in Francis S. Drake, *Tea Leaves: Being a Collection of Letters and Documents, Relating to the Shipment of Tea to the American Colonies in the Year 1773 by the East India Tea Company* (Boston, 1884), pp. lxxi–lxxii.

2. Quoted in Carp, *Defiance of the Patriots*, p. 130.

3. Drake, *Tea Leaves*, p. lxxx.

4. Ibid., p. lxviii.

5. The literature on the political relations between the American colonies and British Imperial authority is vast. The definitive, monumental study of those relations is Lawrence Henry Gipson, *The British Empire Before the American Revolution*, 15 vols. (New York, 1930–1970). Among the most recent works are David Armitage, *The Ideological Origins of the British Empire* (Cambridge, MA, 2000); Eliga H. Gould, *The Persistence of Empire: British Political Culture in the Age of the American Revolution* (Chapel Hill, NC, 2000); and Jack P. Greene, *The Constitutional Origins of the American Revolution* (Cambridge, MA, 2011).

6. The standard account of the Stamp Act crisis is Edmund S. and Helen M. Morgan, *The Stamp Act Crisis: Prologue to Revolution* (Chapel Hill, NC, 1953); see also Pauline Maier, *From Resistance to Revolution: Colonial Radicals and the Development of American Opposition to Britain, 1765–1776* (New York, 1972), esp. pp. 51–112.

7. Douglass Adair and John A. Schutz, eds., *Peter Oliver's Origin and Progress of the American Rebellion: A Tory View* (Stanford, CA, 1961), p. 51. Among the many useful accounts of the political and social conflict between Great Britain and the colonies between 1763 and 1774 are, Maier, *From Resistance to Revolution;* Bernard Bailyn, *Ideological Origins of the American Revolution* (Cambridge, MA, 1967); Gary Nash, *The Urban Crucible: Social Change, Political Consciousness and the Origins of the American Revolution* (Cambridge, MA, 1979); Merrill Jensen, *The Founding of a Nation: A History of the American Revolution, 1763–1776* (New York, 1968); and Ray Raphael, *A People's History of the American Revolution: How Common People Shaped the Fight for Independence* (New York, 2002).

8. Adair and Schutz, eds., *Peter Oliver's Origin*, p. 39; John K. Alexander, *Samuel Adams: The Life of an American Revolutionary* (Lanham, MD, 2011), p. 10; among the other biographies of Adams are Mark Puls, *Samuel Adams: Father of the American Revolution* (New York, 2006); and John C. Miller, *Sam Adams: Pioneer in Propaganda* (Boston, 1936). For an outstanding brief portrait of Sam Adams's personality and political career, see Pauline Maier, "A New Englander as Revolutionary: Samuel Adams," in *The Old Revolutionaries: Political Lives in the Age of Samuel Adams* (New York, 1980), pp. 3–50.

9. Puls, *Samuel Adams*, pp. 26–34.

10. Ibid., p. 34; Alexander, *Samuel Adams*, p. 18.

11. Puls, *Samuel Adams*, p. 30.

12. Nash, *Urban Crucible*, pp. 292–300.

13. Ibid., pp. 169–384; Maier, *From Resistance to Revolution*, pp. 51–228.

14. Sam Adams to Arthur Lee, September 27, 1771, Harry A. Cushing, ed., *Writings of Samuel Adams*, 4 vols. (New York, 1904–1908), 2: 234; Richard D. Brown, *Revolutionary Politics in Massachusetts: The Boston Committee of Correspondence and the Towns, 1772–1774* (New York, 1970), pp. 38–57.

15. Quoted in Puls, *Samuel Adams*, p. 130.

16. Brown, *Revolutionary Politics*, pp. 92ff.

17. Labaree, *Boston Tea Party*, pp. 111–112; Carp, *Defiance of the Patriots*, pp. 89–90.

18. Carp, *Defiance of the Patriots*, pp. 100–102.

19. Labaree, *Boston Tea Party*, p. 133.

20. L.H. Butterfield et al., eds., *The Diary and Autobiography of John Adams*, 4 vols. (Cambridge, MA, 1961), 2: 85–86.

21. For the events following the Boston Tea Party in the other major American seaport cities, see Labaree, *Boston Tea Party*, pp. 146–169; Roger Champagne, *Alexander McDougall and the American Revolution in New York* (Schenectady, NY, 1975), pp. 45–51; Richard Alan Ryerson, *The Revolution Is Now Begun: The Radical Committees of Philadelphia, 1765–1776* (Philadelphia, 1978), pp. 36–40.

22. Carp, *Defiance of the Patriots*, p. 139.

23. Labaree, *Boston Tea Party*, pp. 184–194, 207; Peter D.G. Thomas, *Tea Party to Independence: The Third Phase of the American Revolution, 1773–1776* (Oxford, England, 1991), pp. 55–56. The speaker, Charles Van, was perhaps the most militantly anti-American member of Parliament. The text of his speech can be found in William Cobbett, *The Parliamentary History of England*, 36 vols. (London, 1806–1820), 17: 1178.

24. This account of Franklin's confrontation in the cockpit draws substantially on the insightful analysis by Gordon Wood, in *The Americanization of Benjamin Franklin* (New York, 2004), pp. 135–147; see also Walter Isaacson, *Benjamin Franklin: An American Life* (New York, 2003), pp. 275–279.

25. Wood, *Americanization of Benjamin Franklin*, pp 135–147.

26. The most comprehensive account of the passage of the Coercive Acts can be found in Thomas, *Tea Party to Independence*, pp. 26–87. See also Labaree, *Boston Tea Party*, pp. 170–216.

CHAPTER 2—THE QUEST FOR A UNIFIED AMERICAN RESISTANCE

1. Richard Beeman, *Patrick Henry: A Biography* (New York, 1974), p. 43.

2. Oliver Kuntzleman, "Joseph Galloway: Loyalist" (Ph.D. Diss., Temple University, 1941), p. 96.

3. Labaree, *Boston Tea Party*, p. 238.

4. Champagne, *Alexander McDougall*, pp. 52–66; Carl Becker, *The History of Political Parties in the Province of New York, 1760–1776* (Madison, WI, 1909), pp. 112–141.

5. Peter Force, ed., *American Archives*, 4th series, (Washington, DC, 1837–1846), 1: 342.

6. Boston Committee of Correspondence to the Philadelphia Committee of Correspondence, May 13, 1774, Cushing, ed., *Writings of Samuel Adams*, 3: 109–111; Boyd Stanley Schlenther, *Charles Thomson: A Patriot's Pursuit* (Newark, DE, 1990), pp. 102–104.

7. Schlenther, *Charles Thomson*, p. 104; Milton Flower, *John Dickinson, Conservative Revolutionary* (Charlottesville, VA, 1983), pp. 63–64, 102.

8. Flower, *John Dickinson*, p. 102; Schlenther, *Charles Thomson*, pp. 104–105.

9. Schlenther, *Charles Thomson*, pp. 104–105.

10. Ibid., p. 105; Charles Stille, *The Life and Times of John Dickinson, 1732–1808* (Philadelphia, 1891), pp. 107–108.

11. Flower, *John Dickinson*, pp. 104–105; Ryerson, *Revolution Is Now Begun*, pp. 40–42; Tyler, *"The Common Cause of America,"* pp. 43–46.

12. Tyler, *"The Common Cause of America,"* pp. 45–46; Sam Adams to Charles Thomson, May 30, 1774, Cushing, ed., *Writings of Samuel Adams*, 3: 123–124.

13. Dumas Malone, *Jefferson and His Time: Jefferson the Virginian, Volume One*, 6 vols. (Boston, 1948–1981), 1: 171–173; Douglas Southall Freeman, *George Washington: A Biography*, 7 vols. (New York, 1948–1957), 3: 356–358; Julian P. Boyd, *The Papers of Thomas Jefferson*, 38 vols. to date (Princeton, 1950–), 1: 111–112.

14. Boyd, *Jefferson Papers*, 1: 137–141.

15. This estimate is taken from Gary B. Nash, Billy G. Smith, Merle Brouwer, and Norma Adams Price, "The Population of Eighteenth Century Philadelphia," *Pennsylvania Magazine of History and Biography*, 99 (1975): 362–368. According to these scholars, the population of the city at this time depends on how one defines the boundaries of the city. Philadelphia's population ranged from between 25,000 and 28,000, with that higher figure representing the population not only of the center of Philadelphia but the two areas to the north and south, Southwark and the Northern Liberties. I have used the 28,000 figure for the residents of those two adjoining areas certainly considered themselves residents of "Philadelphia."

CHAPTER 3—THE DELEGATES GATHER IN PHILADELPHIA

1. Adams, *Diary*, Aug. 10, 1774, 2: 97–98; see also John Ferling, *John Adams: A Life* (Knoxville, TN, 1992), p. 102.

2. Benjamin Irvin, *Clothed in the Robes of Sovereignty: The Continental Congress and the People Out of Doors* (New York, 2011), p. 25; Puls, *Samuel Adams*, p. 157; William Vincent Wells, *The Life and Public Service of Sam Adams*, 3 vols. (Boston, 1865), 2: 207–210.

3. James Haw, *John and Edward Rutledge of South Carolina* (Athens, GA, 1997) pp. 61–62; Richard Barry, *Mr. Rutledge of South Carolina* (New York, 1942), pp. 157–158; William Duane, ed., *Extracts from the Diary of Christopher Marshall, 1774–1781* (New York, 1969), p. 9.

4. E. Stanley Godbold, Jr., and Robert H. Woody, *Christopher Gadsden and the American Revolution* (Knoxville, TN, 1982), pp. 120–122. For Gadsden's earlier involvement with the resistance to British policy, see pp. 50–119. Duane, ed., *Diary of Christopher Marshall*, p. 9.

5. Henry Mayer, *A Son of Thunder: Patrick Henry and the American Republic* (New York, 1986), pp. 205–206; Freeman, *George Washington*, 3: 372; Ron Chernow, *Washington: A Life* (New York, 2010), p. 171.

6. Chernow, *Washington*, p. 171; David John Mays, *Edmund Pendleton, 1721–1803: A Biography*, 2 vols. (Cambridge, MA, 1952), 1: 277–278.

7. Barry, *John Rutledge*, pp. 157–158.

8. Adams, *Diary*, Aug. 16, 23, 1774, 2: 100, 109.

9. Ibid., Aug. 29, 1774, 2: 114.

10. Joseph Galloway to William Franklin, Sept. 3, 1774, Smith, *Letters*, 1: 24.

11. Adams, *Diary*, Aug. 29, 1774, 2: 114, 115n.

12. Mayer, *Son of Thunder*, p. 106; Mays, *Pendleton*, 1: 279–282.

13. Silas Deane to Elizabeth Deane, Sept. 10–11, 1774, Smith, *Letters*, 1: 62.

14. Mayer, *Son of Thunder*, pp. 206–207; Freeman, *George Washington*, 3: 373.

15. Only twelve of the thirteen colonies would send delegations to Philadelphia that fall. The colony of Georgia, which had been largely uninvolved with the protests of the previous years, would not send a delegation until the following year.

16. This description of the city relies on Billy G. Smith, *Life in Early Philadelphia: Documents from the Revolutionary and Early National Period* (University Park, PA, 1995), pp. 3–14; George W. Boudreau, *Independence: A Guide to Historic Philadelphia* (Yardley, PA, 2012), passim.; and Richard R. Beeman, *Plain, Honest Men: The Making of the American Constitution* (New York, 2009), pp. 72–79.

17. Billy G. Smith, *"The Lower Sort": Philadelphia's Laboring People, 1750–1800* (Ithaca, NY, 1990), p. 207, and Appendix D. See also Gary B. Nash, *The Urban Crucible*, pp. 313–314; and Boudreau, *Independence*, pp. 287–288. Richard Penn's house was later sold to the wealthy Philadelphia merchant Robert Morris and still later served as the executive mansion for George Washington and John Adams.

18. Adams, *Diary*, Aug. 30, 1774, 2: 116; Irvin, *Clothed in the Robes*, p. 17; Boudreau, *Independence*, pp. 209–213.

19. The best description of the Pennsylvania State House is Charlene Mires, *Independence Hall in American Memory* (Philadelphia, 2002), esp. pp. 4–8, 27–30, 61–62; see also Boudreau, *Independence*, pp. 187–197. For a description of the Walnut Street Jail, see Negley K. Teeters, *The Cradle of the Penitentiary: The Walnut Street Jail at Philadelphia, 1773–1835* (Philadelphia, 1955), passim.

20. Edward Potts Cheyney, *A History of the University of Pennsylvania, 1740–1940* (Philadelphia, 1957), pp. 53–125, esp. pp. 109–100, 119–120.; Isaacson, *Benjamin Franklin*, pp. 103–104, 122–123, 146–148.

21. Peter Thompson, *Rum Punch and Revolution: Taverngoing and Public Life in Eighteenth-Century Philadelphia* (Philadelphia, 1999), pp. 145–181; Beeman, *Plain, Honest Men*, p. 75; *Philadelphia Inns and Taverns, 1774–1780*. Robert E. Graham. ARC (Student Reports, Box 1), LIB, Independence National Historical Park Archives, n.d.

22. Smith, *"The Lower Sort,"* pp. 7–39; Boudreau, *Independence*, pp. 32–35.

23. Silas Deane to Elizabeth Deane, Aug. 31–Sept. 5, 1774, Smith, *Letters*, 1: 15–23.

24. Worthington C. Ford et al., eds., *The Journals of the Continental Congress, 1774–1789* (Washington, DC, 1904–1937), 1: 13–15; Smith, *Letters*, 1: xxvi–xxxii.

25. Tyler, *"The Common Cause of America,"* pp. 90, 114.

26. Ibid., p. 112. Much of the data on the educational background of the delegates has been gathered by looking at the individual biographies of each of the delegates in the Allen Johnson, ed., *Dictionary of American Biography*, 11 vols. (New York, 1964), passim.

27. Tyler, *"The Common Cause of America,"* p. 110.

28. Ibid., p. 111; *Dictionary of American Biography*, passim.

29. Tyler, *"The Common Cause of America,"* p. 115.

CHAPTER 4—TWO DIFFERENT PATHS TO LIBERTY: JOHN ADAMS AND JOHN DICKINSON

1. The legend of Adams as the "Atlas of Independence" comes from a letter from New Jersey Delegate Richard Stockton's son to Adams on Sept. 12, 1821, in which he told Adams that his father had told him that "The Man to whom the Country is most indebted for the great measure of Independence is Mr. John Adams of Boston—I call him the Atlas of American independence." John Hazleton, *The Declaration of Independence: Its History* (New York, 1905), pp. 161–162.

2. There are of course dozens of biographies of John Adams, the most famous being David McCullough's *John Adams* (New York, 2001). Among the Adams biographies that I found most useful are Joseph Ellis, *Passionate Sage: The Character and Legacy of John Adams* (New York, 1993); Page Smith, *John Adams*, 2 vols. (Garden City, NJ, 1962); and Ferling, *John Adams*. More recent studies are James Grant, *John Adams: Party of One* (New York, 2005) and John Patrick Diggins, *John Adams* (New York, 2003). For the details on Adams's early life, I have relied primarily on Ferling's biography. Richard Brookhiser's *America's First Dynasty: The Adamses, 1735–1918* (New York, 2002) is about the Adams family as a whole.

3. A particularly insightful analysis of Adams's youth and the development of his personality is Bernard Bailyn, "Butterfield's Adams: Notes for a Sketch," *William and Mary Quarterly*, 3d. ser., 19 (1962): 238–256; Ferling, *John Adams*, pp. 11–19.

4. The fourth lawyer Adams visited, Benjamin Prat, summarily rejected Adams's request for support, perhaps because he didn't have a letter of recommendation from Putnam. Ferling, *John Adams*, pp. 20–24.

5. Adams, *Diary*, Dec. 18, 1758, January 1759, 1: 63, 68, 73.

6. Ferling, *John Adams*, pp. 28–30.

7. Ibid., pp. 31–34. There are nearly as many studies of Abigail and John Adams the couple as there are of John Adams himself. Among the most recent are Edith B. Gelles, *Abigail and John: Portrait of a Marriage* (New York, 2009); and Joseph Ellis, *First Family: Abigail and John Adams* (New York, 2010).

8. Ferling, *John Adams*, pp. 46–47; McCullough, *John Adams*, pp. 59–61.

9. Adams, *Diary*, Dec. 18, 1765, 1: 263–65.

10. Ferling, *John Adams*, pp. 46–48.

11. Adams, *Diary*, Aug. 15, 1765, 1: 260.

12. Ferling, *John Adams*, pp. 58–59; Hiller B. Zobel, *The Boston Massacre* (New York, 1970), pp. 76–77; Harlow Giles Unger, *John Hancock: Merchant King and American Patriot* (New York, 2000), pp. 129–131.

13. For a complete account of the trial following the Boston Massacre, see Zobel, *Boston Massacre*, pp. 206–294.

14. Adams, *Autobiography*, 3: 293.

15. Ibid., 3: 326.

16. Adams, *Diary*, Aug. 16, 1774, 2: 100.

17. Flower, *John Dickinson*, pp. 63–72; David L. Jacobson, *John Dickinson and the Revolution in Pennsylvania, 1764–1776* (Berkeley, CA, 1965), pp. 43–69. For an easily accessible transcript of Dickinson's *Letters from a Farmer in Pennsylvania to the Inhabitants of the British Colonies* (1767–68) go to http://oll.liberty fund.org/?option=com_staticxt&staticfile=show.php%3Ftitle=690&chapter=10 2299&layout=html&Itemid=27.

18. Flower, *John Dickinson*, pp. 1–29, 76–90. For a carefully nuanced study of the convergence of Dickinson's Quaker family background, intellect and political thought, see Karen Calvert, *Quaker Constitutionalism and the Political Thought of John Dickinson* (New York and Cambridge, 2009), esp. pp. 1–64, 207–246.

19. Flower, *John Dickinson*, pp. 29–75, esp. p. 42; Jacobson, *Dickinson and the Revolution in Pennsylvania*, pp. 9–69.

20. Flower, *John Dickinson*, pp. 105–111; Ryerson, *Revolution Is Now Begun*, pp. 43–59. For the text of the ultimate set of instructions to the Pennsylvania delegates, see Pennsylvania *Gazette*, July 27, 1774.

21. Flower, *John Dickinson*, p. 111.

22. Adams, *Diary*, Aug. 31, 1774, 2: 117.

CHAPTER 5—THE CONGRESS ORGANIZES

1. *JCC*, 1: 13–14; The weather during the period September–October 1774, and May–June 1775 is recorded in Donald Jackson et al., eds., *The Diaries of George Washington*, 6 vols. (Charlottesville, VA, 1976–1979), 3: 281–289, 332–333.

2. Tyler, *"The Common Cause of America,"* pp. 124–125; Adams, *Diary*, Sept. 5, 1774, 2: 122–123.

3. James Duane, "Notes of Debates," Smith, *Letters*, 1: 25. For Galloway's reaction, see Galloway to William Franklin, Sept. 5, 1774, in ibid., 1: 27.

4. *JCC*, 1: 14; John Reardon, *Peyton Randolph, 1721–1775: One Who Presided* (Durham, NC, 1982), pp. 3–23.

5. Reardon, *Peyton Randolph*, pp. 24–54.

6. For an excellent discussion of the evolution of both the meaning and substantive duties of the Continental Congress, see Calvin Jillson and Rick K. Wilson, *Congressional Dynamics: Structure, Coordination, and Choice in the First American Congress, 1774–1789* (Stanford, CA, 1994), esp. pp. 15–67. The only two previous occasions on which a "congress" convened in America had been the abortive effort in Albany, New York, in 1754 to form a plan of union among the colonies in anticipation of the Seven Years' War and then the two-week meeting of the Stamp Act Congress in 1765. Both of these meetings were clearly perceived as temporary gatherings to discuss a particular issue.

7. Ibid.

8. Galloway to William Franklin, Sept. 5, 1774, in Smith, *Letters*, 1: 27; Silas Deane to Elizabeth Deane, Sept. 5, 1774, ibid., 1: 20; Adams, *Diary*, Aug. 30, 1774, 2: 115; see also Schlenther, *Charles Thomson*, pp. 119–122.

9. Schlenther, *Charles Thomson*, pp. 17–22. I am grateful to Gary Nash for sharing with me his unpublished paper, "Patriotism and History: Charles Thomson's Dilemma."

10. Adams, *Diary*, 2: 115; Schlenther, *Charles Thomson*, p. 121.

11. Schlenther, *Charles Thomson*, pp. 205–206.

12. The colonies instructions to their delegates are in *JCC*, 1: 15–24. The instruction quoted is from New Hampshire, but the language of nearly all of the instructions is similar.

13. Ibid., 1: 15–16.

14. Ibid., 1: 21–22.

15. Ibid., 1: 23. For a discussion of Jefferson's role in opposing British policies in Virginia at this time see Malone, *Jefferson the Virginian*, pp. 180–183; Boyd, *Jefferson Papers*, 1: 121. See also Tyler, *"The Common Cause of America,"* pp. 55–56.

16. For a full discussion of the various drafts of Jefferson's proposed resolutions and their eventual printing as a *Summary View of the Rights of British America*, see Boyd, *Jefferson Papers*, 1: 119–144.

17. *JCC*, 1: 23.

18. Mayer, *Son of Thunder*, pp. 210–211; "Notes of Debates," Sept. 6, 1774, Adams, *Diary*, 2: 125.

19. For Henry's life leading up to his service in Congress see Mayer, *Son of Thunder*, pp. 19–24; Beeman, *Patrick Henry*, pp. 1–58; and Thomas Kidd, *Patrick Henry: First Among Patriots* (New York, 2011), pp. 1–25.

20. The phrase "no taxation without representation" was first used by Reverend Jonathan Mayhew in Boston in 1750, and it apparently did become widely used in conversation during the years 1763–1776. However, there appears to be no record of any of America's revolutionary leaders actually using the phrase in print.

21. Beeman, *Patrick Henry*, pp. 132–133.

22. "Notes of Debates," Sept. 6, 1774, Adams, *Diary*, 2: 126.

23. Ibid., 2: 124–126.

24. For an account of John Jay's early life, see Walter Stahr, *John Jay: Founding Father* (New York, 2005), pp. 1–32.

25. Ibid.

26. Ibid., pp. 33–35; Champagne, *Alexander McDougall*, pp. 58–66; Becker, *History of Political Parties*, pp. 112–141. The large size of New York's delegation—nine members—reflects some of the division within New York politics over the direction in which American resistance to England should move.

27. "Notes of Debates," Sept. 6, 1774, Adams, *Diary*, 2: 125.

28. Ibid.

29. Ibid.

30. James Duane, "Notes of Debates," Sept. 6, 1774, in Smith, *Letters*, 1: 30–31. For a clear account of the debate on representation in the Congress, see Burnett, *The Continental Congress*, pp. 36–38.

31. James Duane, "Notes of Debates," Sept. 6, 1774, Smith, *Letters*, 1: 30–31; *JCC*, 1: 25.

32. *JCC*, 1: 26.

CHAPTER 6—"FIGHT AGAINST THEM THAT FIGHT AGAINST ME"

1. *JCC*, 1: 26. Two useful accounts of the "Powder Alarm" are Tyler, *"The Common Cause of America,"* pp. 239–243; and Ray Raphael, *The First American Revolution: Before Lexington and Concord* (New York, 2002), pp. 127–133.

2. James Duane, "Notes of Debates," Sept. 6, 1774, Smith, *Letters*, 1: 31; Robert Treat Paine Diary, Sept. 6, 1774, ibid., 1: 32; Samuel Ward Diary Sept. 6, 1774, ibid., 1: 32–33; "Notes of Debates," Sept. 6, 1774, Adams, *Diary*, 2: 124; John Adams to Abigail Adams, Sept. 8, 18, 1774, *Adams Family Correspondence*, 1: 150–151, 157–158; Samuel Adams to Joseph Warren, Sept. 9, 1774, Smith, *Letters*, 1: 55.

3. Silas Deane to Elizabeth Deane, Sept. 7, 1774, Smith, *Letters*, 1: 34. John Adams to Abigail Adams, Sept. 16, 1774, *Adams Family Correspondence*, 1: 156–157.

4. Adams, *Diary*, Sept. 10, 1774, 2: 131; Sam Adams to Joseph Warren, Sept. 9, 1774, Smith, *Letters*, 1: 55.

5. John Adams to Abigail Adams, Sept. 8, 18, 1774, *Adams Family Correspondence*, 1: 150–151, 157–158.

6. Burnett, *Continental Congress*, pp. 39–41; Tyler, *"The Common Cause of America,"* pp. 139–142.

7. Joseph Galloway, *Historical and Political Reflections on the Rise and Progress of the American Revolution* (London, 1780), pp. 67–68.

8. *JCC*, 1: 27–29; James Duane, "Notes of Debates," Sept. 7, 1774, Smith, *Letters*, 1: 37.

9. For an informed discussion of the committee procedures of the Congress, see Jillson and Wilson, *Congressional Dynamics*, pp. 53–56, 95–99.

10. *JCC*, 1: 27–29.

11. The Subcommittee on Rights was appointed on Sept. 9, and that on "Infringements" on Sept. 17.

12. Richard D. Brown, *Revolutionary Politics in Massachusetts: The Boston Committee of Correspondence and the Towns, 1772–1774* (New York, 1970), pp. 210–211, passim.

13. Samuel Adams Drake, *History of Middlesex County, Massachusetts* (Boston, 1879), pp. 107ff; *American Archives*, 4th ser., 1: 750–752.

14. *JCC*, 1: 31; Sam Adams to the Boston Committee of Correspondence, Sept. 14, 1774, Cushing, ed., *Writings of Samuel Adams*, 3: 154–155.

15. John Alexander, *The Life of an American Revolutionary* (Lanham, MD, 2011), p. 187; Puls, *Samuel Adams*, pp. 156–157, 162, 165, 174–175.

16. Samuel Forman, *Dr. Joseph Warren: The Boston Tea Party, Bunker Hill, and the Birth of American Liberty* (Gretna, LA, 2012), pp. 201–221. Warren's Boston Massacre speeches are quoted from Jensen, *The Founding of a Nation*, p. 413.

17. *JCC*, 1: 31–39.

18. Adams, *Diary*, Sept. 17, 1774, 2: 134–135; John Adams to Abigail Adams, Sept. 18, 1774, *Adams Family Correspondence*, 1: 157–158.

19. A summary of these discussions is in Burnett, *Continental Congress*, pp. 41–42. John Adams and New York delegate James Duane also provided summaries in their notes on the debates: "Notes of Debates," Sept. 8, 1774, Adams, *Diary*, 2: 128–131; James Duane, "Speech to the Committee on Rights," Sept. 8, 1774, Smith, *Letters*, 1: 51–54; see also Samuel Ward's Diary, Sept. 9, 1774, ibid: 1: 59.

20. Duane, "Speech to the Committee on Rights," Sept. 8, 1774, Smith, *Letters*, 1: 51–54. See also Edward Alexander, *A Revolutionary Conservative: James Duane of New York* (New York, 1938), pp. 100–101.

21. "Notes of Debates," Sept. 8, 1774, Adams, *Diary*, 2: 128–131.

22. Adams, *Autobiography*, 3: 308–309.

23. Ibid.

24. John Adams to Abigail Adams, Oct. 9, 1774, *Adams Family Correspondence*, 1: 166–167.

25. *JCC*, 1: 41.

26. Ibid.

27. Charles Thomson failed to record this in the journal, but Adams, *Diary*, Sept. 26, 27, 1774, 2: 103–104, records Lee's motion. See also Tyler, *"The Common Cause of America,"* p. 163.

28. Tyler, *"The Common Cause of America,"* p. 163; *JCC*, 1: 43.

29. Adams, *Diary*, Sept. 26, 27, 1774, 2: 103–104.

30. Ibid.

31. Ibid.

32. Ibid., 2: 105.

CHAPTER 7—GALLOWAY'S LAST STAND

1. John Ferling, *The Loyalist Mind: Joseph Galloway and the American Revolution* (University Park, PA, 1977), pp. 7–25; Oliver Kuntzleman, "Joseph Galloway," pp. 11–94.

2. The best account of the background leading to Galloway's presentation of his Plan of Union is Julian P. Boyd, *Anglo-American Union: Joseph Galloway's Plan to Preserve the British Empire, 1774–1788* (Philadelphia, 1941), pp. 32–38. See also Ferling, *Loyalist Mind*, pp. 26–27; and Kuntzleman, "Joseph Galloway," pp. 103–113.

3. There are two accounts of Galloway's speech in which he presented and defended his plan. One consists of his own "Statement on his Plan of Union," and was probably written a few years after the fact. It is found in *JCC*, 1: 43–48. The other account is "Notes of Debates," Sept. 28, 1774, Adams, *Diary*, 2: 141–144. In spite of the potential biases in each account, the two are generally consistent with one another.

4. The Plan of Union itself is printed in *JCC*, 1: 49–51.

5. Ibid.

6. "Notes of Debates," Sept. 28, 1774, Adams, *Diary*, 2: 141–144.

7. Galloway, "Statement on his Plan of Union," *JCC*, 1: 46.

8. "Notes of Debates," Sept. 28, 1774, Adams, *Diary*, 2, 142. An account of James Duane's political activities from 1764–1774 can be found in Alexander, *James Duane*, pp. 95–98. See also Becker, *Political Parties*, pp. 14–16.

9. "Notes of Debates," Sept. 28, 1774, Adams, *Diary*, 2: 142–143.

10. Ibid., 2, 143.

11. Charles Thomson, true to form, failed to record this action in the congressional journal. But Samuel Ward, delegate from Rhode Island, wrote in his journal that day that "A Plan of Union between G. Britain & the Colonies presented by Mr. Galloway considered, not committed, but ordered to lye on the Table." Smith, *Letters*, 1: 128. See also Tyler, *"The Common Cause of America,"* pp. 166–167; Ferling, *Loyalist Mind*, p. 26.

12. Smith, *Letters*, 1: 112–117n, provides the clearest description of the sequence of events regarding Galloway's proposal.

13. Joseph Galloway, *A Candid Examination of the Mutual Claims of Great Britain and the Colonies: With a Plan of Accommodation of Constitutional Principles* (New York, 1775). Galloway would later publish a similar but even more vituperative pamphlet on the same subject in his *Historical and Political Reflections of the Rise and Progress of the American Revolution* (London, 1780).

14. Galloway, *Candid Examination*, pp. 52–53.

15. Schlenther, *Charles Thomson*, pp. 126–27; Smith, *Letters*, 1: 116n, 325n.

16. Ferling, *Loyalist Mind*, p. 28.

17. Burnett, *Continental Congress*, p. 50.

18. For an analysis of Galloway's last, frustrating days in the Pennsylvania Assembly, see Ryerson, *Revolution is Now Begun*, pp. 107–112. See also Ferling, *Loyalist Mind*, pp. 33–34.

CHAPTER 8—GETTING ACQUAINTED
IN THE CITY OF BROTHERLY LOVE

1. Caesar Rodney to Thomas Rodney, Sept. 9, 1774, Smith, *Letters*, 1: 58.

2. Sam Adams to Joseph Warren, Sept. 25, 1774, Cushing, ed., *Writings of Samuel Adams*, 3: 159.

3. Caesar Rodney to Thomas Rodney, Sept. 9, 1774, Smith, *Letters*, 1: 58; Silas Deane to Elizabeth Deane, Sept. 6, 7, 1774, Cushing, ed., *Writings of Samuel Adams*, 1: 29, 34–35.

4. Samuel Ward to Samuel Ward, Jr., Sept. 9, 1774, Smith, *Letters*, 1: 59.

5. Adams, *Diary*, Sept. 8, 14, 22, 1774, 2: 127, 134, 136.

6. Jensen, *Founding of a Nation*, p. 442; Smith, *Letters*, 1: 67n3.

7. *JCC*, 1: 51–53.

8. Ibid., 1: 55; Tyler, *"The Common Cause of America,"* pp. 168–169; Silas Deane Diary, Oct. 1, 3, 1774, Smith, *Letters*, 1: 133, 138–139.

9. *JCC*, 1: 53–54; Duane's proposed resolution and Lee's resolution in Smith, *Letters*, 1: 134, 140; see also Silas Deane Diary, Oct. 3, 1774, Smith, *Letters*, 1: 138–139.

10. Smith, *Letters*, 1: 138–139.

11. Ibid.

12. Tyler, *"The Common Cause of America,"* p. 169; *JCC*, 1: 53–54.

13. Silas Deane Diary, Smith, *Letters*, 1: 138–139.

14. Sam Adams to Joseph Warren, Sept. 25, 1774, Cushing, ed., *Writings of Samuel Adams*, 3: 158–159; Silas Deane Diary, Oct. 5, 1774, Smith, *Letters*, 1: 144–145.

15. "Notes of Debates," Oct. 6, 1774, in Adams, *Diary*, 2: 148; Sam Adams to Joseph Warren, Sept. 25, 1774, Cushing, ed., *Writings of Samuel Adams*, 3: 158–159.

16. Robert Treat Paine Diary, Oct. 6, 1774, Smith, *Letters*, 1: 154; *JCC*, 1: 55–56.

17. This language comes from Joseph Galloway's retrospective, *Candid Examination*, p. 27.

18. John Adams to William Tudor, Sept. 29, 1774, Robert J. Taylor et al., eds., *Papers of John Adams* (Cambridge, MA, 1977–), 2: 176–177; Sam Adams to General Gage, Oct. 7–8, 1774, Cushing, ed., *Writings of Samuel Adams*, 3: 159–162.

19. John Adams draft letter to General Gage, Oct. 7–8, 1774, is in Smith, *Letters*, 1: 158.

20. Lee's proposal is in Smith, *Letters*, 1: 160–161; John Adams to William Tudor, Oct. 7, 1774, *Adams Papers*, 2: 187–188.

21. *Adams Papers*, 2: 187–188.

22. *JCC*, 1: 59–60.

23. John Adams to Abigail Adams, Oct. 9, 1774, *Adams Family Correspondence*, 1: 166–167.

24. Adams, *Diary*, Oct. 9, 1774, 2: 163–164.

25. Ibid.

26. Adams, *Diary*, Oct. 20, 1774, 2: 155; Flower, *John Dickinson*, p. 115; *JCC*, 1: 74.

CHAPTER 9—POWER TO THE PEOPLE

1. Smith, *Letters*, 1: 193–194n, unravels the complex story of Dickinson's role in the authorship of the Declaration of Rights and Grievances.

2. James Duane, "Notes for a Speech in Congress," Oct. 13, 1774, ibid., 1: 189–191.

3. Samuel Ward, "Notes for a Speech in Congress," Oct. 12, 1774, ibid., 1: 184–189.

4. Adams, *Diary*, Oct. 13, 1774, 2: 151. Tyler, *"The Common Cause of America,"* pp. 175–176 has a concise account of this debate.

5. Adams, *Diary*, Oct. 13, 1774; *JCC*, 1: 63–71. James Duane, "Notes of Debates," Oct. 15–17, 1774, Samuel Ward Diary, Oct. 17, 1774, Smith, *Letters*, 1: 198–200, 206.

6. Many historians of the American Revolution have considered the Quebec Act to be a part of the package of acts that came to be known as the Coercive Acts, but there is little indication that this was Parliament's intention. For

a balanced account of the passage of the Quebec Act, see Thomas, *Tea Party to Independence*, pp. 96–106.

7. James Duane, "Notes of Debates," Oct. 15–17, 1774, Smith, *Letters*, 1: 198–199; Adams, *Diary*, Oct. 17, 1774, 2: 154.

8. Barry, *Mr. Rutledge of South Carolina*, pp. 167, 169; see also Haw, *John and Edward Rutledge*, p. 66.

9. Quoted in Godbold and Woody, *Christopher Gadsden*, p. 126. See also Haw, *John and Edward Rutledge*, p. 66; Tyler, *"The Common Cause of America,"* p. 182.

10. Marston, *King and Congress*, pp. 100–130, presents persuasive evidence detailing the ways in which the creation of the Association enabled the Continental Congress to transform itself from a temporary "convention" to something more closely resembling a governing body.

11. The Fairfax Resolves are printed in W.W. Abbot et al., eds., *The Papers of George Washington, Colonial Series* (Charlottesville, VA, 1983–1995), 10: 128. For Washington's attempts to appease Brian Fairfax, see George Washington to Bryan Fairfax, July 17, 1774, and July 20, 1774, ibid., 10: 114–119, 128–131. See also Chernow, *Washington*, pp. 169–171; Freeman, *George Washington*, 3: 362–368.

12. The full text of the Association is in *JCC*, 1: 75–80.

13. Ibid., 1: 77.

14. This, the seventeenth resolution in the Fairfax Resolves, can be found in *GW Papers*, C.S., 10: 125. There is some irony in the fact that George Mason, the author of those words, owned some three hundred slaves at the time. Helen Hill Miller, *George Mason: Gentleman Revolutionary* (Chapel Hill, NC, 1975), pp. 57–60; Forrest McDonald, *We the People: The Economic Origins of the Constitution* (Chicago, 1958), p. 72.

15. Tyler, *"The Common Cause of America,"* p. 107.

16. Ellis, *His Excellency, George Washington* (New York, 2005), pp. 41, 46, 164–167, 257–264 has an excellent account not only of Washington's acquisition of slaves, but also of the dilemma he faced with respect to freeing his slaves at his death. As Ellis notes, at the time of his death, Washington had legal title to only 124 of his 317 slaves; most of the rest belonged to the family estate of his wife, Martha Custis Washington, and were not legally under his control. See also Chernow, *Washington*, pp. 110–119. The information about the slaveholdings of other delegates to the Congress was gleaned from the individual biographies cited in these notes. For useful discussions of the tensions and contradictions inherent in the Americans' rhetorical abhorrence of British attempts to "enslave" them and the fundamental importance of the institution of slavery to the American economy, see Duncan MacLeod, *Slavery, Race and the*

American Revolution (Cambridge, MA, 1974); Gary Nash, *Race and Revolution* (Lanham, MD, 2001), esp. pp. 3–23; Donald Robinson, *Slavery in the Structure of American Politics, 1765–1820* (New York, 1970), pp. 54–97; David Brion Davis, *The Problem of Slavery in the Age of Revolution* (Ithaca, NY, 1975), esp. pp. 173, 273; and Ira Berlin and Ronald Hoffman, eds., *Slavery and Freedom in the Age of the American Revolution* (Charlottesville, VA, 1983).

17. *JCC*, 1: 77–78.

18. Ibid., 1: 79.

19. Ibid., 1: 78; for an insightful analysis of the way in which Puritan ideals permeated both the rhetoric and the substance of the American resistance to Great Britain, see Edmund S. Morgan, "The Puritan Ethic and the American Revolution," *William and Mary Quarterly*, 3d ser., 24 (1967): 3–43.

20. *JCC*, 1: 79–80. Marston, *King and Congress*, pp. 100–130, presents the most convincing evidence of the ways in which delegating power of enforcement to the people at the local level actually increased the power and authority of the Congress. Timothy H. Breen, *American Insurgents, American Patriots: The Revolution of the People* (New York, 2010), pp. 160–184, though less concerned with the authority of the Congress that authorized the Association, presents compelling evidence about the ways in which local committees implemented the boycott.

21. "Notes of Debates," Oct. 6, 1774, Adams, *Diary*, 2: 149.

22. *JCC*, 1: 80; Galloway, *Candid Examination*, pp. 56, 59. Galloway also expressed his opposition in another pamphlet, *A Reply to an Address to the Author of a Pamphlet, entitled "A Candid Examination of the Mutual Claims of Great Britain and her Colonies"* (New York, 1775), pp. 39–40. See also Ammerman, *In the Common Cause*, pp. 92–93; Tyler, *"The Common Cause of America,"* pp. 182–185; and Smith, *Letters*, 1: 222n.

23. Adams, *Diary*, Oct. 20, 1774, 2: 155.

CHAPTER 10—THE FIRST CONGRESS COMPLETES ITS BUSINESS

1. *JCC*, 1: 82–90. Richard Henry Lee apparently also wrote a draft of an address to the people of Great Britain, but his draft apparently had little influence on Jay's final draft. Lee's draft is in Smith, *Letters*, 1: 174–179. For an analysis of the rather complicated drafting process, see ibid., 1: 179n. See also Stahr, *John Jay*, pp. 40–42.

2. The authorship of the Congress's address to the inhabitants of the American colonies has been a matter of some historical controversy. Most accounts, relying on a letter from Thomas Jefferson (who was not present at the First Continental Congress) to Patrick Henry's biographer, William Wirt, in 1805,

assert that Richard Henry Lee wrote the address. This has a certain logic, since Lee was one of the three members of the committee charged with drafting both the address to the people of Great Britain and that to the people of the colonies, and it would make some sense that there would be a division of labor between Jay and Lee. In fact though, the surviving full-manuscript version of the address to the people of the colonies—seventeen pages in length—is in the hand of John Dickinson, who, though technically not even a member of the Congress until several days after work on the address was begun, was nevertheless an active participant in the delegates' deliberations even before he formally joined the Congress. Dickinson's draft is in Smith, *Letters*, 1: 207–217; for a detailed analysis of the question of authorship of the address, see ibid., 1: 220–221n.

3. *JCC*, 1: 102. George Read to Gertrude Read, Oct. 24, 1774, Smith, *Letters*, 1: 244; Reardon, *Peyton Randolph*, p. 53; Tyler, *"The Common Cause of America,"* p. 189. Charles Thomson stated in the *Journal* that Randolph was unable to attend because of an "indisposition," but we know that Randolph was eager to return to preside over the upcoming meeting of the Virginia House of Burgesses. In fact, the meeting of the Burgesses was delayed because the royal governor, Lord Dunmore, prorogued the legislature until November 7, and then, as the legislature was preparing to meet on the 7th, prorogued it again, delaying its meeting until June 1, 1775.

4. John Dickinson to George Logan, Sept. 15, 1804, in Charles Stille, *The Life and Times of John Dickinson, 1732–1808* (New York, 1891), p. 145. Patrick Henry's and Richard Henry Lee's drafts of the addresses to the king are in Smith, *Letters*, 1: 222–227. Dickinson's is in ibid., 1: 228–231. For an extensive analysis of the question of the authorship of the Address to the King, see Edwin Wolf, II, "The Authorship of the 1774 Address to the King Restudied," *William and Mary Quarterly*, 3d ser., 22 (1965): 189–224.

5. Smith, *Letters*, 1: 226.

6. Ibid., 1: 225, 228–232; Wolf, "Authorship of the 1774 Address," pp. 189–224; Flower, *John Dickinson*, pp. 116–117.

7. Adams, *Diary*, Oct. 24, 1774, 2: 157; *JCC*, 1: 115–121.

8. *JCC*, 1: 104–105, 121–122. The other colonies paying agents to represent their interests in Parliament were New Hampshire (Paul Wentworth), Connecticut (Thomas Life) and South Carolina (Charles Garth); Rhode Island, Delaware, Maryland, Virginia and North Carolina did not have agents at the time. Arthur Lee of Virginia and William Bollan were also in London representing Massachusetts along with Franklin, and Lee was no doubt playing some role in representing Virginia.

9. *JCC*, 1: 105–113. Dickinson's draft of the letter to Quebec is in Smith, *Letters*, 1: 236–244.

10. *JCC*, 1: 121. See also Wolf, "Authorship of the 1774 Address," p. 200. The Virginia delegates who were absent had others sign their names—Richard Henry Lee signing for Patrick Henry and Washington signing for Pendleton, Bland and Harrison. The Congress engrossed two copies of the petition, one to be sent to Benjamin Franklin in London and the other to be hand-carried by a Captain Falconer. The other addresses to the various constituencies were ordered to be published soon after the Congress adjourned, but the petition to the king was not published until after it could be determined that he had actually received it. That petition did not appear in print until Jan. 17 or 18, 1775.

11. Thomas Lynch to Ralph Izard, Oct. 26, 1774, Smith, *Letters*, 1: 247.

12. John Dickinson to Arthur Lee, Oct. 27, 1774, ibid., 1: 250.

13. Ibid. Dickinson wrote a similar letter to Josiah Quincy, Jr., on the following day, ibid., 1: 251–252.

14. Joseph Galloway to Thomas Nickleson, Nov. 1, 1774, ibid., 1: 255.

15. Adams, *Autobiography*, 3: 313.

16. Marston, *King and Congress*, pp. 97–99, 128–130, makes a strong case for this evolution of the Congress's authority and function.

17. *JCC*, 1: 102; Adams, *Diary*, Oct. 28, 1774, 2: 157.

CHAPTER 11—ESCALATION

1. *JCC*, 1: 120–121.

2. Much of my analysis in this book of the British reaction to Congress's actions relies on the meticulous work of Thomas, *Tea Party to Independence*. For Lord Dartmouth's reaction to the American petition, see ibid., pp. 170–175; Tyler, *"The Common Cause of America,"* pp. 200–201; *American Archives*, 4th ser., 1: 1085.

3. Thomas, *Tea Party to Independence*, pp. 188–189; Tyler, *"The Common Cause of America,"* 201–292.

4. King George III to Lord North, Nov. 18, 1774, quoted in Thomas, *Tea Party to Independence*, p. 160.

5. Ibid., pp. 186–187.

6. Ibid., pp. 198–206; Ferling, *Independence*, pp. 102–106; *American Archives*, 4th ser., 1: 1566, 1570, 1590.

7. Burke's remarkable speech has been reprinted numerous times. The quotations in the text are taken from the reprinting in the Library of the Liberty Fund, online at: oll.libertyfund.org/title/796/20357.

8. Thomas, *Tea Party to Independence*, pp. 212–214; Ferling, *Independence*, pp. 104–105.

9. Thomas, *Tea Party to Independence*, pp. 184–186.

10. Hugh T. Lefler and William Powell, *Colonial North Carolina: A History* (New York, 1973), pp. 261–264.

11. Lord Dunmore to Lord Dartmouth, Feb. 15, 1775, in Robert Scribner, Brent Tarter et al., eds., *Revolutionary Virginia: The Road to Independence*, 7 vols. (Charlottesville, VA, 1973–), 3: 66. The precise wording of Henry's famous "give me liberty or give me death" speech will always remain a subject of historical contention. But the standard recounting of that speech is contained in the work of Henry's original biographer, William Wirt, *Sketches of the Life and Character of Patrick Henry* (Philadelphia, 1817), pp. 120–123.

12. Tyler, *"The Common Cause of America,"* pp. 206–207; *American Archives*, 4th ser., 1: 1819–1822; 1837–1842; 2: 677.

13. Becker, *History of Political Parties*, pp. 174–192. Thomas, *Tea Party to Independence*, pp. 222–223. Isaac Low had refused to attend the Provincial Convention, and since only members of that body were eligible to serve in the Continental Congress, he was not able to be elected as a delegate to the Congress. John Haring declined his election.

14. *American Archives*, 4th ser., 2: 1546–1549.

15. There are two, especially useful accounts of the implementation of the Association in localities across America: Breen, *American Insurgents*, esp. pp. 160–184 and Marston, *King and Congress*, esp. pp. 100–130.

16. *JCC*, 1: 79.

17. Marston, *King and Congress*, p. 109; Breen, *American Insurgents*, p. 169. The most thorough research on this subject can be found in Jacob M. Price, "A New Time for Scotland's and Britain's Trade with the Thirteen Colonies and States," *William and Mary Quarterly*, 3d ser., 32 (1975): 325.

18. Breen, *American Insurgents*, pp. 167–169, suggests that the transfer of such significant power over enforcement to local committees may not have been wholly intended by the Congress.

19. Marston, *King and Congress*, pp. 122–130. See also Breen, *American Insurgents*, p. 172.

20. Marston, *King and Congress*, p. 125; Breen, *American Insurgents*, pp. 170–171.

21. Marston, *King and* Congress, p. 125–127.

22. William Duane, ed., *Extracts from the Diary of Christopher Marshall, 1774–1781* (New York, 1969), pp. 51–53. For an extended account of this episode, see Irvin, *Clothed in the Robes of Sovereignty*, pp. 48–50.

23. Dunmore's comments quoted in Breen, *American Insurgents*, pp. 174–176; Josiah Martin to Dartmouth, Sept. 1. 1774, in K.G. Davies, *Documents of the American Revolution* (Shannon, Ireland, 1972–1981), 8: 172; Governor Wright to Dartmouth, August 24, 1774, ibid., 8: 162.

24. Breen, *American Insurgents*, p. 209.

25. Thomas, *Tea Party to Independence*, pp. 223–228; Ferling, *Independence*, pp. 99–100; Breen, *American Insurgents*, pp. 13–14, 88, 156–159, 284–285.

26. *DAR*, 9: 37–41; David Hackett Fischer, *Paul Revere's Ride* (New York, 1994), esp. pp. 95–97. My account of both the events leading to the armed conflict and of the conflict itself is much indebted to Fischer's superb work.

27. Fischer, *Paul Revere's Ride*, pp. 111, 143. See also Samuel A. Forman, *Joseph Warren: The Boston Tea Party, Bunker Hill, and the Birth of American Liberty* (Gretna, LA, 2012), pp. 237, 249, 267.

28. This summary is distilled from Fischer, *Paul Revere's Ride*, pp. 93–260.

29. Ibid., pp. 174–183; Unger, *John Hancock*, pp. 188–194, 198–200.

30. John Hancock to Dorothy Quincy, May 7, 1775, Massachusetts Historical Society, quoted in Ungar, *John Hancock*, pp. 200–201.

31. Miller, *Sam Adams*, p. 336; Unger, *John Hancock*, pp. 202–203; Allan, *John Hancock*, p. 188.

CHAPTER 12—A NEW CONGRESS, CHANGED CIRCUMSTANCES

1. Joseph Hewes to Samuel Johnston, May 11, 1775, Smith, *Letters*, 1: 342–343.

2. *JCC*, 2: 11–20; for the maneuvering behind the appointment of the New York delegation, see Becker, *History of Political Parties*, pp. 174–192; and Champagne, *Alexander McDougall*, pp. 78–81.

3. *JCC*, 2: 44.

4. Galloway, *Candid Examination*, p. 31. For the maneuverings in the Pennsylvania Assembly, see Ryerson, *Revolution Is Now Begun*, pp. 97, 119.

5. *JCC*, 2: 12, 22, 55. Surprisingly, there is no official record of the seating arrangement in the Assembly Room. The historians at Independence National Historical Park, after careful study have instructed their guides to present the seating arrangements of the delegations as noted above. The arrangement suggested by the Independence Park historians is consistent with the arrangement as reported at a later date by Charles Thomson. See the "Report of the Secretary of Congress," May 18, 1782, in Edmund Burnett, *Letters of Members of the Continental Congress*, 8 vols. (Washington, DC, 1921–1936), 6: 349.

6. *JCC*, 2: 13, 24–44.

7. Jillson and Wilson, *Congressional Dynamics*, pp. 59–67, and, more generally, pp. 71–163, have an excellent analysis of the changes in the nature of the business of the two congresses.

8. Silas Deane Diary, May 16, 1774, Smith, *Letters*, 1: 351–352. For Washington's views on the matter of raising an army, see Washington to Fairfax County Committee, May, 16, 1774, *GW Papers*, C.S., 10: 363–365.

9. Silas Deane Diary, May 16, 1774, Smith, *Letters*, 1: 351–352.

10. The bare essentials of Dickinson's speech are in ibid., 1: 352. For more of Dickinson's reasoning, see Dickinson to Arthur Lee, April 29, 1775, ibid., 1: 331–332.

11. Silas Deane Diary, May, 16, 1775, in ibid., 351–352.

12. There are actually two versions of Dickinson's "Notes for a Speech in Congress." Smith, *Letters*, 1: 371–383 and 386–390, presents both of them. Since Dickinson may have spoken several times between May 23 and May 25, these notes may have been incorporated into more than one speech.

13. Ibid., 1: 377.

14. Ibid., 1: 375.

15. Ibid., 1: 377.

16. Silas Deane Diary, May 23, May 24, ibid., 1: 371, 401–402; Adams, *Autobiography*, 3: 315–316.

17. John Adams to Moses Gill, June 10, 1775, Adams to James Warren, July 6, 1775, *Adams Papers*, 3: 20–21, 60–62. For a useful discussion of this debate see Rakove, *Beginnings of National Politics*, pp. 71–79.

18. *JCC*, 2: 64–66. See also Smith, *Letters*, 1: 383–386, for a draft of Dickinson's version of the resolutions.

CHAPTER 13—JOHN HANCOCK ENTERS THE DRAMA

1. Unger, *John Hancock*, 202–203; other biographies of Hancock are: William Fowler, *The Baron of Beacon Hill: A Biography of John Hancock* (New York, 1980); Herbert S. Allan, *John Hancock: Patriot in Purple* (New York, 1948); and Paul D. Brandes, *John Hancock's Life and Speeches: A Personalized Vision of the American Revolution, 1763–1793* (Latham, MD, 1996).

2. John Adams to William Tudor, June 1, 1817, in Charles Francis Adams, ed., *The Works of John Adams*, 10 vols. (Boston, 1850–1856), 10: 260–261.

3. Unger, *John Hancock*, pp. 16–25, 42–45; Allan, *John Hancock*, p. 40.

4. Allan, *John Hancock*, p. 59; Unger, *John Hancock*, pp. 45–50.

5. John Adams to William Tudor, June 1, 1817, in Adams, ed., *Works of John Adams*, 10: 259.

6. Unger, *John Hancock*, pp. 54–59.

7. Ibid., pp. 64–68, 110–111.

8. Hancock's biographers differ on the extent to which the revenues from the House of Hancock depended upon smuggling. Unger, *John Hancock*, pp. 72–73, admits that Hancock, like nearly all New England merchants, engaged in the smuggling of molasses but argues that most of the smuggling carried out in Boston was done by smaller merchant houses, not prosperous ones like the House of Hancock. Allan, *John Hancock*, pp. 45–48, argues that smuggling was a

more fundamental part of the Hancock enterprise. For a general account of American smuggling during the prerevolutionary period, see Lawrence Harper, *The English Navigation Laws: A Seventeenth Century Experiment in Social Engineering* (New York, 1939), pp. 267–270 and passim. See also Jensen, *Founding of a Nation*, pp. 43–50; and Robert Middlekauf, *The Glorious Cause: The American Revolution, 1763–1789* (New York, 1982), pp. 63–66.

9. Unger, *John Hancock*, pp. 118–119.

10. Middlekauf, *Glorious Cause*, pp. 166–169; Unger, *John Hancock*, pp. 19–24, 129–132.

11. Unger, *John Hancock*, pp. 129–132; Ferling, *John Adams*, pp. 58–59.

12. Unger, *John Hancock*, pp. 129–131; Allan, *John Hancock*, pp. 95–96.

13. Unger, *John Hancock*, pp. 121–122; Alexander, *Samuel Adams*, p. 74.

14. Unger, *John Hancock*, pp. 143–146.

15. One of the reasons for the decline in Hancock's interest in the politics of rebellion during this period was no doubt due at least in part to the fact that he was also engaged in the ardent courtship of his future wife, Dolly Quincy, the daughter of one of the colony's most prominent families. Unger, *John Hancock*, pp. 255–256; Allan, *John Hancock*, p. 125; Samuel Adams to Arthur Lee, Sept. 22, 1773, in Cushing, ed., *Writings of Samuel Adams*, 3: 36–37.

16. Richard Brown, *Revolutionary Politics*, pp. 59–61, 66–67; Unger, *John Hancock*, pp. 161–163.

17. Hutchinson's letter is in Hosmer, *Life of Thomas Hutchinson* (Boston, 1896), p. 224. See also Bernard Bailyn, *The Ordeal of Thomas Hutchinson* (Cambridge, MA, 1974), p. 178.

18. Bailyn, *Ordeal of Thomas Hutchinson*, pp. 221ff; Wood, *Americanization of Benjamin Franklin*, pp. 141–146; Puls, *Samuel Adams*, pp. 133–140.

19. Reardon, *Peyton Randolph*, pp. 61–62; Allan, *John Hancock*, p. 190. See also Unger, *John Hancock*, pp. 205–206; Lorenzo Sears, *John Hancock, The Picturesque Patriot* (Boston, 1913), pp. 178–179; Alexander, *Samuel Adams*, p. 243.

20. Reardon, *Peyton Randolph*, p. 67; John Adams to James Warren, Sept. 19, 1775, in *Adams Papers*, 3: 160–161.

CHAPTER 14—CONGRESS ASSUMES COMMAND OF A WAR

1. Ferling, *Independence*, pp. 138–140. See also Ward, *War of the Revolution*, pp. 63–72.

2. Ferling, *Independence*, pp. 138–140.

3. *JCC*, 2: 56–57, 59–61; New York Delegates to Albany Committee of Correspondence, May 18, 1775, Smith, *Letters*, 1: 358; John Hancock to President of New York Provincial Convention, May 26, 1775, ibid., 1: 409.

4. *American Archives*, 4th ser., 2: 696; *JCC*, 2: 59–61, 74; New Hampshire Delegates to Provincial Committee of New Hampshire, May 22, 1775, Smith, *Letters*, 1: 369.

5. *JCC*, 2: 76–78; Marston, *King and Congress*, pp. 258–260.

6. *JCC*, 2: 79, 83–84.

7. John Adams to Moses Gill, June 10, 1775, *Adams Papers*, 3: 20–21; Sam Adams to James Warren, June 10, 1775, Smith, *Letters*, 1: 467–468.

8. John Hancock to Massachusetts Provincial Congress, June 10, 1775, Smith, *Letters*, 1: 472–473.

9. John to Abigail Adams, June 10, 1775, *Adams Family Correspondence*, 1: 213–214.

10. *JCC*, 2: 89–90.

11. Ibid., 2: 91.

12. There are numerous excellent accounts of Washington's military career and of the circumstances surrounding his appointment as commander of the continental army. In my account, I have relied on Freeman, *George Washington*, 3: 418–459; Chernow, *Washington*, pp. 182–192; and Ellis, *His Excellency*, pp. 67–72. Washington's account of the bullets whistling was in a letter to his brother Jack, May 31, 1754, *GW Papers*, C.S., 1: 118.

13. There has been some difference of opinion as to which uniform Washington brought with him to Philadelphia. Freeman, *Washington*, 3: 426, believes that it was the red and blue uniform that Washington wore during the French and Indian War. Chernow, *Washington*, p. 183, believes that it was the blue and buff uniform of the Fairfax County militia. The historians at Washington's Mount Vernon side with Chernow. Benjamin Rush to Thomas Ruston, Oct. 29, 1775 in Butterfield ed., *Letters of Benjamin Rush*, 1: 92.

14. Adams, *Autobiography*, 3: 322–323. See also Ellis, *His Excellency*, pp. 68–69.

15. Adams, *Autobiography*, 3: 322–323.

16. Ibid.; *JCC*, 2: 91.

17. Silas Deane to Elizabeth Deane, June 16, 1775, Eliphalet Dyer to Joseph Trumbull, June 17, 1775, Robert Treat Paine to Artemas Ward, June 18, 1775, Smith, *Letters*, 1: 494, 499–500, 509.

18. Silas Deane to Elizabeth Deane, Sept. 10–11, 1774, Smith, *Letters*, 1: 62.

19. George Washington to Martha Washington, June 18, 1775, George Washington to Burwell Bassett, June 19, 1775, *GW Papers*, R.S., 1: 3–5, 12–13. Patrick Henry's comment is quoted in Freeman, *Washington*, 3: 436.

20. "Address to the Continental Congress," June 16, 1775, *GW Papers*, R.S., 1: 1–3.

21. *JCC*, 2: 93–97. John Adams to Elbridge Gerry, June 18, 1775, John Adams to James Warren, June 20, 1775, *Adams Papers*, 3: 25–26, 34.

22. *JCC*, 2: 99, 103; John Adams to Joseph Warren, June 21, 1775, *Adams Papers*, 3: 44.

23. James Duane to New York Provincial Congress, June 17, 1775, Smith, *Letters*, 1: 498–499; *JCC*, 2: 103; Burnett, *Continental Congress*, p. 82.

24. George Washington to Burwell Bassett, June 19, 1775, George Washington to John Parke Custis, June 19, 1775, George Washington to Martha Washington, June 18, 1775, *GW Papers*, R.S., 1: 4–6, 12–16. A copy of the will has never been found.

25. *JCC*, 2: 100–101.

26. Chernow, *Washington*, pp. 189–190.

27. George Washington to Martha Washington, June 23, 1775, *GW Papers*, R.S., 1: 27.

28. Chernow, *Washington*, p. 191.

29. John to Abigail Adams, June 23, 1775, *Adams Family Correspondence*, 1: 226–227.

CHAPTER 15—DESPERATE EFFORTS AT RECONCILIATION AMIDST AN ESCALATING WAR

1. This brief summary of the much-written-about battle of Bunker Hill has been based on a composite of sources, including: Ward, *War of the Revolution*, pp. 73–98; Ferling, *Almost a Miracle*, pp. 48–60; Middlekauf, *Glorious Cause*, pp. 281–292.

2. See for example, George Washington to the Continental Congress, June 25, 1775, George Washington to John Hancock, June 25, 1775, *GW Papers*, R.S., 1: 32–35. Thomas Jefferson to Francis Eppes, July 4, 1775, Boyd, *Jefferson Papers*, 1: 184–185.

3. Sam Adams to Elizabeth Adams, June 28, 1775, *Writings of Samuel Adams*, 3: 220–221. Sam Adams to James Warren, June 28, 1775, in Smith, *Letters*, 1: 553; John Adams to James Warren, June 27, 1775, *Adams Papers*, 3: 49–50.

4. *JCC*, 2: 105.

5. *JCC*, 2: 107–108; For an extensive discussion of the various drafts of the Declaration of the Causes and Necessity for Taking Up Arms, see Boyd, *Jefferson Papers*, 1: 187–192.

6. Carl Van Doren, *Benjamin Franklin* (New York, 1938), p. 522. See also Isaacson, *Benjamin Franklin*, pp. 286–289.

7. Silas Deane to Elizabeth Deane, July 1, 1775, Smith, *Letters*, 1: 567; John Adams to Abigail Adams, July 23, 1775, *Adams Family Correspondence*, 1: 252–253.

8. John Adams to Abigail Adams, July 23, 1775, *Adams Family Correspondence*, 1: 252–253.

9. The "Vindication" is printed in Smith, *Letters*, 1: 561–566, which includes an informative discussion of the provenance of the document.

10. Jack P. Greene, *Quest for Power: The Lower Houses of Assembly in the Southern Royal Colonies, 1689–1776* (Chapel Hill, NC, 1963), pp. 467–474, esp. p. 470. Malone, *Jefferson the Virginian*, pp. 101–109.

11. The life history, and even the lineage, of Jane Randolph, Jefferson's mother, is surprisingly sketchy. The best, but still fragmented, account of her life is on the website of Jefferson's home, Monticello: http://www.monticello.org /site/jefferson/jane-randolph-jefferson. For Jefferson's early life, see Malone, *Jefferson the Virginian*, pp. 3–48.

12. Ibid., pp. 62–87, esp. p. 73.

13. Ibid., pp. 181–190; Boyd, *Jefferson Papers*, 1: 121–137. Jefferson's *Summary View* had attracted enough attention that Samuel Ward of Rhode Island, when he saw that Jefferson had taken his seat in the Congress, referred to him as "the famous Mr. Jefferson." Samuel Ward to Henry Ward, June 22, 1775, Smith, *Letters*, 1: 535.

14. Joseph Ellis, *American Sphinx: The Character of Thomas Jefferson* (New York, 1997), pp. 24–25, writes that Jefferson traveled to Philadelphia with three slaves—Jesse, Jupiter and Richard. Malone, *Jefferson the Virginian*, pp. 202–203, citing Jefferson's account book, simply says "at least two servants, Jesse, who rode postilion, and Richard, apparently a body servant."

15. *JCC*, 2: 128–157.

16. Ibid.; Livingston's comment is quoted in Malone, *Jefferson the Virginian*, p. 205. The most complete account of the evolution of Jefferson's two drafts, Dickinson's revision, and the eventual outcome of the debate, can be found in Boyd, *Jefferson Papers*, 1: 187–219. See also, Jacobson, *John Dickinson*, pp. 95–98.

17. Boyd, *Jefferson Papers*, 1: 188–189n.

18. Ibid., 1: 217; *JCC*, 2: 128–157.

19. *JCC*, 2: 127; John Adams to James Warren, July 6, 1775, *Adams Papers*, 3: 62; Boyd, *Jefferson Papers*, 1: 190n.

20. John Adams to James Warren, July 10, July 11, 1775, *Adams Papers*, 3: 70–72.

21. *JCC*, 2: 127.

22. Adams, *Autobiography*, 3: 318.

23. John Adams to James Warren, July 6, 1775, *Adams Papers*, 3: 62.

24. *JCC*, 2: 127, 158–162; Paul Leicester Ford, *The Autobiography of Thomas Jefferson, 1743–1790* (New York, 1914), p. 19.

25. John Adams to James Warren, July 24, 1775, *Adams Papers*, 3: 89.

26. *Adams Papers*, 3: 90–93n; George W. Corner, *The Autobiography of Benjamin Rush: His "Travels Through Life" Together with his Commonplace Book for 1789–1813* (Princeton, NJ, 1948), p. 142.

27. *JCC*, 2: 195–199.

28. Isaacson, *Benjamin Franklin*, pp. 299–300; Burnett, *Continental Congress*, p. 90. Smith, *Letters*, 1: 643–644n, has a useful discussion of the provenance of Franklin's proposal, of which there were apparently several copies. See also Isaacson, *Benjamin Franklin*, pp. 299–300; and Burnett, *Continental Congress*, p. 90.

29. Smith, *Letters*, 1: 643–644n; see also Boyd, *Jefferson Papers*, 1: 179–182.

30. *JCC*, 2: 202; Malone, *Jefferson the Virginian*, pp. 198–201; Boyd, *Jefferson Papers*, 1: 223–230.

31. *JCC*, 2: 224–234.

32. Eliphalet Dyer to Joseph Trumbull, July 28, 1775, in Smith, *Letters*, 1: 674.

CHAPTER 16—MANAGING A WAR WHILE SEEKING PEACE

1. Richard Smith Diary, Sept. 12, 1775, Smith, *Letters*, 2: 5; *JCC*, 2: 240–247.

2. Adams, *Diary*, Sept. 15, 1775, 2: 172–173.

3. "List of Delegates," Smith, *Letters*, 2: xvi–xxii.

4. John Adams to James Warren, Sept. 17, 1775, *Adams Papers*, 3: 158–159; Sam Adams to Elbridge Gerry, Sept. 26, 1775, in Cushing, ed., *Writings of Samuel Adams*, 3: 226. I am grateful to John Ferling, *Independence*, p. 182, for revealing this anecdote.

5. Quoted in Marston, *King and Congress*, p. 158.

6. For just a few examples of General Washington's constant complaints about army disciplines, see General Orders, July 4, July 7, July 11, July 16, July 24, July 26, Aug. 1, Aug. 4, 1775, *GW Papers*, R.S., 1: 54–55, 71–74, 106, 122, 163–164, 172, 207, 218–219.

7. George Washington to Lund Washington, Aug. 20, 1775, George Washington to John Hancock, Feb. 9, 1776, *GW Papers*, R.S., 1: 334–337, 3: 275. See also Marston, *King and Congress*, pp. 152–153.

8. Marston, *King and Congress*, p. 157.

9. For a thorough analysis of the committee system—and its various weaknesses—in the Congress, see Jillson and Wilson, *Congressional Dynamics*, pp. 91–131.

10. *JCC*, 2: 254, 255.

11. *JCC*, 3: 265, 266, 270–271.

12. John Adams to James Warren, Oct. 1, 1775, *Adams Papers*, 2: 177; Sam Adams to James Warren, Oct. 3, 1775, Smith, *Letters*, 2: 101–102.

13. Thomas Lynch to Washington, Nov. 13, 1775, Smith, *Letters*, 2: 337–338. See also Chernow, *Washington*, p. 208; and Freeman, *Washington*, 3: 554–556.

14. Ellis, *His Excellency*, pp. 77–78.

15. The shelling by the British of the Port of Falmouth, Maine, lent greater urgency to this matter. For a general history of the creation of the American navy, see George Daughan, *If by Sea: The Forging of the American Navy from the American Revolution to the War of 1812* (New York, 2008).

16. Burnett, *Continental Congress*, pp. 119–120; "Notes of Debates," Oct 5, 1775, Adams, *Diary*, 2: 192–194; James Duane, "Notes of Debates," Oct. 5, 1775, Smith, *Letters*, 2: 113–114.

17. *JCC*, 3: 293–294; Burnett, *Continental Congress*, pp. 119–120.

18. *JCC*, 3: 378–389, 425–427.

CHAPTER 17—WAITING FOR KING GEORGE III

1. This account of George III's background, and much that follows, is drawn from Jeremy Black, *George III: America's Last King* (New Haven, CT, 2006), pp. 6–10.

2. Ibid., pp. 11–21, 43–70.

3. Lord Sandwich's remarks are quoted in McCullough, *1776*, p. 6, from *American Archives*, 4th ser., 1: 1681–1682.

4. Quoted in Thomas, *Tea Party to Independence*, p. 254.

5. Ibid., p. 255.

6. Ibid., 255–258; Ferling, *Independence*, p. 173.

7. Thomas, *Tea Party to Independence*, p. 258.

8. Ibid., pp. 62–63.

9. The full text of the King's speech is in David C. Douglas et al., eds., *English Historical Documents*, 12 vols. (London, 1956–), 9: 850–852.

10. Ibid.; Thomas, *Tea Party to Independence*, pp. 268–270.

11. Thomas, *Tea Party to Independence*, pp. 270–271.

12. Samuel Ward to Henry Ward, Nov. 11, 1775, in Smith, *Letters*, 2: 330–331; Francis Lightfoot Lee to Richard Henry Lee, January 8?, 1776, in ibid., 3: 58.

CHAPTER 18—SMALL STEPS TOWARD INDEPENDENCE

1. Reardon, *Peyton Randolph*, pp. 68–69; *JCC*, 3: 302–303.

2. Breen, *American Insurgents*, pp. 294–299, has an excellent account of this. See also Captain Cochran to Governor Wentworth, Dec. 14, 1775, in *American Archives*, 4th ser., 1: 1041–1042.

3. Breen, *American Insurgents*, pp. 297–298.

4. Marston, *King and Congress*, pp. 260–261.

5. Ibid., pp. 262–265; New Hampshire Delegates to Matthew Thornton, Nov. 3, 1775, Smith, *Letters*, 2: 293; Adams, *Autobiography*, 3: 355; *JCC*, 3: 307.

6. Marston, *King and Congress*, pp. 265–267. For a full account of the "Regulator" movement in the backcountry of South Carolina, see Richard Maxwell Brown, *The South Carolina Regulators* (Cambridge, MA, 1973); and Rachel Klein, *Unification of a Slave State: The Rise of the Planter Class in the South Carolina Backcountry, 1760–1808* (Chapel Hill, NC, 1990), pp. 47–108. For colonial South Carolina politics more generally, see Robert Weir, *Colonial South Carolina: A History* (Columbia, SC, 1997) pp. 291–328; and Eugene Sirmans, *Colonial South Carolina* (Chapel Hill, NC, 1966), pp. 315–357.

7. Marston, *King and Congress*, pp. 269–271; *JCC*, 3: 326–327.

8. Adams, *Autobiography*, 3: 357.

9. Ibid., 3: 357, 358.

10. For an excellent analysis of New Jersey's, and in particular William Franklin's, attempt to negotiate separately with the British, see Smith, *Letters*, 2: 445–446n.

11. *JCC*, 3: 304.

12. Samuel Ward to Deborah Ward, Nov. 1, 1775, in Smith, *Letters*, 2: 283–286. Although Ward's long letter to his wife is dated November 1, it may be that he wrote the section describing the king's response to the petition a day or two later, for that section was apparently added later, as a postscript. See also Samuel Ward to Henry Ward, Nov. 2, 1775, in ibid., 2: 290–292; Sam Adams to James Warren, Nov. 4, 1775, ibid., 2: 297–301.

13. *JCC*, 3: 342–343.

14. At least one delegate, Georgia's John Zubly, may have faced punitive action under the provisions of the new rule of secrecy. On November 10, Zubly left the Congress and returned to Georgia, for reasons, according to some historians, involving a letter that he wrote to Georgia's royal governor James Wright revealing details of the Congress's deliberations. Smith, *Letters*, 2: 328–329n, notes that the supposed letter to the governor has not survived, so there is no direct evidence proving this contention. Nevertheless, there is some evidence that Zubly left under a cloud.

15. Flower, *John Dickinson*, p. 142.

16. "A Proclamation from the Royal Chief Magistracy, May 6, 1775," in Scribner and Tarter, eds., *Revolutionary Virginia*, 3: 100–101.

17. Ibid., 4: 334.

18. Ibid., 4: 435–436.

19. Michael McDonnell, *The Politics of War: Race, Class and Conflict in Revolutionary Virginia* (Chapel Hill, NC, 2007), pp. 161–162.

20. Ibid., pp. 139–144, 156–157, 179–180. While acknowledging that Dunmore's proclamation offering freedom to the slaves was alarming to most white residents of Virginia, McDonnell also stresses the important class divisions among free whites and indentured servants within Virginia at the time.

21. George Washington to John Hancock, Dec. 31, 1775, *GW Papers*, R.S., 2: 623; Chernow, *Washington*, pp. 212–213; Ellis, *His Excellency*, p. 84.

22. *JCC*, 3: 403–404.

23. Ibid., 3: 357.

CHAPTER 19—THE YEAR 1776 DAWNS

1. McDonnell, *Politics of War*, pp. 166ff.

2. The literature on the military campaigns of the American Revolution is of course vast. I have relied on the following for this account of the campaigns. In Montreal and Quebec: Christopher Ward, *The War of the Revolution*, 2 vols. (New York, 1952), 1: 135–201; Ferling, *Almost a Miracle*, pp. 80–99; and Middlekauf, *Glorious Cause*, pp. 304–308.

3. Ward, *War of Revolution*, 1: 163–180.

4. Ibid.; Ferling, *Almost a Miracle*, pp. 96–99.

5. John Hancock to George Washington, Jan. 20, 1776, in *GW Papers*, R.S., 3: 152–153; Thomas Lynch to Philip Schuyler, Jan. 20, 1776, Smith, *Letters*, 3: 125.

6. *JCC*, 4: 241–242; John Hancock to George Washington, Jan. 20, 1776, *GW Papers*, R.S., 3: 152–153.

7. George Washington, Circular to the governments of Massachusetts, Connecticut, and New Hampshire, Jan. 19, 1776, *GW Papers*, R.S., 3: 145; George Washington to John Hancock, Jan. 19, 1776, ibid., 3: 146–147.

8. George Washington to John Hancock, Jan. 30, 1776, ibid., 3: 214–219.

9. Francis Lightfoot Lee to Richard Henry Lee, Jan. 8, 1776, Smith, *Letters*, 3: 58–59; Samuel Ward to his daughter, Jan. 8, 1776, ibid., 3: 61.

10. This account of Drummond's negotiations with members of the Congress is drawn largely from Ferling, *Independence*, pp. 226–230. See also the extended note in Smith, *Letters*, 3: 24–27.

11. Ferling, *Independence*, pp. 227–228; Smith, *Letters*, 3: 24–25. Lord Drummond's Notes, Jan. 3–9, 1776, ibid., 3: 22.

12. Charles Page Smith, *James Wilson, 1742–1798* (Westport, CT, 1956), pp. 36–37, 54–58; Flower, *John Dickinson*, pp. 143–144; see also Smith, *Letters*, 3: 63–64n.

13. Dickinson, "Proposed Resolutions for Negotiating with Great Britain," Jan. 9–24, 1776, Smith, *Letters*, 3: 65–66.

14. Ibid., 3: 66–68.

CHAPTER 20—"THE SCALES HAVE FALLEN FROM OUR EYES"

1. John Hancock to Thomas Cushing, Jan. 17, 1776, Smith, *Letters*, 3: 104–106.

2. Eric Foner, *Tom Paine and Revolutionary America* (New York, 1976), p. 74; Corner, ed., *Autobiography of Benjamin Rush*, pp. 114–115.

3. There have been numerous biographies of Paine. This account has been drawn primarily from Foner, *Tom Paine and Revolutionary America*, pp. 1–17, 71–106; Craig Nelson, *Thomas Paine: Enlightenment, Revolution, and the Birth of Modern Nations* (New York, 2007), pp. 14–100; David Freeman Hawke, *Paine* (New York, 1974), pp. 7–51; and Jack Fruchtman, *Thomas Paine: Apostle of Freedom* (New York, 1994), pp. 15–79.

4. Nelson, *Thomas Paine*, pp. 16–22; Hawke, *Paine*, pp. 10–11.

5. Nelson, *Thomas Paine*, pp. 37–43.

6. Paine, *The Case for the Officers of the Excise* (London, 1772). The passage quoted here is from the online edition of Paine's work, taken from Moncure Daniel Conway, ed., *The Writings of Thomas Paine*, 4 vols. (New York, 1894), vol. IV. http://oll.libertyfund.org/?option=com_staticxt&staticfile=show.php%3Ftitle=1083&chapter=19334&layout=html&Itemid=27.

7. Nelson, *Thomas Paine*, p. 45.

8. Ibid., pp. 48–49.

9. Ibid., p. 48. Nelson, citing the Pennsylvania *Evening Post* of April 30, 1776, says that Paine's ship arrived in Philadelphia sometime between December 7 and 12. Hawke, *Paine*, p. 25, and Foner, *Paine and Revolutionary America*, p. 71, state that he arrived on November 30.

10. Foner, *Paine and Revolutionary America*, pp. 72–73; Nelson, *Thomas Paine*, pp. 64–65.

11. The text of Paine's essay on "Reflections on Titles" can be found in Conway, *Writings of Thomas Paine*, vol. 1, online edition at http://oll.libertyfund.org/?option=com_staticxt&staticfile=show.php%3Ftitle=343&chapter=17011&layout=html&Itemid=27.

12. Nelson, *Thomas Paine*, p. 78.

13. Corner, ed., *Autobiography of Benjamin Rush*, p. 114.

14. Eric Nelson, "Patriot Royalism: The Stuart Monarchy in American Political Thought, 1769–75," *William and Mary Quarterly*, 3d ser., 68 (October 2011): 533–572, has asserted that much of the American rationale for their opposition to British authority during the 1770s was in fact backward-looking, relying on political arguments used to justify the seventeenth-century Stuart monarchy. Although extraordinarily erudite, the argument is unconvincing. For rebuttals to the Nelson's interpretation, see the commentary by Gordon Wood, Pauline Maier, and Jack Rakove in the same issue of the *William and Mary Quarterly*, pp. 573–582, 635–638.

15. Richard Beeman, ed., *Thomas Paine: Common Sense* (New York, 2012), p. 11. All of the citations to *Common Sense* in this chapter are from Beeman's edition.

16. Ibid., p. 13.

17. Ibid., pp. 17–18.

18. Ibid., pp. 18–25.

19. This attack not only on the institution of the monarchy but also on the person of King George III was crucial in breaking Americans' psychological attachment to their king. For a highly perceptive analysis of this psychological process, see Winthrop Jordan, "Familial Politics: Thomas Paine and the Killing of the King, 1776," *Journal of American History*, vol. 60 (Sept. 1973), pp. 294–308.

20. Beeman, ed., *Common Sense*, pp. 33, 43.

21. Ibid., pp. 58, 61.

22. Ibid., p. 48.

23. Ibid., pp. 39–40.

24. Ibid., p. 85.

25. Ibid.

26. George Washington to Col. Joseph Reed, Jan. 31, 1776; *GW Papers*, R.S., 3: 228; see also Nelson, *Thomas Paine*, p. 90.

27. Nelson, *Thomas Paine*, p. 92; Foner, *Paine and Revolutionary America*, p. 79.

28. *Pennsylvania Packet*, Feb. 12, 1776; *Pennsylvania Evening Post*, Feb. 13, March 26, 1776, all quoted in Foner, *Paine and Revolutionary America*, p. 79.

29. Henry Wisner to John McKesson, Jan. 13, 1776, Smith, *Letters*, 3: 90–91; Sam Adams to James Warren, Jan. 13, 1776, ibid., 3: 87.

30. Josiah Bartlett to John Langdon, Jan. 13, 1776, ibid., 3: 87–88; Foner, *Paine and Revolutionary America*, p. 85.

31. John Adams to Abigail Adams, Feb. 18, 1776, *Adams Family Correspondence*, 1: 348. Adams wrote this letter to Abigail from Philadelphia, but he had already sent the pamphlet to her from New York. John Adams to William Tudor, April 12, 1776, *Adams Papers*, 4: 118; John Adams to James Warren, May 12, 1776, ibid., 4: 181.

32. Adams, *Autobiography*, 3: 333.

33. Ibid.

34. Ibid., 3: 334; John Adams to Thomas Jefferson, June 22, 1819, Lester Cappon, ed., *The Adams-Jefferson Letters* (Chapel Hill, NC, 1959), II: 542.

35. Karen Calvert, *Quaker Constitutionalism*, pp. 235–238.

36. Ibid., p. 238.

37. [John Dickinson], *Remarks on a Late Pamphlet Called Plain Truth* (Philadelphia, 1776), p. 2; Jacobson, *Dickinson and the Revolution in Pennsylvania*, pp. 108–109.

38. Flower, *John Dickinson*, p. 143.

CHAPTER 21—"THE CHILD INDEPENDENCE
IS NOW STRUGGLING FOR BIRTH"

1. Benjamin Irvin, in his well-researched and imaginatively argued book, *Clothed in the Robes of Sovereignty*, asserts that the members of the Continental Congress were under the close, and often critical, scrutiny of the residents of Philadelphia, and, indeed, beyond. This may have been the case after independence was declared, but, with only a few exceptions, noted earlier in this book, most of the evidence suggests that the members of the Congress carried out their deliberations in remarkable isolation from the "people out of doors."

2. [New York] *Constitutional Gazette*, April 17, 1776. See also Ryerson, *Revolution Is Now Begun*, pp. 153–154. David Freeman Hawke, *In the Midst of Revolution* (Philadelphia, 1961), pp. 90–94.

3. *Pennsylvania Packet*, April 22, 1776.

4. The full lists of congressional delegates and their terms of service can be found in Smith, *Letters*, 1: xxvi–xxxii, 2: xvi–xxii, 3: xvi–xxii, 4: xv–xxi.

5. Richard Smith Diary, Feb. 13, 1776, ibid., 3: 252.

6. John Adams to Abigail Adams, Feb. 18, 1776, *Adams Family Correspondence*, 1: 348–349; Sam Adams to Samuel Cooper, April 30, 1776, Cushing, ed., *Writings of Samuel Adams*, 3: 284.

7. Thomas, *Tea Party to Independence*, pp. 297–303.

8. Oliver Wolcott to Andrew Adams, March 22, 1776, Smith, *Letters*, 3: 428; Joseph Hewes to Samuel Johnson, March 20, 1776, ibid., 3: 416; John Adams to Horatio Gates, March 23, 1776, *Adams Papers*, 4: 59.

9. For a balanced view of Lord North's intentions in including the possibility of a peace commission in the Prohibitory Act, see Thomas, *Tea Party to Independence*, pp. 297–303.

10. Flower, *John Dickinson*, pp. 144–145; John Adams to Abigail Adams, *Adams Family Correspondence*, 3: 347.

11. Flower, *John Dickinson*, p. 146; Dickinson's drafts of speeches to Congress at this time can be found in Smith, *Letters*, 3: 132–138, 139–145.

12. Oliver Wolcott to Samuel Lyman, Feb. 19, 1776, Smith, *Letters*, 3: 286; Josiah Bartlett to John Langdon, Feb. 21, 1776, ibid., 3: 293; William Whipple to John Langdon, April, 2, 1776, ibid., 3: 479; John Adams to Abigail Adams, April 14, 1776, *Adams Family Correspondence*, 1: 381–383; Sam Adams to Joseph Hawley, April 15, 1776, Cushing, ed., *Writings of Samuel Adams*, 3: 280.

13. Robert Morris to Horatio Gates, April 6, 1776, Smith, *Letters*, 3: 495; Oliver Wolcott to Andrew Adams, March 22, 1776, ibid., 3: 428.

14. George Washington to John Augustine Washington, May 31, 1776, *GW Papers*, R.S., 4: 412.

15. Ferling, *Almost a Miracle*, p. 127; For more information on the Battle of Nassau, see John J. McCusker, "The American Invasion of Nassau in the Bahamas," in *Essays in the Economic History of the Atlantic World* (London, 1997), pp. 258–287.

16. Ferling, *Almost a Miracle*, pp. 104–107; Chernow, *Washington*, pp. 224–227.

17. *JCC*, 4: 191–192, 212–218. Benjamin Franklin to Josiah Quincy, April 15, 1776, Smith, *Letters*, 3: 529; Commissioners to Canada to John Hancock, May 1, 1776, ibid., 3: 611–612.

18. John Hancock to Certain Colonies, June 4, 1776, Smith, *Letters*, 4: 136–137.

19. John Penn to Thomas Person, Feb. 14, 1776, ibid., 3: 254–255.

20. The Virginia Convention had passed its resolution on Jan. 20, 1776, Smith, *Letters*, 3: 262n; *JCC*, 4: 154; "Notes of Debates," Feb. 16, 1776, Adams, *Diary*, 2: 229–230; Richard Smith Diary, Feb. 16, 1776, Smith, *Letters*, 3: 267.

21. Richard Smith Diary, March 22, 1776, Smith, *Letters*, 3: 427; Burnett, *Continental Congress*, p. 139.

22. John Adams to James Warren, Oct. 19, 20, 1775, *Adams Papers*, 2: 215–217.

23. Burnett, *Continental Congress*, pp. 140–142. See also, Jonathan Dull, *A Diplomatic History of the American Revolution* (New Haven, CT, 1985), pp. 3, 49–51; Elmer Bendiner, *The Virgin Diplomats* (New York, 1976), pp. 52–53.

24. Burnett, *Continental Congress*, p. 143. For the elaborate instructions given to Deane by the Secret Committee, see Committee of Secret Correspondence, Minutes of Proceedings, March 2, 1776, Smith, *Letters*, 3: 320–322.

25. *JCC*, 4: 257–259.

26. John Adams to Abigail Adams, April 15, 1776, *Adams Family Correspondence*, 1: 383–385; Sam Adams to James Warren, April 16, 1776, Smith, *Letters*, 3: 340.

CHAPTER 22—FOURTEEN PATHS TO INDEPENDENCE

1. John Adam to James Warren, May 20, 1776, *Adams Papers*, 4: 195.

2. *JCC*, 4: 351, 432; Smith, *Letters*, 3: 670n.

3. Adams, *Autobiography*, 3: 335, 383.

4. "Notes of Debates," May 13–15, 1776, Adams, *Diary*, 239–241.

5. Carter Braxton to Landon Carter, May 17, 1776, Smith, *Letters*, 4: 19; "Delegates Certificate of James Wilson's Conduct in Congress," June 20, 1776, ibid., 4: 271–273.

6. Ryerson, *Revolution Is Now Begun*, pp. 211–216; Flower, *John Dickinson*, p. 151.

7. Flower, *John Dickinson*, pp. 151–152.

8. Ibid., p. 152; Calvert, *Quaker Constitutionalism*, p. 139; John Adams to Benjamin Hichborn, May 29, 1776, *Adams Papers*, 4: 217–218.

9. Flower, *John Dickinson*, pp. 152–153, *Pennsylvania Evening Post*, June 8, 1776.

10. *JCC*, 5: 424–426; Thomas Jefferson, "Notes of Proceedings," Boyd, *Jefferson Papers*, 1: 309.

11. Beeman, *Patrick Henry*, pp. 80–85.

12. *JCC*, 5: 424–426. In mid-January of 1776, Benjamin Franklin and Sam Adams had collaborated on a plan for creating a confederated government, but many in the Congress were convinced that such a plan was, at worst, merely a ruse to push the colonies into independence, or, at best, would unintentionally do so. As a consequence, the proposal went wholly ignored. Marston, *King and Congress*, pp. 192–194.

13. Jefferson, "Notes of Proceedings," Boyd, *Jefferson Papers*, 1: 309–313; Edward Rutledge to John Jay, June 8, 1776, Smith, *Letters*, 4: 174–175.

14. John Dickinson, "Notes for a Speech," June 8, 1776, Smith, *Letters*, 4: 165–169.

15. Ibid.; Jefferson, "Notes of Proceedings," Boyd, *Jefferson Papers*, 1: 309–313.

16. Boyd, *Jefferson Papers*, 1: 309–313; *JCC*, 5: 428–429.

17. *JCC*, 5: 431, 433.

18. Lefler and Powell, *Colonial North Carolina*, pp. 280–281.

19. Burnett, *Continental Congress*, pp. 155–156; Jensen, *Founding of a Nation*, p. 678; Marston, *King and Congress*, pp. 271–272; Weir, *Colonial South Carolina*, pp. 326–328.

20. Burnett, *Continental Congress*, p. 156; Jensen, *Founding of a Nation*, p. 678.

21. Pauline Maier, *American Scripture: Making the Declaration of Independence* (New York, 1997), pp. 61–62.

22. Richard Henry Lee to Patrick Henry, April 20, 1776, Smith, *Letters*, 1: 563–565; Beeman, *Patrick Henry*, pp. 80–85.

23. Thomas Cushing to John Hancock, Jan. 30, 1776, Smith, *Letters*, 3: 106n.

24. Elbridge Gerry to James Warren, March 26, 1776, Smith, *Letters*, 3: 441; John Adams to James Warren, April 16, 22, 1776, *Adams Papers*, 4: 123, 136; James Warren to John Adams, April 30, 1776, ibid., 4: 153; Maier, *American Scripture*, pp. 59–60.

25. Maier, *American Scripture*, pp. 63–64; Jensen, *Founding of a Nation*, p. 692; Smith, *Letters*, 4: 94n.

26. These developments are summarized in Ryerson, *Revolution Is Now Begun*, pp. 228–238; and Flower, *John Dickinson*, pp. 151–154.

27. Marston, *King and Congress*, pp. 289–291; Jensen, *Founding of a Nation*, p. 692.

28. Jensen, *Founding of a Nation*, pp. 692–693; and Marston, *King and Congress*, pp. 291–292.

29. John Adams to Samuel Chase, June 14, 1776, *Adams Papers*, 4: 314; Hoffman, *A Spirit of Dissension: Economics, Politics, and the Revolution in Maryland* (Baltimore, MD, 1973), pp. 164–168.

30. John Adams to Samuel Chase, June 24, 1776, *Adams Papers*, 4: 333; Hoffman, *Spirit of Dissension*, pp. 164–168; Maier, *American Scripture*, pp. 67–68.

31. One of the best accounts of the complicated history of the coming of the Revolution in New York is Becker, *History of Political Parties*, pp. 253–276; see also Jensen, *Founding of a Nation*, pp. 696–699; Marston, *King and Congress*, pp. 292–296.

32. David McCullough, *1776* (New York, 2005), p. 134; Ferling, *Almost a Miracle*, p. 124, claims that over the next forty-eight hours somewhere near 130 British ships had appeared in the harbor.

33. Robert Livingston to John Jay, May 17, 1776, Jay to Livingston, May 29, 1776, Smith, *Letters*, 4: 28–30, 59n. See also Marston, *King and Congress*, p. 294.

34. Marston, *King and Congress*, p. 295.

35. Edward Rutledge to John Jay, June 29, 1776, Smith, *Letters*, 4: 337–339.

CHAPTER 23—"THE GREATEST DEBATE OF ALL"

1. *JCC*, 5: 503.

2. Ibid.; John Adams to Archibald Bulloch, July 1, 1776, John Adams to Samuel Chase, July 1, 1776, *Adams Papers*, 4: 345, 347.

3. Historian Karen Calvert, who has emphasized the importance of Quaker religious and political thought on Dickinson's thinking, notes that his intense fear of dissension and, ultimately, disunion, was a classic Quaker fear, and, more than any other component of his thinking on the question of independence, may have been the most decisive. Many historians of American Quakerism would probably disagree with Calvert's emphasis on fear as a central component of Quaker theology, and, alas, Dickinson, unlike his sometime adversary John Adams, was never very self-revelatory in his writings, so any assertion about the extent to which fear drove his opposition to independence is also purely speculative. Calvert, *Quaker Constitutionalism*, p. 141.

4. Drafts of Dickinson's speech are printed in Smith, *Letters*, 4: 57. See also John H. Powell, "Speech of John Dickinson Opposing the Declaration of Independence, 1 July, 1776," *Pennsylvania Magazine of History and Biography*, 65 (1941): 458–481.

5. John Adams to Samuel Chase, July 1, 1776, *Adams Papers*, 4: 353; Adams, *Autobiography*, 3: 396–397.

6. Adams, *Autobiography*, 3: 396–397.

7. Maier, *American Scripture*, p. 64.

8. Jefferson, "Notes of Proceedings in Congress," July 1–4, 1776, in Boyd, *Jefferson Papers*, 1: 314; *JCC*, 5: 504; John Adams to Samuel Chase, July 1, 1776, *Adams Papers*, 4: 353. Jefferson's notes on the weather in Philadelphia during this period can be accessed online at: http://classroom.monticello.org /kids/gallery/image/342/Jeffersons-notes-on-the-weather-in-Philadelphia -July-1776/.

9. *JCC*, 5: 504.

10. John Adams to Samuel Chase, July 1, 1776, *Adams Papers*, 4: 353; Thomas McKean to Caesar Rodney, Sept. 22, 1813, in Smith, *Letters*, 4: 388n.

11. *JCC*, 5: 506–507.

12. Ferling, *Independence*, pp. 333–334, states that South Carolina's delegation ultimately came around to support independence because they had already made a deal with Jefferson and the Committee of Five with respect to removing the clause critical of the slave trade and the institution of slavery from the list of specific grievances in the Declaration of Independence. There is no persuasive evidence to support this contention. It is more likely that Edward Rutledge, who was the principal holdout, after having received the deference of the Congress in the postponement of a decision on July 1, was now willing to join the common cause. See Haws, *John and Edward Rutledge*, pp. 93–94; Weir, *Colonial South Carolina*, pp. 291–328.

13. Adams, *Diary*, Sept. 3, 1774, 2: 121; John Munroe, *Colonial Delaware* (Millwood, NY, 1978), pp. 249–250; Ferling, *Independence*, p. 328.

14. McKean to Caesar Rodney, Sept. 22, 1813, Smith, *Letters*, 4: 388n.

15. Ibid.; Flower, *John Dickinson*, p. 166; Stille, *Life and Times of Dickinson*, pp. 196–197. Smith, *Letters*, 4: 364–365, while crediting Thomas McKean's description of the voting of the Pennsylvania delegation on July 2, notes that McKean, recollecting the events of that day thirty-seven years after the fact, mistakenly said that the vote in question occurred on July 4, rather than July 2.

16. Page Smith, *James Wilson*, pp. 87–89, 129–139.

17. Morris to Joseph Reed, July 21, 1776, in Smith, *Letters*, 4: 510–511.

18. My interpretation of the motives behind Dickinson's behavior that day mirror those of Flower, *John Dickinson*, p. 166.

19. Ibid., p. 166; Franklin B. Dexter, ed., *The Literary Diary of Ezra Stiles*, 2 vols. (New York, 1901), 2: 282; Calvert, *Quaker Constitutionalism*, p. 242; John Adams to John Winthrop, June 23, 1776, *Adams Papers*, 4: 332.

20. Quoted in Calvert, *Quaker Constitutionalism*, p. 242; and Flower, *John Dickinson*, p. 174.

21. John Adams to Abigail Adams, July 3, 1776, *Adams Family Correspondence*, 2: 27–31.

CHAPTER 24—THOMAS JEFFERSON'S DECLARATION OF INDEPENDENCE

1. Malone, *Jefferson the Virginian*, pp. 25–26; Jefferson to Thomas Page, May 17, 1776, Boyd, *Jefferson Papers*, 1: 293. Jefferson is known as a remarkably prolific correspondent, but in Julian Boyd's edition of the *Jefferson Papers* covering the period from January 1 to the end of May 1776, there are only two letters from Jefferson, and five coming in to him.

2. Boyd, *Jefferson Papers*, 1: 277–284.

3. Malone, *Jefferson the Virginian*, pp. 216–217.

4. "Draft Address to the Foreign Mercenaries," May 1776 [precise date unknown], Smith, *Letters*, 110–112. It appears that Jefferson and George Wythe collaborated in drafting the address; it is in Wythe's hand, but it was found in Jefferson's personal papers.

5. Jefferson to Thomas Nelson, May 16, 1776, Boyd, *Jefferson Papers*, 2: 292–293.

6. Jefferson wrote three drafts of the Virginia Constitution. They are all printed in Boyd, *Jefferson Papers*, 1: 337–364. Though most historians have concluded that George Mason's draft of the Virginia Constitution was the most influential in shaping the final product, Boyd, *Jefferson Papers*, 1: 329–337n, makes a strong case that Jefferson's contribution to the Constitution was greater than historians have recognized.

7. *JCC*, 5: 431; John Adams to Timothy Pickering, Aug. 6, 1822, in Charles Francis Adams, ed., *Works of John Adams, Second President of the United States*, 10 vols. (Boston, 1850–56), 2: 514n.

8. Adams, *Autobiography*, 3: 335.

9. Ibid. Malone, *Jefferson the Virginian*, pp. 219–220, makes a convincing case refuting Adams's claim.

10. Christopher Collier, *Roger Sherman's Connecticut: Yankee Politics and the American Revolution* (Middletown, CT, 1971), pp. 3–64, 85–137.

11. Ibid., p. 94; Max Farrand, ed., *The Records of the Federal Convention of 1787*, 4 vols., rev. ed. (New Haven, CT, 1966), 3: 34, 88–89.

12. For Livingston's evolving views toward independence, see Ferling, *Independence*, pp. 285–289, 294.

13. Adams, *Autobiography*, 3: 336; Adams to Pickering, Aug. 6, 1822, in Adams, ed., *Works of John Adams*, 2: 514n. For an excellent account of these exchanges I am indebted to Maier, *American Scripture*, pp. 99–101.

14. Maier, *American Scripture*, p. 100; Jefferson to James Madison, Aug. 30, 1823, Paul Leicester Ford, ed., *The Writings of Thomas Jefferson* (New York, 1899), 10: 267–269.

15. My account of Jefferson's drafting of the Declaration is based on the superb work of Maier, *American Scripture*, pp. 99–143, 235–241; Carl Becker, *The*

Declaration of Independence: A Study of Political Ideas (New York, 1922), pp. 135–193; and Boyd, *Jefferson Papers*, 11: 413–433.

16. Jefferson to James Madison, Aug. 30, 1823, Ford, ed., *Writings of Jefferson*, 10: 267–269.

17. Jefferson to Benjamin Franklin, June 21, 1776, Boyd, *Jefferson Papers*, 1: 404. For a more general discussion of the sequence of events within the committee see ibid., 1: 413–417; and Maier, *American Scripture*, pp. 101–102.

18. There have been countless books and articles on the intellectual foundations of the Declaration of Independence. Carl Becker, *The Declaration of Independence*, pp. 24–134, is the starting point for understanding the sources of Jefferson's thought. Gary Wills, *Inventing America: Jefferson's Declaration of Independence* (New York, 1978) is a provocative, but ultimately unconvincing argument that the Scottish common-sense philosophers lay at the heart of Jefferson's thought. Jay Fliegelman, *Declaring Independence: Jefferson, Natural Language, and the Culture of Performance* (Stanford, CA, 1993) argues that Jefferson wrote the Declaration in a style that was meant to be read aloud. A helpful survey of these varying perspectives can be found in Maier, *American Scripture*, pp. 123–143.

19. The draft of Jefferson's Declaration being discussed in this paragraph, and in subsequent discussions in this chapter unless otherwise noted, is the so-called "fair copy" that the Committee of Five submitted to the Congress. In fact, that fair copy has not survived, so scholars have used the closest version that they can find—a copy of the committee's draft that Jefferson sent to Richard Henry Lee on July 8, 1776. Jefferson's "original rough draft," reprinted in Boyd, *Jefferson Papers*, 1: 423–427, while more elegant than Mason's, was wordier and not as elegant as the one that emerged from the committee. The version that most likely emerged from the Committee of Five, the so-called fair copy, has been replicated in Becker, *Declaration of Independence*, pp. 174–184 (Becker refers to it as the "Lee Copy") and, in a slightly different form, in Maier, *American Scripture*, pp. 235–241 (which she refers to as the "Jefferson Draft"). The text of the fair copy analyzed in this chapter is reprinted in Appendix A of this volume; it is based on the version printed in Becker, with a few modifications, duly noted.

20. Maier, *American Scripture*, pp. 122–134. For a full discussion of Mason's role in drafting the Virginia Declaration of Rights, see Robert Alan Rutland, *The Birth of the Bill of Rights, 1776–1791* (Chapel Hill, NC, 1955), pp. 33–48; John Selby, *The Revolution in Virginia, 1775–1783* (Williamsburg, VA, 1988), pp. 100–110; Beeman, *Patrick Henry*, pp. 101–109; McConnell, *Politics of War*, pp. 242–243.

21. For the differences between the Committee's "fair copy" and the final version adopted by Congress, see Appendix A.

22. John Locke, *Two Treatises on Government* (London, 1821 ed.), p. 382. The quote from Jefferson's *Summary* View is in Boyd, *Jefferson Papers*, 1: 125; see also Maier, *American Scripture*, pp. 135–137.

23. Maier, *American Scripture*, p. 123, agrees that the preamble was not accorded anywhere near the importance, indeed, the reverence, that it is today. She believes that it was the last paragraph of the Declaration that was the most important and the most oft-quoted, because it, after all, was the paragraph that officially declared independence.

24. The draft of the Virginia Constitution referred to here is Jefferson's "Third Draft," printed in Boyd, *Jefferson Papers*, 1: 356–365. The draft of the Declaration referred to here is the "fair copy" presented by the Committee of Five to Congress and reprinted in Appendix A. See also Boyd, *Jefferson Papers*, 1: 332–333n, and Maier, *American Scripture*, pp. 105–123.

25. Boyd, *Jefferson Papers*, 1: 357. The numbering of the individual grievances in Appendix A is based on the ordering of those grievances in Becker, *Declaration of Independence*, pp. 174–184.

26. For differing views of the intent and impact of this passage, see Becker, *Declaration of Independence*, pp. 212–214, and Maier, *American Scripture*, pp. 121–122.

27. Maier, *American Scripture*, pp. 139–142, has a particularly effective analysis of the anger contained in Jefferson's denunciation of the British people.

CHAPTER 25—AMERICA'S DECLARATION OF INDEPENDENCE

1. Boyd, *Jefferson Papers*, 1: 313–314. The analysis in this chapter, as in Chapter Twenty-Four, draws heavily on the superb analysis of Pauline Maier, in *American Scripture*, esp. pp. 45–46, 143–150.

2. *JCC*, 5: 507.

3. Maier, *American Scripture*, pp. 143–144; Willard Ritz, "From the *Here* of Jefferson's Handwritten Rough Draft of the Declaration of Independence to the *There* of the Printed Dunlap Broadside," *Pennsylvania Magazine of History and Biography*, CXVI (1992): 499–552. See also Boyd, *Jefferson Papers*, 1: 415–417.

4. This, and subsequent analyses of changes made by Congress to the so-called "fair copy" of the document that Jefferson sent to Richard Henry Lee is based on the text of the Declaration, containing Congress's revisions, printed in Becker, *Declaration of Independence*, pp. 174–184. See also, Maier, *American Scripture*, pp. 236–241. Maier's text is a refined version of the version printed in Becker's volume. The version from Becker, with minor adjustments, appears in Appendix A of this volume.

5. Maier, *American Scripture*, pp. 110–111, 146.

6. Boyd, *Jefferson Papers*, 1: 314–315.

7. Maier, *American Scripture*, pp. 146–147. Historians have devoted a huge amount of time and effort in analyzing Jefferson's own views and behaviors on the subject of slavery. Dumas Malone, in his otherwise excellent *Jefferson the Virginian*, p. 228, largely ignores the issue. Jon Meacham, in his recently published biography, *Thomas Jefferson: The Art of Power* (New York, 2012), pp. 105–106, 124, seeks to strike a middle ground, recognizing some of the contradictory qualities of Jefferson's rhetoric, but resists passing judgment. The two most judgmental, and hostile, accounts of Jefferson and slavery are Paul Finkelman, "Jefferson and Slavery: Treason Against the Hopes of the World," in Peter Onuf, ed., *Jeffersonian Legacies* (Charlottesville, VA, 1993), pp. 181–221, and Henry Wiencek, *Master of the Mountain: Thomas Jefferson and His Slaves* (New York, 2012). See also George Van Cleve, *A Slaveholders' Union: Slavery, Politics, and the Constitution in the Early Republic* (Chicago, 2010), pp. 42–45, which, detaching itself from the moral question of slavery, argues that slavery was such a fundamental part of the economic life of America during the colonial period and early Republic that it is hardly surprising that so little progress was made in eliminating the paradox at the nation's core. For a similarly balanced, and morally detached, analysis of this problem, see Peter Onuf and Ari Helo, "Jefferson, Morality, and the Problem of Slavery," *William and Mary Quarterly*, 3d ser., 60 (2003): 583–614.

8. Maier, *American Scripture*, pp. 147–148, 240–241.

9. Ibid., pp. 142, 148–149.

10. Jefferson's reference to the "mutilations" of his draft is contained in a recollection of the events of those days in Jefferson to Robert Walsh, Dec. 4, 1818, in Ford, ed., *Writings of Thomas Jefferson*, 10: 120n; Thomas Jefferson to Richard Henry Lee, July 8, 1776; Lee to Jefferson, July 21, 1776, Boyd, *Jefferson Papers*, 1: 456, 471. My conclusion about the effect of the Congress's alterations to Jefferson's draft closely coincides with that in Maier, *American Scripture*, p. 150.

11. Malone, *Jefferson the Virginian*, p. 229.

12. Jefferson, "Notes on the Proceedings of Congress," July 1–4, 1776, Boyd, *Jefferson Papers*, 1: 315.

13. Jefferson apparently composed his notes on the events of those days shortly before June 1, 1783, at which time he sent them to James Madison. See Boyd, *Jefferson Papers*, 1: 327–329n.

14. *JCC*, 5: 510–516; Robert Treat Paine Diary, July 4, 1776, Paine to Joseph Palmer, July 6, 1776, both in Smith, *Letters*, 4: 386, 399.

15. The only explicit evidence of Hancock's signing is in the rough copy of Thomson's journal, which says: "Signed, by order and in behalf of the Congress, John Hancock, President." It seems likely that Thomson, as secretary, may have signed it that day as well. The most convincing analysis of the timing

of the signing is Smith, *Letters*, 4: 381–383. See also Boyd, *Jefferson Papers*, 1: 304–308; and Hazleton, *Declaration of Independence*, p. 204.

16. Hazleton, *Declaration of Independence*, p. 204; *JCC*, 5: 590–591.

17. *JCC*, 5: 626; Hazleton, *Declaration of Independence*, p. 204.

18. Hazleton, *Declaration of Independence*, pp. 210–21.

19. John Hancock to the New Jersey Convention, July 5, 1776; Hancock to the Pennsylvania Committee of Safety, July 5, 1776; Hancock to "Certain States," July 6, 1776; Smith, *Letters*, 4: 392, 393, 396. See also Ritz, "From the *Here* of Jefferson's Handwritten Rough Draft," pp. 499–512; Maier, *American Scripture*, p. 159.

20. Maier, *American Scripture*, pp. 156–157; Hazleton, *Declaration of Independence*, pp. 242–244; John Adams to Samuel Chase, July 9, 1776, *Adams Papers*, 9: 372. For the contention that the Declaration was read to a small group at the State House, see Ritz, "From the *Here* of Jefferson's Handwritten Rough Draft," pp. 507–510.

21. Hazleton, *Declaration of Independence*, pp. 252–253; George Washington, General Orders, July 9, 1776, George Washington to John Hancock, July 10, 1776, *GW Papers*, R.S., 5: 246, 258; Chernow, *Washington*, p. 237.

INDEX

    as member of committee to draft petition
        to King George, 139–140, 166
    on non-exportation, 154–155
    opinion of Christopher Gadsden, 44
    opposition to John Dickinson's plan for
        reconciliation, 206
    shifting positions on issues of
        'reconciliation,' 206, 224, 251
    social background, 43
    support for new South Carolina
        government, 286

Sandwich, Lord (John Montagu), 274
Schuyler, Philip, 184, 198, 234, 237
Scott, George Lewis, 309
Sea Nymph (ship), 44
Seabury, Samuel, 189
Sears, Isaac, 33, 364, 365
Second Continental Congress
    acting as committee of the whole, 200,
        344, 354, 370, 374, 407
    agenda, 201, 261
    appointment of Washington as
        continental army commander,
        227–228, 230–231
    arming of vessels against British ships,
        337–338
    attendance, decrease in, 294–295
    Committee of Five, 396, 406, 407
    committee to assess military situation,
        265–266
    committee to prepare declaration of
        independence, 354, 387
    committee to prepare form of colonial
        confederation, 354
    committee to prepare plan of treaties
        with foreign powers, 354
    committees to manage war, appointment
        of, 263–264
    Common Sense, reaction to, 320–322
    composition of, 259–260
    continental army, formation, 226–227
    Declaration of Independence, editing,
        408–413
    Declaration of Independence, signing,
        414–416
    delegates' views on independence,
        329–330
    disjunction between Congress and public
        opinion, 327–329

    dispatch of committee to New Jersey, 288
    dispatch of mission to Canada, 335
    distribution of Declaration of
        Independence, 417–418
    English constitution, use of as model for
        government, 312–314
    foreign alliances, importance, 336–337
    foreign alliances, relationship of to
        independence, 339–340
    Fort Ticonderoga, news of capture, 201
    importation resolution, adoption of, 340
    independence, debate of on July 1, 1776,
        371–374
    independence, vote for on July 2, 1776,
        376–379
    John Dickinson, proposals of, 202–206
    John Hancock, election of as president,
        218
    Lord North's "peace plan," response to,
        256–257
    navy, creation of, 267–269
    new governments, resolution calling for
        establishment of, 345
    officers, election of, 199
    Olive Branch petition, 251–253, 276, 277
    peace commission, reaction to
        Parliament's promise, 331–334
    popular support for, 195
    Prohibitory Act, reaction to, 331–332
    proposed resolutions for charting next
        steps, 207–208
    reading of draft of Declaration of
        Independence, 407
    rebuke of New Jersey for intended
        petition to king, 287–288
    recommendation that Virginia form new
        government, 293
    reinforcements for Canadian front,
        299–300
    reluctance to sever ties with Great
        Britain, 280
    resolution to establish new governments,
        adoption, 342
    secrecy, rule of, 289–290
    Secret Committee, 264, 338–339
    use of Pennsylvania State House as
        meeting place, 199, 456n5
    Virginia resolution proposing
        independence, introduction of,
        351–354
    volunteer army, disadvantages, 266–277